Mike Meyers' CompTIA™

Network+™

CERTIFICATION PASSPORT

(Exam N10-008)

SEVENTH EDITION

Mike Meyers' CompTIA

Network+™

CERTIFICATION PASSPORT

(Exam N10-008)

SEVENTH EDITION

Mike Meyers, Series Editor
Jonathan S. Weissman

New York   Chicago   San Francisco   Athens
London   Madrid   Mexico City   Milan
New Delhi   Singapore   Sydney   Toronto

1 2 3 4 5 6 7 8 9   LCR   26 25 24 23 22

Library of Congress Control Number: 2022935403

ISBN   978-1-264-26896-2
MHID   1-264-26896-3

Sponsoring Editor Tim Green	**Acquisitions Coordinator** Caitlin Cromley-Linn	**Proofreader** Richard Camp	**Composition** KnowledgeWorks Global Ltd.
Editorial Supervisor Patty Mon	**Technical Editor** Edward Tetz	**Indexer** Ted Laux	**Illustration** KnowledgeWorks Global Ltd.
Project Editor Rachel Fogelberg	**Copy Editor** Bill McManus	**Production Supervisor** Thomas Somers	**Art Director, Cover** Jeff Weeks

To the three most important people in my life: my beautiful wife, Eva Ann, and our amazing sons, Noah Harrison and Jacob Meir. Thank you for being the best family a guy can have! I love you all so much!

—Jonathan S. Weissman

About the Series Editor

Michael Meyers is the industry's leading authority on CompTIA Network+ certification. He is the president and founder of Total Seminars, LLC, a member of CompTIA, and a major provider of IT fundamentals, PC and network repair, and computer security training and training materials for thousands of organizations throughout the world.

Mike has written numerous popular textbooks, including the best-selling *Mike Meyers' CompTIA A+™ Guide to Managing and Troubleshooting PCs, Mike Meyers' CompTIA Network+™ Guide to Managing and Troubleshooting Networks*, and *Mike Meyers' CompTIA Security+™ Certification Guide*.

Mike has attained numerous industry certifications, including CompTIA A+, CompTIA Network+, CompTIA Security+, CompTIA Cybersecurity Analyst (CySA+), and Microsoft Certified Professional.

About the Author

Jonathan S. Weissman is a senior lecturer in the Department of Computing Security at Rochester Institute of Technology (RIT), where he was awarded the RIT Outstanding Teaching Award in 2014, the RIT B. Thomas Golisano College of Computing and Information Sciences (GCCIS) Outstanding Educator Award in 2018, and RIT Distinguished Teacher Recognition Program Honors in 2019. Weissman developed and teaches three courses for the edX RITx Cybersecurity MicroMasters program to more than 300,000 learners worldwide.

Weissman is also a tenured full professor and the Networking and Cybersecurity program coordinator in the Department of Computing Sciences at Finger Lakes Community College (FLCC), where he was awarded the State University of New York (SUNY) Chancellor's Award for Excellence in Teaching in 2021. All in all, Weissman is the recipient of 11 teaching honors and awards.

In addition to his two full-time teaching positions, Weissman teaches part-time at Syracuse University for the Department of Electrical Engineering and Computer Science and at Nazareth College for the School of Business and Leadership.

Weissman began his teaching career in 2001 and has taught more than 50 graduate and undergraduate courses, which include networking, cybersecurity, routing and switching, systems administration, ethical hacking/pentesting, digital forensics, malware reverse engineering, cryptography, programming, scripting, Web design, database design, computer organization and architecture, operating system design, and many more.

Besides this book (fifth, sixth, and seventh editions), Weissman is the author of *Principles of Computer Security: CompTIA Security+™ and Beyond Lab Manual* and *Mike Meyers' CompTIA Network+ Guide to Managing and Troubleshooting Networks Lab Manual* (fourth, fifth, and sixth editions). He also serves as a technical editor for many industry textbooks, including the textbook and All-in-One Exam Guide in this series.

Furthermore, Weissman is a networking and cybersecurity consultant for local businesses and individuals. Weissman regularly appears on TV news, talk radio, and in articles as a networking and cybersecurity expert. Additionally, he presents at conferences and in webinars, runs workshops, and appears in podcasts.

Weissman has a master's degree in computer science from Brooklyn College and holds 44 industry certifications, including CCNP Enterprise, Cisco Certified Specialist – Enterprise Core, Cisco Certified Specialist – Enterprise Advanced Infrastructure Implementation, CCNA Security, CCNA, CompTIA Security+, CompTIA Network+, CompTIA A+, CompTIA Linux+, CompTIA Server+, EC-Council Certified Ethical Hacker (CEH), EC-Council Computer Hacking Forensic Investigator (CHFI), and IPv6 Forum Certified Network Engineer (Gold), among many others. He was inducted into the IPv6 Forum's New Internet IPv6 Hall of Fame (www.ipv6halloffame.org) as an IPv6 Evangelist in 2021.

Follow Jonathan S. Weissman on LinkedIn at https://linkedin.com/in/jonathan-s-weissman-058b649b/, Twitter at https://twitter.com/CSCPROF, and Instagram at https://instagram.com/cscprof/. Subscribe to his YouTube channel at https://youtube.com/Weissman52.

About the Technical Editor

Edward Tetz graduated in 1990 from Saint Lawrence College in Cornwall, Ontario, with a degree in business administration. Since that time, he has spent his career delivering certified technical training for a Microsoft Training Center and working as a service delivery professional in both Halifax, Nova Scotia, and Ottawa, Ontario. Over his career, Ed has supported Apple Macintosh, IBM OS/2, Linux, Novell NetWare, and all Microsoft operating systems from MS-DOS to Windows Server 2019, as well as hardware from most of the major manufactures. Ed currently works for Microsoft in Customer Success in Ottawa, supporting enterprise and government customers.

When not working with technology, Ed spends time with his wife, Sharon, and his two daughters, Emily and Mackenzie.

Contents at a Glance

1.0 Networking Fundamentals   1

2.0 Network Implementations 129

3.0 Network Operations 191

4.0 Network Security 233

5.0 Network Troubleshooting 311

A   About the Online Content 385

      Index 389

Contents

Acknowledgments xxix
Introduction xxxi

1.0   Networking Fundamentals 1

Objective 1.1 Compare and contrast the Open Systems Interconnection
(OSI) model layers and encapsulation concepts. 2
   OSI Model 2
      Layer 1 – Physical 3
      Layer 2 – Data Link 4
      Layer 3 – Network 7
      Layer 4 – Transport 7
      Layer 5 – Session 7
      Layer 6 – Presentation 8
      Layer 7 – Application 8
   Data Encapsulation and Decapsulation Within the OSI Model Context 8
      Ethernet Header, Internet Protocol (IP) Header, Transmission Control
         Protocol (TCP)/User Datagram Protocol (UDP) Headers, Payload 8
      TCP Flags 11
      Maximum Transmission Unit (MTU) 13
   REVIEW 14
      1.1 QUESTIONS 15
      1.1 ANSWERS 15

Objective 1.2 Explain the characteristics of network topologies
and network types 15
   Bus 16
   Ring 16
   Hybrid 17
   Star/Hub-and-Spoke 19
   Mesh 19

Network Types and Characteristics 21
 Client-Server 21
 Peer-to-Peer 21
 Local Area Network (LAN) 22
 Wide Area Network (WAN) 22
 Metropolitan Area Network (MAN) 22
 Wireless Local Area Network (WLAN) 22
 Personal Area Network (PAN) 22
 Campus Area Network (CAN) 23
 Storage Area Network (SAN) 23
 Multiprotocol Label Switching (MPLS) 23
 Software-Defined Wide Area Network (SDWAN) 24
 Multipoint Generic Routing Encapsulation (mGRE) 24
Service-Related Entry Point 24
 Demarcation Point 25
 Smartjack 26
Virtual Network Concepts 26
 Hypervisor 27
 Virtual Network Interface Card (vNIC) 28
 vSwitch 29
 Network Function Virtualization 30
Provider Links 30
 Satellite 30
 Digital Subscriber Line (DSL) 31
 Cable 32
 Leased Line 33
 Metro-Optical 33
REVIEW 34
 1.2 QUESTIONS 34
 1.2 ANSWERS 35
Objective 1.3 Summarize the types of cables and connectors
and explain which is the appropriate type for a solution 35
Copper 35
 Twisted Pair 35
 Coaxial/RG-6 37
 Twinaxial 39
 Termination Standards 39
Fiber 40
 Single-mode 41
 Multimode 41

Connector Types 42
  Local Connector (LC), Straight Tip (ST), Subscriber Connector (SC),
    Mechanical Transfer (MT), Registered Jack (RJ) 42
  RJ11, RJ45, F-type Connector 43
  Transceivers/Media Converters 43
  Transceiver type 43
Cable Management 44
  Patch Panel/Patch Bay 44
  Fiber Distribution Panel 46
  Punchdown Block 46
Ethernet Standards 47
  Copper 47
  Fiber 50
  REVIEW 53
    1.3 QUESTIONS 54
    1.3 ANSWERS 54

Objective 1.4 Given a scenario, configure a subnet and use
appropriate IP addressing schemes 55
Public vs. Private 55
  RFC 1918 55
  Network Address Translation (NAT) 56
  Port Address Translation (PAT) 57
IPv4 vs. IPv6 59
  Automatic Private IP Addressing (APIPA), Link-Local 59
  Extended Unique Identifier (EUI-64) 60
  Broadcast 62
  Multicast 63
  Unicast 65
  Anycast 66
  Loopback 66
Default Gateway 67
IPv4 Subnetting 67
  Classful 73
  Classless (Variable-Length Subnet Mask) 74
  Classless Inter-Domain Routing (CIDR) Notation 75
IPv6 Concepts 76
  Tunneling 76
  Dual Stack 76
  Shorthand Notation 77
  Router Advertisement, Stateless Address Autoconfiguration (SLAAC) 78

Virtual IP (VIP) 79
Subinterfaces 80
REVIEW 81
1.4 QUESTIONS 81
1.4 ANSWERS 81

Objective 1.5 Explain common ports and protocols, their application, and encrypted alternatives 82
Protocols and Ports 82
Types of Ports 84
Port States 85
Commonly Used Ports 86
IP Protocol Types 89
TCP and UDP 89
Internet Control Message Protocol (ICMP) 92
Generic Routing Encapsulation (GRE) 94
Internet Protocol Security (IPsec) 94
Connectionless vs. Connection-Oriented 94
REVIEW 94
1.5 QUESTIONS 95
1.5 ANSWERS 95

Objective 1.6 Explain the use and purpose of network services 96
DHCP 96
Scope, Scope Options 96
Lease Time, Available Leases 96
Dynamic Assignment 97
Static Assignment 97
Exclusion Ranges 97
Reservation 97
DHCP Relay, IP Helper/UDP Forwarding 98
DNS 99
Zone Transfers 99
Global Hierarchy 100
Time to Live (TTL), DNS Caching 103
Recursive Lookup/Iterative Lookup 103
Record Types 103
Reverse DNS/Reverse Lookup/Forward Lookup 106
Internal vs. External DNS 107
NTP 107
Stratum, Clients, Servers 107
REVIEW 108
1.6 QUESTIONS 108
1.6 ANSWERS 109

Objective 1.7 Explain basic corporate and datacenter network architecture 109
   Three-Tiered 109
      Access/Edge 110
      Distribution/Aggregation Layer 110
      Core 111
   Software-Defined Networking 111
      Control Layer, Infrastructure Layer 112
      Management Plane, Application Layer 113
   Spine and Leaf 113
      Software-Defined Network 114
      Top-of-Rack Switching 114
      Backbone 114
   Traffic Flows 114
      North-South 114
      East-West 115
   Branch Office vs. On-Premises Datacenter vs. Colocation 115
   Storage Area Networks 116
      Connection Types 117
   REVIEW 118
      1.7 QUESTIONS 119
      1.7 ANSWERS 119
Objective 1.8 Summarize cloud concepts and connectivity options . . . 119
   Deployment Models 120
      Public 120
      Private 120
      Hybrid 120
      Community 121
   Service Models 121
      Software as a Service (SaaS) 121
      Infrastructure as a Service (IaaS) 122
      Platform as a Service (PaaS) 123
      Desktop as a Service (DaaS) 123
   Infrastructure as Code 124
      Automation/Orchestration 124
   Connectivity Options 124
      Virtual Private Network (VPN) 124
      Private-Direct Connection to Cloud Provider 125
   Multitenancy 125
   Scalability 125

Elasticity 126
Security Implications 126
REVIEW 127
    1.8 QUESTIONS 127
    1.8 ANSWERS 128

2.0 Network Implementations 129

Objective 2.1 Compare and contrast various devices, their features,
and their appropriate placement on the network 130
    Networking Devices 130
        Layer 2 Switch 130
        Layer 3 Capable Switch 132
        Router 132
        Hub 132
        Access Point 133
        Bridge 133
        Wireless LAN Controller 133
        Load Balancer 134
        Proxy Server 135
        Cable Modem 135
        DSL Modem 136
        Repeater 136
        Voice Gateway 136
        Media Converter 136
        Firewall 137
        Intrusion Prevention System(IPS)/Intrusion Detection System (IDS) Device ... 139
        VPN Headend 141
    Networked Devices 142
        Voice over Internet Protocol (VoIP) Phone 142
        Printer 142
        Physical Access Control Devices 143
        Cameras 143
        Heating, Ventilation, and Air Conditioning (HVAC) Sensors 144
        Internet of Things (IoT) 144
    Industrial Control Systems/Supervisory Control and Data Acquisition (SCADA) 145
    REVIEW 147
        2.1 QUESTIONS 148
        2.1 ANSWERS 149

Objective 2.2 Compare and contrast routing technologies
and bandwidth management concepts 149
    Routing 149
        Dynamic Routing 152
        Static Routing 156

Default Route 156

Administrative Distance 156

Exterior vs. Interior 157

Time to Live 157

Bandwidth Management 157

Quality of Service (QoS), Traffic Shaping 158

REVIEW 158

2.2 QUESTIONS 159

2.2 ANSWERS 160

Objective 2.3 Given a scenario, configure and deploy common Ethernet switching features.............................. 160

Data Virtual Local Area Network (VLAN) 160

Voice VLAN 161

Port Configurations 161

Port Tagging/802.1Q 161

Port Aggregation 162

Duplex 162

Speed 163

Flow Control 163

Port Mirroring 163

Port Security 164

Jumbo Frames 165

Auto-Medium-Dependent Interface Crossover (MDI-X) 166

Media Access Control (MAC) Address Tables 166

Power over Ethernet (PoE)/Power over Ethernet Plus (PoE+) .. 167

Spanning Tree Protocol 168

Carrier-Sense Multiple Access with Collision Detection (CSMA/CD) 169

Address Resolution Protocol (ARP) 170

Neighbor Discovery Protocol 173

REVIEW 174

2.3 QUESTIONS 174

2.3 ANSWERS 175

Objective 2.4 Given a scenario, install and configure the appropriate wireless standards and technologies...................... 175

802.11 Standards 175

a 175

b 176

g 176

n (Wi-Fi 4) 177

ac (Wi-Fi 5) 178

ax (Wi-Fi 6) 178

Frequencies and Range 179
    2.4 GHz 180
    5.0 GHz 180
Channels 180
    Regulatory Impacts 181
Channel Bonding 181
Service Set Identifier (SSID) 181
    Basic Service Set 182
    Independent Basic Service Set (Ad-hoc) 182
    Extended Service Set 182
    Roaming 183
Antenna Types 183
    Omni 183
    Directional 184
Encryption Standards 184
    Wi-Fi Protected Access (WPA)/WPA2 Personal [Advanced Encryption
      Standard (AES)/Temporal Key Integrity Protocol (TKIP)] 184
    WPA/WPA2 Enterprise (AES/TKIP) 186
Cellular Technologies 186
    Global System for Mobile Communications (GSM) 187
    Code-Division Multiple Access (CDMA) 187
    Long-Term Evolution (LTE) 187
    3G, 4G, 5G 188
Multiple Input, Multiple Output (MIMO) and Multi-user MIMO (MU-MIMO) 188
REVIEW 189
    2.4 QUESTIONS 189
    2.4 ANSWERS 190

3.0   Network Operations 191

  Objective 3.1 Given a scenario, use the appropriate statistics
and sensors to ensure network availability 192
Performance Metrics/Sensors 192
    Device/Chassis 192
    Network Metrics 193
SNMP 194
    Management Information Bases (MIBs) 194
    Object Identifiers (OIDs) 194
    Traps 194
Network Device Logs 196
    Log Reviews 197
    Logging Levels/Severity Levels 197

Interface Statistics/Status 198
    Link State (Up/Down) 198
    Speed/Duplex 198
    Send/Receive Traffic 199
    Cyclic Redundancy Checks (CRCs) 199
    Protocol Packet and Byte Counts 199
Interface Errors or Alerts 199
    CRC Errors 200
    Giants 200
    Runts 200
    Encapsulation Errors 200
Environmental Factors and Sensors: Temperature, Humidity, Electrical, Flooding ... 200
Baselines 201
NetFlow Data 202
Uptime/Downtime 202
REVIEW 203
    3.1 QUESTIONS 204
    3.1 ANSWERS 205
Objective 3.2 Explain the purpose of organizational documents
and policies. 205
Plans and Procedures 205
    Change Management 206
    Incident Response Plan 206
    Disaster Recovery Plan 207
    Business Continuity Plan 207
    System Life Cycle 208
    Standard Operating Procedures 208
Hardening and Security Policies 208
    Password Policy 209
    Acceptable Use Policy 209
    Bring Your Own Device (BYOD) Policy 210
    Remote Access Policy 210
    Onboarding and Offboarding Policy 210
    Security Policy 211
    Data Loss Prevention 211
Common Documentation 211
    Physical Network Diagram 211
    Logical Network Diagram 215
    Wiring Diagram 215
    Site Survey Report 216

Audit and Assessment Report 217
Baseline Configurations 217
Common Agreements 218
Non-Disclosure Agreement (NDA) 218
Service-Level Agreement (SLA) 218
Memorandum of Understanding (MOU) 219
REVIEW 219
3.2 QUESTIONS 221
3.2 ANSWERS 221

Objective 3.3 Explain high availability and disaster recovery concepts and summarize which is the best solution. 222

Load Balancing 222
Multipathing 222
Network Interface Card (NIC) Teaming 223
Redundant Hardware/Clusters 223
Switches 224
Routers 224
Firewalls 224
Facilities and Infrastructure Support 224
Uninterruptible Power Supply (UPS) 225
Power Distribution Units (PDUs) 226
Generator 226
HVAC 226
Fire Suppression 227
Redundancy and High Availability (HA) Concepts 227
Cold Site 227
Warm Site 227
Hot Site 227
Cloud Site 228
Active-Active vs. Active-Passive 228
Mean Time to Repair (MTTR) 229
Mean Time Between Failure (MTBF) 229
Recovery Time Objective (RTO) 229
Recovery Point Objective (RPO) 229
Network Device Backup/Restore 230
Configuration 230
State 230
REVIEW 231
3.3 QUESTIONS 232
3.3 ANSWERS 232

4.0 Network Security 233

Objective 4.1 Explain common security concepts 234
Confidentiality, Integrity, Availability (CIA) 234
Threats 235
　Internal 235
　External 235
Vulnerabilities 236
　Common Vulnerabilities and Exposures (CVE) 236
　Zero-Day 236
Exploits 237
Least Privilege 238
Role-Based Access 238
Zero Trust 238
Defense in Depth 239
　Network Segmentation Enforcement 239
　Screened Subnet [Previously Known as Demilitarized Zone (DMZ)] 239
　Separation of Duties 240
　Network Access Control 241
　Honeypot 241
Authentication Methods 242
　Multifactor 242
　Terminal Access Controller Access-Control System Plus (TACACS+) 243
　Remote Authentication Dial-in User Service (RADIUS) 243
　Single Sign-On (SSO) 243
　LDAP 244
　Kerberos 244
　Local Authentication 245
　Extensible Authentication Protocol (EAP) 245
　802.1X 246
Risk Management 247
　Security Risk Assessments 247
　Business Risk Assessments 249
Security Information and Event Management (SIEM) 250
REVIEW 251
　4.1 QUESTIONS 253
　4.1 ANSWERS 254
Objective 4.2 Compare and contrast common types of attacks 254
Technology-Based 254
　Denial-of-Service (DoS)/Distributed Denial-of-Service (DDoS) 254
　On-Path Attack (Previously Known as Man-in-the-Middle Attack) 256

ARP Spoofing 256
DNS Poisoning 257
VLAN Hopping 257
Rogue DHCP 258
Rogue Access Point (AP) 259
Evil Twin 259
Ransomware 259
Password Attacks 260
MAC Spoofing 263
IP Spoofing 263
Deauthentication 264
Malware 266
Human and Environmental 269
Social Engineering 269
REVIEW 274
4.2 QUESTIONS 276
4.2 ANSWERS 276
Objective 4.3 Given a scenario, apply network
hardening techniques 277
Best Practices 277
Secure SNMP 277
Router Advertisement (RA) Guard 277
Port Security 278
Dynamic ARP Inspection 280
Control Plane Policing 280
Private VLANs 280
Disable Unneeded Switchports 281
Disable Unneeded Network Services 281
Change Default Passwords 281
Password Complexity/Length 282
Enable DHCP Snooping 282
Change Default VLAN 282
Patch and Firmware Management 282
Access Control List 284
Firewall Rules 285
Role-Based Access 285
Wireless Security 285
MAC Filtering 286
Antenna Placement 286
Power Levels 287
Wireless Client Isolation 288
Guest Network Isolation 288

Preshared Keys (PSKs) 288
EAP 288
Geofencing 288
Captive Portal 289
IoT Access Considerations 289
REVIEW 292
4.3 QUESTIONS 294
4.3 ANSWERS 294

Objective 4.4 Compare and contrast remote access methods
and security implications 295
Site-to-Site VPN 296
Client-to-Site VPN 296
Clientless VPN 296
Split Tunnel vs. Full Tunnel 296
Remote Desktop Connection 297
Remote Desktop Gateway 298
SSH 298
Virtual Network Computing (VNC) 299
Virtual Desktop 299
Authentication and Authorization Considerations 300
In-Band vs. Out-of-Band Management 300
REVIEW 301
4.4 QUESTIONS 301
4.4 ANSWERS 302

Objective 4.5 Explain the importance of physical security 302
Detection Methods 302
Camera 303
Motion Detection 303
Asset Tags 303
Tamper Detection 303
Prevention Methods 303
Employee Training 304
Access Control Hardware 304
Locking Racks, Locking Cabinets 306
Access Control Vestibule (Previously Known as a Mantrap) 306
Smart Lockers 307
Asset Disposal 307
Factory Reset/Wipe Configuration 307
Sanitize Devices for Disposal 308
REVIEW 308
4.5 QUESTIONS 309
4.5 ANSWERS 309

5.0   Network Troubleshooting   311

Objective 5.1 Explain the network troubleshooting methodology . . .   312

Identify the Problem   312
    Gather Information   313
    Question Users   313
    Identify Symptoms   313
    Determine if Anything Has Changed   313
    Duplicate the Problem, if Possible   314
    Approach Multiple Problems Individually   314
Establish a Theory of Probable Cause   315
    Question the Obvious   315
    Consider Multiple Approaches   315
Test the Theory to Determine the Cause   316
    If the Theory Is Confirmed, Determine the Next Steps
      to Resolve the Problem   317
    If the Theory Is Not Confirmed, Reestablish a New Theory or Escalate . . .   317
    Establish a Plan of Action to Resolve the Problem and Identify
      Potential Effects   317
    Implement the Solution or Escalate As Necessary   318
Verify Full System Functionality and, if Applicable, Implement
    Preventive Measures   318
Document Findings, Actions, Outcomes, and Lessons Learned   319
REVIEW   320
    5.1 QUESTIONS   320
    5.1 ANSWERS   321

Objective 5.2 Given a scenario, troubleshoot common cable
connectivity issues and select the appropriate tools   321

Specifications and Limitations   321
    Throughput   321
    Speed   322
    Distance   323
Cable Considerations   323
    Shielded and Unshielded   323
    Plenum and Riser-Rated   324
Cable Application   324
    Rollover Cable/Console Cable   325
    Crossover Cable   325
    Power over Ethernet   327
Common Issues   327
    Attenuation   328
    Interference   328

Decibel (dB) Loss 329
Incorrect Pinout 330
Bad Ports 330
Open/Short 330
Light-Emitting Diode (LED) Status Indicators 330
Incorrect Transceivers 331
Duplexing Issues 331
Transmit and Receive (TX/RX) Reversed 331
Dirty Optical Cables 331
Common Tools 332
Cable Crimper 332
Punchdown Tool 332
Tone Generator 332
Loopback Adapter 334
Optical Time-Domain Reflectometer (OTDR) 335
Multimeter 336
Cable Tester 336
Wire Map 336
Tap 337
Fusion Splicers 337
Spectrum Analyzers 337
Snips/Cutters 338
Cable Stripper 339
Fiber Light Meter 339
REVIEW 340
5.2 QUESTIONS 343
5.2 ANSWERS 343
Objective 5.3 Given a scenario, use the appropriate network
software tools and commands 344
Software Tools 344
WiFi Analyzer 344
Protocol Analyzer/Packet Capture 344
Bandwidth Speed Tester 346
Port Scanner 347
iperf 348
NetFlow Analyzers 348
Trivial File Transfer Protocol (TFTP) Server 348
Terminal Emulator 349
IP Scanner 349
Command Line Tool 349
ping 349
ipconfig/ifconfig/ip 349

nslookup/dig 351
traceroute/tracert 353
arp 354
netstat 354
hostname 354
route 356
telnet 357
tcpdump 357
nmap 357
Basic Network Platform Commands 357
show interface 357
show config 357
show route 357
REVIEW 358
5.3 QUESTIONS 359
5.3 ANSWERS 360
Objective 5.4 Given a scenario, troubleshoot common wireless
connectivity issues. **360**
Specifications and Limitations 361
Throughput 361
Speed 361
Distance 361
Received Signal Strength Indication (RSSI) Signal Strength 361
Effective Isotropic Radiated Power (EIRP)/Power Settings 362
Considerations 363
Antennas 363
Channel Utilization 364
AP Association Time 364
Site Survey 364
Common Issues 367
Interference 367
Antenna Cable Attenuation/Signal Loss 367
RF Attenuation/Signal Loss 367
Wrong SSID 368
Incorrect Passphrase 368
Encryption Protocol Mismatch 368
Insufficient Wireless Coverage 369
Captive Portal Issues 369
Client Disassociation Issues 369
REVIEW 369
5.4 QUESTIONS 371
5.4 ANSWERS 371

Objective 5.5 Given a scenario, troubleshoot general
networking issues 372
   Considerations 372
      Device Configuration Review 372
      Routing Tables 372
      Interface Status 372
      VLAN Assignment 373
      Network Performance Baselines 373
   Common Issues 373
      Collisions 373
      Broadcast Storm 374
      Duplicate MAC Address 374
      Duplicate IP Address 374
      Multicast Flooding 374
      Asymmetrical Routing 375
      Switching Loops 375
      Routing Loops 375
      Rogue DHCP Server 376
      DHCP Scope Exhaustion 376
      IP Setting Issues 377
      Missing Route 378
      Low Optical Link Budget 378
      Certificate Issues 378
      Hardware Failure 379
      Host-Based/Network-Based Firewall Settings 379
      Blocked Services, Ports, or Addresses 379
      Incorrect VLAN 379
      DNS Issues 379
      NTP Issues 379
      BYOD Challenges 379
      Licensed Feature Issues 380
      Network Performance Issues 380
   REVIEW 381
      5.5 QUESTIONS 383
      5.5 ANSWERS 384
A   About the Online Content 385
   System Requirements 385
   Your Total Seminars Training Hub Account 385
      Privacy Notice 385
   Single User License Terms and Conditions 386

TotalTester Online 387
    Pre-Assessment Test 387
Other Book Resources 388
    TotalSims for Network+ 388
    Mike's Video Training 388
    Mike's Cool Tools 388
Technical Support 388

Index 389

Acknowledgments

Many great people worked together to make this book happen.

My sponsoring editor at McGraw Hill, Tim Green, set the entire book in motion and provided valuable guidance.

My acquisitions coordinator, Caitlin Cromley-Linn, and my project editor, Rachel Fogelberg, helped me keep it all on track and did an outstanding job managing this book through the many phases of development and production.

My technical editor, Ed Tetz, copy editor, Bill McManus, and proofreader, Richard Camp, were exceptional in their findings and suggestions.

Introduction

Whether the CompTIA Network+ certification is your first step toward a career focus in networking or an additional skill credential, this book is your guide to success on the CompTIA Network+ certification exam, the vendor-neutral, industry-standard certification developed for foundation-level networking professionals. Based on a worldwide job task analysis, the exam structure focuses on five domains, as set forth in the official CompTIA Network+ Certification Exam Objectives (Exam Number N10-008):

Domain	Percentage of Examination
1.0 Networking Fundamentals	24%
2.0 Network Implementations	19%
3.0 Network Operations	16%
4.0 Network Security	19%
5.0 Network Troubleshooting	22%

I have structured the content of this book to correspond closely to the outline of the CompTIA Network+ Certification Exam Objectives, including topics and subtopics, with occasional variations in sequence to provide my expert take on the best way to approach the topics.

You can learn more about the exam and download a PDF containing the exam objectives at https://www.comptia.org/certifications/network.

This should *not* be the *first* book you use to study for the CompTIA Network+ Certification Exam, but rather the *last*. I recommend starting with either the *All-in-One CompTIA Network+ Certification Exam Guide, Eighth Edition (Exam N10-008)* or *Mike Meyers' CompTIA Network+ Guide to Managing and Troubleshooting Networks, Sixth Edition (Exam N10-008)* to learn the CompTIA Network+ content in depth. Then, I recommend going through the hands-on labs I wrote in *Mike Meyers' CompTIA Network+ Guide to Managing and Troubleshooting Networks Lab Manual, Sixth Edition (Exam N10-008)* to gain practical experience applying the concepts you learned in the first book you chose.

This book serves a different purpose: it is intended for you to read *after* you've completed your studying and *right before* you take the CompTIA Network+ Certification Exam. It will help you remember the key points and the most important concepts. It will help you focus on what's most important to remember about every one of the exam objectives. Since the book follows the order of the exam objectives, and is not written in an order for learning the content the first time, it also serves as a checklist to make sure you're comfortable with each exam objective.

The book contains some useful items to call out points of interest:

EXAM TIP Indicates critical topics you're likely to see on the actual exam.

NOTE Points out ancillary, but pertinent information, as well as areas for further study.

KEY TERM Describes special terms, in detail, and in a way you can easily understand.

CAUTION Warns you of common pitfalls, misconceptions, and potentially harmful or risky situations in working with the technology in the real world.

Cross-Reference

Directs you to other places in the book where concepts are covered, for your reference.

ADDITIONAL RESOURCES Points to where you can find books, Web sites, and other media for further assistance.

The end of each objective gives you handy tools. The Review section covers each objective with a synopsis—a great way to quickly review the critical information. Then, the Questions and Answers sections enable you to test your newly acquired skills. For further study, this book includes access to online practice exams that will help you to prepare for taking the exam itself. All the information you need for accessing the exam questions is provided in the appendix. I recommend that you take the practice exams to identify where you have knowledge gaps and then go back and review as needed.

Teaching is my absolute passion! Not only am I passionate about teaching, I also am extremely passionate about the subjects I teach. I am fortunate to live by the famous proverb, "Choose a job you love, and you will never have to work a day in your life."

My classes, like the process for studying for the CompTIA Network+ Certification Exam, consist of a mix of lecture and lab. In my opinion, you can't attempt any lab without having fundamental knowledge learned through the lecture. Furthermore, knowledge by itself is not enough. Being able to apply knowledge to hands-on lab scenarios, simulating real-world environments, offers you the best chance at success!

As I say at the end of all my courses, "Once a student of mine, always a student of mine." Please get in touch and stay in touch with me. I'd love to hear how this book helped you!

—Jonathan S. Weissman

Networking Fundamentals

DOMAIN 1.0

Domain Objectives

- **1.1** Compare and contrast the Open Systems Interconnection (OSI) model layers and encapsulation concepts.

- **1.2** Explain the characteristics of network topologies and network types.

- **1.3** Summarize the types of cables and connectors and explain which is the appropriate type for a solution.

- **1.4** Given a scenario, configure a subnet and use appropriate IP addressing schemes.

- **1.5** Explain common ports and protocols, their application, and encrypted alternatives.

- **1.6** Explain the use and purpose of network services.

- **1.7** Explain basic corporate and datacenter network architecture.

- **1.8** Summarize cloud concepts and connectivity options.

Objective 1.1 ## Compare and contrast the Open Systems Interconnection (OSI) model layers and encapsulation concepts

Networking takes a lot of pieces, both hardware and software, to get anything done. Just making Google appear in your Web browser is the culmination of decades of research, development, and technological progress. Whenever we encounter highly complex technologies, we need to simplify the overall process by breaking it into discrete, simple, individual processes. We do this by using models.

Modeling is critical in networking. We use models to understand and communicate with other techs about networks. What functions define all networks? What details can you omit without rendering the model inaccurate? Does the model retain its usefulness when describing a network that does not employ all the layers of the model?

In the early days of networking, different manufacturers made unique types of networks that functioned fairly well. But each network had its own naming conventions, cabling, hardware, drivers, applications, and many other unique features. Back then, a single manufacturer provided everything for a customer when the customer purchased a network solution: cabling, NICs, hubs (which are long since obsolete), switches, routers, servers, drivers, and all the software, in one complete and expensive package. Although these networks worked fine as stand-alone networks, the proprietary nature of the hardware and software made it difficult—to put it mildly—to connect networks of multiple manufacturers. To interconnect networks and improve networking as a whole, someone needed to create a guide, a model that described the functions of a network, so that people who made hardware and software could work together to make networks that worked together well.

OSI Model

The International Organization for Standardization (ISO) created a framework into which the major network hardware and software components and protocols could be placed, to give every item a common reference point. This framework, a seven-layer model called the *OSI model* (Open Systems Interconnection model), provides a means of relating the components and their functions to each other and a way of standardizing components and protocols.

ADDITIONAL RESOURCES   ISO is often expanded as the International Standards Organization, but that's not correct. The International Organization for Standardization, founded in London in 1946, wanted to use three official languages. The ISO founders didn't want to use different acronyms in different languages (IOS in English, OIN in French, and MOC in Russian), so they used ISO as the short form of the organization's name. According to the ISO Web site, ISO is derived from the Greek word *isos*, meaning "equal," and is not an acronym. Standards bodies look to promote equality, which is why this organization chose to be known as ISO. However, this fact has been called into question, since the word "equal" never came up when the organization was founded. Read more at https://fstoppers.com/originals/myths-iso-423056, https://www.iso.org/files/live/sites/isoorg/files/about%20ISO/docs/en/Friendship_among_equals.pdf, and https://www.iso.org/about-us.html.

The OSI model provides a critical common language that network hardware and software engineers can use to communicate and ensure that their equipment will function together. Each layer of the model represents a particular aspect of network function.

EXAM TIP   The CompTIA Network+ exam expects you to know the layers by name, how they function in relation to each other, and what they represent.

As well as helping to standardize the design elements of network components, the OSI model helps describe the relationships between network protocols. As you'll see, more than one protocol or action is needed to get your data onto a network.

Let's run through the layers and an overview of their tasks and responsibilities. Figure 1.1-1 summarizes the layers and their functions.

Layer 1 – Physical

Layer 1 of the OSI model, the *Physical* layer, defines the network standards relating to the electrical, light, or wireless signals that travel the network cables, the connectors, and the media types (cables or wireless technologies) themselves. The Physical layer also determines the way that data is placed on the network media.

For the CompTIA Network+ exam, you need to know examples of components that run at each layer of the OSI model. Cables are an example of a network component that is considered part of the Physical layer. Wireless transmission also uses the Physical layer. Hubs operated at this layer in their heyday.

Also operating at Layer 1 are SONET/SDH, Bluetooth, Wi-Fi, and more.

Frames are turned into 1s and 0s and transmitted at bits and bytes at Layer 1.

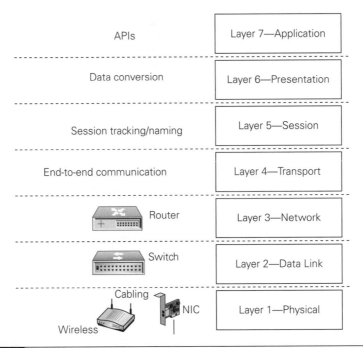

APIs	Layer 7—Application
Data conversion	Layer 6—Presentation
Session tracking/naming	Layer 5—Session
End-to-end communication	Layer 4—Transport
Router	Layer 3—Network
Switch	Layer 2—Data Link
Cabling / Wireless / NIC	Layer 1—Physical

FIGURE 1.1-1   The seven-layer OSI model

Layer 2 – Data Link

Layer 2, the *Data Link* layer, defines the rules for gathering and completing all the elements that make up a data frame and putting the whole thing together, so that it can be passed to a Physical-layer device and on to the network, for traffic leaving a machine. For traffic coming into a machine, the Data Link layer strips the frame off and passes the resulting packet up to Layer 3.

The magic of a network starts with the *network interface card*, or *NIC* (pronounced "nick"), which serves as the interface between the PC and the network. NICs come in a wide array of shapes and sizes. On older systems, a NIC truly was a separate card that snapped into an expansion slot, which is why they were called network interface *cards*. Even though they've been built into the motherboard for decades, they are still called NICs.

There needs to be a mechanism that gives each system a unique identifier—like a telephone number—so data is delivered to the right system. That's one of the NIC's most important jobs. Inside every NIC, burned onto a type of ROM chip, is special firmware containing a unique identifier with a 48-bit value called the *MAC (media access control) address*.

Each NIC vendor/manufacturer/organization purchases an OUI (Organizationally Unique Identifier) from the Institute of Electrical and Electronics Engineers (IEEE), who won't give more than one vendor/manufacturer/organization the same OUI. In some cases, however, a NIC vendor/manufacturer/organization can assign the same device ID to more than one NIC, but it will ship NICs with the same address to various parts of the United States or world, ensuring that two NICs with the same MAC address don't wind up on the same network. MAC addresses are locally significant just to the network they're on. Furthermore, a NIC can be configured with a locally administered address by an administrator or user. From the other side, MAC addresses can be spoofed by an attacker.

In print, we represent the MAC address as 12 hexadecimal digits, with each group of two separated by a dash; for example: A0-AF-BD-BB-10-52. The first six digits, in this example A0-AF-BD, represent the number of the NIC manufacturer, which is Intel in this case. The last six digits, in this example BB-10-52, are the manufacturer's unique serial number for that NIC, the *device ID*.

 NOTE   Would you like to see the MAC address of your NIC? Open a command prompt/terminal. On a Windows machine, execute **ipconfig /all** and look at the value for Physical Address. On a Linux box, execute **ip a** and look for the value for link/ether. On a Mac, execute **ifconfig** and look for the value for ether. Linux and Mac use a colon delimiter between each two hex characters, while Windows uses a dash. Cisco IOS (Internetwork Operating System) is even more unique, and represents a MAC address with three groups of four hex digits separated by a dot.

So how is a MAC address used? Ah, that's where the fun begins! Recall that computer data is binary, which means it's made up of streams of 1s and 0s. NICs send and receive this binary data as pulses of electricity, light, or radio waves. The NICs that use electricity to send and receive data are usually taught first, so let's consider that type of NIC now. The specific process by which a NIC uses electricity to send and receive data is exceedingly complicated but, luckily for you, not necessary to understand. Instead, just think of a *charge* on the wire as a *one* and *no charge* as a *zero*.

Once you understand how data moves along the wire, the next question is how the network gets the right data to the right system. All networks transmit data (Web pages, files, print jobs, etc.) by transmitting a series of bits, 1s and 0s, across the Physical layer. These bits and bytes represent discrete chunks called frames, which is what they're known as at Layer 2. A *frame* is basically a container for data and metadata moving across a network. The NIC creates and sends, as well as receives and reads, these frames.

Switches exist at Layer 2 and carefully read frames sent from NICs, learning and associating source MAC addresses in the frames to the physical ports on the switch (not to be confused with the logical ports that programs and services listen on) they were heard on. This allows switches to send frames just to the devices that should get the traffic, unlike the old, obsolete Layer 1 hubs that sent all frames to all connected ports (except the port that the frame originated on). The exact contents (payload/data) of the frame will vary, but Ethernet frames, as shown in Figure 1.1-2, have a header that includes the physical MAC address of the receiving machine, the physical MAC address of the sending machine, and the type of protocol encapsulated in the frame (for data frames, not control frames, it will be Internet Protocol [IP] or Address Resolution Protocol [ARP]). After the header comes the actual payload/data

Destination MAC 6 bytes	Source MAC 6 bytes	Type 2 bytes	Data 46–1500 bytes	Frame Check Sequence 4 bytes

FIGURE 1.1-2   Ethernet frame

(ARP frame or IP packet), followed by a trailer that contains an error-detection mechanism, the *frame check sequence (FCS)*, which implements a cyclic redundancy check (CRC) algorithm, to make sure that no part of the data was changed accidentally during transmission. 802.11 frames have equivalents of all of these, as well as many other fields.

Cross-Reference

You'll learn how the switches learn MAC addresses and make decisions based on them, with a MAC address table, in Objective 2.3.

The Data Link layer on the sending machine assembles outgoing frames and calculates the FCS by applying a standard mathematical formula called *cyclic redundancy check (CRC)* to the contents of the frame. The CRC value is placed in the Ethernet trailer, known as the FCS. The receiving machine performs the same calculation for incoming frames, enabling the receiving machine to verify the validity of the data by comparing its locally generated FCS value with that sent in the frame. If the values don't match, the frame is discarded. Upper layers and their protocols deal with error correction and retransmissions.

The Data Link layer also determines how data is placed on the wire by using an access method. The wired access method, *carrier-sense multiple access with collision detection (CSMA/CD)*, was once used by all wired Ethernet networks, but is automatically disabled on switched full-duplex links, which have been the norm for decades. *Carrier-sense multiple access with collision avoidance (CSMA/CA)* is used by wireless networks, in a similar fashion.

The Data Link layer is divided into two sublayers:

- **Logical Link Control (LLC)**   The LLC sublayer is responsible for flow control and error management functions, which were used in the past by now obsolete protocols. It was also used to multiplex protocols, when IP wasn't the end-all-be-all protocol as it is today. You'll only see the 802.2 LLC header today for management protocols, like VTP (VLAN Trunking Protocol), CDP (Cisco Discovery Protocol), and STP (Spanning Tree Protocol).

- **Medium/Media Access Control (MAC)**   The MAC sublayer is responsible for addressing network devices by using the physical address—that's the MAC address burned in to the ROM chip of each NIC. The physical address for both the sending and receiving devices are placed in the Layer 2 frame header. This layer also adds and verifies the FCS.

Operating at Layer 2 are ARP, CDP, Ethernet, STP, VTP, 802.1Q (VLANs), and more.

Layer 3 – Network

Layer 3, the *Network* layer, is responsible for logical addressing and routing functions. The Network layer IP addresses identify not only a device, but also the network on which the device resides. Routers use the network identification to determine how to send packets to destination networks.

If the data being sent is bigger than the MTU (maximum transmission unit, discussed in more depth later in this objective) allowed by the Layer 2 protocols (for Ethernet, it's 1500 bytes), the Network layer breaks the packet into smaller ones that will fit inside two or more frames. Breaking up data into smaller chunks at Layer 3 is known as *fragmentation*.

 EXAM TIP   Examples of Layer 3 components are Internet Protocol, IP addresses, and routers.

Operating at Layer 3 are IPv4, IPv6, ICMP (Internet Control Message Protocol), IGMP (Internet Group Message Protocol), IPsec (IP Security), and more. (More information on IPv4 and IPv6 is coming up in Objective 1.4.)

Layer 4 – Transport

Layer 4, the *Transport* layer, is where the sending application chooses between connection-oriented TCP (Transmission Control Protocol) and connectionless UDP (User Datagram Protocol) for end-to-end communication. To see the Transport layer in action, strip away the IP addresses from an IP packet. What's left is a chunk of data in yet another unit called a TCP segment or a UDP datagram.

Operating at Layer 4 are TCP and UDP.

 KEY TERM   An **IP packet** exists at Layer 3. Packets don't exist at any other layer, so don't say "Ethernet packet," "TCP packet," or "UDP packet."

Layer 5 – Session

Layer 5, the *Session* layer, is responsible for establishing, maintaining, and terminating connections, called sessions, between programs on communicating devices. The combination of an IP address, port, and Layer 4 protocol (TCP or UDP) is known as a socket, which represents a session in the form of an endpoint of an active communication link for each side of a connection. The `netstat` utility is used for displaying this socket information.

Layer 6 – Presentation

Layer 6, the *Presentation* layer, used to be responsible for the conversion of data, including compression/decompression, encryption/decryption, and formatting, but these functions are now performed elsewhere. This layer is the layer that has the least relevance to modern communication today, but it simply can't be removed from the model.

Layer 7 – Application

Layer 7, the *Application* layer, represents the network-related program code and functions running on a computer system that either initiate the request on the sending system or service the request on the receiving system.

The Application layer does not refer to actual applications like Wireshark, Zoom, or Microsoft Word. Instead, it refers to the protocols or application programming interfaces (APIs) on which those programs rely. For example, IMAP (Internet Message Access Protocol) and SMTP (Simple Mail Transfer Protocol) are important Application layer protocols for e-mail, but many different end-user applications use those protocols, such as Microsoft Outlook and Mozilla Thunderbird.

At the Application layer are the previously mentioned APIs, which are shared libraries that allow programs on one machine to communicate with other programs on the same machine, the operating system, and even programs on other machines.

Operating at Layer 7 are DNS (Domain Name System), DHCP (Dynamic Host Configuration Protocol), FTP (File Transfer Protocol), HTTP (Hypertext Transfer Protocol), HTTPS (HTTP over TLS – Transport Layer Security), LDAP (Lightweight Directory Access Protocol), SSH (Secure Shell), SNMP (Simple Network Management Protocol), and more.

Data Encapsulation and Decapsulation Within the OSI Model Context

Given that the OSI model's functions are largely hidden from our eyes, it's sometimes difficult to appreciate how each discrete layer performs a necessary step of the data delivery process. Nonetheless, it's important for you to understand just how the OSI model operates. Understanding *data encapsulation and decapsulation within the OSI model context* is one of the keys to understanding modern networking technology.

Ethernet Header, Internet Protocol (IP) Header, Transmission Control Protocol (TCP)/User Datagram Protocol (UDP) Headers, Payload

Think of the last time you were in an airport, waiting to board a flight. Finally, you hear, over the airport speakers, "Flight 260, now boarding." You ready your boarding pass and carry-on luggage and then get in line. You're not flying. You're getting ready to fly. That's the Application layer (Layer 7). As mentioned earlier, APIs, not applications, exist at the Application layer. When you start the ball rolling for networking, API calls are made. You're not sending traffic across networks yet, but you're starting the process. That's just like boarding the flight. You're not flying (networking), but you're getting ready to! The data/*payload* that has just been formed at the Application layer is now passed to the layer below, the Presentation layer.

Think of the last time you prepared for a job interview. You got your clothes ready, your hair ready, and your face ready. That's the Presentation layer (Layer 6). Compression and decompression used to be done at this layer. Encryption and decryption, too. Formatting as well. Just about all of the old functions at this layer have been offloaded to other parts of the networking story, but this layer remains for backward compatibility. The data/payload generated at this layer is added to what came from the layer above and is sent to the layer below, the Session layer.

 NOTE   The terms data and payload are often used interchangeably. Technically speaking though, the payload is the actual transmitted data that is encapsulated inside a protocol of a layer below it. This data is the actual message, but needs to be encapsulated in another protocol of a layer below it. The protocol at the layer below the payload puts a header in front of the data that serves as metadata for the data itself. Layers 1–4 each have a protocol data unit (PDU), which is a single unit of information. At Layer 4, the PDU could be either a segment (if TCP is used) or a datagram (if UDP is used). At Layer 3, the PDU is a packet. At Layer 2, the PDU is a frame. At Layer 1, the PDU is simply bits and bytes. The PDU for Layers 5–7 is simply known as data.

Back when I used dial-up, many years ago, downloading a file often took a great amount of time. Occasionally, someone in the house would suddenly pick up the phone as a file was downloading. Oh no! The download stopped. I would yell "You ruined my download!" In reality, it is the Session layer (Layer 5) that establishes, maintains, and terminates connections between programs on different machines. Data/payload generated at this layer is added to what came from the two layers above and is sent to the layer below, the Transport layer.

At this point, the data/payload faces a pivotal moment. It will be encapsulated in a TCP segment or a UDP datagram at the Transport layer (Layer 4). For applications that require accuracy and integrity, TCP will be chosen. For applications that require speed, UDP will be chosen. If TCP is chosen, the data/payload, which could be quite large at this point, is chopped up into different parts (a process called segmentation) and is placed inside of multiple segments. If UDP is chosen, the data/payload will not be chopped up here, but rather at the Network layer. TCP segments and UDP datagrams vary greatly, but they do share an addressing component in common—ports. A source port and destination port will be added in each. Data/payload generated at this layer is added to what came from the three layers above and is sent to the layer below, the Network layer.

Transmission Control Protocol (TCP)/User Datagram Protocol (UDP) headers (which-ever one is used for a specific communication) and their payloads are placed inside of an IP packet, consisting of an *Internet Protocol (IP) header* and payload, at the Network layer (Layer 3). The IP header contains source IP address and destination IP address fields, among others. Routers operate at this layer. If the packet is too large (usually UDP at this point will be the culprit), the packet is fragmented into multiple packets. Data/payload generated at this layer is added to what came from the four layers above and is sent to the layer below, the Data Link layer.

Everything that came from above is placed inside of a frame—an Ethernet frame, consisting of an *Ethernet header* and payload, on a wired network, or an 802.11 frame, consisting of an 802.11 header and payload, on a wireless network—at the Data Link layer (Layer 2). The frame contains destination MAC address and source MAC address fields, among others. Switches operate at this layer. NICs partially operate at this layer, since that's the device from where the MAC address comes. Data/payload generated at this layer is added to what came from the five layers above and is sent to the layer below, the Physical layer.

The frame at this point is transmitted from the NIC (the other layer it exists at, since it transmits and receives network traffic here) out to the network medium, wired or wireless, representing frames in the form of bits and bytes, 1s and 0s, at the Physical layer (Layer 1). The traffic moves through switches and out of the local network through a router. After passing through multiple routers, the traffic reaches a switch on the destination's network and finds its way to the destination machine.

Unlike the other PDUs, frames also have a field that comes after the data/payload, a trailer. When the frame (frames are destroyed and re-created at each hop, so this is not the original frame sent by the source if the destination is on a different network) gets to the destination, the destination checks the FCS, the field in the trailer of the frame, implemented through a CRC. The purpose of this CRC is to detect accidental changes in the frame and its payload. A numeric value, based on the remainder of polynomial division of the contents, is placed in the trailer. The destination computes the same algorithm. If the computed value doesn't match the value in the trailer, the frame is discarded.

If the computed value matches the value in the trailer field, the frame has integrity. Then, the destination checks the destination MAC address field in the frame. If that address is not a broadcast, a multicast supported by this NIC, or the unicast address of this NIC, the frame is discarded. Otherwise, the frame is removed and the contents are analyzed. The Type field identifies what's inside the frame, which for data frames (not control frames) will be either ARP frames (which exist at Layer 2) or IP packets (which exist at Layer 3). This happens at each hop as the packet and its payload repeatably get encapsulated with new frames.

The destination IP address in the packet is scrutinized the same way. If it passes the check, the packet is stripped off and the OS looks at the destination port number in the TCP segment or UDP datagram. The Layer 4 header is stripped off at this point, and the actual data or payload is sent to the destination application or service. Any fragmented packets or segmented segments need to be reassembled before moving up the OSI model.

TCP Flags

At Layer 4 of the OSI model, TCP establishes a connection between two systems (referred to as client and server in this section) before any data is transferred, requires every message to be acknowledged, and guarantees data delivery through the TCP three-way handshake.

In nontechnical terms, the client says, "Hey, I want to talk to you (SYN)!" The server says back, "I want to talk to you as well (SYN), and, yes, you can talk to me (ACK)!" Then the client says, "Sure, let's rock (ACK)!"

TCP flags in the TCP header represent specific control information, each represented by a single bit. Turning a flag on (or setting it) means giving that bit a value of 1. Turning a flag off (or clearing it) means giving that bit a value of 0. There are six standard flags in the TCP header (as well as three specialty ones).

Cross-Reference

You'll learn about how routers and switches work in Objective 2.1.

As detailed in Objective 1.5, TCP establishes a connection between source and destination with the TCP three-way handshake. This process involves two TCP flags that correspond to other fields in the TCP header. First, the SYN (Synchronize) flag is used in conjunction with the Sequence Number field in the TCP header. Second, the ACK (Acknowledgment) flag is used in conjunction with the Acknowledgement Number field in the TCP header.

During the TCP three-way handshake each side will come up with a 4-byte pseudorandom number, put it in the Sequence Number field, and send it with the SYN flag set. Each side will also acknowledge the other side's sequence number by adding 1 to it, putting it in the Acknowledgment Number field, and sending it with the ACK flag set. This is done in three steps, hence the term TCP three-way handshake.

This process is often described as SYN, SYN/ACK, ACK, in relation to the flags that are set at each of the three steps. Notice in the second step, there is both a SYN and an ACK, as that side acknowledges the SYN it received in the first step at the same time as it sends its own sequence number. The ACK in the third step acknowledges the SYN set in the second step.

After the TCP three-way handshake completes, the SYN flag is not seen anymore. However, during the data exchange process (which follows the TCP three-way handshake) and the TCP teardown process (which closes the connection), the ACK flag will be set in every TCP segment.

During the data exchange process, the corresponding Acknowledgment Number field will increment the number of the last byte received from the other side and instruct the other side to use that Acknowledgment Number value as its next Sequence Number value.

Now, let's take a look at the other flags:

- **URG**   The URG flag is a relic of the past and is not really used by modern protocols. It used to be a way to tell a destination system to prioritize data in a segment, at a location specified by the Urgent Pointer field in the TCP header.

- **PSH**   The PSH flag is used to tell the sending system to push the data down and out immediately without waiting for a buffer to accumulate (which would normally happen for efficient data transfer when many TCP segments are sent), as well as to tell the receiving system to push the received data up to the receiving application without waiting for a buffer to accumulate (which would normally happen for efficient data transfer when many TCP segments are received). The PSH flag is used at the end of an HTTP or TLS session, when there's no more data to be sent or received, as well as during an SSH session, where the keystrokes need to be sent immediately to a remote system, in addition to other instances. Without the PSH flag there could be significant latency, making the communication unbearable.

- **FIN**   The FIN flag is used to tear down an established TCP connection in a similar fashion to the way that the SYN flag is used to establish the connection. The teardown process uses four steps (two separate two-way handshakes), unlike the TCP three-way handshake, which uses three steps. First, the side that starts the TCP connection termination (also known as the TCP teardown) sends a TCP segment with the FIN flag set. Second, the other side sends a TCP segment with the ACK flag set. Third, the same side that sent the segment with the ACK flag set in the second step now sends another segment, this time with the FIN flag set. Fourth, the side that started the teardown sends a segment with the ACK flag set.

    Sequence and acknowledgment numbers are used here as well. The sequence numbers pick up from where they were at the end of the data exchange process, and the acknowledgment numbers increment the sequence numbers sent with the FINs by 1.

- **RST**   A TCP connection can be terminated gracefully with the FIN flag from each side or abruptly with the RST flag. Reasons for sending an RST to abort a connection include receiving an invalid header, not having enough resources present to support the connection, not receiving any response from the other side, and even optimizing—getting rid of the other side as quickly as possible instead of a graceful close with FINs that take more time and resources.

 EXAM TIP   You can remember the six standard TCP flags (there are three specialty flags as well) with the phrase, Unskilled Attackers Pester Real Security Folks (URG, ACK, PSH, RST, SYN, FIN)!

Maximum Transmission Unit (MTU)

The *maximum transmission unit (MTU)* of Ethernet is 1500 bytes, which means that more than 1500 bytes, consisting of an IP header and data, can't be placed inside of an Ethernet frame. DSL customers have an MTU of 1492 outgoing toward their ISP, because an additional 8 bytes, in the form of a PPPoE (Point-to-Point Protocol over Ethernet) header, is added.

If a packet exceeds an MTU, the packet has to be broken up into multiple packets that stay under or at the MTU. This process is known as *fragmentation*. IPv4 routers can fragment IPv4 packets 68 bytes or larger (they must be able to forward packets less than 68 bytes without fragmentation) if a link to another router/network has an MTU that's customized to a number lower than the size of an IP packet that needs to be sent across the link. For example, if an MTU between two routers is 1000 bytes, and an IP packet is 500 bytes, the first router can break up a 1500-byte packet into two smaller-sized packets, such as one consisting of 1000 bytes and the other consisting of 500 bytes. The packets are reassembled when they reach the destination by three fields in the IP header that contain fragmentation information:

- **Identification (2-byte value)**   Fragments of the same packet are linked together with the same value, which acts as a label to group these fragments together.
- **Flags (1-bit values)**   This field consists of Reserved bit (always 0), Don't Fragment (more on this in a bit—pun intended), and More Fragments (all fragments but the last will have a value of 1, indicating to the destination that more fragments are on the way).
- **Fragment offset (2-byte value)**   This field helps the destination put received fragments in order. The first fragment offset is 0, and each subsequent offset increases by the size of the previous fragment. For example, fragments in a sequence could have offsets of 0, 1480, 2960, and 4440. These numbers allow the fragments to be reassembled, like puzzle pieces, should they arrive in nonsequential order (which is common).

Path MTU Discovery, described in RFC 1191, takes a different approach. Imagine the path between a Web server and Web client has an MTU of 1000 between two routers. The Web server would send 1500 bytes in a single packet, which would be fragmented into two packets, and then reassembled at the destination. When routers fragment packets and when hosts reassemble fragments, this creates latency. A Web server and Web client would both prefer to cut down on the latency.

According to RFC 1191, it would make more sense for TCP-related traffic (like HTTP and TLS) to first discover the smallest MTU in a path than to have every packet larger than the smallest MTU broken up into multiple packets (fragmentation). That's why the IP header will have the "Don't Fragment" flag bit turned on for TCP-related traffic. This flag, when turned on, instructs IPv4 routers to not fragment the packet, but rather to discard it and send an ICMP error message (Fragmentation Needed) back to the source with the MTU that was exceeded. Now the source won't send packets that exceed that size. So, in our Web server example, the Web server, when it gets this ICMP Fragmentation Needed message, will send packets of size 1000 bytes or less. Even though it's less bytes at a time than the 1500 bytes originally being sent, the overall throughput will be higher and latency will be lower, because no time is needed for the routers to fragment the packets and for the destination to reassemble the packets.

The process described in RFC 1911 is the default behavior for IPv6 routers. Instead of fragmenting packets, they send ICMPv6 error messages (Packet Too Big) to the hosts that sent the packets to notify them that an MTU was exceeded. The hosts then perform fragmentation on their own. IPv6 routers can send these messages for IPv6 packets that are 1280 bytes or larger (they must be able to forward packets less than 1280 bytes without fragmentation).

NOTE The MTU of an IP packet is 65,535, because the Total Length field in the IP header is 2 bytes (16 bits long), and the highest number that can be represented with 2 bytes is 65,535. The MTU of a TCP segment payload (MSS, maximum segment size) is 1460 bytes. Ethernet frames can have a payload between 46 and 1500 bytes, and a total size of 1518 bytes (counting the Ethernet header and trailer) or 1522 bytes (counting a VLAN header). IP headers can range between 20 and 60 bytes, although nowadays, they're always 20 bytes, because the additional options (which raise the minimum size of 20 bytes) are not used anymore (mostly due to security concerns). ICMP headers are 8 bytes long. UDP headers are also 8 bytes long. TCP headers can range between 20 and 60 bytes, like IP headers. The MSS, which is like an MTU for a TCP payload, is 1460 bytes, because that allows for the minimum size TCP header (20 bytes) and the minimum size IP header (20 bytes). 1460 + 20 + 20 = 1500, which is the MTU of Ethernet. Amazing how it all relates, isn't it?

REVIEW

Objective 1.1: Compare and contrast the Open Systems Interconnection (OSI) model layers and encapsulation concepts

- The *International Organization for Standardization (ISO)* created a framework into which the major network hardware and software components and protocols could be placed, to give every item a common reference point. This framework, a seven-layer model called *Open Systems Interconnection (OSI) model*, provides a means of relating the components and their functions to each other and a way of standardizing components and protocols.
- The OSI model layers include, from top (7) to bottom (1): Application, Presentation, Session, Transport, Network, Data Link, and Physical.
- Data from Layers 7 through 5 is encapsulated in a TCP segment or UDP datagram at Layer 4. The segment or datagram is encapsulated in an IP packet at Layer 3. The packet is encapsulated inside a frame at Layer 2. The frame is transmitted as 1s and 0s at Layer 1.
- TCP flags include URG, ACK, PSH, RST, SYN, and FIN.
- The MTU defines the level of data that can be encapsulated in various protocols.

1.1 QUESTIONS

1. Which layer of the OSI model are routers found at?
   A. 1
   B. 2
   C. 3
   D. 4

2. What is encapsulated directly inside of a frame?
   A. TCP segment
   B. IP packet
   C. UDP datagram
   D. ICMP packet

3. Which TCP flag is set in the first step of the TCP three-way handshake?
   A. ACK
   B. FIN
   C. RST
   D. SYN

1.1 ANSWERS

1. **C**   Routers are found at Layer 3, the Network layer, of the OSI model.
2. **B**   An IP packet is encapsulated directly inside of a frame.
3. **D**   The SYN (Synchronize) flag starts off the TCP three-way handshake.

Objective 1.2 **Explain the characteristics of network topologies and network types**

A network *topology* provides a general description of how the devices on the network link to each other, either physically or logically. A *physical topology* describes precisely how devices connect, such as how the wires run from machine to machine. The devices could all connect to a single central box, for example, or in a daisy chain of one computer to another. A *logical topology*, also known as a *hybrid topology*, in contrast, describes how the signals used on the network travel from one computer to another.

Topologies can be wired or wireless. Topologies do not define specifics about how to implement a network installation. They provide only a very high-level look at how network nodes connect. To move from a theoretical overview to a working solution, you must implement a

specific network standard. Furthermore, the type of network can be described with acronyms like LAN, MAN, WAN, and others, where the last two letters stand for "area network" and the first letter stands for a word that describes the scope/geographical reach of the network.

This objective also covers service-related entry point entities, virtual network concepts, and provider links.

Bus

The bus topology has been obsolete for decades.

If you can imagine your laundry hanging on a long, straight clothesline, you have a pretty good idea of how a *bus* topology network was constructed. Everything hung off one long run of cable, as shown in Figure 1.2-1.

A bus topology network used a single cable (i.e., the *bus*) that connected all the computers in a line.

In bus topology networks, data from each computer simply went out on the whole bus. A network using a bus topology needed termination at each end of the cable (as shown in Figure 1.2-2) to prevent a signal sent from one computer from reflecting at the ends of the cable and quickly bringing the network down.

Ring

The ring topology has been obsolete for decades.

In a true *ring* topology, all computer systems were connected together in a complete loop, as shown in Figure 1.2-3. A ring topology network connected all computers on the network with a ring of cable.

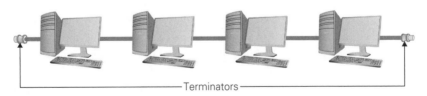

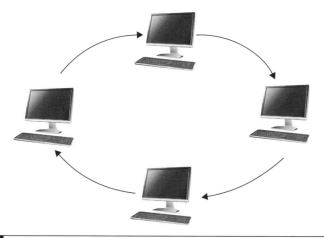

FIGURE 1.2-3   Ring topology

 CAUTION   Topologies are diagrams, much like an electrical circuit diagram. Real network cabling doesn't go in straight lines or perfect circles.

In a ring topology network, in contrast to a bus topology, data traffic moved in a circle from one computer to the next in the same direction (as you can see in Figure 1.2-3). With no end to the cable, ring networks required no termination. The main selling point for ring networks was the deterministic method of communication. Devices on the ring played nicely and accessed the ring when it was their turn. A device's turn was when it had the token, which was passed around. After transmitting, or if the device had nothing to transmit, the device passed the token to the next device in the ring. No token, no talk.

Bus and ring topology networks suffered from the same problem: the entire network stopped working if the cable broke at any point, as shown in Figure 1.2-4. The broken ends on a bus topology network didn't have the required termination, which caused reflection between computers that were still connected. A break in a ring topology network simply broke the circuit, stopping the data flow.

Hybrid

Before the advent of the switch, early network designers saw that the benefits of a star topology were overwhelming, motivating the development of ways to use a star topology without requiring a major redesign.

The ring topology network designers struck first by taking the entire ring and shrinking it into a small box called a multistation access unit (MAU), as shown in Figure 1.2-5.

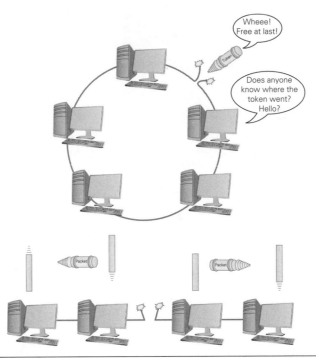

FIGURE 1.2-4   Nobody is talking!

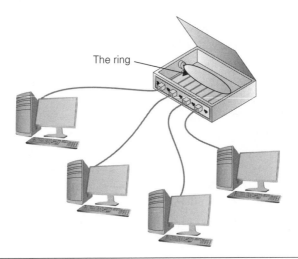

FIGURE 1.2-5   Star-ring hybrid topology

This was quickly followed by the bus topology folks, who, in turn, shrunk their bus (better known as the segment) into their own box called a hub, as shown in Figure 1.2-6.

Physically, these hybrid topologies created with a MAU and a hub looked like a star topology, but if you examined them as an electronic schematic, the signals acted like a ring

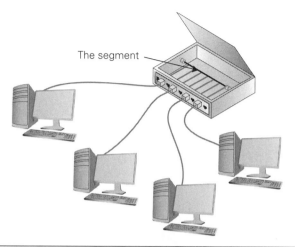

The segment

FIGURE 1.2-6   Star-bus hybrid topology

or a bus. Clearly the old definition of topology needed a little clarification. That's why we use one expression for how the cables physically look, the physical topology, and another for how the signals travel electronically, the logical topology, also known as a *hybrid* topology.

The hybrid topology has been obsolete for decades.

Star/Hub-and-Spoke

The *star/hub-and-spoke* topology uses a central switch for all the computers on the network, as shown in Figure 1.2-7.

Star topologies have a huge benefit over ring and bus topologies by offering fault tolerance—if one of the cables breaks, all of the other computers can still communicate.

In Figure 1.2-7, Host C cannot communicate with any other node, but Hosts A, B, D, E, and F can communicate with each other just fine.

The star topology, with a switch as the central device, has been the norm for decades.

Cross-Reference

The switch's improvements over a hub are discussed in Objective 2.1.

Mesh

The wired *mesh* topology connects each node with multiple links, providing multiple paths between any two nodes. The wired mesh topology is not seen in LANs because of cost: it requires so many separate links. A partial mesh, however, is used to connect networks together, as shown in Figure 1.2-8. In essence, any series of interlinked networks where more than one possible data path exists between network locations can be considered to be using a mesh

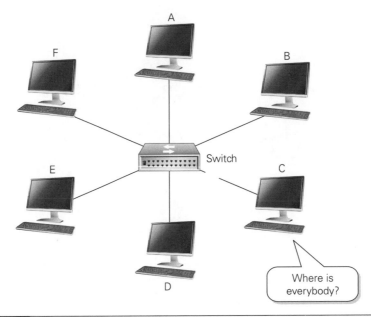

FIGURE 1.2-7 Star topology

FIGURE 1.2-8 Mesh topology

topology. Because mesh topologies support multiple paths between networks, the level of fault tolerance improves as the number of paths increases.

You won't find partial mesh networks in an office setting, using redundant connections between computers. However, many large companies have implemented mesh designs in the infrastructure backbone, with multiple redundant links between routers and switches, making use of multiple technologies to support a multipath solution for network traffic. At the switching level, overkill on a Spanning Tree Protocol (covered in Objective 2.3) implementation would be a partial mesh. Another example would be internal use of multiple backup routing paths to internal routers (if the network is heavily routed rather than switched). This sometimes goes into edge network closets, where closets can be interconnected, but completely applies to network devices within a server room or datacenter.

NOTE In this book "datacenter" is one word, following the CompTIA Network+ exam objectives, but it's two words in many instances in industry.

 EXAM TIP You're more likely to see the term "mesh" used to describe connections among networks over distance, like on a university campus. You won't see a full mesh network at all outside of the CompTIA Network+ exam.

Topologies aren't just for wired networks. Wireless networks also need topologies to get data from one machine to another, but using radio waves instead of cables involves somewhat different topologies.

In a *wireless mesh* network, nodes including clients (devices like laptops and phones) and routers are connected together. Generally speaking, mesh refers to the bridge-to-bridge connections, while another term, ad hoc, refers to the client-to-client connections.

Network Types and Characteristics

Networks come in many sizes and vary widely in the number of computers attached to them. People connect computers at home so that they can share files or play games together, while companies that have thousands of employees in dozens of countries need to network their computers together to get work done. Network folks put most networks into one of two categories: LANs and WANs. You'll find quite a few other groupings as well. *Network types and characteristics* vary greatly.

Client-Server

Klara accesses servers to do her job; her laptop runs client services of those server services. This scenario describes a classic *client-server* network type. When you are using protocols like DNS, DHCP, FTP, SSH, TLS, and more, you're using a client-server architecture. The client requests from the server, and if the request is proper and the client is authorized, the server serves.

Peer-to-Peer

In some circumstances, however, Klara might access resources distributed on many computers. In turn, her computer might share some of those resources with others. This alternative network type, typified by the BitTorrent file sharing protocol, is called *peer-to-peer*.

 EXAM TIP Look for a question on the CompTIA Network+ exam that contrasts client-server and peer-to-peer networking.

Local Area Network (LAN)

A *local area network (LAN)* covers a small area and contains a modest number of computers. A LAN is usually contained in a single building. Examples of typical LANs include home networks and school networks. A LAN is simply a single network or a broadcast domain that represents nodes that can hear each other's broadcast transmissions. Routers never forward broadcasts between LANs.

Wide Area Network (WAN)

Interconnecting computers over distances, especially when the connections cross borders or jurisdictions, creates a *wide area network (WAN)*, though the term is pretty flexible. A WAN is composed of two or more LANs connected together. A WAN can be as simple as a bunch of LANs interconnected on a single campus, or a WAN can cover a large geographical area and have a substantial number of devices. All of the LANs in all of the schools in a city school district, for example, link together to form a WAN. Computers in a WAN usually connect through some type of public network. The largest WAN in existence is the *Internet*, which is a worldwide network that connects billions of devices from different networks.

Metropolitan Area Network (MAN)

A *metropolitan area network (MAN)* is a group of networks connected together in a smaller distance than a WAN, such as a network of municipal offices in a town or city. MANs can range in size from a few city blocks to entire cities. Sites on a MAN are usually interconnected using fiber-optic cable or some other high-speed digital circuit, and the MAN itself may carry voice as well as data traffic.

Wireless Local Area Network (WLAN)

What do you call the network at your local coffee shop? It's a local area network (LAN) for sure, but there's nowhere for ordinary customers to plug their laptops into the network. Thus, it's a *wireless local area network (WLAN)*. The thing to note here is that a WLAN is always going to be a Wi-Fi 802.11-based network and will be able to serve a number of clients.

Personal Area Network (PAN)

Think about all the devices you might be carrying around that communicate with each other. Your phone might communicate with your laptop or tablet. How about a phone that communicates with a watch? These are examples of a *personal area network (PAN)*, which is a bunch of devices, on or around your person, sending network traffic to each other. Furthermore, with a PAN, one device can connect all the other devices to a LAN or even the Internet.

A WPAN (wireless personal area network) is a PAN that uses technologies such as *Bluetooth* and *infrared (IR)* that, while they all use some form of wireless communication, are designed to make a single point-to-point connection, and only at very short ranges. Bluetooth may go as far as 100 meters for the most powerful Bluetooth connections to as little as 5 cm for NFC (near field communication) devices.

PANs that are not wireless use wired interfaces, like USB.

Campus Area Network (CAN)

A *campus area network (CAN)* is a group of interconnected LANs within a small geographical area, such as a school campus, university, hospital, or military base.

Storage Area Network (SAN)

A *storage area network (SAN)* is a dedicated network used for servers to access a shared storage array, using storage protocols that appear to the server to be local storage at the server. This technology started out using Fibre Channel switches and low-overhead protocols. You can now use standard switches and a dedicated host bus adapter (HBA) to access storage. An HBA is a like an Ethernet NIC, but connects a system to block level storage devices like Fibre Chanel and iSCSI (instead of Ethernet), discussed more along with SANs in Objective 1.7.

 KEY TERM   If you had to describe the difference between **LAN**, **WAN**, **MAN**, **PAN**, and **CAN** in one word, it would be "distance" or "geography." Distance is also a great way to differentiate all WLANs from each other, as well as explain how a **SAN** works, by treating different hard drives, physically located in different places, as one logical volume.

Multiprotocol Label Switching (MPLS)

In an IP network, routers receive incoming IP packets, check the destination IP address, consult their routing tables, and then forward the packets to the next hop. Nothing in the IP packet tells the router details about how to get to that destination. This router-intensive analysis of where to send each packet happens at every hop that packet takes from its source to its destination. This works great for a typical IP network, but years ago applications like video conferencing suffered over distances. This has changed a lot today, but go with me here on the motivation for something better.

In a private network, a few destinations can use a different switching technology to make direct or more efficient connections. *Multiprotocol Label Switching (MPLS)* provides a platform-agnostic labeling system to greatly improve performance compared to an IP network.

MPLS adds an MPLS label that sits between the Layer 2 header and the Layer 3 header. The MPLS header consists of four parts:

- **Label**   A unique identifier, used by MPLS-capable routers to determine how to move data.
- **Experimental Bits (Exp)**   A relative value used to determine the importance of the labeled packet to be able to prioritize some packets over others.

- **Bottom of Label Stack (S)** In certain situations, a single packet may have multiple MPLS labels. This single bit value is set to 1 for the initial label.
- **Time to Live (TTL)** A value that determines the number of hops the label can make before it's eliminated

The original idea for MPLS was to give individual ISPs a way to move traffic through their morass of different interconnections and switches more quickly and efficiently by providing network-wide quality of service (QoS). MPLS-capable routers avoid running IP packets through their full routing tables and instead use the header information to route packets quickly. Where "regular" routers use QoS on an individual basis, MPLS routers use their existing dynamic routing protocols to send each other messages about their overhead, enabling QoS to span an entire group of routers.

Software-Defined Wide Area Network (SDWAN)

One interesting use of MPLS networks is to provide Internet connectivity to a back office or satellite location via a public-facing router at the central office, a backhaul connection. This keeps the full security in place (the good part about MPLS and private WANs), but the connection will most likely be slow compared to a direct Internet connection.

Another disadvantage of MPLS is that it's expensive to acquire and install dedicated connections between the central office and the various back offices or satellites. The public Internet eclipsed any performance advantage of dedicated networks, so the only thing superior in the latter is security.

A *software-defined wide area network (SDWAN)* enables traffic over the Internet that incorporates a lot of the features of MPLS, with efficient addressing and routing for a lot of traffic. An SDWAN maintains high security as well.

Multipoint Generic Routing Encapsulation (mGRE)

The *multipoint generic routing encapsulation (mGRE)* protocol can be paired with IPsec for encryption to create a virtual private network (VPN). You can use GRE to make a point-to-point tunnel connection that carries all sorts of traffic over Layer 3, including multicast and IPv6 traffic.

While GRE is a point-to-point protocol, mGRE allows one interface to be used for many tunnels, as much as you need. While you can't set a GRE tunnel destination interface in advance, with multipoint GRE (mGRE), you now have one interface terminating with more than one tunnel.

Service-Related Entry Point

The outside world needs to interface with your internal networks at some point, known as a *service-related entry point*. There are multiple ways that can be accomplished, as detailed next.

Demarcation Point

Connections from the outside world—whether network or telephone—come into a building at a location called a *demarcation point*, known simply as demarc. The demarc refers to the physical location of the connection and marks the dividing line of responsibility for the functioning of the network. You take care of the internal functioning; the person or company that supplies the upstream service to you must support connectivity and function on the far side of the demarc.

 EXAM TIP   You might get a question about the location of a demarc on the CompTIA Network+ exam. You'll find the demarc located in the *service-related entry point* for a network.

In a private home, the equipment (cable modem, optical network terminal, etc.) supplied by your ISP is a network interface unit (NIU) that serves as a demarc between your home network and your ISP. In an office environment, the demarc is usually more complex, given that a typical building simply has to serve a much larger number of telephones and computers. Figure 1.2-9 shows the demarc for a midsized building, including both Internet and telephone connections coming in from the outside.

 NOTE   The best way to think of a demarc is in terms of responsibility. If something breaks on one side of the demarc, it's your problem; on the other side, it's the ISP's problem.

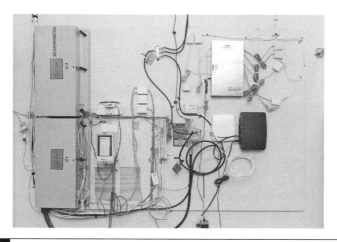

FIGURE 1.2-9   Office demarc

Smartjack

One challenge to companies that supply Internet services is the need to diagnose faults in the system. An intelligent network interface device (INID) known as a *smartjack* is used set up a remote loopback—critical for loopback testing when you were at one end of the connection and the other connection was blocks or even miles away. A smartjack is a demarc for T1 lines, which are disappearing in all but the most extreme situations. T1 doesn't appear in the Network+ objectives.

Virtual Network Concepts

There are many *virtual network concepts*. In the simplest terms, virtualization is the process of using special software—a class of programs called hypervisors—to create a complete environment in which a guest operating system can function as though it were installed on its own computer. That guest environment, which virtualizes the hardware for the guest operating system, is called a virtual machine (VM).

There are many great advantages to virtualization:

- With each VM running on the same hardware, hardware dependency issues are eliminated.
- To make a copy of a VM, simply copy the files and folders that comprise it.
- Consolidating servers from many physical machines into VMs reduces the power consumption, carbon footprint, and business expenses (expensive hardware, for example) of datacenters. Datacenters can even be expanded with VMs on an as-needed basis and contracted when those additional resources are no longer needed.
- Some hypervisors can perform dynamic load balancing, allocating requests to VMs that are not as busy as others, and can even dynamically allocate more resources to VMs that are very busy.
- Instead of hours or days needed to replace or fix a physical machine affected by a disaster, a VM can quickly be provisioned and deployed in minutes by replicating or cloning the affected machine. Reducing downtime is huge for the availability of an organization.
- Installing, updating, and maintaining environments is more efficient, allowing the IT staff to be more productive.
- A VM can be easily deployed for a developer to test programs and patches in a certain environment.
- Troubleshooting software on various platforms can be done with multiple VMs, which is, of course, much easier than doing it through multiple physical machines running various OSs.
- Security settings can limit malware attacks or software glitches on a VM from affecting other VMs. Furthermore, if one VM suffers a malware attack, an earlier saved copy of that VM can be restored.

Hypervisor

A normal operating system uses programming called a supervisor to handle very low-level interactions among hardware and software, such as task scheduling, allotment of time and resources, and so on.

Because virtualization enables one machine—called the host system—to run multiple operating systems in virtual machines simultaneously, full virtualization requires an extra layer of sophisticated programming called a hypervisor to manage the vastly more complex interactions.

A hypervisor is a program that runs virtual machines, which exist as a set of files. The CPU, RAM, hard drive, and other physical hardware are virtualized for the guest operating systems that run through a hypervisor.

A hypervisor has to handle every input and output that an operating system would request of normal hardware. With a good hypervisor like VMware Workstation Pro, you can easily add and remove virtual hard drives, virtual network cards, virtual RAM, and so on.

Virtualization even goes so far as to provide a virtualized BIOS and system setup utility for every virtual machine.

 NOTE The host system allocates real RAM and CPU time to every running virtual machine. A host system can only handle a finite number of simultaneous VMs before experiencing degraded performance. A single hypervisor on a single system will happily run as many VMs as its RAM, CPU, and drive space allow (RAM is almost always the main limiting factor). A VM that's shut down is just files sitting on a hard drive.

Type 1 Hypervisors vs. Type 2 Hypervisors

VMware Workstation Player requires an underlying operating system, so it functions essentially like a very powerful desktop application. Hypervisors that operate in this fashion are called *Type 2 hypervisors*.

What if you could remove the OS altogether and create a bare-metal implementation of virtualization? VMware introduced ESX in 2002 to accomplish this goal. ESX is a hypervisor that's powerful enough to replace the host operating system on a physical box, turning the physical machine into a machine that does nothing but support virtual machines. Hypervisors that operate in this fashion are called *Type 1 hypervisors*. Power up the server; the server loads ESX. In short order, a very rudimentary interface appears where you can input essential information, such as a master password and a static IP address.

VMware came out with a free version of ESX, called ESXi, in 2008. This strategic move allowed administrators to use, publicize, and get comfortable with ESXi at no cost. There is a non-free version of ESXi as well, which is highly recommended for production networks. Although there are still some ESX machines out there, in 2010 VMware discontinued development on ESX and strongly urged its customers to move over to ESXi, which is the only platform now supported by VMware vSphere (explained next).

KEY TERM   For all you acronym lovers, **ESX** officially means nothing. Unofficially, it stands for "Elastic Sky," which is probably why it officially means nothing.

Don't let ESXi's small size fool you. It's small because it only has one job: to host virtual machines. ESXi is an extremely powerful bare-metal hypervisor.

Powerful hypervisors like ESXi are not administered directly at the box. Instead, you use tools such as VMware's vSphere Client, so you can create, configure, and maintain VMs on the hypervisor server from the comfort of a client computer running this program. Once the VM is up and running, you can close the vSphere Client, but the VM will continue to run happily on the server. So you now really have two different ways to virtualize: using hypervisors such as VMware Workstation Pro to manage virtual desktops and using powerful hypervisors such as ESXi to manage virtual servers.

NOTE   Type 1 hypervisors include Microsoft Hyper-V, VMware ESXi, Proxmox Virtual Environment, Xen, and Kernel-based Virtual Machine (KVM). Type 2 hypervisors include VMware Workstation Player, VMware Workstation Pro, Parallels Desktop for Mac, and Oracle VM VirtualBox. KVM is a kernel module that converts the host operating system to a Type 1 hypervisor. Since Linux operating systems have applications vying with each other for resources, KVM can also be thought of as a Type 2 hypervisor.

EXAM TIP   Make sure you understand the difference between Type 1 and Type 2 hypervisors for the exam.

Virtual Network Interface Card (vNIC)

Let's say you install VMware Workstation Player on a Windows machine, and open Network and Sharing Center on the host system. To do that on a Windows 10 host system, click the Start button or in the search box and type **sharing**. Click Manage Advanced Sharing Settings, click Network And Sharing Center in the address bar, click Change Adapter Settings on the left, and look at all of your interfaces.

Besides your physical interfaces, you now have two new VMware Network Adapters, each of which is a *virtual network interface card (vNIC)*. In bridged networking, the host system and VM are on the same LAN, so no virtual adapter is needed on the host system, since the physical NIC is on the same subnet as the VM.

NAT networking uses a virtual router running NAT between the host system and the VM, which will be on a different network than the host system. However, your host system is already configured for a default gateway on a router that doesn't know about another virtual network behind VMware's NAT router. Therefore, to allow the host system to send traffic to the VM in

NAT networking, a vNIC, VMware Network Adapter VMnet8, is created for the host system. This virtual adapter has an IP address on the subnet of the VM running in NAT networking, which allows the host system to send traffic directly to the VM (and vice versa), without the need of a router (physical or virtual).

Host-only networking, which allows the VM to talk with just the host system, uses the same concept of a virtual NIC on the host system, and this one is called VMware Network Adapter VMnet1. Like in NAT networking, the VM is on a different network than the host system. If the host system wants to communicate with the VM in host-only networking, the host system uses the vNIC for host-only networking, because again, the default gateway of the host does not know about the existence of this remote network that the VM is on.

vSwitch

A *vSwitch* (virtual switch) can allow multiple VMs to access to the Internet. The VMs need their own IP addresses, but the host machine only has a single NIC.

The simplest way is to bridge the NIC with a *vSwitch*. A vSwitch is a switch implemented in software that passes traffic from the real NIC to a virtual one, as shown in Figure 1.2-10. Like a physical Ethernet switch, a vSwitch operates at Layer 2 of the OSI model, so each vNIC gets a legitimate, unique MAC address to which the Layer 3 IP address will be associated.

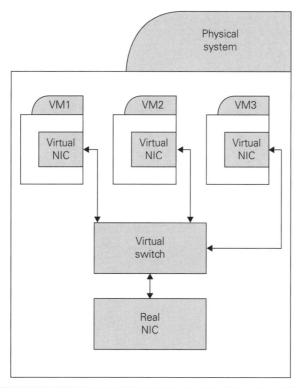

FIGURE 1.2-10 vSwitch

Network Function Virtualization

Network function virtualization (NFV) is where virtual machines take the place of network appliance hardware, like routers, switches, IDSs, load balancers, firewalls, gateways, and more. By separating the services from the physical hardware devices (routers, switches, etc.), new services can be spun up quickly on an as-needed basis, without having to worry about purchasing and deploying new hardware. This turns months of work into hours, and saves a lot of money in the process!

The various parts of the virtual network are programmed and automatically provisioned through software with a hypervisor or software-defined networking (coming up in Objective 1.7).

An NFV architecture consists of three parts:

- **A centralized virtual network infrastructure**   Network function virtualization infrastructure (NFVI) represents all hardware and software used to build the NFV environment. NFVI allows you to tie several NVF objects together for consolidated management of all objects.
- **Software implementations for network functions**   Virtualized network functions (VNFs) represent these applications and are deployed on an NFVI.
- **A framework for NFV management and orchestration**   Known as MANO (management, automation, and network orchestration), this framework allows for the management and orchestration of NFVI and VNFs.

 NOTE   Hardware switches are still a part of our "virtual" network, so don't let that confuse you. Just because we can replace some hardware boxes with virtual machines, that doesn't mean we can eliminate all networking hardware! We still need a way to move network traffic between our servers and up to the Internet.

Provider Links

Various technologies enable individuals and organizations to tap into wide area networks, such as the Internet. These technologies enable connections to Internet service providers (ISPs), businesses that lease direct connections and in turn provide a public onramp—provider links—to the Internet. This section explores *provider links*, the connections most frequently termed the last mile—literally the connection options from a telco central office to the premises.

Satellite

Living in the countryside may have its charms, but you'll have a hard time getting high-speed Internet out on the farm. For those too far away to get anything else, *satellite* may be your only option. Satellite access comes in two types: one-way and two-way. One-way means that you download via satellite, but you must use a PSTN (public switched telephone network)/ dial-up modem connection for uploads. Two-way means the satellite service handles both the uploading and downloading.

 NOTE Companies that design satellite communications equipment haven't given up on their technology. The standard HughesNet products advertise download speeds up to 25 Mbps. Viasat download speeds are advertised at 12–100 Mbps. The SpaceX Starlink service claims potential download speeds of 50–150 Mbps worldwide, though it's still in beta.

Satellite requires a small satellite antenna, identical to the ones used for satellite television. This antenna connects to a satellite modem, which, in turn, connects to your PC or your network.

Digital Subscriber Line (DSL)

Many telephone companies offer a digital subscriber line (DSL) connection, a fully digital, dedicated (no phone number) connection. DSL represented the next great leap forward past ISDN for telephone lines. A physical DSL connection manifests as just another PSTN connection, using the same telephone lines and RJ-11 jacks as any regular phone line. DSL comes in a number of versions, but the two most important to know for the CompTIA Network+ exam are symmetric DSL (SDSL) and asymmetric DSL (ADSL).

SDSL

SDSL provides equal upload and download speeds and, in theory, provides speeds up to 15 Mbps, although the vast majority of ISPs provide packages ranging from 192 Kbps to 9 Mbps.

ADSL

ADSL uses different upload and download speeds. ADSL download speeds are much faster than the upload speeds. Most small office and home office (SOHO) users are primarily concerned with fast *downloads* for things like Web pages and can tolerate slower upload speeds. ADSL provides theoretical maximum download speeds up to 15 Mbps and upload speeds up to 1 Mbps. Real-world ADSL download speeds vary from 384 Kbps to 15 Mbps, and upload speeds go from as low as 128 Kbps to around 768 Kbps. ADSL is less expensive than SDSL.

DSL Features

One nice aspect of DSL is that you don't have to run new phone lines. The same DSL lines you use for data can simultaneously transmit your voice calls.

All versions of DSL have the same central office–to–end user distance restrictions as ISDN—around 18,000 feet from your demarc to the central office. At the central office, your DSL provider has a device called a DSL Access Multiplexer (DSLAM) that connects multiple customers to the Internet.

The DSL modem in your house is considered a termination point, a demarc and NIU that enables loopback testing so the ISP can remotely check your line and box.

Installing DSL

DSL operates using your preexisting telephone lines (assuming they are up to specification). This is wonderful but also presents a technical challenge. For DSL and your run-of-the-mill POTS (plain old telephone service) line to coexist, you need to filter out the DSL signal on the POTS line. A DSL line has three information channels: a high-speed downstream channel, a medium-speed duplex channel, and a POTS channel.

Segregating the two DSL channels from the POTS channel guarantees that your POTS line will continue to operate even if the DSL fails. You accomplish this by inserting a filter on each POTS line, or a splitter mechanism that allows all three channels to flow to the DSL modem but sends only the POTS channel down the POTS line. The DSL company should provide you with a few POTS filters for your telephones. If you need more, most computer/electronics stores stock DSL POTS filters.

A common early DSL installation consisted of a DSL modem connected to a telephone wall jack and to a standard network interface card (NIC) in your computer. The DSL line ran into a DSL modem via a standard phone line with RJ-11 connectors. Today you'd add a router, which connects to the DSL modem, which connects to the wall jack.

The DSL modem connects to the gateway router with a patch cable, which, in turn, connects to the company's switch.

The first generation of DSL providers used a bridged connection; once the DSL line was running, it was as if you had snapped an Ethernet cable into your NIC. You were on the network. Those were good days for DSL. You just plugged your DSL modem into your NIC and, assuming your IP settings were whatever the DSL folks told you to use, you were running.

The DSL providers didn't like that too much. There was no control—no way to monitor who was using the DSL modem. As a result, the DSL folks started to use Point-to-Point Protocol over Ethernet (PPPoE), a protocol that was originally designed to encapsulate PPP frames into Ethernet frames. The DSL people adopted it to make stronger controls over your DSL connection. In particular, you could no longer simply connect; you now had to log on with an account and a password to make the DSL connection. PPPoE is now predominant on DSL. If you get a DSL line, your operating system has software to enable you to log onto your DSL network. Most SOHO routers come with built-in PPPoE support, enabling you to enter your username and password into the router itself.

Cable

The first big competition for ADSL came from the *cable* companies. A majority of houses in America have a coax cable for cable TV. In a moment of genius, the cable industry realized that if it could put the Home Shopping Network and the History Channel into every home, why not provide Internet access? The entire infrastructure of the cabling industry had to undergo some major changes to deal with issues like bidirectional communication, but cable modem service quickly became common in the United States. Cable modems are now as common as cable TV boxes.

Cable modems have the impressive benefit of phenomenal top speeds. These speeds vary from cable company to cable company, but most advertise speeds in the 5 to 200 Mbps range. Many cable modems provide a throughput speed of 30 to 200 Mbps for downloading and 5 to 10 Mbps for uploading—there is tremendous variance among different providers.

In a cable modem installation, the cable modem connects to an outlet via a coaxial cable. It's separate from the one that goes to the television. It's the same cable line, just split from the main line as if you were adding a second cable outlet for another television. A cable modem connects to a router, which in turn connects to a PC using a standard NIC and UTP cabling.

Cable modems connect using coax cable to a headend, similar to a telephone company's central office. Headends, in turn, connect to the cable company's network. This network uses a unique protocol called Data Over Cable Service Interface Specification (DOCSIS). The current specification is DOCSIS 4.0. Starting with DOCSIS 3.1, gigabit Internet speeds on cable modems became a reality.

ADDITIONAL RESOURCES   Check out the following links, detailing gigabit Internet over cable modems:
https://pickmymodem.com/all-about-docsis-3-1-and-docsis-3-1-cable-modems/
https://www.spectrum.net/support/internet/gig-speed-support/
https://stopthecap.com/2018/04/25/spectrum-launches-gigabit-upgrades-across-upstate-new-york-dozens-of-other-cities/
https://www.cablelabs.com/gigabit-internet-speeds
https://www.tomsguide.com/us/gig-speed-internet,review-5134.html

Leased Line

Many organizations connect far-flung network resources through private connections, rather than across the Internet. The purchase of dedicated connections—using a *leased line*—from telecommunication companies enables these organizations to secure network communication with no fear of hackers accessing network resources. These dedicated connections are expensive, as you might imagine, but ideal for many businesses. Several technologies provide the underpinnings for private WANs: MPLS, SDWAN, and metro Ethernet (the first two were discussed earlier in this objective, and the last one is discussed next).

Metro-Optical

A metro Ethernet network creates a secure, private network within a city using fiber-optic cabling and Ethernet technology. CompTIA refers to this networking technology as *metro-optical*. The metropolitan area network (MAN) created does not use the Internet to connect and thus doesn't require security. The use of Ethernet substantially reduces the cost of implementing a metro-optical network compared to implementing an MPLS or SDWAN network. Typically, a provider runs fiber in a city only in areas where the provider expects to be able to sell or onboard customers. That would all be based on the provider's calculated business benefit. Availability will vary by market and location.

 NOTE   A metro-optical network can connect offices and individuals and provide Internet connectivity.

REVIEW

Objective 1.2: Explain the characteristics of network topologies and network types

- Physical topologies describe the way the network looks, while logical/hybrid topologies describe how the network behaves in regard to network traffic.
- The difference between a LAN, WAN, MAN, CAN, and PAN is geography or distance.
- Switches, NICs, and entire network functions can be virtualized.
- Provider links include satellite, digital subscriber line (DSL), cable, leased line, and metro-optical.

1.2 QUESTIONS

1. Which of the following wired topologies is used today to connect devices of the same network together?
   A. Bus
   B. Ring
   C. Mesh
   D. Star

2. Where do connections from the outside world come into the building?
   A. Client-server
   B. Demarc
   C. Virtual network interface card (vNIC)
   D. Leased line

3. What manages the interaction between a VM and a host system?
   A. Hypervisor
   B. Supervisor
   C. vSwitch
   D. Network function virtualization (NFV)

1.2 ANSWERS

1. **D**   On networks today, the switch acts as the central device in a star topology.

2. **B**   Connections from the outside world—whether network or telephone—come into a building at a location called a demarcation point, known simply as demarc. The demarc refers to the physical location of the connection and marks the dividing line of responsibility for the functioning of the network.

3. **A**   A hypervisor is a program, existing as a set of files, that runs virtual machines.

 # Summarize the types of cables and connectors and explain which is the appropriate type for a solution

Wireless is popular, but serious solutions require networked systems linked together using some type of cabling. Different types of networks over the years have used a number of different types of cables—and you need to learn about all these cables to succeed on the CompTIA Network+ exam!

All cables used in the networking industry can be categorized in two distinct groups: copper (with names like UTP, STP, and coax) and fiber-optic. All styles of cables have distinct connector types that you need to be familiar with.

Copper

The most common form of cabling uses copper wire wrapped up in some kind of protective sheathing, thus the term *copper* cables. The two primary types of copper cabling used in industry are coaxial and twisted pair (UTP and STP are different types of twisted pair cabling).

Twisted Pair

Many modern networks use a telephone-type cable known as unshielded twisted pair (UTP). UTP network cables, as shown in Figure 1.3-1, have four pairs of *twisted pair* wires. The twists in the cable pairs reduce crosstalk and also act as a partial shield. As you might have guessed from the name, UTP has no metal shielding—just the cable pairs inside the covering. UTP cable is popular because it is relatively cheap and simple to install. Better still, the same wiring infrastructure can be used for data and voice/telephony. That means if UTP cable is installed as part of a building's infrastructure, the same cabling system can be used for many of the building's services, such as computer networks, security systems, telephones, and so on.

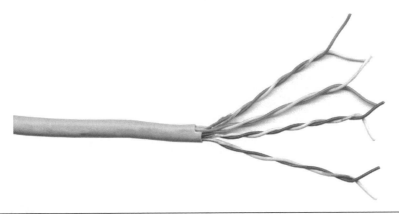

FIGURE 1.3-1 Four-pair UTP cable

 KEY TERM **Crosstalk** is an unwanted interaction, or interference, between two electrical signals.

Cat 5, Cat 5e, Cat 6, Cat 6a, Cat 7, Cat 8

UTP comes in a variety of grades, called *categories*, numbered Category 1 through Category 8, including *Cat 5*, *Cat 5e*, *Cat 6*, *Cat 6a*, *Cat 7*, and *Cat 8*, as summarized in Table 1.3-1. These categories define the maximum supported data speed of the cable, and they have been developed over the years to cater to faster and faster network designs.

TABLE 1.3-1 Cat Ratings for UTP

Cat Rating	Max Frequency	Max Bandwidth	Status with Telecommunications Industry Association (TIA)
Cat 5	100 MHz	100 Mbps	No longer recognized
Cat 5e	100 MHz	1 Gbps	Recognized
Cat 6[1]	250 MHz	10 Gbps	Recognized
Cat 6A[2]	500 MHz	10 Gbps	Recognized
Cat 7	600 MHz	10+ Gbps	Not recognized
Cat 7A[3]	1000 MHz	40–100 Gbps	Not recognized
Cat 8	2000 MHz	25–40 Gbps	Not recognized

[1] Cat 6 cables can use the full 100-meter length when used with 10/100/1000BASE-T networks. With 10GBASE-T networks, Cat 6 is limited to 55 meters.
[2] Cat 6A cables can use the full 100-meter length with networks up to 10GBASE-T.
[3] Cat 7A cables can theoretically support 40 Gbps at 50 meters; 100 Gbps at 15 meters.

EXAM TIP   TIA doesn't recognize anything past Cat 6A, while the CompTIA Network+ exam only includes Cat 5, Cat 5e, Cat 6, Cat 6A, Cat 7, and Cat 8.

Most new cabling installations use Cat 6 or Cat 6A cabling, because they support all current (and planned) data speeds and standards. The category level of a piece of cable normally is written on the cable itself or on the box.

All cable accessories, such as the wall- or pillar-mounted data ports, must also match the category of the cable being used. Mixing Cat 6A cable with Cat 3 wall sockets, for example, could cause that part of the network not to work properly. The post-installation network testing should pick up this type of mismatch, but it is better to get things right the first time rather than find out later you need to replace all your data outlets!

EXAM TIP   For the exam, be sure to know the UTP category cable types and their associated transfer rates.

Cross-Reference

Shielded twisted pair (STP) cabling is discussed in Objective 5.2.

Coaxial/RG-6

Coaxial cable, better known as "coax," is the granddaddy of all mainstream network media types. Coax was very much associated with the original designs of the popular Ethernet networking standard, developed in 1973, although today you'll only see it used with broadband Internet solutions.

EXAM TIP   A *baseband* network means that only a single signal travels over the wires of the network at one time, occupying the lowest frequencies. Ethernet networks are baseband. Contrast this with *broadband*, where you can get multiple signals (a.k.a. channels) to flow over the same wire at the same time, modulating to higher frequencies. Broadband is how cable television and cable Internet work.

Coaxial cable has a central conducting core surrounded by a protective, insulating layer; an outer metal screen made of a woven copper mesh; a metal-covered plastic or foil (or both); and an overall insulating jacket, as shown in Figure 1.3-2.

The metal screen helps shield the data traveling down the central core from being corrupted by external signals, such as radio waves, and other sources of electromagnetic interference

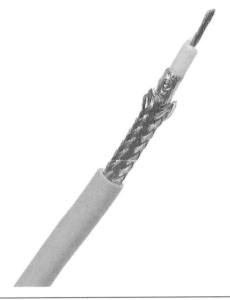

FIGURE 1.3-2 Coaxial cable

(EMI), such as high-current power cables, cell phones, electric motors, fluorescent tubes, and local electrical storms. The screen also reduces the amount of data signals that can radiate from the cable to become another source of EMI and thus cause problems for other data cables and systems. The cable is referred to as *coaxial* (or simply *coax*) because both the center wire and the braided metal shield share a common axis, or centerline.

Coax is considered old technology and isn't used these days for new LANs, except in proprietary solutions in specialized settings such as elevator shafts. Coax has and will crop up for connecting a LAN to an Internet connection provided by your local cable company, because high-speed Internet through the cable lines has become a popular broadband solution.

 EXAM TIP Coax is often preferred when connections need to run through elevator shafts because it's resistant to radio noise and is much cheaper than fiber.

A mind-boggling number of different types of coax are available, each one suitable for a specific purpose, such as audio, video, TV, satellite, cable, radio, or data. Each coax type has its own characteristics, closely matched to the type of signal that cable is designed to carry. These coax types are called *radio-grade (RG)*.

Coaxial cables have used many types of connectors over the years. Modern coaxial cables use screw-on *F connectors* (shown in Figure 1.3-3 and discussed later in this objective).

FIGURE 1.3-3   Coaxial cable with the common F connector

Coax cable was originally baseband and was used on digital computer networks as a medium for data transmissions. Nowadays, the only type of coax cable you'll see is broadband, which is not used for data transmission on digital networks, but rather for broadband services, like TV and Internet coming into homes.

Coax comes in a variety of grades, called types. Broadband coax has evolved from the uses the *RG-6* type. The nominal impedance—a measure of the wire's resistance that shows how much the cable impedes or resists the flow of electric current—is one of the factors that determines the RG type, and for RG-6 is 75 ohms.

Twinaxial

Twinaxial cable is a type of coaxial cable that contains two central copper conductors wrapped around a single shield. You'll see it used as a substitute for short fiber connections, generally between equipment within a rack, like switches. For such uses, it's substantially cheaper than fiber and associated hardware. Twinaxial cable used this way is called a *direct attached cable (DAC)*.

Termination Standards

It probably won't come as a surprise to know that UTP connectors and wiring have associated color codes and wiring schemes, as well as *termination standards*. Each wire inside a UTP cable must connect to the proper pin on the connector at each end of the cable. The wires are color-coded to assist in properly matching the ends; each pair of wires has a solid-colored wire and a striped wire: blue/blue-white, orange/orange-white, brown/brown-white, and green/green-white. Two industry organizations, the Telecommunications Industry Association (TIA) and the Electronic Industries Alliance (EIA), developed a variety of standard color codes to facilitate installation. EIA disbanded in 2011, but you will still hear the term TIA/EIA or EIA/TIA used by technicians. Furthermore, the former duo is still listed together in the CompTIA Network+ exam objectives. Read on…

TIA/EIA-568A, TIA/EIA-568B

Two major wiring standards, *TIA/EIA-568A* and *TIA/EIA-568B* (really T568A and T568B today), determine the order of the wires placed in the RJ45 connector. Using an established color-code scheme ensures that the wires match up correctly at each end of the cable. This consistency makes troubleshooting and repair easier.

 EXAM TIP The CompTIA Network+ exam objectives use the full acronyms of the organizations (*TIA/EIA*) instead of just *T*, which is contrary to the official standards.

The T568A wiring standard has the wires in the order white/green, green, white/orange, blue, white/blue, orange, white/brown, and finally brown. The most common wiring standard in use today is known as the T568B standard and has the wires in the order shown in Figure 1.3-4.

Fiber

Optical *fiber* is relatively expensive to purchase and install because it requires specialized handling and connection techniques. For this reason alone, fiber is not usually installed for desktop network connections unless a special need exists, such as locations with high levels of EMI. In general, fiber will be used where one or more of the following apply:

- Long distances need to be covered; depending on the type of fiber-optic cable, this can be in the tens of kilometers (km).
- A link is needed between buildings, and other options, such as microwave and laser, are impractical (no line of sight, for example), too expensive, or electrically unworkable.
- High speeds (10 Gigabit Ethernet and beyond) are required.
- Security is a concern. Optical fibers don't radiate signals that can be picked up by listening equipment, and it is difficult to tap a fiber without being detected.
- The general environment is electrically unfriendly to data—that is, full of EMI, such as in a factory or in a radio/TV/radar transmitter room.
- Any potential for an electrical spark must be eliminated, such as in a laboratory using flammable gases and other volatile chemicals.

FIGURE 1.3-4 The T568B wiring standard

FIGURE 1.3-5   Duplex optical fiber cabling

An optical fiber cable has three components: the fiber itself; the cladding, which actually makes the light reflect down the fiber; and the insulating jacket. Fiber cabling is specified by its mode of operation and a two-number designator representing the core and cladding diameter in microns (µm, or millionths of a meter). The most common size used for general networking is multimode 62.5/125 µm, which can be used for cable runs of up to 275 meters. Almost all fiber networking standards require two fibers, and a pair is often connected together as duplex optical fiber cabling (see Figure 1.3-5). Longer cable runs are possible with other types of fiber-optic cabling (up to 80 km as of this writing, though not through an IEEE 802.3 standard).

Data can be sent down an optical fiber cable as either infrared or laser light, according to the system in use and the maximum distances involved. Each type of system requires a specific type of media; infrared LED systems use multimode fiber (MMF), whereas laser-diode-based systems (mainly used for high-speed, long-haul data and telecom links) use single-mode fiber (SMF) cable.

 CAUTION   Infrared and laser-diode light sources can cause eye damage if you stare at them directly, so never look down a fiber cable to see if it's working. Professional testing kits use optical sensors and/or cameras. If you don't have the proper equipment available, test for faults by replacing suspect fiber leads with known good ones.

Single-mode

Single-mode fiber (SMF) uses a single cohesive frequency (ray) of laser light, known as a *mode*, to carry the transmission over long distances (up to as much as around 40 km).

Multimode

Multimode fiber (MMF) uses multiple rays of light (modes) simultaneously, with each ray of light running at a different reflection angle to carry the transmission over short distances (under 2 km). MMF is cheaper than SMF and is typically used within a building or between buildings of a campus, due to the short distances required.

EXAM TIP Remember that SMF is used to reach long distances, whereas MMF transmits over shorter distances.

Connector Types

Copper and fiber cables have a wide variety of *connector types*. Let's take a look…

Local Connector (LC), Straight Tip (ST), Subscriber Connector (SC), Mechanical Transfer (MT), Registered Jack (RJ)

Because they are optical rather than electrical, fiber cables have their own series of connector types. The two most common types of fiber-optic connectors are the *straight tip (ST)* and *subscriber connector (SC)* types (see Figure 1.3-6). ST connectors have a keying mechanism to stop them from being impaled on their sockets and twisted with total abandon. If you do get carried away, you can snap the ceramic connector body—so easy does it!

You'll also find other fiber connectors, such as the fiber *local connector (LC)*, ferrule connector (FC), and *Mechanical Transfer Registered Jack (MT-RJ)*. These connectors are similar to other connector types, such as the RJ and fiber SC shape. The fiber LC is the preferred connector of the two for communications exceeding 1 Gbps due to its small form factor.

Aside from the various connection types (LC, MT-RJ, and so on), fiber connectors vary in the connection point. The standard connector type today is called a physical contact (PC) connector because the two pieces of fiber touch when inserted. These connectors replace the older

FIGURE 1.3-6 ST and SC fiber connectors

flat-surface connector that left a little gap between the connection points due to imperfections in the glass. PC connectors are highly polished and slightly spherical, reducing the signal loss at the connection point.

Angled Physical Contact (APC), Ultra-Physical Contact (UPC)

Two technologies have dropped in price and have replaced PC connectors in some implementations: UPC and APC. *Ultra-physical contact (UPC)* connectors are polished extensively for a superior finish. These reduce signal loss significantly over PC connectors. *Angled physical contact (APC)* connectors add an 8-degree angle to the curved end, lowering signal loss further. Plus, their connection does not degrade from multiple insertions, unlike earlier connection types.

RJ11, RJ45, F-type Connector

You'll have a hard time telling a cable modem from a DSL modem. The only difference, other than the fact that one will have "cable modem" printed on it whereas the other will say "DSL modem," is that the cable modem has a coax *F-type connector* and an RJ45 connector; the DSL modem has an *RJ11* connector and an *RJ45* connector.

Transceivers/Media Converters

A *transceiver* plugs into networking devices, enabling conversion from one media type to another.

The Gigabit Ethernet folks created a standard for modular ports, a *media converter* called a gigabit interface converter (GBIC). With many Gigabit Ethernet switches and other hardware, you can simply pull out a GBIC transceiver that supports one flavor of Gigabit Ethernet and plug in another. You can replace an RJ45 port GBIC, for example, with an SC GBIC, and it'll work just fine. In this kind of scenario, electronically, the switch or other gigabit device is just that—Gigabit Ethernet—so the physical connections don't matter. Ingenious!

Transceiver type

Transceivers come in multiple types, including small form-factor pluggable (SFP), enhanced form-factor pluggable (SFP+), quad small form-factor pluggable (QSFP), and enhanced quad small form-factor pluggable (QSFP+).

Small Form-Factor Pluggable (SFP), Enhanced Form-Factor Pluggable (SFP+)

The *small form-factor pluggable (SFP)*—also known as a mini-GBIC—and *the enhanced form-factor pluggable (SFP+)* transceivers work in a similar fashion as GBICs and include connectors for the 10 Gigabit standards, among others. SFPs are smaller than GBICs so manufacturers can pack more slots onto a networking device, and they're backed by many different manufacturers.

Quad Small Form-Factor Pluggable (QSFP), Enhanced Quad Small Form-Factor Pluggable (QSFP+)

Gigabit bidirectional (BiDi) transceivers typically use SFP optics. Most 10GBASE BiDi transceivers use SFP+ connectors. 40GBASE BiDi transceivers use a unique transceiver called *quad small form-factor pluggable (QSFP)*.

Way back in 2010, the IEEE 802.3ba committee approved standards for 40- and 100-Gb Ethernet, 40 Gigabit Ethernet (40 GbE) and 100 Gigabit Ethernet (100 GbE), respectively. Both standards, in their many varieties, use the same frame as the slow-by-comparison earlier versions of Ethernet, so with the right switches, you've got perfect interoperability. The 40 GbE and 100 GbE standards are primarily implemented in backbones.

Common 40 GbE runs on OM3 or better multimode fiber, uses laser light, and uses various four-channel connectors. A typical connector is called an *enhanced quad small form-factor pluggable (QSFP+)*, essentially taking four SFP+ transceivers and squashing them into a single, wider, transceiver. Other 40 GbE standards run on single-mode fiber and can do distances up to 10 km. Still other 40 GbE connections run on Cat 8 UTP for an underwhelming 30 meters. This is 40 GBASE-T and shows up in the CompTIA Network+ exam objectives.

100 GbE standards employ both MMF and SMF with various connectors. A typical connector is the QSFP28 that has four channels of 25 Gb each. You'll sometimes see this connector referred to as a QSFP100 or 100G QSFP.

Cable Management

While we might see the network cables that carry data, including the connection into our NICs, it's not common to see the other side of the cable. What happens to that cable after it goes into a wall plate? Where does that cable run end? *Cable management* is important!

Patch Panel/Patch Bay

Ideally, once you install horizontal cabling, you should never move it. As you know, UTP horizontal cabling has a solid core, making it pretty stiff. Solid-core cables can handle some rearranging, but if you insert a wad of solid-core cables directly into your switches, every time you move a cable to a different port on the switch, or move the switch itself, you will jostle the cable. You don't have to move a solid-core cable many times before one of the solid copper wires breaks, and there goes a network connection!

Luckily for you, you can easily avoid this problem by using a patch panel. A *patch panel* is simply a box with a row of female ports in the front and permanent connections in the back, to which you connect the horizontal cables. Figure 1.3-7 shows a line connecting the uplink port and a port labeled 2X. You may use only one of those two ports, not both at the same time.

Not only do patch panels prevent the horizontal cabling from being moved, but they are also your first line of defense in organizing the cables. All patch panels have space in the front for labels, and these labels are the network tech's best friend! Simply place a tiny label on the

FIGURE 1.3-7   Typical uplink port

patch panel to identify each cable, and you will never have to experience that sinking feeling of standing in the telecommunications room of your nonfunctioning network, wondering which cable is which. Figure 1.3-8 shows a typical patch panel.

The patch panel needs a patch cable, which is nothing but a short, stranded, straight-through cable, to connect between a port on the front of the patch panel and a port on a switch. When a computer connects to the network jack in the wall, the patch cable is used to map that system to the port on the switch. The concept of the patch panel allows ease of administration and flexibility in moving systems from one switch to another without visiting the workstation.

Proper patch panel cable management means documenting everything clearly and carefully. This way, any competent technician can follow behind you and troubleshoot connectivity problems.

Networks that include audio/video components have a second set of wires running to the telecommunications room. These runs of coaxial or fiber connect to a *patch bay*, a dedicated block with A/V connections rather than twisted pair and fiber network connections.

FIGURE 1.3-8   Typical patch panel in a server room

Fiber Distribution Panel

Fiber-optic cables are terminated in a *fiber distribution panel*, where there often is additional fiber, connectors, and splicers.

Punchdown Block

A *punchdown block* can come in different varieties.

66

A *66* block is used for wiring the telephone system.

110

A *110* block is used to wire the patch panel for UTP cable.

Krone

The *Krone* LSA-PLUS proprietary European telecommunication connector offers an alternative to the 110 block. Developed by the German telecommunications company The Krone Group (CommScope Inc., today) in the 1970s, Krone connectors enable networking as well as audio interconnections. Figure 1.3-9 shows a couple of Krone blocks.

Bix

The Building Industry Cross-connect (BIX) block is another alternative to the 110 block. It's a proprietary networking interconnect developed by the now defunct Nortel Networks.

Similar in function to a 110 punchdown block, a BIX block is installed on a wall rather than in a rack. Figure 1.3-10 shows BIX blocks and connectors.

FIGURE 1.3-9 Krone blocks

FIGURE 1.3-10 BIX blocks and connectors

Ethernet Standards

The quest to break 10-Mbps network speeds in *Ethernet standards* started in the early 1990s. By then, 10BASE-T Ethernet, created by the IEEE 802.3 committee, had established itself as the most popular networking technology (although other standards, such as IBM's Token Ring, still had some market share). The goal was to create a new speed standard that made no changes to the actual Ethernet frames themselves. By doing this, the 802.3 committee ensured that different speeds of Ethernet could interconnect, assuming you had something that could handle the speed differences and a media converter if the connections were different.

The frame size and elements have stayed precisely the same when going from 10-megabit standards to 100-megabit (and beyond). This standardization ensures communication and scalability.

 ADDITIONAL RESOURCES   The official IEEE 802.3 Ethernet Working Group page is at www.ieee802.org/3/.

Copper

The CompTIA Network+ exam expects you to be familiar with older and newer *copper* standards.

10BASE-T

In 1990, the IEEE 802.3 committee created a version of Ethernet called *10BASE-T* that rapidly became the most popular network technology in the world, replacing competing and now long-gone competitors with names like IBM's Token Ring and Apple's LocalTalk.

The classic 10BASE-T network consisted of two or more computers connected to a central hub. The NICs connected with wires as specified by the 802.3 committee.

The name 10BASE-T follows roughly the same naming convention used for earlier Ethernet cabling systems. The number *10* refers to the speed: 10 Mbps. The word *BASE* refers to the signaling type: baseband. *Baseband* (digital) means that the cable only carries one signal. Contrast this with *broadband* (analog)—as in cable television—where the cable carries multiple signals or channels.

The letter *T* refers to the type of cable used: twisted pair. 10BASE-T used unshielded twisted pair (UTP) cabling.

Officially, 10BASE-T required the use of Cat 3 (or higher), two-pair, UTP cable. One pair of wires sent data to the hub while the other pair received data from the hub. Even though 10BASE-T only required two-pair cabling, everyone installed four-pair cabling to connect devices to the hub as insurance against the possible requirements of newer types of networking.

Most UTP cables (then and now) come with stranded Kevlar fibers to give the cable added strength, which, in turn, enables installers to pull on the cable without excessive risk of literally ripping it apart.

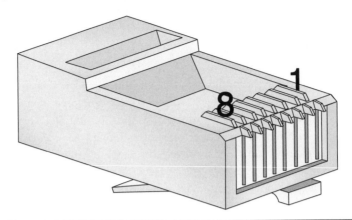

FIGURE 1.3-11 Pins 1 through 8

10BASE-T also introduced the networking world to the *RJ45 connector*. Each pin on the RJ45 connects to a single wire inside the cable; this enables devices to put voltage on the individual wires within the cable. The pins on the RJ45 are numbered from 1 to 8, as shown in Figure 1.3-11.

Like any other Ethernet standard, 10BASE-T had limitations, both on cable distance and on the number of computers. The key distance limitation for 10BASE-T was the distance between the hub and the computer. The twisted-pair cable connecting a computer to the hub could not exceed 100 meters in length. In fact, that limitation applies to all twisted-pair cable standards today.

A 10BASE-T hub could connect no more than 1024 computers, although that limitation rarely came into play. It made no sense for vendors to build hubs that large—or more to the point, that *expensive*.

100BASE-TX

When it came time to come up with a new standard to replace 10BASE-T, network hardware makers forwarded a large number of potential standards, all focused on the prize of leading the new Ethernet standard. As a result, two twisted-pair Ethernet standards appeared: 100BASE-T4 and 100BASE-TX. 100BASE-T4 used Cat 3 cable, whereas 100BASE-TX used Cat 5. By the late 1990s, 100BASE-TX became the dominant 100-megabit Ethernet standard. 100BASE-T4 disappeared from the market and today has been forgotten. As a result, we never say 100BASE-TX, simply choosing to use the term *100BASE-T*.

 NOTE   100BASE-T is also known as *Fast Ethernet*. The term still sticks to the 100-Mbps standards even though there are now much faster versions of Ethernet.

Upgrading a 10BASE-T network to 100BASE-T was not a small undertaking. First, you needed Cat 5 cable or better. Second, you had to replace all 10BASE-T NICs with 100BASE-T NICs. Third, you needed to replace the 10BASE-T hub or switch with a 100BASE-T hub or switch. Making this upgrade cost a lot in the early days of 100BASE-T, so people clamored for a way to make the upgrade a little easier and less expensive. This was accomplished via multispeed, auto-sensing NICs and hubs/switches.

When a typical multispeed, auto-sensing 100BASE-T NIC from the late 1990s first connected to a network, it negotiated automatically with the hub or switch to determine the other device's highest speed. If they both did 100BASE-T, then you got 100BASE-T. If the hub or switch only did 10BASE-T, then the NIC did 10BASE-T. All of this happened automatically.

NOTE   If you want to sound like a proper tech, you need to use the right words. Techs don't actually say "multispeed, auto-sensing," but rather "10/100/1000." As in, "Hey, is that a 10/100/1000 NIC you got there?" Now you're talking the talk!

Distinguishing a 100BASE-T NIC from a 1000BASE-T NIC without close inspection was impossible. You had to look for something on the card to tell you its speed. Some NICs has extra link lights to show the speed. Of course, you could always simply install the card and see what the operating system says it sees.

You'll also have trouble finding a true 10BASE-T or 100BASE-T NIC any longer because multispeed NICs have been around long enough to have replaced any single-speed NIC. All modern NICs are multispeed and auto-sensing.

Fast Ethernet at 100 Mbps makes sense for simple networks where you share small data, like documents and spreadsheets. Some LANs around the world continue to soldier on at 100-megabit speeds. A lot of network-connected devices, such as printers, function just fine on Fast Ethernet as well. Still, Fast Ethernet is dead in new installations, so let's turn to the current standard.

1000BASE-T

By the end of the 1990s, the true speed junkie needed an even more powerful version of Ethernet. In response, the IEEE created *Gigabit Ethernet*, which today is the most common type of Ethernet found on new NICs.

The IEEE approved two different versions of Gigabit Ethernet. The most widely implemented solution, published under the IEEE *802.3ab* standard, is called *1000BASE-T*. The other version, published under the *802.3z* standard and known as *1000BASE-X*, is divided into a series of standards, with names such as 1000BASE-SX and 1000BASE-LX.

1000BASE-T uses four-pair UTP or STP cabling to achieve gigabit performance. Like 10BASE-T and 100BASE-T, 1000BASE-T has a maximum cable length of 100 meters on a segment. 1000BASE-T connections and ports look exactly like the ones on a 10BASE-T or 100BASE-T network. 1000BASE-T is the dominant Gigabit Ethernet standard.

KEY TERM The term **Gigabit Ethernet** is more commonly used than *1000BASE-T.*

EXAM TIP The vast majority of network rollouts in offices use 1000BASE-T connections (or *drops,* as you'll hear them called). You can imagine any number of appropriate scenarios for using 1000BASE-T. Many offices also add in wireless today.

10GBASE-T

Developers continue to refine and increase Ethernet networking speeds, especially in the LAN environment and in backbones. *10GBASE-T* offers speeds of up to 10 gigabits per second, over STP or UTP copper cables.

While 10 Gigabit Ethernet (10GbE) was designed with fiber optics in mind, copper 10 GbE can still often pair excellent performance with cost savings. As a result, you'll find a mix of fiber and copper in datacenters today.

40GBASE-T

40GBASE-T is supported by Cat 8 copper cabling up to 30 meters, as defined in IEEE 802.3bq. You'll really only see it between network switches in datacenters.

Fiber

When utilizing standards above 1000 Mbps, the cable will most likely be *fiber.* As such, there are a plethora of standards.

100BASE-FX

Most Ethernet networks use unshielded twisted pair (UTP) cabling, but quite a few use fiber-based networks instead. In some networks, using fiber simply makes more sense.

UTP cabling cannot meet the needs of every organization for three key reasons. First, the 100-meter distance limitation of UTP-based networks is inadequate for networks covering large buildings or campuses. Second, UTP's lack of electrical shielding makes it a poor choice for networks functioning in locations with high levels of *electromagnetic interference (EMI)*—disturbance in electrical signals caused by electrical radiation coming from nearby devices. Finally, the Jason Bournes and James Bonds of the world find UTP cabling (and copper cabling in general) easy to tap, making it an inappropriate choice for high-security environments. To address these issues, the IEEE 802.3 standard provides for a flavor of 100-megabit Ethernet using fiber-optic cable, called 100BASE-FX.

The *100BASE-FX* standard saw quite a bit of interest for years, as it combined the high speed of 100-megabit Ethernet with the reliability of fiber optics. Outwardly, 100BASE-FX looked exactly like its predecessor, 10BASE-FL (introduced in Chapter 3). 100BASE-FX uses multimode fiber-optic cabling, and SC or ST connectors. 100BASE-FX offers improved data speeds over 10BASE-FL and equally long cable runs, supporting a maximum cable length of 2 km.

 EXAM TIP   There is no scenario today where you would install Fast Ethernet networking components, except perhaps to make use of donated equipment. However, you will definitely find Fast Ethernet gear installed and functioning in some organizations.

100BASE-SX

100BASE-SX was a short-distance, LED-based alternative to 100BASE-FX. It ran on OM1 or OM2 fiber at 850 nm (nanometer) and used ST, SC, or LC connectors. It was completely backward compatible to 10BASE-FL, so was touted as a viable upgrade from the even older tech. 100BASE-SX is long gone but appears in the CompTIA Network+ exam objectives for some reason, so it's included here for completeness.

1000BASE-SX

Many networks upgrading to Gigabit Ethernet use the *1000BASE-SX* standard. 1000BASE-SX uses multimode fiber-optic cabling to connect systems, with a generous maximum cable length of 220 to 500 meters; the exact length is left up to the various manufacturers. 1000BASE-SX uses an 850-nm wavelength LED to transmit light on the fiber-optic cable. 1000BASE-SX devices look similar to 100BASE-FX devices, and although both standards can use several types of connectors, 1000BASE-SX devices commonly use LC, while 100BASE-FX devices frequently use SC.

1000BASE-LX

1000BASE-LX is the long-distance carrier for Gigabit Ethernet. 1000BASE-LX uses lasers on single-mode cables to shoot data at distances up to 5 km—and some manufacturers use special repeaters to increase that to distances as great as 70 km! The Ethernet folks are trying to position this as the Ethernet backbone of the future, and already some large carriers are beginning to adopt 1000BASE-LX. You may live your whole life and never see a 1000BASE-LX device, but odds are good that you will encounter connections that use such devices in the near future. 1000BASE-LX connectors look like 1000BASE-SX connectors.

10GBASE-SR, 10GBASE-LR

When the IEEE members sat down to formalize specifications on Ethernet running at 10 Gbps, they faced an interesting task in several ways. First, they had to maintain the integrity of the Ethernet frame. Data is king, after all, and the goal was to create a network that could interoperate with any other Ethernet network. Second, they had to figure out how to transfer those frames at such blazing speeds. This second challenge had some interesting ramifications because of two factors. They could use the traditional Physical layer mechanisms defined by the Ethernet standard. But a perfectly usable ~10-Gbps fiber network, called SONET, was already in place and being used for WAN transmissions. What to do?

The IEEE created a whole set of 10 GbE standards that could use traditional LAN Physical layer mechanisms, plus a set of standards that could take advantage of the SONET infrastructure and run over the WAN fiber. To make the 10-Gbps jump as easy as possible, the IEEE also recognized the need for different networking situations. Some implementations require data transfers that can run long distances over single-mode fiber, for example, whereas others can make do with short-distance transfers over multimode fiber. This led to a lot of standards for 10 GbE.

The 10 GbE standards are defined by several factors: the type of fiber used, the wavelength of the laser or lasers, and the Physical layer signaling type. These factors also define the maximum signal distance.

The IEEE uses specific letter codes with the standards to help sort out the differences so you know what you're implementing or supporting. All the standards have names in the following format: "10GBASE-" followed by two other characters, what we'll call xy. The x stands for the type of fiber (usually, though not officially) and the wavelength of the laser signal; the y stands for the Physical layer signaling standard. The y code is always either R for LAN-based signaling or W for SONET/WAN-based signaling. The x differs a little more, so let's take a look.

10GBASE-S*y* (Table 1.3-3) uses a short-wavelength (850 nm) signal over multimode fiber. The maximum fiber length is 400 meters, although this length will vary depending on the type of multimode fiber used. *10GBASE-SR* is used for Ethernet LANs, and *10GBASE-SW* is used to connect to SONET devices.

10GBASE-L*y* (Table 1.3-4) uses a long-wavelength (1310 nm) signal over single-mode fiber. The maximum fiber length is 10 km, although this length will vary depending on the type of single-mode fiber used. *10GBASE-LR* connects to Ethernet LANs and *10GBASE-LW* connects to SONET equipment. 10GBASE-LR is the most popular and least expensive 10 GbE media type.

10GBASE-E*y* (Table 1.3-5) uses an extra-long-wavelength (1550 nm) signal over single-mode fiber. The maximum fiber length is 40 km, although this length will vary depending on the type of single-mode fiber used. *10GBASE-ER* works with Ethernet LANs and *10GBASE-EW* connects to SONET equipment.

TABLE 1.3-3   10GBASE-S*y*

Standard	Fiber Type	Wavelength	Physical Layer Signaling	Maximum Signal Length
10GBASE-SR	Multimode	850 nm	LAN	26–400 m
10GBASE-SW	Multimode	850 nm	SONET/WAN	26–400 m

TABLE 1.3-4   10GBASE-L*y*

Standard	Fiber Type	Wavelength	Physical Layer Signaling	Maximum Signal Length
10GBASE-LR	Single-mode	1310 nm	LAN	10 km
10GBASE-LW	Single-mode	1310 nm	SONET/WAN	10 km

TABLE 1.3-5	10GBASE-E*y*				
Standard	**Fiber Type**	**Wavelength**	**Physical Layer Signaling**	**Maximum Signal Length**
10GBASE-ER	Single-mode	1550 nm	LAN	40 km
10GBASE-EW	Single-mode	1550 nm	SONET/WAN	40 km

The 10 GbE fiber standards do not define the type of connector to use and instead leave that to manufacturers.

Bidirectional Wavelength Division Multiplexing (WDM), Dense Wavelength Division Multiplexing (DWDM), Coarse Wavelength Division Multiplexing (CWDM)

Still want more throughput? Many fiber devices use a very clever feature called *bidirectional wavelength division multiplexing (WDM)* or its newer and more popular version, *dense wavelength division multiplexing (DWDM)*. DWDM enables an individual single-mode fiber to carry multiple signals by giving each signal a different wavelength (using different colors of laser light). The result varies, but a single DWDM fiber can support ~150 signals, enabling, for example, a 51.8-Mbps OC-1 line run at 51.8 Mbps × 150 signals = 7.6 *gigabits per second*! DWDM has been very popular for long-distance lines as it's usually less expensive to replace older SONET/OC-*x* equipment with DWDM than it is to add more fiber lines.

 NOTE   DWDM isn't just upgrading SONET lines; DWDM works just as well on long-distance fiber Ethernet.

A related technology, *coarse wavelength division multiplexing (CWDM)*, also relies on multiple wavelengths of light to carry a fast signal over long distances. It's simpler than DWDM, which limits its practical distances to a mere 60 km. You'll see it used in higher-end LANs with 10GBASE-LX4 networks, for example, where its lower cost (compared to direct competitors) offers benefits.

In the mid-life of the Internet, backbone runs were largely composed of SONET links. Today, SONET has mostly been replaced with a mix of ever-improving optical links such as 100 Gigabit Ethernet, 400 Gigabit Ethernet, and others.

REVIEW

Objective 1.3: Summarize the types of cables and connectors and explain which is the appropriate type for a solution

- Networks, today, use *unshielded twisted pair (UTP)* cabling.
- Fiber cable is used on backbones, over large distances.

- Connectors vary by cable type. Copper cable can be connected with a multitude of connectors, including RJ45, RJ11, DB-9, DB-25, and F-type. Fiber cables use many connectors, too, including LC, ST, SC, and MT-RJ. PC connectors are now being replaced in some implementations by APC and UPC connectors.
- A transceiver plugs into networking devices, enabling conversion from one media type to another. Examples include SFP, SFP+, QSFP, and QSFP+.
- There are various copper cable standards, with Cat 6A being the latest TIA recognized standard (although Cat 7 and Cat 8 appear in the exam objectives).
- Various Ethernet standards, such as 100BASE-T, 1000BASE-T, 1000BASE-LX, 1000BASE-SX, 10GBASE-T, and more, ensure communication and scalability.

1.3 QUESTIONS

1. Which of the following fiber technologies is used to reach long distances?
   A. SMF
   B. MMF
   C. ST
   D. RG-58

2. Which of the following is not a type of punchdown block?
   A. 66
   B. 110
   C. Krone
   D. DIX

3. Which of the following standards is likely to be associated with the NIC inside your computer?
   A. 10BASE-T
   B. 100BASE-T
   C. 1000BASE-T
   D. 10GBASE-T

1.3 ANSWERS

1. **A** Single-mode fiber is used to reach long distances.
2. **D** DIX represents Digital Equipment Corporation, Intel, and Xerox, the companies that worked together on Ethernet.
3. **C** Gigabit Ethernet is the standard for NICs today.

Objective 1.4 # Given a scenario, configure a subnet and use appropriate IP addressing schemes

IP addresses are assigned in multiple ways, used in many ways, and represent different entities. IPv6 addressing and usage is radically different than the IPv4 counterparts. Let's take a look!

Public vs. Private

Some IP addresses are not routed on the Internet. Private addressing started with RFC 1918, which drew the line in terms of *public vs. private* addresses.

RFC 1918

In 1996, the Internet Engineering Task Force (IETF) set out specific ranges of IP addresses, known as private IP addresses, in *RFC 1918* (https://datatracker.ietf.org/doc/html/rfc1918). An RFC is a *Request for Comments*, a document used to define just about everything involving computer networking. The motivations for RFC 1918 were as follows:

- Increasing numbers of enterprises using TCP/IP just for intra-enterprise communications, without needing to connect to other enterprises or the Internet.
- A concern that the globally unique address space will be exhausted.
- A concern that routing overhead will be more than ISPs can provide.
- The likelihood that when an organization would get globally unique IP addresses, it would need to renumber IP addresses for all public hosts, regardless if the addresses were originally globally unique or not.
- It was becoming harder to acquire additional address space without proper justification.

The RFC then grouped hosts into one of three categories:

> Category 1: Hosts that don't need to access hosts in other enterprises or the Internet
>
> Category 2: Hosts that need to access some outside services like e-mail, FTP, etc.
>
> Category 3: Hosts that need Network layer access outside the enterprise

Category 1 and Category 2 describe private hosts, while Category 3 describes public hosts. The ranges of addresses that are designated as private IP addresses are shown in Table 1.4-1.

TABLE 1.4-1		Private IP Address Ranges		
Address Block Start	**Address Block Stop**	**Prefix Representation**	**Meaning in Binary**	**Meaning in English**
10.0.0.0	10.255.255.255	10.0.0.0/8	First 8 bits must be 0000101010	1 Class A network (10.0.0.0/8)
172.16.0.0	172.31.255.255	172.16.0.0/12	First 12 bits must be 10101100.0001	16 Class B networks (172.16.0.0/16 through 172.31.0.0/16) where the second octet can have a value of 16 through 31
192.168.0.0	192.168.255.255	192.168.0.0/16	First 16 bits must be 11000000.10101000	256 Class C networks (192.168.0.0/24 through 192.168.255.0/24) where the third octet can have a value of 0 through 255

NOTE   There are, in fact, other reserved IP addresses. Check this link for more IPv4 reserved address ranges: https://www.iana.org/assignments/iana-ipv4-special-registry/iana-ipv4-special-registry.xhtml. On a related note, IPv6 reserved address ranges can be found at this link: https://www.iana.org/assignments/iana-ipv6-special-registry/iana-ipv6-special-registry.xhtml.

EXAM TIP   Make sure you can quickly tell the difference between a public IP address and a private IP address for the CompTIA Network+ exam. The objectives mention the distinction as *public vs. private.*

Network Address Translation (NAT)

Routers running some form of *network address translation (NAT)* enable devices using private addresses to communicate over the Internet. NAT extended the useful life of IPv4 addressing on the Internet for many years and is extremely common and heavily in use. NAT is a feature in addition *to* the core capability of routing implemented by routers. NAT is not routing, but a separate technology.

Here's the situation. You have a LAN with five computers that need access to the Internet. With classic TCP/IP and routing, several things have to happen. First, you need to get a block

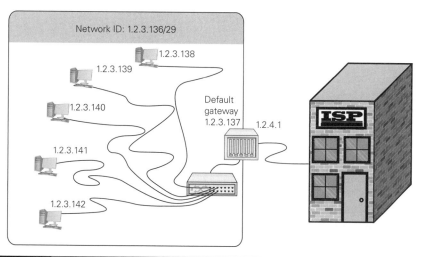

FIGURE 1.4-1   Network setup

of legitimate, unique, expensive IP addresses from an ISP. You could call up an ISP and purchase a network ID—say, 1.2.3.136/29. Second, you assign an IP address to each computer and to the LAN connection on the router. Third, you assign the IP address for the ISP's router to the WAN connection on the local router, such as 1.2.4.1. After everything is configured, the network looks like Figure 1.4-1. All of the clients on the network have the same default gateway (1.2.3.137). This router interface on the LAN side acts as the default gateway for a number of client computers.

This style of network mirrors how computers in LANs throughout the world connected to the Internet for the first 20+ years, but the major problem of a finite number of IP addresses worsened as more and more computers connected.

Port Address Translation (PAT)

Most internal networks today don't have one machine, of course. Instead, they use a block of private IP addresses for the hosts inside the network. They connect to the Internet through one or more public IP addresses.

The most common form of NAT that handles this one-to-many connection—called *port address translation (PAT)*—uses port numbers to map traffic from specific machines in the network. Let's use a simple example to make the process clear.

The JSW Corporation has a network that uses the private IP addressing space of 192.168.1.0/24. All the computers in the private network connect to the Internet through a single router using PAT, with the global IP address of 203.0.113.52/24. Table 1.4-2 represents the NAT/PAT translation table, which is dynamically generated on the router running NAT.

TABLE 1.4-2   JSW Corporation Using NAT

Host	IP Address	Source Local Socket	Source Translated Socket	Destination Remote Socket
A	192.168.1.10	192.168.1.10:60536 TCP	203.0.113.52:60536 TCP	129.21.1.40:443 TCP
B	192.168.1.11	192.168.1.11:60246 TCP	203.0.113.52:60246 TCP	129.21.1.40:443 TCP
C	192.168.1.12	192.168.1.12:60246 TCP	203.0.113.52:60247 TCP	129.21.1.40:443 TCP

There are three hosts, labeled A through C. Each host's IP address starts with 192.168.1, as there are three network octets in this /24 network. The fourth octet is a host octet, with 8 host bits. Notice each host's IP address.

Now, let's say Host A and Host B both send traffic to 129.21.1.40, the IP address of the Rochester Institute of Technology (RIT) Web server. The source local socket, which combines the source IP address with a source port, and also includes the Layer 4 protocol, TCP in this case, is shown in Table 1.4-2. Observe that for the source translated socket, the private inside IP addresses are replaced with the single public outside IP address of 203.0.113.52. In this case, the source ports remain the same. Also notice that the destination remote socket is the same for Host A and Host B, since they're both sending traffic to the same Web server.

When traffic comes back to the network from the RIT Web server, traffic destined for Host A and Host B will have a destination IP address of 203.0.113.52. However, the router running NAT will notice the destination ports, and use each of those as an index in the NAT table. Seeing port 60536 will trigger NAT to change the destination IP address to 192.168.1.10 and send the traffic out of the LAN interface as such. Seeing port 60246 will trigger NAT to change the destination IP address to 192.168.1.11 and send the traffic out of the LAN interface as such.

Let's imagine that at the same time Host A and Host B went to the RIT Web server, Host C did as well. Let's also imagine that Host C, by some coincidence, used the same local port that Host B used, 60246. If the source port is used as an index (when it comes back as a destination port) to find the correct inside host IP address, and if each source translated socket uses the same, single public IP address, how can traffic for Host B and Host C now be differentiated? Easy! NAT will replace the Layer 4 source port number of Host C, to make it unique in the source translated socket, 60247 in this case. When traffic with that destination port is seen in return traffic, both the Layer 4 port and the Layer 3 IP address will now be translated back to what they were, and traffic will be sent out of the router's LAN interface, reaching the appropriate inside host.

Sometimes NAT will change the source port, even without a conflict with what's in the table already.

Well, how does NAT work with ICMP, if ICMP is a Layer 3 protocol, which means there is no Layer 4 header (TCP or UDP) with port information? For ICMP messages that have queries and replies (ICMP Echo request/ICMP Echo reply, for example), the ICMP Query ID value will be treated like an actual TCP or UDP port number. ICMP messages that are one-way, error messages, have no ICMP ID. However, ICMP error messages contain the complete IP header and at least the first 8 bytes of the payload of the packet that caused the ICMP error message. In those cases, NAT will use the actual port number of the encapsulated TCP segment or UDP datagram.

ADDITIONAL RESOURCES   NAT is not a security mechanism, nor has it ever been. See the following links for more details:
https://weberblog.net/why-nat-has-nothing-to-do-with-security/
https://0day.work/an-example-why-nat-is-not-security/
https://blog.ipspace.net/2011/12/is-nat-security-feature.html
https://www.f5.com/services/resources/white-papers/the-myth-of-network-address-translation-as-security
https://youtu.be/v26BAIfWBm8

IPv4 vs. IPv6

IPv4 vs. IPv6 isn't just an increase in address size, from the 32 bits in an IPv4 address to the 128 bits in an IPv6 address. It's an entirely new paradigm of Layer 3. Here are some of the many differences.

Automatic Private IP Addressing (APIPA), Link-Local

Talk about polar opposites! The way IPv4 and IPv6 deal with the concept of *Automatic Private IP Addressing (APIPA)* is drastically different. In the world of IPv4, you never want one of these addresses, while in the world of IPv6, the equivalent of an APIPA address is always used for local communication.

IPv4

DHCP (Dynamic Host Configuration Protocol) is very convenient and, as such, very popular. It's so popular that you'll very rarely see a user's computer on any network using static addressing.

NOTE   Servers and router interfaces should always be configured with static IP addresses, so they never change and they don't become inaccessible in the event that a DHCP server goes down and can't renew a lease.

You should know how to deal with the problems that arise with DHCP. The single biggest issue is when a DHCP client tries to get a DHCP address and fails. You'll know when this happens because the operating system will post some form of error telling you there's a problem and the DHCP client will have a rather strange address in the 169.254.0.0/16 network ID range.

This special IP address is generated by a version of *zero-configuration networking (zeroconf)*. Microsoft's implementation is called Automatic Private IP Addressing (APIPA).

 KEY TERM   Zero-configuration networking (zeroconf) is a generic term that refers to devices auto-configuring themselves (as administrators have zero to configure). Microsoft's implementation of zeroconf is **APIPA**.

All DHCP clients are designed to generate an APIPA address automatically if they do not receive a response to multiple DHCP Discover messages. The client only generates the last two octets of an APIPA address. A client sends a gratuitous ARP to see if another device already has the IP address the client is trying to give itself. If the ARP request gets an ARP reply, the client picks another IP address on the 169.254.0.0/16 subnet. If the ARP request gets no ARP reply, the client starts using the IP address it gave itself. This at least allows the dynamic clients on a single network to continue to communicate with each other because they are on the same network ID.

Unfortunately, APIPA cannot issue a default gateway (since no router interface will ever be configured with an IP address on 169.254.0.0/16), so you'll never get on the Internet using APIPA. That provides a huge clue to a DHCP problem scenario: you can communicate with other computers on your network that came up *after* the DHCP server went down, but you can't get to the Internet or access computers that retain the DHCP-given address. More details on DHCP are coming up in Objective 1.6.

IPv6

All IPv6 hosts use a *link-local* address (fe80::/10) for traffic on the same link (the IPv6 term for network). This is the equivalent of IPv4's APIPA/zeroconf address in the 169.254.0.0/16 block that you never want to have. Link-local addresses in IPv6 are always used for on-link communications! Your default gateway's IPv6 address will be a link-local address. Routers send routing updates to other routers using this type of address.

Extended Unique Identifier (EUI-64)

The concept of Extended Unique Identifier (EUI-64), unlike APIPA, does not apply to both IPv4 and IPv6.

IPv4

EUI-64 has no relevance in IPv4. The host ID portion of an IPv4 address never uses part of the MAC address of the host.

IPv6

When a computer running IPv6 first boots up, it gives itself a link-local address. The first 64 bits of a link-local address are always fe80::/10, followed by 54 zero bits. That means every address always begins with fe80:0000:0000:0000.

The second 64 bits of a link-local address, called the *interface identifier (interface ID)*, are generated in two ways. Windows clients since Windows Vista generate a random 64-bit number. Other operating systems, such as Mac OS X Lion (10.7) or later and Windows Server 2008 and beyond, also use random numbers. Cisco router interfaces, and very old operating systems such as Windows XP and Windows Server 2003, used the device's 48-bit MAC address in part to create a 64-bit number called an *Extended Unique Identifier (EUI-64)*. Linux distros used to default to EUI-64, but now use randomized identifiers.

With stateless address autoconfiguration (SLAAC), coming up later in this objective, the host can generate a 64-bit interface ID with either the EUI-64 process or a random 64-bit value. Here's the process for EUI-64, which was the original method and is still supported by routers but not by Windows, macOS, or most distributions of Linux:

1. The host splits its 48-bit MAC address in the middle, with six hex digits representing the OUI on one side, and six hex digits representing the device ID on the other side. As an example, let's take 00-03-6b-18-f0-0d and split it in the middle:

    `00-03-6b    18-f0-0d`

2. In the middle, the host puts fffe, a special reserved value specifically meaning that the MAC address was used in this process (the formatting of the address includes a dash between the ff and fe):

    `00-03-6b-ff-fe-18-f0-0d`

3. The seventh bit from the left is known as both the Universally/Locally (U/L) bit and the Local/Global bit. A 0 in this bit position means the IEEE assigned this address. A 1 means it's locally administered by a company. Looking at what we have so far, again:

    `00-03-6b-ff-fe-18-f0-0d`

    The first two hex digits (00) in binary are 00000000 (notice that the seventh bit is **in bold**).

    When you flip this seventh bit, it becomes 0000 0010 (notice again that the seventh bit is **in bold**). Turning the binary back into hex, since the bit flipped is in the 2s column of the second hex digit, the second hex digit becomes a 2 (**bolded below**):

    `02-03-6b-ff-fe-18-f0-0d`

    From section 2.5.1 of RFC 2373 (https://datatracker.ietf.org/doc/html/rfc2373):

    The motivation for inverting the "u" bit when forming the interface identifier is to make it easy for system administrators to hand configure local scope identifiers when hardware tokens are not available. This is expected to be case for serial links, tunnel end-points, etc. The alternative would have been for these to be of the form 0200:0:0:1, 0200:0:0:2, etc., instead of the much simpler ::1, ::2, etc.

Now imagine using your laptop on various networks. Your NIC's MAC address, if part of an IPv6 address, can be tracked, aggregated, and correlated on all the networks you connect to.

It will be in log files and network traces. That fear lead to RFC 4941 (https://datatracker.ietf.org/doc/html/rfc4941), "Privacy Extensions for Stateless Address Autoconfiguration in IPv6," which states:

> Any time the same identifier is used in multiple contexts, it becomes possible for that identifier to be used to correlate seemingly unrelated activity. For example, a network sniffer placed strategically on a link across which all traffic to/from a particular host crosses could keep track of which destinations a node communicated with and at what times. Such information can in some cases be used to infer things, such as what hours an employee was active, when someone is at home, etc.

In addition to generating randomized interface IDs, devices will also generate temporary addresses to be used as source IPv6 addresses for short periods of time, to further aid in privacy. An IPv6 address that does not change will be assigned by the host for incoming connections.

A host can have more than one GUA (global unicast address, the IPv6 equivalent term for IPv4's public IP address) on one or more links in addition to a link-local address for each link. Furthermore, multiple temporary addresses can be in play to allow existing connections to continue while a new temporary address is used for future connections.

Broadcast

A *broadcast* message is sent to and read by each device on a network.

IPv4

A broadcast is sent to every node on the network. The destination MAC address for a broadcast is all Fs: FF-FF-FF-FF-FF-FF. The flooded broadcast address in the world of IP addresses is 255.255.255.255. A targeted subnet broadcast address has all ones in the host portion, but this type of broadcast address is more of a relic of the past nowadays.

Broadcasting is not a good thing. Switches flood broadcasts out of all ports except the port on which the message originated, thus extending the broadcast domain. A PC that sees a broadcast, reads it, and in many cases like ARP requests, drops the message when it realizes that the message is not meant for itself. Thus, the PC just wasted resources like processing, slowing it down from what it would have normally been doing.

Notable protocols that use broadcasts (for some of their messages) are ARP and DHCP.

IPv6

There is no such thing as broadcasting in IPv6. It has been completely eliminated. That's a very good thing!

| TABLE 1.4-3 | Important IPv4 Multicast Addresses |

Address	Description
224.0.0.1	All hosts
224.0.0.2	All routers
224.0.0.5	All OSPF (Open Shortest Path First) routers
224.0.0.6	All OSPF DR/BDR (designated router/backup designated router) routers
224.0.0.22	IGMPv3 (Internet Group Management Protocol version 3)
224.0.0.10	All EIGRP (Enhanced Interior Gateway Routing Protocol) routers
224.0.0.18	VRRP (Virtual Router Redundancy Protocol)

Multicast

A *multicast* is sent to and read by more than one destination, but it is not sent to every device on the network (which is what a broadcast is).

IPv4

Addresses in the 224-239 Class D range are reserved for multicast addresses.

Internet Group Management Protocol (IGMP) is used by hosts to join multicast groups and by routers to send multicast messages to the intended recipients. Table 1.4-3 lists some important IPv4 multicast addresses.

 NOTE   You can view IANA's IPv4 Multicast Address Space Registry at https://www.iana.org/assignments/multicast-addresses/multicast-addresses.xhtml.

Multicast addresses from Internet Assigned Numbers Authority (IANA) have corresponding MAC addresses that start with 01-00-5E.

IPv6

IPv6 multicast addresses start with ff, are followed by a 0 for permanent, well-known IANA-assigned address or a 1 for dynamically assigned multicast addresses, and then, either a 2 for link-local scope or a 5 for site-local scope.

Multicast Listener Discovery (MLD) is used by IPv6 devices in the same way that IPv4 devices use IGMP. Table 1.4-4 lists some important IPv6 multicast addresses.

Like IPv4 multicast addresses, IPv6 multicast addresses have corresponding Ethernet MAC addresses. A multicast MAC address corresponding to an IPv6 address always starts with 33-33, with the rest of the MAC address (the lower 32 bits) corresponding to the lower 32 bits of the IPv6 multicast address. For example:

- 33-33-00-00-00-01 is the MAC address for ff02::1 (All-devices).
- 33-33-00-00-00-02 is the MAC address for ff02::2 (All-routers).

| TABLE 1.4-4 | Important IPv6 Multicast Addresses |

Address	Description
ff02::1	All nodes
ff02::2	All routers
ff02::5	All OSPFv3 (Open Shortest Path First version 3) routers
ff02::6	All OSPFv3 DR/BDR (designated router/backup designated router) routers
ff02::a	All EIGRP (Enhanced Interior Gateway Routing Protocol) routers
ff02::d	PIM (Protocol Independent Multicast) routers (PIM is used to join and leave multicast distribution trees)
ff02::12	VRRPv3 (Virtual Router Redundancy Protocol version 3)
ff02::16	MLDv2 reports
ff02::1:2	All DHCPv6 servers and relay agents
ff05::1:3	All DHCP servers

NOTE   The reason for multicast MAC addresses starting with four 3s is explained in RFC 7042 (https://datatracker.ietf.org/doc/html/rfc7042) as follows:
Historical note: It was the custom during IPv6 design to use "3" for unknown or example values, and 3333 Coyote Hill Road, Palo Alto, California, is the address of PARC (Palo Alto Research Center, formerly "Xerox PARC"). Ethernet was originally specified by the Digital Equipment Corporation, Intel Corporation, and Xerox Corporation. The pre-IEEE [802.3] Ethernet protocol has sometimes been known as "DIX" Ethernet from the first letters of the names of these companies.

Besides these assigned multicast addresses, another type of multicast address, solicited-node multicast address, is a major entity in IPv6.

In IPv6, there is no broadcast traffic, just unicast, multicast, or anycast. How, then, can hosts get the MAC addresses of the devices they wish to communicate with, given an IP address that they will have (they can be told of the actual IP address or can use DNS to resolve a fully qualified domain name [FQDN] into its corresponding IP address). ARP requests are broadcasts, so that can't be how it's done in IPv6.

The answer is Neighbor Discovery Protocol, which is run through ICMPv6 (ICMP for IPv6, not the sixth version of ICMP), specifically:

- Neighbor Solicitation (NS, the IPv6 equivalent of an ARP request)
- Neighbor Advertisement (NA, the IPv6 equivalent of an ARP reply)

Let's say an IPv6 device has to send a packet to 2001:db8:f00d:1::200/64. That's the destination IPv6 address that will be found in the IPv6 header of the packet. The packet, of course, must be encapsulated inside of a frame, and the source needs the destination's MAC address for the frame.

The source first checks its neighbor cache, the IPv6 equivalent of the IPv4 ARP cache. If the binding is there, it's used, just like the ARP cache is used for IPv4. If it's not, the source sends a Neighbor Solicitation message to the destination's solicited-node multicast address. In this case, it's ff02::1:ff00:200.

We started with 2001:db8:f00d:1::200/64.

Without shortcut notation, that's 2001:db8:f00d:0001:0000:000:0**00:0200**/64.

We took the last 24 bits (six hex digits) to make the following solicited-node multicast address (notice the bold):

> ff02:0000:0000:0000:0000:0001:ff**00:0200**

Now let's take the last 32 bits (eight hex digits) of that address (notice the bold):

> ff02:0000:0000:0000:0000:0001:**ff00:0200**

and put them after 33-33 (notice the bold):

> 33-33 **ff-00-02-00**

That is the MAC address placed in the frame, corresponding to the solicited-node multicast address in the packet.

With the use of a Layer 2 multicast address now instead of a broadcast ARP request (which is read in addition to the Ethernet frame by all devices), the NIC can filter NS messages quickly and easily. The IPv6 header and the ICMPv6 packet need not be consulted.

Now, of course, it is possible, although not likely, to have more than one interface with the same last six hex digits. The interface ID is 64 bits long, so these interfaces will differ in their highest 40 bits of the interface ID. If so, these interfaces will have the exact solicited-node multicast address and the exact multicast MAC address. That's not an issue, because inside of the ICMPv6 Neighbor Solicitation message is a Target Address field, and the interface not matching the value in that field will drop the NS at that point.

Unicast

A *unicast* address is a specific address bound to a NIC.

IPv4

In IPv4, a unicast address is used for one-to-one communication. A system can have only one unicast address, which can be either statically or dynamically configured.

IPv6

In IPv6, a unicast address is also used for one-to-one communication. However, a system can have more than one unicast address, including multiple addresses from one or more categories:

- **Global unicast address (GUA)**   A public IPv6 address that is routable on the Internet. The address assigned to the host must be unique on the Internet. This address type is equivalent to a public IP address with IPv4. This address always starts with a hex character of 2 or 3.
- **Link-local unicast address**   An address that's automatically assigned to the system and is used to communicate only with other nodes on the link (a term that means network/subnet/LAN in the world of IPv6). Link-local addresses always start with fe80. This address type is equivalent to an APIPA address (169.254.0.0/16) with IPv4. The big difference is that APIPA addresses are never desired in IPv4, because it indicates the inability to contact a DHCP server, and therefore a lack of routing capabilities. In IPv6, the link-local address is the actual address used for communicating with nodes on your same network.
- **Unique local address**   An address that's similar to the RFC 1918 private IPv4 addresses, but is not meant to be translated to a GUA to be routed across the Internet. It uses the fc00::/7 prefix, where the first hextet can range between fc00::7 and fdff::/7.

 NOTE   Loopback, unspecified, and embedded IPv4 are other types of IPv6 unicast addresses.

Anycast

An *anycast* address is applied to a group of systems (sharing the same unicast IP address) providing a service. Clients that send data to the anycast address have their communication routed to the nearest server that's a part of the anycast address, through BGP (Border Gateway Protocol).

IPv4 and IPv6

Both IPv4 and IPv6 make use of the anycast in many ways, including the IP addresses of the 13 root name servers, located at the top of the DNS (Domain Name System) hierarchy. (DNS is coming up in Objective 1.6.)

Loopback

The *loopback* address is used to test the TCP/IP stack on a system. It's pure software, and has nothing to do with any hardware, including the NIC.

IPv4

When you tell a device to send data to 127.0.0.1, you're telling that device to send the packets to itself. The loopback address has several uses. Besides testing out a system's TCP/IP stack, browsing to 127.0.0.1 can test a Web server running on that same device. In fact, any server service can be accessed with a destination IP address of 127.0.0.1.

 EXAM TIP   Even though, by convention, you use 127.0.0.1 as the loopback address, the entire 127.0.0.0/8 subnet is reserved for loopback addresses. You can use any address in the 127.0.0.0/8 subnet as a loopback address.

IPv6

While the address changes from IPv4's 127.0.0.1 to ::1 in IPv6, its purpose and functionality remain the same.

Default Gateway

Every TCP/IP LAN that wants to connect to another TCP/IP LAN must have a router connection. There is no exception to this critical rule. A router, therefore, needs an interface IP address on the LANs that it serves, so it can correctly route packets. That router interface, on each LAN, is known as the *default gateway*. Outgoing packets will be encapsulated in frames with a destination MAC address of the default gateway. Incoming packets will be encapsulated in frames with a source MAC address of the default gateway.

IPv4

The default gateway IP address for an IPv4 host will be an address on the LAN/subnet of the host.

IPv6

The default gateway IP address for an IPv6 interface will be an address in the link-local fe80::/10 range, in the scope of the interface.

IPv4 Subnetting

When it comes to IP addressing, the IP address is only half of the story. The other component is the subnet mask. Network hosts need both an IP address and a corresponding subnet mask in order to communicate on a network. There were problems with classful addressing (see the Classful section coming up for more), though, that came to light almost immediately. *IPv4 Subnetting* involves taking a single network ID and chopping it up into multiple smaller networks, also known as *subnets*. IPv4 subnetting also provides great benefits, as well. Network speed and overall performance will go up, since instead of one large broadcast domain, you'll have multiple subnets separated by routers. Routers never forward broadcasts. This is why college courses are taught in their own individual rooms (like subnets that contain their own broadcast traffic), as opposed to many classes taught in a single lecture hall (like one big broadcast domain/LAN without subnets). I don't want my students to hear the broadcast traffic from other professors while I teach, just mine!

Other benefits of IPv4 subnetting include:

- It cuts down on network congestion, because the traffic in each subnet goes down.
- You could filter traffic at Layer 3 with router ACLs (access control lists) and more.
- You could control how the network grows by using custom subnet masks.
- Administration is easier in terms of keeping track of devices and troubleshooting, since with multiple networks it won't be like looking for a needle in a haystack, but rather smaller sections.

 EXAM TIP You need to know how to subnet to pass the CompTIA Network+ exam.

The cornerstone to subnetting lies in the subnet mask.

You take an existing /8, /16, or /24 subnet and extend the subnet mask by adding more 1s by taking away the corresponding number of 0s. For example, let's say you have an Internet café with 50 computers, 40 of which are for public use and 10 of which are used in the back office for accounting and such (see Figure 1.4-2). Your network ID is 192.168.4.0/24. You want to prevent people using the public systems from accessing your private machines, so you decide to create subnets. You also have Wi-Fi and want to separate wireless clients (never more than 10) on their own subnet.

You need to keep two things in mind about subnetting. First, start with the given subnet mask and add more ones to the right (replacing the 0s with 1s) until you have the number of subnets you need. Second, forget the dots. They no longer define the subnets.

Never try to subnet without first converting to binary. Too many techs are "victims of the dots." They are so used to working only with class licenses that they forget there's more to subnets than just /8, /16, and /24 networks. There is no reason network IDs must end on the dots. The computers, at least, think it's perfectly fine to have subnets that end at points between the periods, such as /26, /27, or even /22. The trick here is to stop thinking about network IDs and subnet masks just in their dotted decimal format and instead return to thinking of them as binary numbers.

Let's begin subnetting the café's network of 192.168.4.0/24. Start by changing a 0 to a 1 on the subnet mask so that the /24 becomes a /25 subnet:

11111111111111111111111110000000

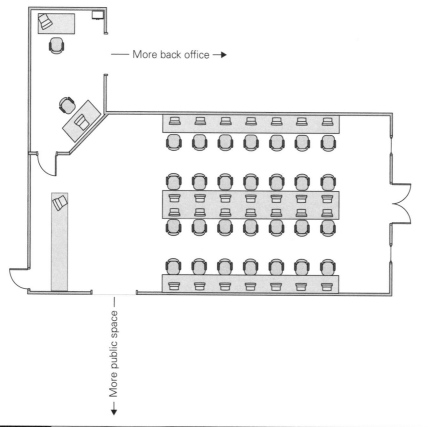

FIGURE 1.4-2   Layout of the network

Calculating Hosts

Before going even one step further, you need to answer this question: On a /24 network, how many hosts can you have? Well, if you used dotted decimal notation, you might say

192.168.4.1 to 192.168.4.254 = 254 hosts

But do this from the binary instead. In a /24 network, you have eight 0s that can be the host ID:

00000001 to 11111110 = 254

There's a simple piece of math here: $2^x - 2$, where x represents the number of 0s in the subnet mask:

$2^8 - 2 = 254$

If you remember this simple formula, you can always determine the number of hosts for a given subnet. This is critical! Memorize this!

If you have a /26 subnet mask on your network, what is the maximum number of hosts you can have on that network?

Because a subnet mask always has 32 bits, a /26 subnet means you have 6 0s left after the 26 1s: $2^6 - 2 = 62$ total hosts.

Excellent! Knowing how to determine the number of hosts for a particular subnet mask will help you tremendously, as you'll see in a moment.

Making Subnets

Let's now make some subnets. All subnetting begins with a single network ID. In this scenario, you need to convert the 192.168.4.0/24 network ID for the café into three network IDs: one for the public computers, one for the private computers, and one for the wireless clients.

 CAUTION You cannot subnet without using binary!

The primary tool for subnetting is the existing subnet mask. Write it out in binary. Place a line at the end of the 1s, as shown in Figure 1.4-3.

Now draw a second line one digit to the right, as shown in Figure 1.4-4. You've now separated the subnet mask into three areas. The first area consists of the original network bits (ones) in the subnet mask. The second area contains the first host bit (the first 0) in the subnet mask. The third area contains the remaining seven host bits (the last seven 0s).

Now, turn that 0 in the second area into a 1, which changes it from a host bit to a network bit. This process is known as "borrowing," but I call it "stealing," since you're never going to give it back! You now have a /25 subnet mask. At this point, most people first learning how to subnet start to freak out. They're challenged by the idea that a subnet mask of /25 isn't going to fit into one of the three pretty subnets of 255.0.0.0, 255.255.0.0, or 255.255.255.0. They think, "That can't be right! Subnet masks are made of only 255s and 0s." That's not correct.

Subnet mask 11111111.11111111.11111111.00000000

FIGURE 1.4-3 Step 1 in subnetting

Subnet mask 11111111.11111111.11111111.00000000

FIGURE 1.4-4 Organizing the subnet mask

A subnet mask is a string of 1s followed by a string of 0s. People only convert it into dotted decimal to read, understand, and configure. So, convert /25 into dotted decimal. First write out 25 1s, followed by 7 0s, with periods in between every group of eight digits:

11111111.11111111.11111111.10000000

Then convert the result into dotted decimal:

```
255.255.255.128
```

Get used to the idea of subnet masks that use more than 255s and 0s. Here are some examples of perfectly legitimate subnet masks. Try converting these to binary to see for yourself.

```
255.255.255.224
255.255.128.0
255.248.0.0
```

Calculating Subnets

When you subnet a network ID, you need to follow the rules and conventions dictated by the good folks who developed TCP/IP to ensure that your new subnets can interact properly with each other and with larger networks. All you need to remember for subnetting is this: start with an initial subnet mask and keep borrowing bits until you have the number of subnets you need. The formula for determining how many subnets you create is 2^y, where y is the number of bits you turn from host bits (0s) to network bits (1s) in the subnet mask.

Figure 1.4-4 shows a starting subnet of 255.255.255.0, with 1 bit in the second area, ready to be flipped from a 0 to a 1, turning it from a host bit into a network bit.

Changing 1 bit will only give you two subnets. You have only one problem—the café needs three subnets, not just two! So, let's take the original /24 and borrow 2 bits, forming a /26 subnet mask, as shown in Figure 1.4-5.

Borrowing 2 bits creates four new network IDs: $2^2 = 4$. To see each of these network IDs, first convert the original network ID—192.168.4.0—into binary. Then add the four different patterns of 2 bits to the end of the network ID portion, as shown in Figure 1.4-6.

Subnet mask   11111111.11111111.11111111.11000000

FIGURE 1.4-5   The new /26 subnet mask

Original network ID: 192.168.4.0 /24
Translates to this in binary:
11000000.10101000.00000100.00000000

```
11000000.10101000.00000100.|00|000000
11000000.10101000.00000100.|01|000000
11000000.10101000.00000100.|10|000000
11000000.10101000.00000100.|11|000000
```

FIGURE 1.4-6   Creating the new network IDs

Now convert these four network IDs back to dotted decimal, as shown in the first column of Table 1.4-5.

The network IDs increment by the multiplier, also known as the spacing and the magic number. This value is the column of the furthermost right 1 bit. In this case, looking back at Figure 1.4-4, it's the 64s column of the fourth octet. Notice, in Table 1.4-5, how we start with the original network ID for the first subnet (the numbering starts with 0, so the first subnet is subnet 0), but now increment the column in which the borrowing stopped in by that multiplier: 0 + 64 = 64, 64 + 64 = 128, 128 + 64 = 192. Adding 64 to 192 will give you 256, a number that you can't make with 8 bits (the highest value for 8 bits is 255), which makes sense, since we have already established the fact that borrowing 2 bits creates only four subnets.

The host ranges start with the first address available after the network ID. The first one is obvious, because the network ID ends with 0 in the fourth octet, so the first host would have a 1 in the fourth octet. The last number available in the host range is one number before the broadcast address for that subnet, which itself is one number before the next network ID.

The formula for determining how many hosts on each subnet there are (each subnet will always have the same number of hosts) is $2^x - 2$, where x is the number of host bits. With this /26 example, there are 6 host bits left, which means there are $2^6 - 2 = 62$ host addresses available for each of the four subnets. Looking at the Host Range column in Table 1.4-5 shows just that.

Congratulations! You've just taken a single network ID, 192.168.4.0/24, and subnetted it into four new network IDs!

You may notice that the café only needs three subnets, but you created four—you have an extra subnet now. Because subnets are created by powers of two, you will often create more subnets than you need—welcome to subnetting.

TABLE 1.4-5   Completed Subnetting

Subnet Number	Network ID	Host Range	Broadcast Address
0	192.168.4.0/26	192.168.4.1–192.168.4.62	192.168.4.63
1	192.168.4.64/26	192.168.4.65–192.168.4.126	192.168.4.127
2	192.168.4.128/26	192.168.4.129–192.168.4.190	192.168.4.191
3	192.168.4.192/26	192.168.4.193–192.168.4.254	192.168.4.255

CAUTION   In terms of this example, the unused network ID sets the café up for scalability. If the café grows and needs another subnet, it's already there for the café to use without messing with the existing subnets.

Classful

To support the dispersion of IP addresses and to make sure that no organizations used duplicate IP addresses on the Internet, the Internet Assigned Numbers Authority (IANA) was formed to track and disperse IP addresses to those who need them. IANA was initially handled by a single person (Jon Postel) until 1998, when the Internet Corporation for Assigned Names and Numbers (ICANN) was established to oversee IANA.

IANA has grown dramatically, and now oversees five Regional Internet Registries (RIRs) that parcel out IP addresses to large ISPs and major corporations. The RIR for the United States, Canada, and many Caribbean and North Atlantic islands is the American Registry for Internet Numbers (ARIN).

ADDITIONAL RESOURCES   Read the blog post I wrote for ARIN at https://www.arin.net/blog/author/jweissman/.

NOTE   The Internet Corporation for Assigned Names and Numbers (ICANN) manages IANA.

IANA originally passed out IP addresses in a *classful* fashion, outlined in Table 1.4-6 (notice that the entire 127.0.0.0/8 range has been reserved for the loopback address, as described earlier).

TABLE 1.4-6   Classful Addressing

	First Octet Value	**Addresses**	**Hosts per Network ID**
Class A	1–126	1.0.0.0–126.255.255.255	16,777,214
Class B	128–191	128.0.0.0–191.255.255.255	65,534
Class C	192–223	192.0.0.0–223.255.255.255	254
Class D	224–239	224.0.0.0–239.255.255.255	Not assigned to hosts; used for multicasting
Class E	240–255	240.0.0.0–255.255.255.255	Not assigned to hosts; used for experimental purposes

EXAM TIP   Make sure you memorize the IP class ranges! You should be able to look at any IP address and know its class. Here's a trick to help: the first binary octet of a Class A address always begins with a 0 (0xxxxxxx); for Class B, it begins with a 10 (10xxxxxx); for Class C, it begins with 110 (110xxxxx); for Class D, it begins with 1110 (1110xxxx); and for Class E, it begins with 1111 (1111xxxx).

A Class A network block, with a subnet mask of 255.0.0.0, uses the first octet (8 bits) to define the network ID and the last three octets (24 bits) for the host ID. All hosts in network 10.0.0.0, for example, would have the first number in common. Having three octets to use for hosts means you have an enormous number of possible hosts—over 16 million different number combinations (not that you would ever make a network with 16 million hosts).

A Class B block, with a subnet mask of 255.255.0.0, uses the first two octets to define the network ID. All hosts in network 172.30.0.0, for example, would have the first two numbers in common. This leaves two octets to define host IDs, which means each Class B network ID can have up to 65,534 different hosts.

A Class C block, with a subnet mask of 255.255.255.0, uses the first three octets to define only the network ID. All hosts in network 192.168.1.0, for example, would have the first three numbers in common. Only the last octet defines the host IDs, which leaves only 254 possible unique addresses.

Multicast class blocks are used for one-to-many communication, such as in streaming video conferencing, as well as when routers talk to each other, with routing protocols.

Classless (Variable-Length Subnet Mask)

CIDR (Classless Inter-Domain Routing), and its *classless (variable-length subnet mask)* related concepts, was introduced in 1993 to solve the following three problems, as listed originally in RFC 1338 (https://datatracker.ietf.org/doc/html/rfc1338):

> As the Internet has evolved and grown over in recent years, it has become painfully evident that it is soon to face several serious scaling problems. These include:
>
> 1. Exhaustion of the class-B network address space. One fundamental cause of this problem is the lack of a network class of a size which is appropriate for mid-sized organization; class-C, with a maximum of 254 host addresses, is too small while class-B, which allows up to 65534 addresses, is to large to be widely allocated.
>
> 2. Growth of routing tables in Internet routers beyond the ability of current software (and people) to effectively manage.
>
> 3. Eventual exhaustion of the 32-bit IP address space.

As previously mentioned, there are five RIRs around the world that assign IP address blocks, in their geographical locations, to ISPs and large organizations. The first problem, exhaustion of the Class B network address space, was solved by subnetting at the RIR and ISP level, using variable-length subnet masking (VLSM), a component of CIDR that allows arbitrary-length prefixes instead of the fixed-length prefixes of classful addressing. Since these prefixes don't fit nicely into the classful addressing scheme, they are called *classless*. This made it possible to create subnets with different host sizes and not use the wasteful Class A, Class B, and Class C fixed host lengths.

Underneath the hood, VLSM is the process of subnetting a subnet. For example, instead of one organization getting a single Class B network, consisting of a possible 65,534 hosts (which would be subnetted, of course), an RIR could subnet that Class B network, and then subnet the subnets differently, creating networks of many different sizes. Now, networks of appropriate sizes can be assigned to organizations, proportional to their sizes and actual host requirements.

Furthermore, VLSM can be done internally by an organization, based on its needs. Traditional subnetting creates subnets of the same size. VLSM allows an organization to create subnets of variable lengths. For example, a subnet can be further subnetted to allow for just two hosts on a network, and networks of those sizes could be assigned to router interfaces that are directly connected together. There's no need for more than two host IP addresses on those networks consisting of just two router interfaces. Other subnets of an organization can be subnetted to allow for different host sizes, like 14, 62, or 126.

The second problem, unmanageable growth of routing tables in Internet routers, was solved with a concept known as supernetting, summarizing multiple network IDs in the router routing tables when possible to cut down on the number of entries. For example, if all North American IP addresses start with 198.0.0.0 (using the subnet mask of 255.0.0.0), all routers from South America could have one entry pointing to routers in North America for all addresses that start with 198.0.0.0 (regardless of the values of other octets). Then, all North American routers will have more specific routes for each ISP. For example, one ISP could be in control of all 198.133.0.0 (using the subnet mask of 255.255.0.0) addresses, and another ISP could be in control of all 198.134.0.0 (using the subnet mask of 255.255.0.0) addresses. Then, each ISP will have more specific routes for each of its customers. For example, the first ISP could have customers with IP addresses starting with 198.133.1.0 (using the subnet mask of 255.255.255.0), 198.133.2.0 (using the subnet mask of 255.255.255.0), etc.

The third problem was solved with a new protocol known as IPv6, discussed in the upcoming "IPv6 Concepts" section.

Classless Inter-Domain Routing (CIDR) Notation

With CIDR, came *Classless Inter-Domain Routing (CIDR) notation*. In CIDR notation, the IP address is followed by the subnet mask, represented with a / (forward slash) followed by a number that corresponds to the number of network bits in the IP address (which also represents the number of ones in the subnet mask in binary). For example, 192.168.5.0/24 means there are 24 network bits. /24 is a lot easier to say and write than 255.255.255.0.

Instead of writing out the subnet mask in dotted decimal base 10 notation, like 255.255.255.0, and saying it like "Two fifty-five, dot, two fifty-five, dot, two fifty-five, dot, zero," you can write it like /24 and say "slash twenty-four." In other words, take the network ID, put a slash after it, and then put a number that represents how many 1s are in the subnet mask. For example, 192.168.1.0/24.

IPv6 Concepts

IPv6 concepts of tunneling and dual stack allow for IPv6 to coexist with IPv4; the IPv6 concept of shorthand notation allows for the ease of representing an IPv6 address in a simpler way; and the IPv6 concepts of router advertisement and stateless address autoconfiguration (SLAAC) allow for an interface to give itself an IPv6 address.

Tunneling

All modern operating systems and routers (including small home routers) support IPv6. However, not all routers on the Internet have IPv6 support.

In order for IPv6 to work, every router and every computer on the Internet needs to support IPv6, but the Internet is not yet there. The problem is that some routers and DNS servers between your IPv6-capable computer and the other IPv6-capable computers to which you would like to connect are not yet ready for IPv6. How do you get past this IPv6 gap?

To get on the IPv6 Internet, you need to circumvent this gap with *tunneling*, by implementing an IPv4-to-IPv6 tunnel. The folks who developed IPv6 have a number of ways for you to do this, using one of many IPv4-to-IPv6 tunneling standards. An IPv4-to-IPv6 tunnel works like any other tunnel, encapsulating one type of data into another. In this case, you are encapsulating your IPv6 traffic into an IPv4 tunnel to get to an IPv6-capable router.

An overlay tunnel enables two IPv6 networks to connect over an existing IPv4 infrastructure, like the Internet.

Dual Stack

The routers that connect the IPv6 networks to the IPv4 infrastructure run a *dual stack* architecture—both IPv4 and IPv6—and can encapsulate the traffic from the local network into IPv4 packets. Those IPv4 packets travel over the IPv4 infrastructure and the router at the other end of the tunnel strips the IPv4 stuff off the packet and sends the remaining IPv6 packet on its merry way.

Hosts also can be dual stacked, sending IPv6 traffic when DNS returns an AAAA record, and sending IPv4 traffic when DNS just returns an A record, or as a fallback when the IPv6 host can't be reached by IPv6 but can also be reached by IPv4. Record types are discussed in Objective 1.6.

Shorthand Notation

The 32-bit IPv4 addresses are written as 197.169.94.82, using four octets. IPv6 addresses have 128 bits, so octets are gone. IPv6 addresses are written like this:

```
2001:0db8:0000:0000:0800:200c:00cf:1234
```

IPv6 uses a colon as a separator, instead of the period used in IPv4's dotted decimal format. Each 16-bit group—called a quartet or hextet—is a hexadecimal number between 0000 and ffff.

EXAM TIP   You'll see the hexadecimal letters in IPv6 written both uppercase and lowercase. It doesn't matter to the computer, but the people behind IPv6 insist (per RFC 5952) that notation should be lowercase. That's the convention used here. You might see the letters uppercase on the CompTIA Network+ exam. It's all the same, so don't get thrown off.

An IPv6 address generally splits into two 64-bit sections. The first 64 bits is the network prefix (serving the same purpose as IPv4's network ID). The second 64 bits is the interface ID (serving the same purpose as IPv4's host ID).

NOTE   For those who don't play with hex regularly, one hexadecimal character represents 4 bits; so four hexadecimal characters make a 16-bit group.

A complete IPv6 address always has eight groups of four hexadecimal characters. If this sounds like you're going to type in really long IP addresses, don't worry, IPv6 offers a *shorthand notation* that provides shortcuts.

First, leading 0s can be dropped from any group, so 00cf becomes cf, 0db8 becomes db8, and 0000 becomes 0. Let's rewrite that IPv6 address using the leading 0 rule:

```
2001:db8:0:0:800:200c:cf:1234
```

To write IPv6 addresses containing strings of 0s, you can use a pair of colons (::) to represent one or more consecutive groups with a value of 0. For example, using the double colon rule, you can write the IPv6 address

```
2001:db8:0:0:800:200c:cf:1234
```

as

```
2001:db8::800:200c:cf:1234
```

Double colons are very handy, but you have to be careful when you use them. Take a look at this IPv6 address:

```
fe80:0000:0000:0000:00cf:0000:ba98:1234
```

You can convert it to

```
fe80::cf:0:ba98:1234
```

Note that you cannot use a second :: to represent the last group of four 0s—only one :: is allowed per address! There's a good reason for this rule. If more than one :: was used, how could you tell how many sets of 0s were in each group? Answer: you couldn't.

NOTE If there are more than one contiguous strings of hextets of all 0s, RFC 5952, Section 4.2.3, states

When there is an alternative choice in the placement of a "::", the longest run of consecutive 16-bit 0 fields MUST be shortened (i.e., the sequence with three consecutive zero fields is shortened in 2001: 0:0:1:0:0:0:1). When the length of the consecutive 16-bit 0 fields are equal (i.e., 2001:db8:0:0:1:0:0:1), the first sequence of zero bits MUST be shortened. For example, 2001:db8::1:0:0:1 is correct representation.

IPv6 uses the "/x" prefix length naming convention, similar to the CIDR naming convention in IPv4. Here's how to write an IP address and prefix length for a typical IPv6 host:

```
fe80::cf:0:ba98:1234/64
```

The /64 tells the reader that the network prefix is 64 bits. The address starts with fe80 followed by some number of hextets of all 0s: 0000. With the /64, you know to make the prefix thus:

```
fe80:0000:0000:0000
```

Here's an example of a very special IPv6 address that takes full advantage of the shorthand notation, the IPv6 loopback address:

```
::1
```

Without using the double-colon notation, this IPv6 address would look like this:

```
0000:0000:0000:0000:0000:0000:0000:0001
```

Router Advertisement, Stateless Address Autoconfiguration (SLAAC)

In the world of IPv4, you could filter some or all of the ICMP messages and still have a functional network. You just can't do that in IPv6.

Neighbor Discovery Protocol, which is implemented through ICMPv6 (ICMP for IPv6), is a way of life for IPv6.

When an IPv6 host has an interface enabled, it sends a router solicitation (RS) to the all-routers multicast address of ff02::2 in hopes of receiving a *router advertisement* (RA) in response. The RA can either be sent either the all-hosts multicast address of ff02::1, or it can be configured to be sent to the link-local unicast address of the host. The host's MAC address is included in the RS as well, so the router has all it needs. Routers also send unsolicited router advertisements in regular time intervals.

RA messages let hosts know how to go ahead with dynamic addressing and contain a prefix (the IPv6 term for network ID), prefix length (the IPv6 term for subnet mask, which should always be /64 to allow hosts to autoconfigure themselves with SLAAC—coming up in this section), default gateway, and other information for configuration. A router can also be configured to send IP addresses of DNS servers in an option in an RA.

 NOTE IPv4 does have an IPv4 router advertisement concept, implemented through ICMP Internet Router Discovery Protocol (IRDP), but it hasn't really ever seen the light of day.

There are three important flags in the RA:

- **Address Autoconfiguration flag (A flag)**   A 1 (default) instructs a host to create its global unicast address (GUA—the IPv6 term for public IP address) with SLAAC (described following this list). The RA contains a 64-bit prefix, which will be followed by a 64-bit interface ID generated by the host during the SLAAC process.
- **Other Configuration Flag (O flag)**   A 1 instructs a host to get information other than an actual GUA (like DNS server IPv6 addresses and domain name information) from a stateless DHCPv6 (DHCP for IPv6) server.
- **Managed Address Configuration flag (M flag)**   A 1 instructs a host to use a stateful DHCPv6 server for everything, including its GUA and other configuration information, just like an IPv4 host would use a DHCP server. However, the source IPv6 address in the RA becomes the host's default gateway address. DHCPv6 servers do not give out default gateway information.

With *stateless address autoconfiguration (SLAAC)*, the host can generate a 64-bit interface ID with either the EUI-64 process or a random 64-bit value. In addition to generating randomized interface IDs, devices will generate temporary addresses to be used as source IPv6 addresses for short periods of time to further aid in privacy. An IPv6 address that does not change will be assigned by the host for incoming connections.

A host can have more than one GUA (on one or more links) in addition to a link-local address for each link. Furthermore, multiple temporary addresses can be in play to allow existing connections to continue while a new temporary address is used for future connections.

Virtual IP (VIP)

Clients need to be configured with the IP address of the default gateway, or their traffic will never be sent off their network, and traffic intended for them, from other networks, won't be delivered onto their network.

A first hop redundancy protocol (FHRP) allows two or more routers to provide backup for the default gateway IP address given to hosts. Let's say the default gateway's IP address given to hosts is 192.168.1.1, and a single router has that IP address statically configured on its interface on the LAN. If that router goes down, no host from the LAN will be able to send or receive traffic to or from different LANs. That's a single point of failure.

Cross-Reference

FHRPs are discussed in Objective 3.3.

Now imagine two, three, or more routers having their own IP addresses bound to each of their LAN interfaces. The router interfaces could have the following addresses: 192.168.1.2, 192.168.1.3, 192.168.1.4, and 192.168.1.5. Each router would provide support for the default gateway address, a *virtual IP (VIP)* address, assigned to hosts: 192.168.1.1.

Within a few seconds of a failure of an active router, a backup router will spring into action, keeping the *virtual IP (VIP)* address 192.168.1.1 functioning.

The more common FHRPs include the following:

- **Hot Standby Router Protocol (HSRP)**   Cisco proprietary.
- **Virtual Router Redundancy Protocol (VRRP)**   An open standard that's very similar to HSRP.
- **Gateway Load Balancing Protocol (GLBP)**   Cisco proprietary protocol that allows for load balancing by default too, by having multiple active routers as opposed to HSRP and VRRP, where only one router is active at a time, unless multiple groups are configured.

 CAUTION   HSRP and VRRP by default don't support load balancing, but can be made to support load balancing by configuring multiple (HSRP or VRRP) groups. However, that is not the easiest thing to pull off. Half of the clients will be configured to get one gateway IP address, while the other half of clients will be configured to get a different gateway IP address. There's just no easy way to do that. GLBP, though, is "plug and play load balancing" from the start.

Subinterfaces

When you take an actual physical interface and divide it into logical interfaces, known as *subinterfaces*, it's as if that physical interface becomes multiple physical interfaces. Before the advent of multilayer switches, subinterfaces were used for VLAN traffic in a router-on-a-stick/one-armed router setup, to allow traffic from multiple VLANs to be routed. Older NBMA (non-broadcast multiple access) WAN implementations, like frame relay and ATM (Asynchronous Transfer Mode), also made use of subinterfaces.

REVIEW

Objective 1.4: Given a scenario, configure a subnet and use appropriate IP addressing schemes

- RFC 1918, along with NAT/PAT, was able to extend the life of IPv4.
- There are many differences between IPv4 and IPv6, including the use of APIPA by IPv4 versus the use of a link-local address by IPv6, the use (IPv4)/non-use (IPv6) of broadcasting, and more.
- Classless addressing replaced classful addressing in the 1990s, but you still need to understand how classful addressing works to fully understand concepts like subnetting.
- IPv6 can be tunneled from a device without native IPv6 connectivity.
- A system that's running both IPv4 and IPv6 is said to be dual stacked.
- IPv6 addresses can be written with two shortcuts.
- Using router advertisements and SLAAC, interfaces can give themselves their own IPv6 addresses.

1.4 QUESTIONS

1. Which of the following is not an RFC 1918 private address?
   - **A.** 10.0.0.1
   - **B.** 172.16.17.18
   - **C.** 192.168.1.3
   - **D.** 224.0.0.2

2. What's the prefix for an IPv6 link-local address?
   - **A.** fe10::/8
   - **B.** fe80::/10
   - **C.** fe80::/8
   - **D.** fe10::/10

3. Which of the following is not an FHRP that deals with a virtual IP (VIP) address?
   - **A.** HSRP
   - **B.** VRRP
   - **C.** GLBP
   - **D.** CIDR

1.4 ANSWERS

1. **D**   224.0.0.2 is a multicast address.
2. **B**   fe80::/10 is the prefix for all IPv6 link-local addresses.
3. **D**   Classless Inter-Domain Routing solved multiple problems with IP addressing in 1993 and is not a first hop redundancy protocol.

Objective 1.5 # Explain common ports and protocols, their application, and encrypted alternatives

Creating a network from the ground up requires a huge number of hardware and software technologies to work together to get the data from one machine to another. Enabling these technologies to interact requires, in essence, sets of rules of what a network should do and how it should be accomplished. These sets of rules—and the software written to follow these rules—are broken down into individual rules called *protocols*. When a series of protocols are specifically designed to work together, they are called a *protocol suite*. These protocol suites invariably are named with some form of *protocol name/protocol name* format.

The dominant protocol suite for today's network is called Transmission Control Protocol/ Internet Protocol (TCP/IP). In 1973, the U.S. Defense Advanced Research Projects Agency (DARPA) first proposed TCP/IP as a standard for connecting various existing networks so that they could exchange information. One aim was to develop a common standard to replace the growing number of proprietary and incompatible networks that were emerging as part of the Advanced Research Projects Agency Network (ARPANET). The work undertaken, led by Vint Cerf and Bob Kahn, eventually led to the development of the TCP/IP protocol suite and the Internet as we know it today.

Despite DARPA's effort to establish a common standard, in the early days of local area networks (LANs), many protocol suites competed with TCP/IP for LAN market share. Microsoft networks used NetBIOS/NetBEUI, Apple networks used AppleTalk, Novell networks used IPX/SPX, and Digital Equipment Corporation used DECnet. The problem was that no one agreed on how a network should communicate and run. The rise and commercialization of the Internet, which depended on TCP/IP, forced LAN vendors to all switch to TCP/IP.

Protocols and Ports

Protocols and ports are closely related.

 NOTE This section doesn't have a structure that corresponds to the official exam objective outline as the previous ones have. After an introduction, the contents of Objective 1.5 are presented in tabular format, which makes it easier to compare the protocols and ports than if they were in paragraph format.

The way network communication goes in and out of a machine physically (at Layer 1, the Physical layer of the OSI model) is through the network interface card (NIC). Those 1s and 0s are entering and exiting your machine through the NIC (that exists at both Layer 1 and

Layer 2, the Data Link layer, of the OSI model), which is the connection from your machine to the rest of the world. The way network communication goes in and out of a machine logically, though, is through a program or service.

A service is a program that runs in the background, independent of a sign-in, in Windows. In Linux, the term daemon is used instead of service (and in Linux, the term service refers to a command that calls scripts that control daemon processes). A process is an instantiation of a program or service and can be further broken down into threads. Windows client machines, for instance, have a workstation service running in the background that allows them to create and maintain network connections with the Server Message Block (SMB) protocol to server services that allow for access to remote files and printers.

When you start a Web server, you're starting a specific server service that isn't tied to a specific account. This way, when the server reboots, the service automatically starts, without the need to sign in.

NOTE Technically speaking, a server is a service (software) that responds to client service requests. The term server, though, is often used for the machines (hardware) on which server services run.

Well, how does network communication go in and out of a program or service?

Let's say a single machine is running both a File Transfer Protocol (FTP) server and a Web server. If they are both accessible by the same IP address, how does the traffic for the FTP server get to the FTP server and the traffic for the Web server get to the Web server?

Think about an apartment building with a mailbox grid in the lobby. The man in apartment 21, Frank Thomas Peterson, checks his mail with a key to box 21, and the woman in apartment 80, Helen Theresa Thomasina Parker, checks her mail with a key to box 80. The mailman brought their mail to the same building. They both live in the same building with the same street address. This is like two different servers that are accessible through the same IP address. However, when traffic is destined for the man in apartment 21, it is noted on the front of the envelope. The same goes for mail addressed to the woman in apartment 80. Similarly, the way into and out of a program or service is through a port. A port is a logical endpoint of communication that identifies a program or service and is represented by a port number.

NOTE The term port is used instead of port number. For example, you'd see or hear "port 21" instead of "port number 21."

So, in addition to source and destination MAC addresses and source and destination IP addresses, there are source and destination ports. MAC addresses are found in frame headers at Layer 2 (Data Link) layer of the OSI model. IP addresses are found in IP packet headers at Layer 3 (Network layer) of the OSI model. Port numbers are found in either TCP segment headers or UDP datagram headers at Layer 4 (Transport layer) of the OSI model.

TABLE 1.5-1	Port Categories

0–1023	Well-known port numbers
1024–49151	Registered ports
49152–65535	Dynamic or private ports

Based on the destination port, the operating system on the destination machine knows which program or service to send the data to, in the same way that the mail carrier knows to put the mail for apartment 21 in the box for apartment 21, and the mail for apartment 80 in the box for apartment 80.

Types of Ports

Ports are organized into three categories, as identified in Table 1.5-1.

Well-Known Ports

Well-known ports use port numbers 0–1023 (0 is used by programming APIs as a wildcard to find an available port, but not directly by hosts) and are reserved for major protocols and services. FTP servers send and receive control traffic on port 21 (which explains why I chose to name the man in apartment 21 Frank Thomas Peterson). Web servers running Hypertext Transfer Protocol (HTTP) send and receive unencrypted traffic on port 80 (which is why I chose to name the woman in apartment 80 Helen Theresa Thomasina Parker). Web servers send and receive encrypted traffic on port 443, with Transport Layer Security (TLS).

KEY TERM   An **IP address** gets data to the right device. A **port number** gets the data to the right program/service on that device.

Registered Ports

Registered ports use port numbers 1024–49151 and are assigned by the Internet Assigned Numbers Authority (IANA) for specific organizations that want a common port to be used for their programs or protocols. However, these port numbers can be used by any system if not in use. In fact, operating systems will use port numbers in this range and treat them like dynamic ports (described next). Registered port numbers are locally significant to a system. It's not like using a registered IP address, which has global scope.

ADDITIONAL RESOURCES   Here's the form to apply for a port number from IANA: https://www.iana.org/form/ports-services.

Dynamic Ports

Dynamic ports use port numbers 49152–65535 and are used by client applications on an as-needed basis. For example, a browser might open port 60000 to send a request to a Web server that will be listening for requests either on port 80, unencrypted, normal HTTP, or on port 443, encrypted HTTP over Transport Layer Security (TLS), known as HTTPS.

The Web server's response is sourced from port 80 or 443 and is destined for the port the browser opened. After the communication between the browser and the Web server is complete, the browser will close the port it opened, but the Web server's port will remain open for new incoming connections. The browser, or any other program/service running on the machine, will subsequently open a different port in that dynamic range for its next request. As mentioned earlier, operating systems sometimes use unused ports in the registered port number range for the same purpose.

Port States

A port can be classified as being in one of three states: open, closed, or filtered. There's really just one difference between an open port and a closed port. Open ports have programs or services listening on them, whereas closed ports don't. For example, if you start a FileZilla FTP server, port 21 is open. Stop the FileZilla FTP server, and port 21 is closed. If you start an Apache Web server, port 80 is now open. Stop the Apache Web server, and port 80 is now closed.

A filtered port is a port that's either open or closed, but it can't be determined because packet filtering keeps the scans from getting to the port. The filtering could come from a dedicated firewall device, router rules, or a host-based firewall. Sometimes an ICMP error message will be sent in response to a filtered port. However, often, filters will just drop traffic and won't send responses. Therefore, sometimes these probes will need to be sent multiple times to make sure that the lack of responses was due to filtering and not network congestion. This slows down the scanning process greatly.

Firewalls don't open ports. Firewalls don't close ports. Firewalls filter ports.

If a network-based firewall is set to deny some or all traffic to a Secure Shell (SSH) server that sends and receives traffic on port 22, you still have an SSH server running on the machine. The firewall didn't close port 22 on the machine. If you run netstat on the SSH server, you'll see that port 22 is indeed open. Any hosts inside the network, therefore, will be able to access the SSH server, since the network-based firewall-filtering port 22 doesn't affect them. When a host-based firewall on the SSH server is filtering either some or all incoming traffic on port 22, if the service is started, port 22 is still open.

Let's say I'm teaching a class in the Finger Lakes Community College (FLCC) Victor Campus Center. Think of the class in the Networking and Cybersecurity Lab as a program or service that's running. Think of the room number (VC206) as the port number that lets students know where to enter. While class is in session, the port is open. After class, we all leave. The lights go off and the door is locked. The port is closed.

Picture yourself trying to enter FLCC's Victor Campus Center, but the security guard at the front door doesn't let you in. That guard is the firewall. You can't get to my classroom door to even determine whether class is in session (open port) or not (closed port) because you're being filtered by the firewall (filtered port).

 NOTE Don't confuse these logical ports with physical ports into which connectors are plugged in.

This section discusses the seven-layer OSI model. Jump back to Objective 1.1 for a complete discussion of OSI.

Commonly Used Ports

Table 1.5-2 lists the protocols and corresponding port(s) identified in Objective 1.5, and describes their purpose.

 EXAM TIP You should definitely memorize the protocols, their functions, and their corresponding port numbers listed in Table 1.5-2.

TABLE 1.5-2 CompTIA Network+ Ports Listed in Objective 1.5 *(continued)*

Protocol	Port(s)	Purpose
File Transfer Protocol (FTP)	20/21	Transfers files between clients and servers. Port 20 is only used in active mode for data transfer by the server (mostly deprecated today). In passive mode, the server uses a dynamic port instead of 20. Port 21 is used by the server in both modes for control information.
Secure Shell (SSH)	22	Remote shell login and command execution with encryption. Replaces Telnet, which sent communications (including usernames and passwords) in plaintext.
Secure File Transfer Protocol (SFTP)	22	An extension to SSH that provides secure file transfer and file system access.
Telnet	23	Obsolete, replaced by SSH. Remote shell login and command execution which sent communications (including usernames and passwords) in plaintext.
Simple Mail Transfer Protocol (SMTP)	25	Sends e-mail off a domain.

TABLE 1.5-2   CompTIA Network+ Ports Listed in Objective 1.5 *(continued)*

Protocol	Port(s)	Purpose
Domain Name System (DNS)	53	Resolves FQDNs (fully qualified domain names) into their corresponding IP addresses, and performs other types of resolution like finding a domain's DNS servers, finding a domain's mail servers, and performing reverse lookups, matching IP addresses to FQDNs.
Dynamic Host Configuration Protocol (DHCP)	67/68	Provides clients configuration information including IP address, subnet mask, default gateway, IP addresses of DNS servers, and more. DHCP servers use port 67, and in a very rare and unique client assignment, DHCP clients use port 68.
Trivial File Transfer Protocol (TFTP)	69	Simplified version of FTP used primarily today to boot from a LAN with PXE (Preboot eXecution Environment), and to upload and download router and switch images and configurations.
Hypertext Transfer Protocol (HTTP)	80	Defines the formatting, transmission, and actions done by Web servers and clients. Passes everything in plaintext.
Post Office Protocol v3 (POP3)	110	Obsolete, replaced by IMAP. Retrieves e-mail from a server, removing it from the server and storing it on the local machine. When you check your e-mail, later, from another device, the previously stored messages are no longer available on the server. If the option of "Leave a copy of messages on the server" is selected, you'll always see the messages as new on each new device mail is checked from.
Network Time Protocol (NTP)	123	Synchronizes clocks between networked devices.
Internet Message Access Protocol (IMAP)	143	Retrieves mail from a server to an e-mail client, but you're working directly on the server the entire time. You're able to check your mail from multiple devices and have all devices synched to the messages and their status (read vs. unread, deleted vs. not deleted) on the server. Folders are created on the server, and will appear on each new client, as opposed to folders when using POP3, which will only appear on the client that they're created on.

TABLE 1.5-2   CompTIA Network+ Ports Listed in Objective 1.5 *(continued)*

Protocol	Port(s)	Purpose
Simple Network Management Protocol (SNMP)	161/162	Collects information from networking devices for management and monitoring purposes.
Lightweight Directory Access Protocol (LDAP)	389	Accesses and maintains distributed directory information services related to users, groups, computers, printers, and more. Implemented on Microsoft Windows servers through Active Directory.
Hypertext Transfer Protocol Secure (HTTPS) [Secure Sockets Layer (SSL)]	443	Provided authentication, confidentiality, and integrity to exchanges between Web servers and clients. Used HTTP over SSL to prevent on-path (aka man-in-the-middle) attacks, securing accounts, and keeping communications, identities, and browsing private. Note: This objective lists TLS's obsolete predecessor, SSL.
HTTPS [Transport Layer Security (TLS)]	443	For many years HTTPS has been HTTP over TLS, SSL's successor.
Server Message Block (SMB)	445	Provides shared access to files, printers, and more.
Syslog	514	A message logging standard that separates the software generating the messages, the system storing the messages, and the software reporting and analyzing the messages.
SMTP TLS	587	Secures SMTP with TLS.
Lightweight Directory Access Protocol (over SSL) (LDAPS)	636	Secured LDAP with SSL (and later with TLS), but is now deprecated.
IMAP over SSL	993	Secures IMAP with TLS (the objective lists TLS's obsolete predecessor, SSL, though).
POP3 over SSL	995	Secures POP3 (obsolete itself) with TLS (the objective lists TLS's obsolete predecessor, SSL, though).
Structured Query Language (SQL) Server	1433	Port 1433/TCP connects to the SQL database instance of Microsoft's SQL Server. Port 1434/UDP, incidentally, allows for the automatic discovery of SQL by the clients.
SQLnet	1521	The Oracle server listener that clients connect to.

| TABLE 1.5-2 | CompTIA Network+ Ports Listed in Objective 1.5 | |

Protocol	Port(s)	Purpose
MySQL	3306	The MySQL RDBMS (relational database management system) server that clients connect to.
Remote Desktop Protocol (RDP)	3389	Microsoft protocol that allows for connecting to another computer through a GUI (graphical user interface).
Session Initiation Protocol (SIP)		Establishes, modifies, and terminates VoIP (Voice over IP) calls. Port 5060 is used for non-encrypted signaling traffic, while port 5061 is used for TLS encrypted traffic.

 ADDITIONAL RESOURCE   Port numbers are maintained by IANA at https://www.iana.org/assignments/service-names-port-numbers/service-names-port-numbers.xhtml.

IP Protocol Types

Each of the protocols listed in Table 1.5-2 in the previous section is placed inside another protocol at Layer 4, either a TCP segment or a UDP datagram. TCP segments and UDP datagrams are always placed inside of IP packets. In addition, ICMP messages are placed inside IP packets for informational and error reporting. *IP protocol types* (what's directly inside the IP packet) are indicated by the protocol field in the IP header. For example, 1 is ICMP, 6 is TCP, and 17 is UDP.

TCP and UDP

At Layer 4 of the OSI model, all applications use either *TCP* segments or *UDP* datagrams to encapsulate and send data coming from Layers 5, 6, and 7.

TCP establishes a connection between the source and destination devices for reliable data transfer and flow control, sending data at a rate that is acceptable to both the source and destination devices. UDP is connectionless and has no flow control.

All bytes sent with TCP are ordered and sequenced. TCP guarantees that every single byte sent will be received with integrity and processed in the correct order. So, actually, there are three things guaranteed in life: death, taxes, and…TCP. UDP doesn't offer any such guarantee.

TCP segments are acknowledged, so the sender knows the destination got the traffic. If an acknowledgement, specifically referencing byte numbers of the data sent, doesn't come back, TCP resends the unacknowledged bytes. UDP doesn't do this.

TCP is used for file transfers (FTP), e-mail (IMAP/SMTP), and going to Web sites (HTTP, TLS). In these cases, accuracy is important. If bytes are lost or corrupted, the whole message could be destroyed.

UDP is used for real-time communications, conferencing, and streaming. Furthermore, two major network protocols, DNS and DHCP, use UDP.

If every byte sent needed to be acknowledged on a VoIP call over the Web, there could be problems with lost messages, or even lost acknowledgements. TCP, on the source, would think the destination didn't get the message, and would resend it. So the destination would hear "Hello," and send its acknowledgment back to the source. Let's say that acknowledgement got lost. The destination would hear the subsequent words from the voice call that were already sent by the source, "How are you doing today?" but then the source would send "Hello" back again. That would be a very frustrating phone call! You'd have the past coming back into the current conversation!

As you can imagine, all audio and video that is delivered in real time and streaming over the Internet in UDP datagrams still has to be ordered, to ensure that it is processed in the correct order. Real-Time Streaming Protocol (RTSP), which exists at Layer 7, does the ordering for UDP.

Using RTSP just for the ordering of the UDP datagrams involves significantly less overhead than TCP would require. If TCP was used, a connection would have to be established and maintained, flow control would need to be added, and acknowledgements would need to be sent. The communication would slow down based on these and other factors. With UDP, if bytes are lost, we don't care. They're just a fleeting moment in time. We might not even notice. We might notice a slight degradation in image quality or sound quality, but even if that's the case, we just accept it, instead of slowing down the entire communication for the additional overhead that TCP requires.

TCP has much more overhead than UDP and is deliberately slower, striving for accuracy and integrity. UDP has no overhead and is quicker, striving for efficiency.

The TCP header contains many fields that have functions that add latency, whereas the UDP header has only a few fields with no additional overhead.

So how exactly does TCP establish a connection between a source and destination? It's called the TCP *three-way handshake*. In nontechnical terms, the source says, "Hey, I want to talk to you," the destination replies, "Okay, you can talk to me. Can I talk to you?," and the source says, "Sure, let's rock!" Take a look at Figure 1.5-1, as we'll focus on certain fields of the TCP header to describe the three-way handshake.

The first two fields of the TCP header contain the source and destination ports, indicating the program or service that the message comes from on the source and is headed to on the destination. Next are two important fields, Sequence Number and Acknowledgement Number.

To understand how these fields are used, we need to look at the flags section, which comes after the Data Offset field, representing the size of the TCP header, and the Reserved field, which is just three 0 bits. Flags in the TCP header represent specific control information conveyed to and from the connected machines. Like a flag on a mailbox, these flags could be raised or lowered. TCP flags, however, are not red. They're represented by a single bit. Turning a flag

TCP Header

Offsets	Octet	0								1								2								3							
Octet	Bit	0	1	2	3	4	5	6	7	8	9	10	11	12	13	14	15	16	17	18	19	20	21	22	23	24	25	26	27	28	29	30	31
0	0	Source Port															Destination Port															
4	32	Sequence Number																															
8	64	Acknowledgement Number																															
12	96	Data Offset				Reserved 000			N S	C W R	E C E	U R G	A C K	P S H	R S T	S Y N	F I N	Window Size															
16	128	Checksum															Urgent Pointer															
20	160	Options																															
...	...	...																															

FIGURE 1.5-1 TCP header

on means setting that bit to a value of 1. Turning a flag off means setting that bit to a value of 0. There are nine flags in the TCP header (six standard ones and three specialty ones). We're going to focus on two of them here, shown in Figure 1.5-1 to the right of the Data Offset field (representing the size of the TCP header) and the Reserved field (which is just three 0 bits).

In the first step of the three-way handshake (shown in Figure 1.5-2), the source (client) sets the SYN (Synchronize) flag on by placing a 1 in that bit position, and generates a pseudo-random sequence number that it places in the Sequence Number field. Let's say it's 52 for this example. The source places the TCP header in an IP packet, places the packet in a frame, and, assuming remote communication, sends the frame to the default gateway.

When the TCP segment arrives at the destination, step two of the TCP three-way handshake takes place, with the destination (server) saying "Roger that!" by sending its own TCP header. In the second step of the three-way handshake (shown in Figure 1.5-2), the destination turns on the ACK (Acknowledgment) flag and increments the sequence number that the

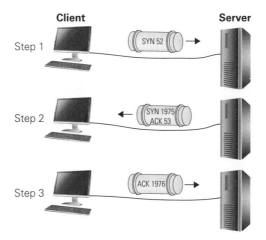

FIGURE 1.5-2 TCP three-way handshake

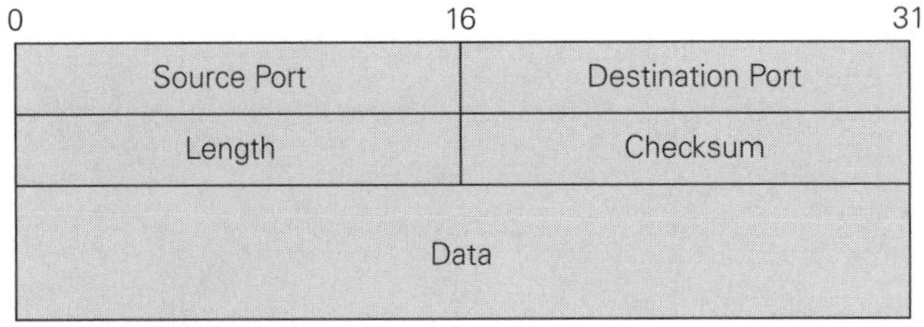

0		16		31
Source Port		Destination Port		
Length		Checksum		
Data				

FIGURE 1.5-3 UDP header

source sent, by one, in the Acknowledgment Number field. In this example the source's initial sequence number is 52, so the destination puts 53 (52 + 1) in the Acknowledgement Number field. In reality, both the sequence number and acknowledgment number are 4-byte values.

In the same TCP header, the destination also raises the SYN flag and comes up with its own pseudo-randomly generated sequence number, let's say 1975, which it places in the Sequence Number field. This is the destination saying "Can I talk to you too?" This TCP segment is sent to the source.

In the third step of the three-way handshake (shown in Figure 1.5-2), the source responds to this by sending another TCP segment with the ACK flag on, incrementing the sequence number sent by the destination by one in the Acknowledgement Number field, in our example to 1976.

At this point, the two systems are connected. The TCP segments in the three steps didn't have any data. It was just control messages in the TCP header. Now when actual data is transmitted by either station, be it HTTP, TLS, SSH, FTP, or anything else, it's encapsulated inside the TCP headers. In fact, the sequence numbers now go up by the size of the data sent, and the acknowledgements increment the number of the last byte sent by one. Every bit sent is acknowledged. If not, it's resent. That's how TCP follows through on its guaranteed data delivery claim!

When querying your DNS server to resolve a name to an IP address or querying your DHCP server to get or renew a lease for an IP address, if no reply comes back to your client, your client will simply ask again. There's no need to for additional overhead.

The UDP header, shown in Figure 1.5-3, contains only four simple fields: Source Port, Destination Port, Length, and Checksum (for error checking).

Internet Protocol encapsulates all messages at Layer 3 in a unit called a *packet*. It delivers packets from source to destination based on the IP addresses in the IP header portion of the packet. The data portion contains the upper-layer headers and data.

As shown in Figure 1.5-4, the IP header contains many fields, some of which we'll explore in a subsequent domain.

Internet Control Message Protocol (ICMP)

Internet Control Message Protocol (ICMP) is used by utilities like `ping` and `tracert` (on Windows)/traceroute (non-Windows) to provide control information to IP. The ping utility sends ICMP echo request messages to a destination. If the destination gets those messages, it

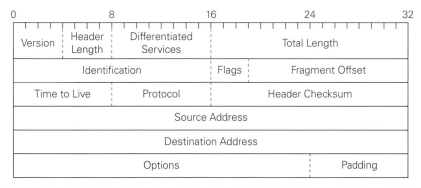

FIGURE 1.5-4   IP header

sends back ICMP echo reply messages to the source. This confirms that the source can reach the destination. If no ICMP echo replies come back, it means either the source can't reach the destination or the replies from the destination are not able to reach the source.

ICMP messages are encapsulated directly inside of IP headers and come in two types: informational messages, such as the ICMP Echo reply messages, and error messages, such as destination unreachable messages, which are generated for many reasons (for example, when the router doesn't have a route for the destination network).

Every ICMP header starts off with the same three fields—Type, Code, and Checksum—and then varies based on the situation (see Figure 1.5-5).

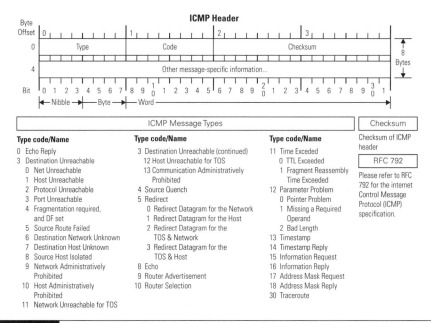

FIGURE 1.5-5   ICMP header

Generic Routing Encapsulation (GRE)

For VPNs, the *Generic Routing Encapsulation (GRE)* protocol is paired with IPsec for encryption. You can use GRE to make a point-to-point tunnel connection that carries all sorts of traffic over Layer 3, including multicast and IPv6 traffic.

Internet Protocol Security (IPsec)

Many VPN technologies use *Internet Protocol Security (IPsec)* tunneling for VPNs.

 NOTE   The *Internet Engineering Task Force (IETF)* oversees the IPsec protocol suite, managing updates and revisions. One of those specifications regards the acronym for the protocol suite, calling it *IPsec* with a lowercase "s" rather than IPS or IPSec (the form CompTIA prefers). This ensures that IPsec won't be confused with an intrusion prevention system (IPS), covered in Objective 2.1.

Authentication Header (AH)/ Encapsulating Security Payload (ESP)

IPsec is a suite of two protocols used for authentication and encryption of packets. The *Authentication Header (AH)* protocol only performs authentication, while the *Encapsulating Security Payload (ESP)* protocol performs both authentication and confidentiality (through encryption). As such, AH hasn't been used much, and it is obsolete today.

Connectionless vs. Connection-Oriented

As mentioned, TCP is *connection-oriented*, whereas UDP is *connectionless*.

TCP is used when programs require integrity and accuracy. UDP is used for programs that require quick performance and can live with lost packets here and there.

Furthermore, IP is connectionless, and gets connection-oriented information from ICMP.

REVIEW

Objective 1.5: Explain common ports and protocols, their application, and encrypted alternatives

- The purpose of ports is to represent a logical way for traffic to move into and out of a program or service on a machine.
- Port numbers are found in either a TCP header or a UDP header. They are used at Layer 4 to correspond with a program or service on a machine that's sending or receiving traffic. For example, Web servers listen for incoming traffic and send their own traffic on port 80 (unencrypted) or 443 (encrypted with TLS), while FTP servers listen for incoming traffic and send their own traffic on port 21.

- Protocols are used by devices to send and receive different types of communication. The purpose of a common TCP/IP protocol suite is to allow any device to talk to any other device.

- TCP segments and UDP datagrams are encapsulated in IP packets at Layer 3.

- ICMP provides informational and error reporting.

1.5 QUESTIONS

1. Which port number would be opened by a Web browser?
    A. 22
    B. 80
    C. 443
    D. 50000

2. Which application would TCP be used for?
    A. DHCP
    B. DNS queries
    C. FTP
    D. VoIP

3. Which protocol is connection-oriented?
    A. TCP
    B. UDP
    C. ICMP
    D. IP

1.5 ANSWERS

1. **D** 50000 is in the dynamic port range. 22 is for SSH servers, while 80 (unencrypted) and 443 (encrypted with TLS) are for Web servers, not Web clients (browsers).

2. **C** FTP requires TCP, as accuracy and integrity are more important than speed for file transfers. The other applications use UDP, because in those cases, speed is more important.

3. **C** TCP is the only option that is connection-oriented.

Objective 1.6 Explain the use and purpose of network services

DHCP (Dynamic Host Configuration Protocol) allows clients to automatically get IP addresses, instead of being statically configured.

DNS (Domain Name System) resolves FQDNs to IP addresses and much more.

NTP (Network Time Protocol) synchronizes clocks.

It's time to explore all three!

DHCP

Dynamic IP addressing, implemented through Dynamic Host Configuration Protocol *(DHCP)*, automatically assigns an IP address whenever a computer connects to the network.

Scope, Scope Options

When a DHCP client boots up, it automatically sends out a DHCP Discover UDP datagram to the broadcast address, 255.255.255.255. This DHCP Discover message asks "Are there any DHCP servers out there?" The client can't send unicast traffic yet, as it doesn't have a valid IP address that can be used.

A DHCP server is designed to respond to DHCP Discover requests with a DHCP Offer, which, depending on various factors, could either be unicast or broadcast. The DHCP server is configured to pass out IP addresses from a range (called a DHCP *scope* or pool) and a subnet mask. It also passes out other information, known generically as *scope options*, that covers a large number of choices, such as default gateway, DNS server, NTP server, and more.

The DHCP client sends out a DHCP Request as a broadcast. The client still can't unicast, but as an added benefit of broadcasting here, if multiple offers came from multiple servers (which is very possible), this lets one server know the client wants its IP address, and it also lets the other server know the client doesn't want its IP address. That server can now return the address to the pool for a future request, and not have it in an in-between state.

The DHCP server then sends a DHCP Ack and starts the lease for the DHCP client, associating the DHCP client's MAC address with the IP address from the scope.

At the end of the four-step DHCP dance, *DORA (Discover, Offer, Request, and Ack),* the DHCP client gets a *DHCP lease.*

Lease Time, Available Leases

A DHCP *lease time* is set for a fixed amount of time, generally one to eight days. The number of *available leases* is dependent on the number of addresses in the scope. Fifty percent into the lease, the DHCP client will send another DHCP Request. The DHCP server, then, will send back a DHCP Ack, and the lease will be renewed. If, within the lease period (stored in a Registry key in Windows), the DHCP client is rebooted or powered on after a shutdown, a DHCP Request will be triggered, to renew the lease, as well.

Literally 50 percent (1/2) into the lease the DHCP client will send out a DHCP Request as a unicast (during DORA it's a broadcast), hoping to have its lease renewed. If that DHCP doesn't respond, at 87.5 percent (7/8) into the lease, the DHCP client will send out DHCP Requests as broadcasts (as it did during DORA), in hopes that another DHCP server will renew the lease. If the lease fully elapses, the client gives itself an APIPA address (169.254.0.0/16), as discussed in Objective 1.4, and periodically sends out DHCP Discover messages, in hopes of starting DORA again.

 EXAM TIP   DHCP uses *UDP* ports 67 (servers) and 68 (clients).

Dynamic Assignment

DHCP clients get IP addresses and more from DHCP servers through *dynamic assignment*. DHCP clients need to be configured to receive addresses in this dynamic fashion.

Static Assignment

A client that is not configured for dynamic assignment uses *static assignment*, the manual configuration of an IP address, subnet mask, default gateway, DNS servers, and more. Servers and router interfaces should be statically configured. You don't want their IP addresses potentially changing, which could be the case with dynamic addressing. Furthermore, reservations, covered shortly, which allow a device to get the same dynamic IP address, still pose a problem. If the DHCP server(s) goes down, the servers and router interfaces that rely on the reservations won't be able to renew leases (and will become inaccessible using a 169.254.0.0/16 APIPA address), making static assignment a much better option. A system statically assigned an IP address can send still out DHCP Inform messages (asking for other information, like DNS server IP addresses) if the DHCP client service is running.

Exclusion Ranges

Exclusion ranges represent an IP address or range of IP addresses from the pool of addresses that are not to be given out by the DHCP server. Exclusions should be made for the static addresses manually configured on servers and router interfaces, so these IP addresses won't be offered to DHCP clients.

Reservation

DHCP servers can be set up to reserve addresses for specific machines through what's called, appropriately, a *reservation*. Best practice with servers, though, is to use static IP addresses, so that they're reachable if the DHCP server goes down, as previously mentioned.

A good use case for an actual reservation is a lab, where, for example, you always want Computer #13 to get the IP address 192.168.1.13.

DHCP Relay, IP Helper/UDP Forwarding

For small networks, when there's a single subnet, it's a given that the DHCP server will be on that network. That's what's typically found in SOHO networks, a DHCP server on the same network as the DHCP clients.

However, in an internetwork, where there are multiple subnets, it's not practical to put a DHCP server or pair of DHCP servers on each subnet.

If you have a pair of DHCP servers on a specific subnet, though, how are clients, without IP addresses at the start, going to reach these DHCP servers? They can't send any traffic to a remote DHCP server using IP routing, because they don't have a routable IP address, they don't know the IP address of a router, and they don't know the IP address of a DHCP server. Furthermore, routers don't forward broadcasts, so the DHCP Discover messages would not get to the right place.

The solution is to configure router interfaces (which will eventually become default gateways to clients on those subnets) as *DHCP relay* agents. In Cisco IOS, the command is

```
ip helper-address 1.2.3.4
```

where 1.2.3.4 represents the IP address of a DHCP server.

The DHCP client sends a DHCP Discover broadcast, which is heard by all devices on that network, including the router interface acting as the relay agent. Remember, though, that routers don't forward broadcasts. This relay agent was configured with the IP addresses of the DHCP servers, and now it receives the DHCP Discover broadcast.

What happens next is the turning point as the DHCP relay agent, also referred to as an *IP helper* (due to the `ip helper-address` configuration command) performs a special kind of *UDP forwarding*. The relay agent takes the DHCP Discover message and the UDP datagram that encapsulates it, and strips them away from both the broadcast packet and broadcast frame that they are encapsulated in. Now the relay agent places the UDP datagram with the DHCP Discover message in a new IP packet. This packet, though, is a unicast packet, sent to the actual IP address of a DHCP server. In other words, the relay agent takes the broadcast traffic and turns it into unicast traffic, it doesn't simply "forward the broadcast."

 NOTE   An IP helper can turn broadcasts into unicasts for 8 protocols/UDP port numbers (not just for a DHCP relay agent) including Time (port 37, note that this is not NTP), TACACS/TACACS+ (port 49, note that this is for the UDP implementation only, as most TACACS+ implementations today use TCP), DNS (port 53), BOOTP/DHCP server (port 67), BOOTP/DHCP CLIENT (port 68), TFTP (port 69), NETBIOS Name Service (port 137), and NETBIOS Datagram Service (port 138).

The client's MAC address is preserved in the DHCP Discover message payload. The DHCP server is able to determine the scope to use for an IP address in the DHCP Offer, because the relay agent placed its IP address in the Gateway IP Address field of the DHCP Discover.

The DHCP server replies to the client by sending the DHCP Offer to the relay agent, using unicast transmission. The relay agent then sends the DHCP Offer to the client.

The DHCP Request and DHCP Ack follow the same process.

DNS

An autonomous system usually has two Domain Name System (*DNS*) servers for the entire network. These DNS servers have a zone file that lists all the hostnames on the domain and their corresponding IP addresses, along with other resource record types. Each server is known as an authoritative name server for the domain.

Imagine how busy the google.com domain is—it needs lots of DNS servers to support all the incoming DNS queries. In this case a single domain will have a single primary name server but a number of other secondary DNS servers. Both a primary DNS server and a secondary DNS server are authoritative for the domain. That means they don't rely on cache to give out answers, as they have the answers in a file. The difference between the two is that the systems administrator makes changes to the zone files on the primary DNS server, and those changes are copied upon request to the secondary DNS servers, in a process known as a zone transfer. But again, the secondary servers are still authoritative, because they answer from the zone file, and not from a cache in RAM.

Zone Transfers

The primary DNS server's job is to make sure that the secondary DNS server is updated for changes. Let's say you add a new computer called rochester to the jonathansweissman.edu domain, with the IP address 192.168.19.82. As an administrator, you would add this data to the primary DNS server. The primary DNS server, through *zone transfers*, will distribute this information to the secondary DNS servers in the domain. Timers in the SOA resource record (coming up) will determine how often the secondary DNS server queries the primary for updates. In addition, if configured, triggered updates can be sent from the primary DNS server to the secondary that the zone file has changed. Zone transfers are a pull technology, not push, so the primary will say something like the following to the secondary DNS server: "The zone file has changed. Please ask me for an update."

 NOTE   Both primary and secondary DNS servers are considered authoritative, because they don't rely on cache. They have the static files.

In the early years of the Internet, DNS worked interchangeably with IP addressing. You could surf to a Web site, in other words, by typing in the fully qualified domain name (FQDN) or the IP address of the Web server.

Modern Web sites don't really function well without DNS. The Web server that houses a domain also hosts many other domain names on the same machine. If you try to access one of these Web sites by IP address, the Web server won't know what to do, as a single IP address for a Web server without a host, like www.google.com, specified is ambiguous. Today, this concept of a Web server running many Web sites is found within a content delivery network (CDN), like Akamai Technologies, that runs many worldwide servers that replicate Web sites. This way, when browsers request Web sites, they're directed to the nearest server geographically to them, improving performance and reducing latency. For example, if Jonathan in Rochester, New York, goes to www.cnn.com, and Kushal in Sunnyvale, California, goes to www.cnn.com, each will see the same content, albeit from different servers.

For a Web server with a single host, though, connecting by IP address will work. For example, open up a browser and go to 129.21.1.40 to see the RIT (Rochester Institute of Technology) Web site. You'll also find this 1:1 correlation of DNS name to IP address with simpler devices like IP security cameras. These are cameras with an Ethernet connection, a public IP address, and a built-in interface for viewing and control.

Once you get into how computers communicate on the Web, name resolution becomes an integral part of the process. When you type in a Web address, your browser must resolve that name to the Web server's IP address to make a connection to that Web server. It can resolve the name by consulting its own DNS resolver cache or querying a DNS server.

Let's say you type **www.microsoft.com** in your Web browser. To resolve the name www .microsoft.com, the host contacts its DNS server and requests the IP address.

To request the IP address of www.microsoft.com, your PC needs the IP address of its DNS server. This information is given out by a DHCP server, when it gives a client its IP address, subnet mask, and default gateway.

Alternatively, DNS information can be manually entered, even if you are using DHCP for an IP address.

Global Hierarchy

DNS works in a *global hierarchy* fashion.

Consider the fully qualified domain name (FQDN) www.flcc.edu, for the Finger Lakes Community College (FLCC) Web server. In this example, the FQDN consists of the hostname of the machine, www (a common hostname for machines that run Web servers); followed by the second-level domain (SLD) of flcc; and, finally, the top-level domain (TLD) of .edu. Most Web sites are set up in DNS in a way that if www is left off the URL (uniform resource locator, Web site address), the Web server's IP address will be given by default. A URL starts with a transfer protocol, including HTTP, HTTPS, and FTP. After the transfer protocol in a URL comes the FQDN. The FQDN in the URL may be followed by a specific path including a folder or folders and sometimes even a filename.

See if you can identify all of the parts of this URL (you can check it out online, too) from the preceding description: https://www.flcc.edu/pdf/catalog/2021-2022-FLCC-Catalog.pdf

If I'm at Rochester Institute of Technology (RIT), connected to an RIT network, and I type www.flcc.edu into my browser's URL bar, my DNS client service will check my machine's DNS

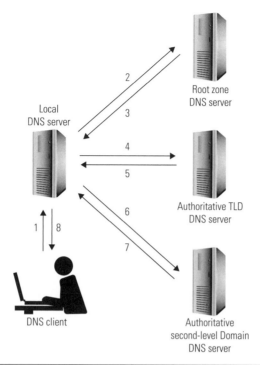

Local
DNS server

2

Root zone
DNS server

3

4

5

Authoritative TLD
DNS server

1 8

6

7

DNS client

Authoritative
second-level Domain
DNS server

FIGURE 1.6-1   The DNS hierarchy

resolver cache (also referred to simply as DNS cache), which is stored in RAM, to see if it has an IP address that corresponds with www.flcc.edu.

If the entry for www.flcc.edu exists in the DNS resolver cache, my machine's DNS client service will not query a DNS server at all and will immediately start a TCP three-way hand-shake with the machine running the Web server service. If there is no such entry in the DNS resolver cache, my DNS client service will generate a DNS query for an RIT DNS server (step 1 of Figure 1.6-1). Usually, there will be two local DNS servers for fault tolerance and load balancing, to get DNS information for the internal DNS clients. Each domain should also have two other DNS servers that are authoritative for the zone (two, again for fault tolerance and load balancing) for external queries from other domains. That function, in this story, will be served by the authoritative DNS server for the flcc.edu domain.

If the RIT DNS server has the answer in its DNS resolver cache (from a previous query it issued on behalf of another client), it will return the answer to the DNS client. If the RIT DNS server does not have the answer in its DNS resolver cache, it begins some heavy lifting, by first asking the same query to one of the 13 root servers, also known as root name servers, that reside in the root zone (step 2 of Figure 1.6-1).

Root DNS Servers

In reality, there are hundreds of servers around the world using 1 of 13 IP addresses assigned to the *root DNS servers*, which are preprogrammed into a company's internal DNS servers that do the querying and caching for their clients. Using anycast addressing (multiple nodes sharing the same public IP address), DNS queries can be routed to the nearest root server using that IP address by BGP (Border Gateway Protocol), the routing protocol used by the infrastructure of the Internet between autonomous systems. It's like finding the nearest gas station, the nearest bank, the nearest Dunkin', the nearest Starbucks, and so on from where you are currently located.

There are only 13 IP addresses for root servers because when DNS was designed (with only IPv4 32-bit addresses in existence, pre-IPv6), it was determined that up to 512 bytes of DNS information should be placed in a UDP (User Datagram Protocol) datagram. An Internet standard (RFC 791) requires each host to accept packets of 576 bytes or less (in whole or in fragments). The IPv4 header can range from 20 to 60 bytes, although the options that raised the size of the IPv4 header beyond the minimum of 20 bytes are no longer used today. UDP headers are 8 bytes long. When you start with 576 bytes that a host must accept, then subtract 8 (for the UDP header), and then subtract 60 (for the largest possible size of an IP header), you get 508. The nearest binary value is 512. When you put 13 domain names, 13 IPv4 addresses, and information about those resource records (such as TTL and type) in the payload of a single UDP datagram, they fit quite well within that 512-byte limitation (although the math does allow for a 14th as well).

Authoritative Name Servers

A root server will give the RIT DNS server a referral to one of the *authoritative name servers*, in this case an authoritative DNS server for the .edu TLD (step 3 of Figure 1.6-1), and the RIT DNS server will issue the same query to this server (step 4 of Figure 1.6-1) as well.

Note that each TLD has its own registry. If your query was for a .com TLD in this step, the referral would be for a .com authoritative TLD DNS server, not a .edu authoritative TLD DNS server. Each TLD has multiple machines working together to perform the authoritative name resolution. This level of the DNS hierarchy is only responsible for knowing the "point of contact" for each SLD in their TLD, specifically, the IP addresses of the authoritative DNS servers that have the zone files for each domain in that TLD.

The response will be a referral to an authoritative DNS server for flcc.edu (step 5 of Figure 1.6-1), and the RIT DNS server will once again issue the same query to this server (step 6 of Figure 1.6-1).

 NOTE Notice how distributed and hierarchical DNS really is. The root servers only need to know the IP addresses of each TLD's authoritative DNS servers. The root servers can't be expected to know the IP address of every resource on the planet. The authoritative TLD DNS servers only need to know the IP addresses of each SLD's authoritative DNS servers. The authoritative TLD DNS servers can't be expected to even know the IP addresses of every resource in their TLD. Furthermore, the SLDs wouldn't even want their resource records stored on the TLD servers anyway (security, liability, configuration, and other concerns). The SLD DNS servers are where the zone files are, containing the static DNS resource records.

Without root servers, whenever a new TLD is created, every systems administrator on the planet would need to add information about that new TLD on their local DNS servers. With root servers, the local DNS servers just need information about these 13 logical IP addresses that, in turn, will have the responsibility of knowing about new TLDs.

If I'm at home, and I type www.flcc.edu into my browser's URL bar, that will cause my ISP's DNS server to go down the chain and get the answer for me.

If I'm using a public DNS server, such as Google's 8.8.8.8 or 8.8.4.4, Cloudflare's 1.1.1.1 or 1.0.0.1, or IBM's (and others') 9.9.9.9, again, those servers would do the heavy lifting.

Once the answer comes either to the RIT DNS server, to my ISP's DNS server, or to one of the public DNS servers (step 7 of Figure 1.6-1), those servers cache the answers, so they don't have to do the heavy lifting for subsequent queries; they then return the answer to the DNS client (step 8 of Figure 1.6-1). This answer is also cached on the client machine, so the DNS client doesn't need to query a DNS server for this address in the near future.

 EXAM TIP   Be very comfortable with the hierarchical way DNS works.

Time to Live (TTL), DNS Caching

The *Time to Live (TTL)* field, in the DNS message, encapsulated in a UDP datagram is for *DNS caching*, and specifies how long resource records should be cached. This is not to be confused with the TTL field in the IP header, which isn't even a measurement of time, but rather is a hop count. The DNS TTL is set by the systems administrator of the second-level domain (like flcc.edu) being queried.

Recursive Lookup/Iterative Lookup

Steps 1 and 8 in Figure 1.6-1 use a *recursive lookup* process. The client's local DNS server puts the client on hold, acts as the client, and then gives the answer back to the client in the end.

Steps 2–7 use an *iterative lookup* process. The client's local DNS server is asking three separate DNS servers in an iterative fashion, getting further along and closer to the actual answer each time.

Record Types

Part of the power and flexibility of DNS comes from the use of resource *record types*. Each resource record type helps different aspects of DNS do their job.

Address (A vs. AAAA)

A (IPv4 host address) resource records map hostnames or FQDNs to IPv4 addresses.

Individual hosts each get their own unique A resource record. A resource records are the workhorse resource records in any forward lookup zone. A Web server on a forward lookup zone, for example, usually gets an A resource record called www, if for no other reason than users expect a Web site URL to start with www.

When you open a browser and enter www.rit.edu in the URL bar, your system asks your DNS server for the A resource record of www.rit.edu. Assuming nothing is in cache anywhere, your DNS server then asks this same query to a root name server, an authoritative TLD DNS server, and finally the authoritative DNS server for the rit.edu domain.

The query for www.rit.edu will be replied to with the answer of 129.21.1.40, first from an authoritative DNS server of the rit.edu domain to your DNS server, and then your DNS server to you.

For this specific FQDN, though, there is another resource record type, CNAME (discussed shortly), that comes into play.

AAAA (IPv6 host address) resource records map hostnames or FQDNs to IPv6 addresses. For example, the AAAA query for www.rit.edu will be replied to with the answer of 2620:8d:8000:0:aba:ca:daba:217.

If you have a global unicast address (GUA) IPv6 address (instead of or in addition to an IPv4 address), your browser will issue separate queries for both the A resource record and the AAAA resource record for a Web site.

 NOTE   The resource record type is named AAAA because IPv6 addresses are four times the length of IPv4 addresses (32 bytes × 4 = 128 bytes).

Canonical Name (CNAME)

Canonical name (CNAME) resource records act like aliases. They map a hostname or FQDN to another hostname or FQDN. For example, if you query for the A resource record of www .rit.edu, you'll actually be given a CNAME response of web01www01.rit.edu. The RIT Web server's hostname is web01www01 (for whatever reason), but the RIT systems administrators knew that it would be annoying for users to type, so they created a CNAME resource record to map any query for www.rit.edu to web01www01.rit.edu. The CNAME response plays the "think ahead game" and gives the A resource record for web01www01.rit.edu as well, which is 129.21.1.40. Therefore, in this case, the same Web page can be accessed by its actual hostname, its aliased hostname, and its IP address.

Mail Exchange (MX)

Mail exchange (MX) resource records are used to map a domain to the FQDNs of that domain's mail servers.

When your SMTP server has to send e-mail to another domain, it issues a DNS query to your domain's DNS server for the MX resource record of the destination domain. For example, if I want to send an e-mail to my RIT (Rochester Institute of Technology) e-mail account from my FLCC (Finger Lakes Community College) e-mail account, my FLCC e-mail server will issue a query to the FLCC DNS server, asking for the MX resource record of the rit.edu domain. One of the answers coming back will be mx03a-in01r.rit.edu. Yes, the answer to the query for an MX resource record will always be an FQDN. Now the FLCC SMTP server will need to issue a query for the A resource record for the IP address of mx03a-in01r.rit.edu, to get its corresponding IP address of 129.21.3.76. In some cases, based on configuration, to cut down on the extra traffic that would be needed, the RIT DNS server does a recursive lookup for the A resource record itself and presents it with the reply to the MX query, to the FLCC DNS server, which then presents all this information to the FLCC SMTP server.

 **CAUTION** The only device querying for an MX resource record will be your own SMTP server.

Start of Authority (SOA)

Start of authority (SOA) resource records contain a zone's administrative information, including the name of the zone, the primary server information, the e-mail address of the zone administrator, and values related to a zone transfer (how primary DNS servers replicate information to secondary DNS servers).

Pointer (PTR)

Pointer (PTR) resource records map IP addresses to their corresponding hostnames or FQDNs. This resource record enables a system to determine an FQDN by knowing the IP address. It does the exact reverse of what DNS normally does!

The value being queried is formed by taking an IP address, reversing the order of the four octets, and adding a unique TLD called "in-addr.arpa." For example, a query for 129.21.1.40 becomes 40.1.21.129.in-addr.arpa, and will be mapped to the corresponding FQDN, which will be sent in a DNS response. The reason the octets have to be reversed is because IP addresses go from general (the network ID) to specific (the host ID), but FQDNs go from specific to general (the computer name, then the SLD, then the TLD).

One place you'll see PTR resource records in action is when you do a tracert/traceroute. Instead of just seeing the IP addresses, whenever possible, a PTR resource record will turn those IP addresses into FQDNs, to make the output more meaningful. PTR resource records are also used.

Text (TXT)

Text (TXT) resource records map text (without any specifications or requirements) to a hostname or FQDN, or simply more text.

One great usage of the TXT resource record is for Sender Policy Framework (SPF), which allows receiving SMTP servers to check that incoming mail from a domain comes from a host authorized by that domain's administrators. Authorized sending hosts and IP addresses for a domain are specified in a specially formatted TXT resource record, which is checked by receiving SMTP servers. This can prevent e-mail spoofing, spam, and phishing that forge "From:" addresses.

A second great use of the TXT resource record is for DomainKeys Identified Mail (DKIM), which authenticates e-mail and, like SPF, prevents e-mail spoofing, spam, and phishing. In this case, the owner of a domain uses a public/private key pair just for signing outgoing messages. The public key is listed in a DNS TXT resource record, while the private key is allowed to be accessed by the DKIM-enabled outbound e-mail server. When an authorized domain user sends an e-mail, the server uses the private key to generate a digital signature of the message, which becomes the message's header.

The DKIM-enabled receiving e-mail server examines the signature and claimed From: domain, and then retrieves the public key from the DNS system for the claimed From: domain, to verify the signature. A match proves that the e-mail was sent from, and with the permission of, the claimed domain and that the message headers and content, including attachments, haven't changed in transit. The message might be deleted if the signature does not match.

A third great use of the TXT resource record is for DMARC (Domain-based Message Authentication, Reporting and Conformance), which enables domain owners to protect their domains from e-mail spoofing and other unauthorized-use attempts. This is done by publishing a policy, with a DNS TXT resource record, that specifies what should happen in the event that SPF and/or DKIM verification fail.

One final usage of the TXT resource record is how some cloud service providers, such as Azure, validate ownership of custom domains. You are provided with data to include in your TXT record, and once that is created, the domain is verified and able to be used. The thought is that if you control the DNS, then you own the domain name.

Service (SRV)

Service (SRV) resource records map a service to a hostname or FQDN and a port number.

For example, SRV resource records can be used to allow clients to find a domain controller implementing Lightweight Directory Access Protocol (LDAP) through Active Directory, by mapping that service to a hostname of a domain controller.

Name Server (NS)

Name server (NS) resource records map a domain to the FQDNs of the authoritative DNS for that domain. When a root name server gives your DNS server a referral to a TLD DNS server, it gives your DNS server the FQDNs of the authoritative TLD DNS servers. Your DNS server now has to individually query for the A resource records of each of them, to ask the next question, to one of them.

Reverse DNS/Reverse Lookup/Forward Lookup

Forward lookup zones contain all DNS resource records mentioned in the previous section except for PTR resource records.

Reverse DNS involves a reverse lookup zone, which maps an FQDN to an IP address. This is the reverse of what's done with IP addresses and FQDNs in a forward lookup zone, which maps IP addresses to FQDNs.

The only resource records found in a reverse lookup zone are SOA (start of authority, also found in forward lookup zones, containing administrative information), NS, and PTR, all of which are discussed in the next section.

Internal vs. External DNS

If done correctly, an organization will have a pair of public DNS servers (for external requests) and a separate pair of private DNS servers (for internal requests). *Internal vs. external DNS* relates to who is asking the queries and who is giving the answers.

The public DNS servers are needed to be authoritative for external hosts accessing inside resources, like a Web server that the company wants the outside world to access.

However, for clients inside that zone that need access to external resources, like another company's Web page, private internal DNS servers will act as resolvers, as well as caching servers for the internal clients. Furthermore, these private inside DNS servers could have resource records for private inside resources, not to be accessed by external outside networks.

From a security standpoint, having two separate servers protects you from a single point of failure.

In another usage of internal vs. external, as far as DNS is concerned, consider the following situation. Instead of using an internal authoritative DNS server to resolve queries about resources in your domain, as has been described so far, another option is using a cloud-based DNS provider from another company (putting your resource records on their servers and having queries for resources in your domain go to those servers to be resolved), like Dyn for scalability, predictability, and even to avoid a distributed denial of service (DDoS) DNS attack. However, Dyn itself was the target of a series of major DDoS attacks on October 21, 2016, and hundreds of sites, some of them major Internet sites no less, that depended on Dyn for DNS services were inaccessible.

NTP

Network Time Protocol (*NTP*) is used to synchronize the clocks of devices on an internetwork for important services like Kerberos, so that authentication works properly. It's also important when aggregating log files, and for verification of digital certificates.

Stratum, Clients, Servers

NTP and its lightweight sidekick, Simple Network Time Protocol (SNTP), use UDP. If a device requires NTP/SNTP, you will be able to enter the IP address for an NTP/SNTP server. NTP/SNTP uses port 123.

NTP operates in a hierarchical fashion or clock strata. At the highest end, *stratum* 0 devices—like atomic clocks or the Global Positioning System (GPS) satellites—keep near perfect time. The servers that connect to stratum 0 devices, called stratum 1 servers, synchronize to within a few milliseconds of the stratum 0 time. Stratum 1 servers in turn enable connection by stratum 2 clients—which are a little less perfectly synchronized—that enable connection by stratum 3 clients. This hierarchy continues until stratum 15; after that, devices are not synchronized with the clock. NTP usually employs *clients* and *servers* for the hierarchy described here, but also enables peer-to-peer connections at each stratum level for backup and sanity checks.

REVIEW

Objective 1.6: Explain the use and purpose of network services

- The four-step DORA process allows a DHCP client to get a lease from a DHCP server.
- Static addressing should be used for servers and router interfaces.
- A DHCP relay agent/IP helper is a router interface that turns a broadcast into a unicast, so it can reach a DHCP server on a remote network.
- DNS is mostly known for turning a FQDN into its corresponding IP address with A and AAAA resource records, but other resource records like CNAME, MX, SOA, PTR, TXT, SRV, and NS perform other functions.
- DNS is hierarchical and global, and uses both recursion and iteration.
- NTP is used to synchronize the clocks of devices on an internetwork for important services like Kerberos, so that authentication works properly. NTP is also important when aggregating log files, and for verification of digital certificates.

1.6 QUESTIONS

1. Which of the following is not given to a DHCP client from a DHCP server's scope options?
   A. Port number
   B. IP address
   C. Default gateway IP address
   D. DNS server IP address

2. How do DNS root name servers respond to DNS queries?
   A. Check authentication
   B. Give referrals
   C. Give actual answers to queries
   D. Query another server on behalf of their clients

3. Which of the following is at the highest end of NTP with nearly perfect time keeping?
   A. Stratum 0
   B. Stratum 1
   C. Stratum 3
   D. Stratum 15

1.6 ANSWERS

1. **A** Port numbers are determined by the application and operating system. The IP addresses in the other choices are given to DHCP clients from a DHCP server.

2. **B** DNS root name servers give referrals to the appropriate authoritative TLD DNS server.

3. **A** At the highest end, stratum 0 devices—like atomic clocks or the GPS satellites—keep near perfect time.

Objective 1.7 # Explain basic corporate and datacenter network architecture

Datacenters consist of servers, such as mail servers, DNS servers, and proxy servers. They also consist of routers and switches that allow the outside world to access these servers. In addition, datacenters contain firewalls, VPN gateways, IDSs, IPSs, and much more.

Three-Tiered

In a simple world where a datacenter consists of a couple of servers, there isn't much in the way of architecture. You have servers, a switch, a router, and an ISP connection.

As the number of servers in your datacenter begins to grow, you must have an organization to your servers, switches, and routers, as well as many support systems (HVAC and power especially). After decades of different architectures, the architecture most adopted by traditional datacenters is Cisco's *three-tiered* architecture. A three-tiered architecture consists of three layers, access layer, distribution layer, and core layer, as shown in Figure 1.7-1.

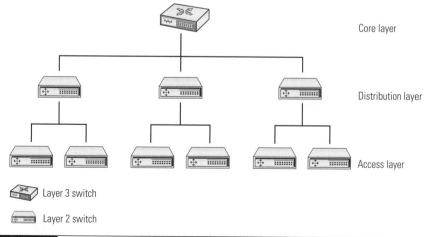

FIGURE 1.7-1 Three-tiered architecture

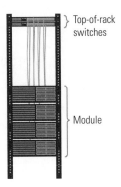

FIGURE 1.7-2 Typical rack with switch

Access/Edge

The *access/edge* layer acts as the primary connection between the datacenter connectivity and the servers. The access layer includes the cables and the access switches closest to the systems. A common implementation of access switches is top-of-rack switching, as shown in Figure 1.7-2. With top-of-rack switching, every equipment rack uses one (or two for redundancy) Layer 2 switches sitting at the top of the rack, connecting to all the systems on the rack. Top-of-rack switches are co-resident in the rack with servers, as compared to switches that reside in a separate rack.

Top-of-rack switches—dedicated switches—help keep cable runs short and well organized. Top-of-rack switching does not require that the switches be physically at the top of the rack (although they usually are). Each group of computers connected to the same access switch is known as a module. Multiple VLANs should be configured for each access layer switch.

Client devices comprise the biggest part of the edge in corporate networks, which have edge switches in wiring closets near the devices (often on each floor of a large building), then connected back to the distribution layer switches in the server room/datacenter. Consider an installation that involves putting five 48-port switches in the wiring closet on each floor. In most cases those five switches are stacked using proprietary interconnects for management, but they also have two or more connections back to the distribution layer (perhaps leveraging LACP, or RSTP, or both).

Distribution/Aggregation Layer

Datacenters have tens, hundreds, or in some cases thousands of racks in a single facility. With top-of-rack switches on all the racks, you need to provide a method to interconnect and distribute data to all the systems, acting as the connection between the access layer and the core layer. The *distribution/aggregation layer*, as shown in Figure 1.7-3, provides that connectivity. Distribution switches are usually multilayer and conduct forwarding from Layer 2 on the access side to Layer 3 for the core side. Cisco best practices recommend always having two distribution switches for each access switch. The two switches provide redundancy in case of the failure of the distribution switch or the cables that connect the distribution and

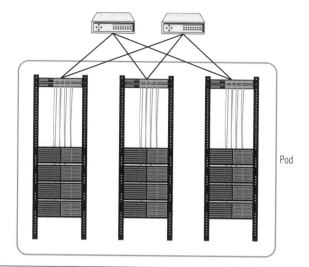

FIGURE 1.7-3   Distribution layer

access switches. Every group of modules that share the same connection to their distribution switches is known as a pod.

Core

The *core* layer ties together all the switches at the distribution layer and acts as the point of connection to the external connections, including the Internet. All systems at this level run exclusively at OSI Layer 3 (Network layer). The interconnections here are the highest speed and the highest bandwidth and are therefore defined as the *backbone*. Just as with distribution, Cisco best practices recommend always having two core switches accessible to each access switch. Again, the redundancy here is warranted because of the criticality of the core switches.

Software-Defined Networking

Traditionally, hardware routers and switches were designed with two closely integrated parts: a control plane that decides how to move traffic, and a data plane that executes those decisions. The control plane on a router is what you log into to configure it. The control plane runs the software that actually speaks routing protocols, like OSPF and BGP, and builds the routing tables that it gives to the data plane. The router's data plane (also known as the forwarding plane) reads incoming packets and uses the routing table to send them to their destination. *Software-Defined Networking* changes everything.

NOTE   Some sources use *layer*, some use *plane*, and others, like the CompTIA Network+ exam objectives, here, mix them.

Control Layer, Infrastructure Layer

Software-defined networking (SDN) cuts the *control layer* of individual devices out of the picture and lets an all-knowing program (running on a server, probably in the cloud) called a network controller dictate how both physical and virtual network components move traffic through the network. SDN requires components (think routers, switches, firewalls) with an *infrastructure layer* (also known as the data layer) designed to take instructions from the network controller instead of their own control plane.

While it's important enough that SDN allows for a master controller (such as the one shown in Figure 1.7-4—though large networks may also distribute the controller's workload over multiple servers), the revolutionary idea behind SDN is that the network controller is programmable. We can write code (or use software designed by others) that controls how the entire network behaves.

SDN is about automation of provisioning and management of devices. With SDN, like with a Cisco WLAN controller, I could give the instruction, "Create a VLAN across the network," and SDN will reach out to all devices and, regardless of the actual commands, take care of the

FIGURE 1.7-4   Management interface for UISP network controller from Ubiquiti

configuration. If a device fails, I could give the instruction "Here is the replacement device," and SDN will take care of the configuration. Cisco is expanding this premise to move to Intent-based configuration, where more broad terms for wants and needs can be specified to configure the network. With SDN, programming is mostly configuring, and not actually programming/coding.

Management Plane, Application Layer

To manage the complexity that comes with separating the infrastructure and control planes, SDN introduces a few new planes for us to keep straight. The most important are the *management plane* and *application plane*. The management (or administration) layer is responsible for setting up network devices to get their marching orders from the right controller. The application layer, which sits on top of this entire framework, is where the actual network-behavior-controlling software runs. Applications that run here often do jobs like load balancing, optimizing the flow of traffic, monitoring, enforcing security policy, threat protection, and so on.

Spine and Leaf

Virtualization and SDN freed the datacenter from the three-tiered model. In particular virtualization removes the need for the distribution/aggregation layer. With a *spine-and-leaf* architecture, every spine switch connects to every leaf switch in a two-tiered mesh network, as shown in Figure 1.7-5. The mesh network removes the need for dedicated connections between the spine *backbone* switches, because traffic moves seamlessly from spine to leaf to spine, regardless of how many spine or leaf switches are on the network.

Virtualization moved much of the access layer into the virtualization product, which makes a two-layer hierarchy easier to support. A product like VMware manages the connection of 10–20+ virtual servers internally, and only using two or four external NICs.

The spine and leaf architecture has some real benefits compared to three-tiered architecture. First, the spine and leaf architecture reduces the number of necessary devices. Every step

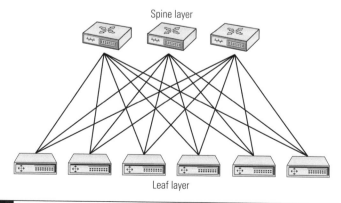

FIGURE 1.7-5 Spine and leaf architecture

from the spine to leaf is a single hop, which reduces latency and creates completely predictable connections. Also, there's no longer a concern for loops, making Spanning Tree Protocol (STP) unneeded. Virtual servers today rely heavily on data from other servers in the same datacenter, adding far more east-west traffic (see below) than is easily handled by three-tiered architecture. The spine and leaf architecture handles east-west traffic with ease. Spine and leaf architecture uses protocols such as *Equal-Cost Multipath (ECPM)* to provide load balancing across the paths.

Finally, spine and leaf architecture makes adding capacity simpler than in a three-tiered architecture. You can add another spine switch and connect it to every leaf switch through the mesh network; new leaf switches that are added simply slot in to reduce the load on all the other leaf switches.

Software-Defined Network

A *software-defined* network, implementing the concepts described in the Software-defined networking section above, can be implemented in a spine and leaf architecture.

Top-of-Rack Switching

Spine and leaf can also be the architecture of a common implementation of access switches, *top-of-rack switching*, previously discussed in the "Access/Edge" section.

Backbone

A third spine and leaf implementation is the *backbone*, which is implemented by the core layer, as previously discussed in the "Core" section. The traditional network backbone was the connection between all of the device switches, the center bone to which all others were attached.

Traffic Flows

All the switches, cables, and routers that populate your typical datacenter have a single job: to move a lot of data. To help those who design datacenters, the industry has established common terms to define the movement of the data into/out of and around the datacenter. These are called *traffic flows*.

North-South

North-south traffic describes data moving into and out of the datacenter. While there is some variance in terms, the industry defines north-south traffic as any data leaving and entering and the datacenter. Breaking down this term even more, northbound traffic leaves the datacenter and southbound traffic enters the datacenter.

 NOTE Network devices involved in north-south traffic include edge routers, edge firewalls, and load balancers.

East-West

East-west traffic is defined as any traffic that moves between systems within the datacenter. Unlike north-south traffic, there is no separate east traffic or west traffic. It's all just east-west. Examples of east-west are backup traffic, intrusion detection system (IDS) alerts, and logs.

 NOTE Network devices involved in east-west traffic include internal routers, internal firewalls, and switches.

Branch Office vs. On-Premises Datacenter vs. Colocation

So, where does the datacenter physically exist? That answer varies based on where and how an organization stands in terms of growth. A tiny company might leave all of its data sitting on a single computer in the founder's garage, but beyond that, very simple initial choices must be made. As a company grows and its data requirements grow, does it build an on-premises datacenter—that is, a dedicated datacenter at the company's site?

For many organizations, the next step means to build a rack and throw a few servers and some mass storage into a handy room—in essence, building a mini datacenter. That is perfectly fine for small organizations, but as data and server needs progress even further, a true datacenter is required. It's time to take the servers and move them into a proper, secure, reliable, classic datacenter.

But where to place this beast? An *on-premises datacenter* is wildly expensive in terms of both the building and the associated maintenance and upkeep. Back in the day, there really weren't any other viable choices. Over time, however, clever entrepreneurs (or folks who had already built datacenters and had extra capacity) began to offer public, third-party datacenters where anyone could place their own servers, a process known as *colocation*.

There's one more step in the growth of an organization that will affect the datacenter: multiple locations. As an organization grows into multiple locations, there's usually a central location (often corporate headquarters) that contains an organization's single datacenter. This datacenter serves outlying offices, each called a *branch office*. The branch offices themselves store very little data.

 EXAM TIP Expect a question on the CompTIA Network+ exam that compares branch office vs. on-premises datacenter vs. colocation. That would be remote connections to a datacenter vs. an on-site datacenter vs. a datacenter hosted by a third party.

Storage Area Networks

All that data moving north, south, east, and west sometimes needs to rest someplace, and that's where data storage comes into play. For the most part, all data storage in a classic datacenter focuses on the mass storage devices that store the terabytes or petabytes of 1s and 0s that make up the data. *Mass storage devices* in a traditional datacenter include *hard drives, tape backups,* and *optical media*. Tape backups and optical media are now rare (or completely gone), making hard drives and SSDs the main technologies used to store data in datacenters.

So, where are all these mass storage devices located in the datacenter, and what are their jobs? To be sure, every system is going to have a boot drive, in most cases a single M.2 drive mounted to the motherboard, but that drive does no more than boot the operating system. For the actual data storage, most traditional datacenters use *storage area networks* (SANs). A SAN is a network that connects individual systems to a centralized bank of mass storage, as depicted in Figure 1.7-6. But don't think of a SAN as simply a networked hard drive! You might remember from CompTIA A+ that hard drive storage is broken up into tiny sectors, but you might not know that these sectors are also known as *blocks*. You might also remember that to access the hard drive, you have to plug it into an interface like SATA, which your operating system uses to read and write to blocks on the disk. A SAN is a *pool of mass storage devices*, presented over a network as any number of logical disks. The interface it presents to a client computer pretends to be a hard disk and enables the client's operating system to read and write blocks over a network.

 NOTE A lot of newer techs or techs-in-training confuse the terms SAN and NAS. Both are mass storage technologies and use the same three letters, so it's understandable. But let's clear up the difference right now. SANs, covered in this objective, are high-end data storage structures that create usable and configurable storage blocks for virtual drives, virtual desktops, and more. Network attached storage (NAS) refers to a generally much smaller dedicated network appliance with two, four, six, or eight hard disk drives configured into some sort of array. A NAS attaches to a network switch (usually) via Ethernet and appears as available storage on the network. A NAS is used for local backups, media serving on the LAN, and other personal duties.

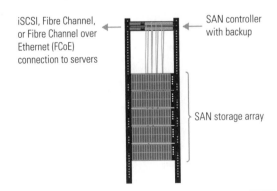

iSCSI, Fibre Channel, or Fibre Channel over Ethernet (FCoE) connection to servers

SAN controller with backup

SAN storage array

FIGURE 1.7-6 SAN in action

Most major SAN providers (EMC/NetApp) offer a NAS option on many of their SAN products, since they would like to hold all of your data. NetApp, for instance, allows you to allocate a portion of your storage for NAS operations, and the controller then takes care of presenting SMB or NFS shares to devices on the data network. This allows you to leverage SAN functionality of data replication, snapshots, and data deduplication, while still providing block-level services on the SAN to your servers. SAN-based management of NAS shares means that a company saves on creating file servers, which would be another physical server, with a SAN-based storage disk, and that requires companies to pay for the server and server license and to use up SAN block-level storage (which does not have the features that NAS has).

Think of creating a RAID array, where you create the array and then create and present "disks" or volumes to the server. Three physical drives in a array can be presented to the OS of the server they are attached to as anything between 1 and 10+ disks. With the SAN, this presentation is done to a specific server HBA over the SAN.

One of the benefits of using a SAN is that, by just reading and writing at the block level, it avoids the performance costs of implementing its own file system. The SAN leaves it up to the client computers to implement their own file systems—these clients often use specialized shared file system software designed for high volume, performance, reliability, and the ability to support multiple clients using one drive.

Connection Types

When it comes to the infrastructure to support a SAN, there are currently two *connection types*: Fibre Channel (FC)/Fibre Channel over Ethernet (FCoE) and Internet Small Computer Systems Interface (iSCSI).

Fibre Channel, Fibre Channel over Ethernet (FCoE)

Fibre Channel (FC) is, for the most part, its own ecosystem designed for high-performance storage. It has its own cables, protocols, and switches, all increasing the costs associated with its use. While more recent developments like *Fibre Channel over Ethernet (FCoE)* make Fibre Channel a little more flexible within a local wired network, long-distance Fibre Channel is still clumsy without expensive cabling and hardware.

FCoE really means you can use slightly less expensive data network switches and NICs instead of FC switches and NICs, but at the cost of the overhead of Ethernet frames being used. For performance and scale, you still need to go with very high-end equipment and not something like TRENDnet switches and NICs.

Internet Small Computer Systems Interface (iSCSI)

Internet Small Computer Systems Interface (iSCSI) is built on top of TCP/IP, enabling devices that use the SCSI protocol to communicate across existing networks using cheap, readily available hardware. Because the existing networks and their hardware weren't built as a disk interface, performance can suffer. Part of this performance cost is time spent processing frame headers. We can ease some of the cost of moving large amounts of data around the network at standard frame size by using jumbo frames. Jumbo frames are usually 9000 bytes long—though technically anything over 1500 qualifies—and they reduce the total number of frames moving through the network.

 NOTE   The physical connections between the systems and the SAN are usually fiber optics.

Moving a server's data storage physically apart from the server adds some risk. If the SAN fails, the server won't function. To address this risk, most SAN solutions provide more than one connection or path between the server and the SAN, what's called multipathing. If either connection fails, the other connection continues to keep the server connected to the SAN. A SAN is developed with high availability in mind, so it often includes features such as redundant controllers and power supplies, plus shared memory. All this is in addition to multipathing, which applies to all SAN technologies. There should also be redundant switches. The standard base design is one storage array, two controllers, two switches, and two HBA interfaces on each server (either one dual or two single HBAs). Anything that can have redundant power should be configured as such, too.

Critical connections to FC, FCoE, and iSCSI should not use the infrastructure of a general data network, but rather should be isolated for both efficiency and security (even though efficiency and security are inversely proportional).

REVIEW

Objective 1.7: Explain basic corporate and datacenter network architecture

- After decades of different architectures, the architecture most adopted by traditional datacenters is Cisco's three-tiered architecture. A three-tiered architecture consists of three layers: access/edge layer, distribution/aggregation layer, and core layer.
- Software-defined networking (SDN) cuts the control layer of individual devices out of the picture and lets an all-knowing program (running on a server, probably in the cloud) called a network controller dictate how both physical and virtual network components move traffic through the network.
- North-south traffic describes data moving into and out of the datacenter. East-west traffic is defined as any traffic that moves between systems within the datacenter.
- The datacenter can exist in a branch office, on-premises, or as part of a colocation setup.
- SAN connection types include Fibre Channel, Fibre Channel over Ethernet (FCoE), and Internet Small Computer Systems Interface (iSCSI).

1.7 QUESTIONS

1. Which of the following is at the top of the three-tiered architecture?

    A. Access/edge

    B. Distribution/aggregation layer

    C. Core

    D. Control layer

2. Which layer is responsible for setting up network devices to get their orders from a controller?

    A. Application

    B. Control

    C. Infrastructure

    D. Management

3. Which of the following is an alternative to the three-tiered architecture?

    A. Spine and leaf

    B. Top-of-rack

    C. STP

    D. Backbone

1.7 ANSWERS

1. **C** The core layer ties together all the switches at the distribution layer and acts as the point of connection to the external connections, including the Internet. All systems at this level run exclusively at OSI Layer 3.

2. **D** The management (or administration) layer is responsible for setting up network devices to get their marching orders from the right controller.

3. **A** Spine and leaf architecture has some real benefits compared to three-tiered architecture.

Objective 1.8 Summarize cloud concepts and connectivity options

Cloud concepts and connectivity options depend on deployment models, service models, connectivity options, and more.

Deployment Models

Organizations have differing needs and capabilities, of course, so cloud *deployment models* can vary greatly. When it comes to cloud computing, organizations have to balance cost, control, customization, and privacy. Some organizations also have needs that no existing cloud provider can meet. Each organization makes its own decisions about these trade-offs, but the result is usually a cloud deployment that can be categorized in one of four ways.

Public

Most folks usually just interact with a *public* cloud, a term used to describe software, platforms, and infrastructure delivered through networks that the general public can use. When we talk about *the* cloud, this is what we mean. Out on the open, public Internet, cloud services and applications can collaborate in ways that make it easier to think of them collectively as *the cloud* than as many public clouds. The public doesn't *own* this cloud—the hardware is often owned by companies like Amazon, Google, and Microsoft—but there's nothing to stop a company like Netflix from building its Web application atop the IaaS (infrastructure as a service) offerings of all three of these companies at once.

Private

If a business wants some of the flexibility of the cloud, needs complete ownership of its data, and can afford both, it can build an internal cloud the business actually owns—a *private* cloud. A security-minded company with enough resources could build an internal IaaS network in an onsite datacenter. Departments within the company could create and destroy virtual machines as needed, and develop SaaS (software as a service) to meet collaboration, planning, or task and time management needs all without sending the data over the open Internet. A company with these needs but without the space or knowledge to build and maintain a private cloud can also contract a third party to maintain or host it.

Hybrid

Not all data is crucial, and not every document is a secret. Needs that an organization can only meet in-house might be less important than keeping an application running when demand exceeds what it can handle onsite. We can build a *hybrid* cloud by connecting some combination of public and private clouds, allowing communication between them. Using a hybrid cloud model can mean not having to maintain a private cloud powerful enough to meet peak demand—an application can grow into a public cloud instead of grind to a halt, a technique called cloud bursting. But a hybrid cloud isn't just about letting one Web application span two types of cloud—it's also about integrating services across them. Let's take a look at how Bob could use a hybrid cloud to expand his business.

Bob runs a national chain of sandwich shops and is looking into drone-delivered lunch. He'll need a new application in his private cloud to calculate routes and track drones, and that application will have to integrate with the existing order-tracking application in his private cloud. But then he'll also need to integrate it with a third-party weather application in the public cloud to avoid sending drones out in a blizzard, and a flight-plan application running in a hybrid cloud to avoid other drones, helicopters, and aircraft (and vice versa). The sum of these integrated services and applications *is* the hybrid cloud that will power Bob's drone-delivered lunch.

Community

A *community* cloud is more like a private cloud paid for and used by more than one organization with similar goals or needs (such as medical providers who all need to comply with the same patient privacy laws).

Service Models

There are three different types of traditional cloud services, *service models*, used for different things today: SaaS, PaaS, and IaaS. Each has its own unique flavor of cloud computing that allows for greater flexibility than ever before. A newcomer to the service model game is DaaS.

Software as a Service (SaaS)

Remember the days of downloading Microsoft Office or going to the store to buy it on optical disc? Remember having to download and install updates? Then, a few years later, it became obsolete, and you needed a new version! Now, with Microsoft Office 365, you use a browser to access the latest and greatest of the Office suite in the cloud, with security patches applied immediately. Furthermore, you don't have to uninstall the previous version and install the current version. Google's G Suite offers a similar set of cloud tools with Google Docs, Google Sheets, and Google Slides, which are free for consumers, but enterprise features, options, tools, and settings, and support come at different pricing levels.

The *software as a service (SaaS)* model provides access to necessary applications wherever you have an Internet connection, often without having to carry data with you (the data can be stored in the cloud, as well) or regularly update software. At the enterprise level, the subscription model of many SaaS providers makes it easier for organizations to budget software expenses and to keep hundreds or thousands of computers up to date (Figure 1.8-1) with office software, messaging software, payroll processing software, database management software, management software, and much more.

In exchange for the flexibility of using public, third-party SaaS, you often have to trade strict control of your data. Security might not be crucial when someone uses Google Drive to draft a blog post, but many companies are concerned about sensitive intellectual property or business secrets traveling through untrusted networks and being stored on servers they don't control.

Specific examples of SaaS include any Web-based e-mail provider (like Gmail and Yahoo!), Dropbox, Box, Slack, Google Docs, Google Sheets, Google Slides, and Office 365.

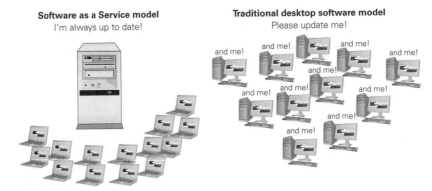

FIGURE 1.8-1 SaaS vs. every desktop for themselves

Cross-Reference

If you've never used Google Docs before, try it now: https://docs.google.com. Web versions of Office apps are free as well: https://www.microsoft.com/en-ca/microsoft-365/free-office-online-for-the-web.

Infrastructure as a Service (IaaS)

Large-scale global *infrastructure as a Service (IaaS)* providers use virtualization to minimize idle hardware, protect against data loss and downtime, and respond to spikes in demand. Companies can use big IaaS providers, like Amazon Web Services (AWS), to launch new virtual servers using an operating system of choice on demand for pennies an hour. The beauty of IaaS is that you no longer need to purchase expensive, heavy hardware. You are using Amazon's powerful IaaS.

For example, think about certain holidays and times of the year when there's an increase in online shopping (Black Friday, pre-Christmas, etc.). An online retailer might need to temporarily extend their current datacenter infrastructure to handle a spike in traffic for a certain period of time. Instead of investing in the hardware, software, and more, which is not needed all year round, companies can use AWS, for example, to provide many of the services needed to drive popular, complex Web applications—unlimited data storage, database servers, caching, media hosting, and more—all billed by usage. After Black Friday, retailers can delete those machines and pay nothing. If your machine is built and turned off, you still have some residual fees for OS licenses and data storage of your disks, but you are saving any access costs and the like.

The hitch is that, while you're no longer responsible for the hardware, you're still responsible for configuring and maintaining the operating system and software of any virtual machines you create. This can provide a lot of flexibility to tune it for yours needs, but it also requires knowledge of the underlying OS and time to manage it.

NOTE   Sometimes you'll see *aaS or *xaaS* used to refer generically to any type of as-a-service cloud computing, like SaaS, PaaS, and IaaS.

Platform as a Service (PaaS)

Web applications are built by programmers. Programmers do one thing really well: they program. The problem for programmers is that a Web application needs a lot more than a just programmer. To develop a Web application, we need people to manage the infrastructure: system administrators, database administrators, general network support, and more. A Web application also needs more than just hardware and an operating system. It needs development tools, monitoring tools, database tools, and potentially hundreds of other tools and services. Getting a Web application up and running is a big job.

A *platform as a service (PaaS)* provider gives programmers all the tools they need to deploy, administer, and maintain a Web application. They have some form of infrastructure, which could be provided by an IaaS, but on top of that infrastructure the PaaS provider builds a platform: a complete deployment and management system to handle every aspect of a Web application.

The important point of PaaS is that the infrastructure underneath the PaaS is largely invisible to the developer. The PaaS provider is aware of their infrastructure, but the developer cannot control it directly, and doesn't need to think about its complexity. As far as the programmer is concerned, the PaaS is just a place to deploy and run their application.

Heroku, one of the earliest PaaS providers, creates a simple interface on top of AWS's Amazon Elastic Compute Cloud (EC2), further reducing the complexity of developing and scaling Web applications. Heroku's management console enables developers to increase or decrease the capacity of an application with a single slider, or easily set up add-ons that add a database, monitor your logs, track performance, and more. It could take days for a tech or developer unfamiliar with the software and services to install, configure, and integrate a set of these services with a running application; PaaS providers help cut this down to minutes or hours.

Desktop as a Service (DaaS)

Desktop as a Service (DaaS) enables us to move user workstations into the cloud and manage them as flexibly as other cloud infrastructure.

DaaS isn't really a new idea—it's just the latest form of a kind of virtualization we've been doing for a while now. Desktop virtualization replaces direct access to a system's local desktop environment with a client that can access a virtualized desktop running in a VM. You could technically run that VM on the same device, but benefits like flexible management come from centralizing the desktop VMs on a smaller number of servers—a pattern called virtual desktop infrastructure (VDI). This server/client VDI pattern is roughly what cloud providers bundle up and sell as DaaS.

Even though you can accomplish the same goals with in-house VDI, cloud services do have some distinct benefits. For example, DaaS makes it possible to onboard new employees even when there's no space on the internal servers. The ability to host virtual desktops closer to users all around the world, even when you don't have an office nearby, can also help them have a smooth experience because of the reduction in lag. Some services also have distinct options—users of Azure Virtual Desktop, for example, can support legacy apps on copies of Windows 7 that still get regular security updates from Microsoft (this ESU—Extended Security Updates—program has an associated cost outside of Azure infrastructures).

Infrastructure as Code

Infrastructure as code (IaC) does away with manual processes and allows the management and provisioning of the cloud infrastructure to be performed entirely through code. Using configuration files with infrastructure specifications makes it easier to modify and deploy configurations, while also guaranteeing that all provisioned environments will be the same. It also allows for breaking up an infrastructure into modular components and using automation to combine them. This can be done with automation and orchestration.

Automation/Orchestration

One way that infrastructure as code can be implemented is through *automation*, which uses software to replace human interaction with systems, which cuts down on cost, complexity, and especially errors. The term automation refers to this process related to one task.

Another way that infrastructure as code can be implemented is through *orchestration*, which refers to automating a process or workflow with many steps across different systems. This involves configuring, managing, and coordinating systems, applications, and services through automation.

Connectivity Options

Unless your organization manages to chug along just fine without any cloud resources—or only needs to use resources that can be publicly accessible—it'll probably have to support interconnecting resources running locally with those running in the cloud. The security implications of an always-on connection are very concerning. There are two *connectivity options* that the exam objectives focus on: a virtual private network (VPN) and a private-direct connection to the cloud provider. Those options are better than simply connecting over the Internet directly.

Virtual Private Network (VPN)

The most convenient way to connect your network to the public cloud is the tried-and-true *virtual private network (VPN)*, which creates an encrypted tunnel between two networks over another, less secure, network. A site-to-site VPN can establish a permanent tunnel (often using IPsec) between your local network and a virtual network in the cloud.

VPN tunnels are relativity simple to set up because they use off-the-shelf technology like IPsec. This makes them easy to integrate with existing site-to-site WAN infrastructure or even an SDWAN service.

Private-Direct Connection to Cloud Provider

VPNs are easy, but big-time organizations often need big-time pipes. To meet this need, providers such as AWS and Azure offer a *private-direct connection to cloud provider*, links between leased lines from a telco/third party to the cloud provider's datacenter. The main thing to keep in mind is that the traffic for a private-direct connection never goes over the public Internet. It's a private line between your datacenter and your cloud provider's datacenter.

Multitenancy

Multitenancy is the ability to support multiple customers on the same infrastructure at the same time—and it's both a blessing and a curse. It's a blessing because one of the great benefits of cloud computing is that someone who needs a teeny-tiny server that does almost no work can pay for a likewise teeny-tiny fraction of the resources of a huge server for a few pennies a day. The curse, though, is that you have neighbors, and you don't get much say in who they are.

Your server may run really well on a quiet system with polite neighbors, or struggle for CPU time on a system where every neighbor keeps demanding more server resources. And then there's the question of *malicious* neighbors (or perhaps just nice neighbors who have been hacked). Hypervisors do a good job of isolating one VM from another, but this isn't perfect (and containers are less isolated).

There is a steady stream of new exploits that could enable a bad neighbor to snoop on your app or service. This isn't a big deal if you're just hosting some cat videos, but it can be a huge problem if you work with tightly regulated data such as patient medical records. In the latter case, the regulations may require you to pay a little more for *dedicated* instances (potentially using more secure facilities, networks, or hardware) that spare you from sharing the same infrastructure with other tenants. Of course you don't see these issues with AWS or Azure, where physical security is treated as a high priority, as is isolation of customers from each other, monitoring of loads, data security, and network security.

Scalability

One of the cool things virtualization enables us to do (especially in the cloud) is take the same virtual machine and run it with more or less of its host machine's resources, or even move it to a more powerful machine. This benefit is called *scalability,* because it enables us to scale "up" an application or service without needing to run it on more than one server.

Scaling includes both scaling up (more resources for a machine) and scaling out (more machines). With PaaS you can scale both ways for an application. Not all cloud providers may provide easy scaling options for something like PaaS, although Azure and AWS do. With Azure's IaaS and PaaS, you can choose to change the size of virtual server manually, which only requires a restart of the server (or WebApp), allowing you to scale the server up or down. This does not require the reinstallation of the server or the transfer of data. With PaaS, you can also scale the number of devices/instances hosting the application, which will then support load balancing. This is scaling from the customer point of view. The platform provider is also providing continual scaling of the datacenters, but typically scalability is considered from the customer perspective.

Elasticity

Elasticity is automation on the scaling operations, so that if the load on an application exceeds a certain percentage, scaling automatically increases capacity (either up or out, but typically out), and when load drops below a certain percentage, scaling automatically reduces resources.

Regarding the Black Friday example mentioned earlier, a company will add resources to the frontend Web apps to handle load, and after Cyber Monday, the resources they are paying for will automatically go back down. With only manual scaling options, the company would be increasing resources for Black Friday, but would be paying for those resources until they remember to relinquish them, incurring unnecessary costs. Some cloud providers may support scaling without support for elasticity, but the big providers like Azure and AWS support both.

Security Implications

Using a particular cloud provider means you are putting complete faith and trust in the cloud provider. *Security implications* are important. For example, insider threats at the cloud provider could be more damaging than insider threats at your own organization, so you need to be assured that the cloud provider has internal controls to prevent insider threats. Before you choose a cloud provider, you need to explore various security implications and get answers from potential providers regarding how they handle security. For example, is the cloud provider prepared to respond if it's hit with a denial of service (DoS) attack? How do the providers intend to encrypt your data? How quickly will they react to patch vulnerabilities and deal with threats? Will they comingle your data, meaning your data is on the same server as another company's data, or even using shared RAM? If so, how do they keep it segregated? Who owns what in the cloud? There is a lack of standards covering cloud providers, so it is up to you to investigate a potential cloud provider's security posture.

 EXAM TIP   The CompTIA Network+ exam will likely be very interested in your understanding of the security implications of cloud computing.

REVIEW

Objective 1.8: Summarize cloud concepts and connectivity options

- The software as a service (SaaS) model provides access to necessary applications wherever you have an Internet connection, often without having to carry data with you or regularly update software
- A platform as a service (PaaS) provider gives programmers all the tools they need to deploy, administer, and maintain a Web application. They have some form of infrastructure, but on top of that infrastructure the PaaS provider builds a platform: a complete deployment and management system to handle every aspect of a Web application.
- Large-scale global infrastructure as a service (IaaS) providers use virtualization to minimize idle hardware, protect against data loss and downtime, and respond to spikes in demand.
- Most folks usually just interact with a public cloud, a term used to describe software, platforms, and infrastructure delivered through networks that the general public can use.
- If a business wants some of the flexibility of the cloud, needs complete ownership of its data, and can afford both, it can build an internal cloud the business actually owns—a private cloud.
- We can build a hybrid cloud by connecting some combination of public and private clouds, allowing communication between them.
- Connectivity methods to a cloud provider include connecting over the Internet directly, using a VPN, and using a separate connectivity provider to set up a direct, private connection.
- Multitenancy, elasticity, scalability, and security implications are all factors in determining a cloud service.

1.8 QUESTIONS

1. Google Docs is an example of which of the following?
   A. SaaS
   B. PaaS
   C. IaaS
   D. VPN

2. Which one of these is not a cloud delivery model?
   A. Public
   B. Private
   C. Hybrid
   D. Mesh

3. Which of the following is a use case for IaaS?
   A. Running programs over the Internet
   B. Web site development
   C. A company that needs extra servers to handle a spike in traffic for holiday shopping
   D. Backing up files

1.8 ANSWERS

1. **A**   Software available over the Internet is software as a service.

2. **D**   There is no mesh cloud delivery model.

3. **C**   Infrastructure as a service provides a company an extension to its onsite datacenter.

Network Implementations

DOMAIN 2.0

Domain Objectives

- **2.1** Compare and contrast various devices, their features, and their appropriate placement on the network.

- **2.2** Compare and contrast routing technologies and bandwidth management concepts.

- **2.3** Given a scenario, configure and deploy common Ethernet switching features.

- **2.4** Given a scenario, install and configure the appropriate wireless standards and technologies.

Compare and contrast various devices, their features, and their appropriate placement on the network

Networking devices enable nodes to send and receive packets. There are various networking devices whose placement, installation, and configuration you need to understand in a given scenario.

Networking Devices

There are many distinctions between *networking devices*: wired vs. wireless, Layer 1 vs. Layer 2 vs. Layer 3, required for communication vs. required for security, used for voice traffic vs. used for data traffic, and even modern vs. obsolete.

Layer 2 Switch

A *Layer 2 switch* connects devices of the same network together. Think of switches as the local streets of a city, connecting entities (such as homes, office buildings, banks, coffeehouses, and supermarkets) in the same vicinity. These entities are like the end devices on a network. End devices are the sources or destinations of traffic and have IP addresses. End devices are connected by switches and include desktops, laptops, printers, cameras, mobile devices, and so on. Just like the streets of a city allow you to easily go from a bank to a coffeehouse, switches allow network traffic (for example, a document) to go from your computer to a network printer. Just like a set of streets can lead to another part of a city, switches connect to other switches, extending the network's reach. Of course, a network must have a switch that connects to a router, that takes traffic destined for other networks off the network (by forwarding the traffic to another router) and brings traffic from other networks onto that network (after receiving traffic from another router).

To see a switch in action, check out Figure 2.1-1. When you first turn on a switch, it knows nothing. However, as frames come in from computers directly connected to that switch, the switch copies the source MAC addresses and quickly creates a table of the MAC addresses to ports of each computer directly connected to that switch. The table is called a MAC address table, source address table (SAT), or content addressable memory (CAM) table .

NOTE Switches use the source MAC address in the frame to learn where hosts are, and use the destination MAC address in the frame to decide where to send the frames to (based on the port associated with the source MAC address that was learned when that device sent frames into the switch).

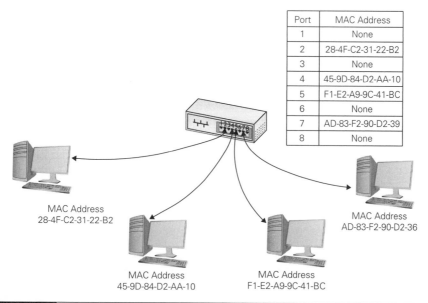

Port	MAC Address
1	None
2	28-4F-C2-31-22-B2
3	None
4	45-9D-84-D2-AA-10
5	F1-E2-A9-9C-41-BC
6	None
7	AD-83-F2-90-D2-39
8	None

MAC Address
28-4F-C2-31-22-B2

MAC Address
AD-83-F2-90-D2-36

MAC Address
45-9D-84-D2-AA-10

MAC Address
F1-E2-A9-9C-41-BC

FIGURE 2.1-1   Layer 2 switch

When a computer sends into a switch a frame destined for another computer on the same switch, the switch acts like a telephone operator, creating something similar to an on-the-fly connection between the two devices. When a computer sends into a switch a frame destined for another computer on a different switch (directly or indirectly connected to the first switch), the frame will reach the actual destination through switch-to-switch links. If two switches are connected together, all devices on the first switch will have their MAC addresses associated with the port on the second switch that's connected to the first switch, and vice versa.

Each port on a switch is in its own collision domain, plus the switch can buffer incoming frames. That means that two nodes connected to the switch can send data at the same time and the switch will handle it without any collision.

With older, obsolete half-duplex switches, collisions could occur and the rules of CSMA/CD applied (see Objective 2.3 for coverage of CSMA/CD). These collisions could only happen between the switch and a node (not between two nodes) in the event that the switch tried to send a frame to a node at the same time as the node tried to send a frame to the switch. For decades, switches have been full-duplex, and with full-duplex enabled, CSMA/CD is disabled. No collisions can occur, and each node always gets the full band-width of the network.

Unicast messages always go only to the intended recipient when you use a switch. The switch sends all broadcast and multicast (unless pruned) messages out of all ports, except the port on which the message originated. Furthermore, an unknown unicast, where the switch doesn't know which port the destination MAC address is associated with, is treated like a broadcast and flooded out of all ports, except the port on which the message originated.

Layer 3 Capable Switch

Once you've configured a switch to support multiple VLANs, each VLAN is its own broadcast domain (each VLAN should be a separate IP subnet as well), just as if the multiple VLANs were on completely separate switches, networks, and physical infrastructures.

This is where a *Layer 3 capable switch* (also known as a multilayer switch, since it operates at both Layer 2 and Layer 3) comes into play. A Layer 3 capable switch allows you to create switched virtual interfaces (SVIs), which are IP addresses assigned to VLANs that serve as default gateways for devices plugged into the switch, as well as physical routed ports (a simple interface configuration mode command—`no switchport`—can change a default Layer 2 switched port into a Layer 3 routed port), to interconnect these VLANs with each other and other VLANs and subnets. Routing on the switch will need to be enabled with the global configuration mode `ip routing` command.

Router

A *router* forwards packets based on their destination IP address. Routers work, therefore, at Layer 3 (Network layer) of the OSI model.

Think of routers as the highways that connect different cities and states together. Unlike switches, routers don't connect devices together. Routers connect networks together. Routers also connect to other routers that are connected to other routers that are connected to other routers, and so forth. This allows traffic from one network to be sent to any interconnected network via any number of routers and allows the return traffic to make its way back to the device that initiated the traffic on the originating network. Just like highways allow you to go from Rochester to Staten Island, routers allow your network traffic to reach devices on other networks that could be in the same building, another state, or another country or continent.

Classically, routers are dedicated boxes that contain at least two connections, although many routers contain more connections.

Most techs today get their first exposure to routers with the ubiquitous small office/home office (SOHO) wireless routers that enable PCs to connect to a cable modem, DSL modem, or, for fiber ISPs, an optical network terminal (ONT). The typical SOHO router, however, serves multiple functions, often combining a router, a switch, and other features like a firewall, a DHCP server, a DNS server, a NAT gateway, an access point, and much more into the box we simply call router.

Hub

A classic 10BASE-T network with a *hub* could only have one message on the wire at any time. When two computers sent traffic at the same time, the hub dutifully repeated both signals. The nodes recognized the collision and, following the rules of CSMA/CD, attempted to resend. Add in enough computers and the number of collisions increased, lowering the effective transmission speed for the whole network. A busy network became a slow network because all the computers shared the same collision domain.

Hubs are obsolete, and have been for decades. Furthermore, in 2011, the IEEE 802.3 Working Group ordered the networking world to not use hubs anymore. Collisions are obsolete today too, as full-duplex, which replaced half-duplex decades ago, disables CSMA/CD.

Access Point

An *access point (AP)*, also known as a wireless access point (WAP), is a device designed to interconnect wireless network nodes with wired networks. A basic access point operates like a hub and works at Layer 1. As mentioned in the "Router" section, the access point functionality is incorporated into many SOHO wireless routers.

Creating a basic service set (BSS) network with a single access point and multiple clients works in a relatively small area, but you can extend a Wi-Fi network in a couple of ways if you have difficult spaces—with lots of obstructions, for example—or a need to communicate beyond the range of the wireless network. Most commonly, you'd add one or more access points to create an extended service set (ESS). You can also install a wireless bridge to connect two or more wired networks.

Bridge

A wireless *bridge* is used to connect two wireless network segments together, two wired network segments together, or to join wireless and wired network segments together in the same way that wired switches do. You can also use wireless bridges to provide access to other networked devices, such as printers.

Wireless bridges come in two different flavors: point-to-point and point-to-multipoint. Point-to-point bridges can only communicate with a single other bridge and are used to connect two wireless network segments. Point-to-multipoint bridges can talk to more than one other bridge at a time and can connect multiple network segments.

 EXAM TIP Besides a hub, there was another networking device that predated the switch, the *bridge*. PCs were wired into hubs, and hubs were wired into bridges. Each side of the bridge was a collision domain. CSMA/CD and the MAC address table worked the same on bridges as described in relation to switches. The switch eliminated the hub/bridge combination, as PCs were wired into the single switch. Think of a switch as a multiport bridge. If you see a question about a bridge on the exam, you can be pretty sure that it's referring to a wireless bridge, because wired bridges have been obsolete for decades.

Wireless LAN Controller

An enterprise wireless infrastructure is almost certainly going to consist of a large number of access points. It's impossible to administer a large number of access points when you have to access each one individually. Imagine something as simple as changing the password on a WPA2-encrypted ESSID (extended service set identifier) on a wireless network with 50+ access points. The job would take forever!

The wireless industry long ago appreciated the complexity of enterprise-level wireless networks and created tools to make administration easier. The important point to any wireless network is that all of the access points, at least on a single SSID, connect to a single switch or group of switches. What if we offload the job of configuration to a device that's designed to handle a number of access points simultaneously? We call this type of switch a *wireless LAN controller* (WLC).

Any access point that you can access directly and configure singularly via its own interface is called a thick access point. An access point that can only be configured by a wireless controller is called a thin access point.

For years, these centralized configuration methods were proprietary for each wireless manufacturer, making for little or no cross-brand interoperability. This incompatibility in thin and thick clients was a common wireless issue back in the day. Today, most manufacturers use the Lightweight Access Point Protocol (LWAPP) to ensure interoperability. Given LWAPP's broad acceptance, most access points will accept commands from any wireless controller.

 NOTE   Managing large wireless networks without a WLC is easily doable, but the issue, bigger than passwords, is channel balancing, especially in the 2.4 GHz range. This ties in nicely with the discussion on software-defined networking in Objective 1.7. When you define access points managed in each SSID, the WLC pushes out a consistent configuration to every access point. Changing out access points means that you only need to tell the WLC to remove the old one and add the new one. Channel balancing and signal strength can be done continually and automatically, as well as advanced features like rogue access point detection and remediation. These are all features of most WLC software.

Load Balancer

Popular Web servers need to support hundreds of thousands to, in some cases, millions of requests per day. The Web servers need to send text, images, videos, and more to Web browser clients as quickly as possible. Multiple servers, therefore, are needed to provide the same service. How do the requests get spread across these servers acting in parallel? That's where a *load balancer* comes into play. The load balancer sends requests to the servers in an efficient way that maximizes speed and capability, making sure that no single server is overburdened. If a server goes down, the load balancer doesn't redirect traffic to it, and when a new server comes up, the load balancer adds it to the group.

Sometimes the load balancer decides on which server to send traffic to by a round robin algorithm, simply going through all servers one by one. Another criteria used by load balancers is to send traffic to the server with the least number of current connections to clients. More advanced methods include sending traffic to a server based on a hash of the client's IP address.

Load balancers can be either hardware based or software based.

Proxy Server

A *proxy server* sits in between clients and external servers, essentially pocketing the requests from the clients for server resources and making those requests itself. The client computers never touch the outside servers and thus stay protected from any unwanted activity. A proxy server usually does something to those requests as well. The biggest reasons for using a proxy server are that it can filter the requests based on content in the request or the return data and can perform caching.

Let's see how proxy servers work using HTTP, one of the oldest uses of proxy servers.

Since proxy serving works by redirecting client requests to a proxy server, you first must tell the Web client not to use the usual DNS resolution to determine the Web server and instead to use a proxy. Every Web client comes with a program that enables you to set the IP address of the proxy server.

Once the proxy server is configured, HTTP requests move from the client directly to the proxy server. Built into every HTTP request is the URL of the target Web server, so the Web proxy knows where to get the requested data once it gets the request. In the simplest format, the proxy server simply forwards the requests using its own IP address and then forwards the returning packets to the client.

This simple version of using a proxy server prevents the Web server from knowing where the client is located—a handy trick for those who wish to keep people from knowing where they are coming from, assuming you can find a public proxy server that accepts your HTTP requests (there are plenty!). There are many other good reasons to use a proxy server. One big benefit is caching. A proxy server keeps a copy of the served resource, giving clients a much faster response.

A forward proxy server acts on behalf of clients, getting information from various sources and handing that info to the clients. The sources (servers) don't know about the clients, only the proxy server.

If a proxy server caches a Web page, how does it know if the cache accurately reflects the real page? What if the real Web page was updated? In this case, a good proxy server uses querying tools to check the real Web page to update the cache.

A reverse proxy server, in contrast, acts on behalf of its servers. Clients contact the reverse proxy server, which gathers information from its associated server(s) and hands that information to the clients. The clients don't know about the servers behind the scenes. The reverse proxy server is the only machine with which they interact.

A proxy server might inspect the contents of the resource, looking for inappropriate content, malware, or just about anything else the creators of the proxy might desire it to identify.

HTTP proxy servers are the most common type of proxy server, but any TCP application can take advantage of proxy servers. Numerous proxy serving programs are available.

Cable Modem

A modem (modulator-demodulator) is a device that converts both digital bit streams into analog signals (modulation) and incoming analog signals back into digital signals (demodulation). The traditional modem connects telephone lines to computers.

A *cable modem* is a device that enables customers to connect to their cable ISP using Data Over Cable Service Interface Specification (DOCSIS).

DSL Modem

A *DSL modem* is a device that enables customers to connect to their DSL (digital subscriber line) ISP using Point-to-Point Protocol over Ethernet (PPPoE).

Repeater

Various manufacturers market a *repeater* (also known as a wireless range extender and Wi-Fi extender) that picks up the Wi-Fi signal and repeats it into a wider space.

 ADDITIONAL RESOURCES   Check out the article "How to Extend Wi-Fi to Your Outdoor Space," from marthastewart.com, in which I explain the concept: https://www.marthastewart.com/7989513/how-extend-wifi-range-outside.

 NOTE   The original repeater, in the world of networking, was replaced by a hub, which was a multiport repeater.

Voice Gateway

A *voice gateway*, also known as a Voice over IP (VoIP) endpoint, represents a location at which a call terminates, which could be an IP phone, an application, or even a server.

Media Converter

A variety of Ethernet deployment standards exist (for example, 100BASE-T, 1000BASE-T, 1000BASE-LX, 1000BASE-SX, 10GBASE-T), each of which can use different cabling and devices. The common denominator is that they all use Ethernet frames at Layer 2. As a result, interconnecting flavors of Ethernet is common with a *media converter* (Figure 2.1-2).

Cross-Reference

Ethernet standards were covered in Objective 1.3.

Most media converters are plain-looking boxes with a port or dongle on either side. They come in all flavors:

- Single-mode fiber (SMF) to UTP/STP
- Multimode fiber (MMF) to UTP/STP
- Fiber to coaxial
- SMF to MMF

FIGURE 2.1-2 Typical copper-to-fiber Ethernet media converter (photo courtesy of TRENDnet)

Firewall

A *firewall* manifests either as a dedicated physical hardware device or as software running on a host. Firewalls filter traffic based on rules. Filtering, as far as firewalls are concerned, means that certain packets are not let into a network. It also means that packets on the way out of a network can be blocked from leaving. Certain packets will not be filtered. So, we can say that firewalls permit or deny traffic both inbound and outbound.

Firewalls can filter by source IP addresses, destination IP addresses, protocols, ports, and other criteria. Firewalls sit on the border between the trusted inside and the untrusted outside. One side of the firewall is under the administrator's control. The other side is connected to the big bad unknown. Firewalls help prevent unauthorized access to or from a system or a network. This includes malware that might attack your computer, sent by cybercrminals or downloaded unknowingly by users.

Network activity, in both directions, is logged by the firewall for a potential forensic investigation. Malware is restricted inbound and outbound—inbound to protect the organization's resources, outbound so the organization can't be accused of originating an attack in the event of a worm propagating, as well as to prevent installed malware from communicating back to an attacker and opening up a reverse shell.

Firewalls (like proxy servers) are also a way to restrict employees from visiting certain Web sites like Facebook and YouTube, and at the same time prevent them from downloading malware.

Hardware-based firewalls are also referred to as network-based firewalls. One side is the network that the firewall is trying to protect, and the other is the untrusted outside. This type of firewall can be strategically placed between the corporate edge router, which connects to the ISP, and the internal network. Network-based firewalls can also be placed on one side of an internal corporate router that doesn't connect to the ISP. In that case, the untrusted outside would be not only the untrusted Internet, but also certain internal networks as well.

That still leaves a network vulnerable to malicious traffic originating from that very network. The use of software-based firewalls, also known as host-based firewalls, is one way to deal with malicious traffic originating on that very network. They only protect a single system. They can mitigate the risk of an attack spreading from one machine to another. Operating systems have software-based firewalls built in.

In this case the trusted inside would just be the local machine, and the untrusted outside would not only be the Internet, and other networks, but all devices on the current network as well. The border of untrusted to trusted is essentially the device's NIC. Anything on the other side of the NIC, as far as a host-based firewall is concerned, is the untrusted outside.

Firewalls can use different techniques to filter traffic, regardless if they are hardware network-based firewalls or software host-based firewalls. Packet filtering looks at each packet that enters or leaves a network. The firewall will permit or deny the packet based on user-defined rules, like source IP address, destination IP address, protocol, and port.

 EXAM TIP Filter means to block. When firewalls filter certain packets, they block them. Packets that the firewalls don't filter are let into a network or let out of a network.

Stateless vs. Stateful

Packet filtering can be further broken down into two subcategories. The first is stateless packet filtering, which is sessionless. Each packet is treated by itself as an isolated piece of communication. This requires less memory and time. There is low overhead and high throughput. However, this type of firewall technique cannot make complex decisions based on a communication stage, just on access control lists referencing IP addresses, protocols, and ports. If an attacker spoofs an IP address, a stateless packet filter can be fooled.

Stateful packet filtering, on the other hand, uses sessions, can understand stages of a TCP connection, and can be aware of a cybercriminal who tries to spoof an IP address. For TCP-based traffic, after a connection has been established, packets can flow between the hosts without further checking.

ALG

An application layer gateway (ALG) applies security mechanisms based on a certain application, like HTTP, TLS, FTP, DNS, and VoIP. So instead of just looking at IP addresses, protocols, and ports, ALGs look deeper into the protocols to see if they're being used properly. ALGs understand how specific protocols should work and look at Layer 7, and can filter offensive or disallowed commands in the data stream. They are stateful.

DPI Deep Packet Inspection (DPI) is done by an ALG to examine, in great detail, the contents of the data being sent. Some examples include making sure that data is sent in the right format and that no malware is attached. Other uses include snooping and censoring. In fact, some ISPs have been known to use DPI to scan the contents of a packet and reroute or drop packets meeting certain criteria. ISPs in certain countries use DPI to look for keywords and Web addresses for censorship purposes. High-bandwidth communications, like those involving Zoom or YouTube, can be prioritized over regular HTTP traffic.

DCI DPI has actually evolved into Deep Content Inspection (DCI), which examines an entire file or e-mail attachment, looking for new generations of malware, spam, data exfiltration, keywords, and other content. In other words, DPI just looks into the actual protocols and their behavior, instead of relying on just headers from the lower layers. That's great, but DCI puts together parts of actual objects that are transmitted in parts of different packets, like PDFs and images. DCI even decodes and decompresses files. This is a much greater form of intelligence than partial data at Layer 7 that DPI deals with.

UTM Appliance vs. NGFW/Layer 7 Firewall

There's been tons of confusion and contradiction among industry experts relating to the distinction, if any, between a unified threat management (UTM) appliance and a next-generation firewall (NGFW)/Layer 7 firewall. Some say there's not a single difference between the two, calling them the same technologies with the same capabilities marketed and promoted differently by different companies and industries (mid-market versus enterprise/carrier grade). Others say NGFWs are firewalls with IPS and application intelligence, whereas UTM appliances have those features plus more, including e-mail security, URL filtering, wireless security, Web application firewalls, and VPNs. This opinion thinks of NGFWs as simply components of UTMs.

Intrusion Prevention System(IPS)/Intrusion Detection System (IDS) Device

An *intrusion prevention system (IPS)/intrusion detection system (IDS) device* complements firewalls.

IDSs and IPSs are important for two reasons related to firewalls. First, how can you protect each network from malicious traffic that originates inside of those networks themselves? Firewalls sit on the border between the trusted inside network and the untrusted outside.

The malicious traffic that originates on the inside can't be filtered by a firewall that's at the edge. It's already in! Furthermore, what happens to traffic that evades the firewalls?

The IPS is inline (see Figure 2.1-3), so original traffic must pass through the IPS. An IPS adds some latency, since traffic is processed live.

An IDS is out-of-band (see Figure 2.1-3) and simply gets copies of network traffic. It can be as simple as a system getting copies of traffic to inspect, through a switch configured to send all traffic to the IDS. Since the IDS is out-of-band, it doesn't add latency.

If the IDS sensor goes down (possibly after a targeted attack on the IDS itself), traffic still flows. If an IPS is targeted, attacked, and brought down, traffic stops right there. An IDS can alert an administrator, and even automatically instruct a firewall to block traffic, based on what it observes. An IPS can do the same, but can stop traffic dead in its tracks as well. The IPS will still report back to a firewall so that traffic can be filtered a lot earlier than where the IPS is located.

The obvious question is, if an IPS can do what an IDS can do, but better, why does an IDS still exist today? Well, an IDS can be like a window into your network traffic. It sits, listens, and collects data that can be used for forensics and analysis. Think of an IPS as a control device, and an IDS as a visibility device. Packets collected by the IDS can be subsequently analyzed to gain insight into past, or even possible future, violations when lots of events are linked together.

Both IDSs and IPSs are vulnerable to false positives, which is when normal traffic is flagged as malicious, and false negatives, which is when malicious traffic is ignored as normal.

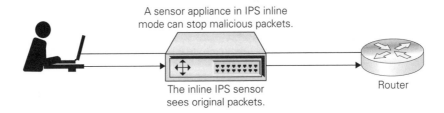

A sensor appliance in IPS inline mode can stop malicious packets.

The inline IPS sensor sees original packets.

Router

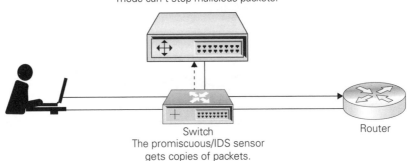

A sensor appliance in promiscuous/IDS mode can't stop malicious packets.

Switch
The promiscuous/IDS sensor gets copies of packets.

Router

FIGURE 2.1-3 IPS vs. IDS

IDSs and IPSs need to be constantly tuned to minimize both false positives, which will send out lots of incorrect alerts, and false negatives, which won't send out alerts when something malicious is happening.

Since IDSs are out-of-band, a false positive won't stop legitimate traffic in its tracks, which is another reason why IDSs are used together with IPSs to form a great defense-in-depth setup.

IDSs and IPSs, like firewalls, can be either host based or network based. Thus far, we've been talking only about network-based IDSs (NIDSs) and network-based IPSs (NIPSs).

A host-based IDS (HIDS) or IPS (HIPS) resides on a particular computer or server and monitors activity on just the host system. It benchmarks and monitors the access, creation, modification, and deletion of key system files, and also monitors system configuration databases, like the Windows registry. Unlike a NIDS or NIPS, a HIDS or HIPS can deal with encrypted traffic that will have been decrypted on the host for processing. It can also detect attacks that may elude a NIDS or NIPS. As you can imagine, this does slow a system down. The difference between a HIDS and a HIPS is that a HIDS doesn't stop network traffic in its tracks, whereas a HIPS does.

Just like a NIDS or NIPS can catch malicious traffic that either evaded the network-based firewall or originated from within the network, a HIDS or HIPS can catch malicious traffic that either evaded the host-based firewall or originated from the inside of the machine.

Signature-based IDSs and IPSs act just like antivirus software, trying to detect attacks by looking for patterns, for example, with certain instructions on a host machine or usage of protocols or content. The obvious problem is that unknown patterns can't be detected and adversaries are constantly changing their code to avoid simple signature detection. Furthermore, the signature database needs to be updated constantly.

Anomaly-based IDSs compare an established baseline to something that might be malicious. However, false positives and false negatives are big issues that need to be dealt with through monitoring and tweaking. The latest anomaly-based IDSs and IPSs can detect malicious insiders, as well as machines or accounts that have been compromised from outsiders.

 EXAM TIP Make sure you understand the differences between an IDS and IPS for the exam.

VPN Headend

A *VPN headend* (also known as a VPN concentrator) can be thought of as a router with special capabilities that can connect endpoints from multiple VPN tunnels simultaneously (thousands, in some cases) and manage those connections. In addition, the VPN concentrator can authenticate users, assign IP addresses, and encrypt and decrypt data.

Networked Devices

As opposed to networking devices, which are the middlemen, dealing with packets between the source and destination endpoints, *networked devices* are those endpoints themselves. As you might imagine, there are many varied types of networked devices.

Voice over Internet Protocol (VoIP) Phone

Many years ago, TCP/IP-based communications began to replace the traditional PBX-style phone systems in most organizations. This switch enabled companies to minimize wire installation and enabled developers to get more creative with the gear. Technologies such as Voice over Internet Protocol (VoIP) made it possible to communicate by voice right over an IP network, even one as big as the Internet. Today, TCP/IP communications encompass a range of technologies, including voice, video, and messaging. On the cutting edge (led by Cisco) is the field of unified communication (UC).

Early VoIP systems usually required multiple cables running to each drop to accommodate the various services offered. These drops would often even go to their own separate switches, and from there into separate VoIP gateways that would interface with old-school PBX systems or directly into the telephone network if the latter used VoIP PBX. These are the typical purposes and use case scenarios for computer telephony integration (CTI).

A typical UC network consists of three core components: UC devices, UC servers, and UC gateways.

A UC device is what we used to call the *Voice over Internet Protocol (VoIP) phone*. In a well-developed UC environment, the UC device handles voice, video, and more.

A UC server is typically a dedicated box that supports any UC-provided service. In small organizations this might be a single box, but in larger organizations there will be many UC servers. UC servers connect directly to every UC device on the LAN. It's not uncommon to see all the UC servers (as well as the rest of the UC devices) on a separate VLAN.

A UC gateway is an edge device, sometime dedicated but often nothing more than a few extra services added to an existing edge router. That router interfaces with remote UC gateways as well as with PSTN systems and services.

Printer

Traditional network printing, where employees can use a *printer* over a network connection, is still common in many offices and large corporations.

Taking it to the next level, a smart printer connects directly to the Internet, not so much to control efficient communication but to enable it. You can print from a laptop or smartphone directly. You can scan a document, save it as a PDF, and immediately upload it to an Internet location, from the print device.

Physical Access Control Devices

Physical access control devices, such as smart garage door openers that enable you to open or close the garage door from an app, are a great form of convenience. Normally you'd use the app in a local setting, but you can even monitor, open, and close the door for a delivery that you wouldn't want left on the front porch. A smart garage door opener is an example of a physical access control device installed at a house.

NOTE   More commonly, you'll see security gates, door locks, turnstiles, and such described as examples of physical access control devices. An authorized person swipes a card on a network device that validates the card and corresponding physical access rights against a security control server, which maintains the access data.

Cameras

In the context of networked devices, *cameras* are commonly used for monitoring and are considered IoT devices (covered in an upcoming section). Hardening IoT devices decreases the danger of loss or downtime on the devices and increases the protection of personal information and company data. Generally, hardening means to keep the devices current (software and firmware), use physical security precautions, and apply internal security options.

Consider a scenario in which an organization uses many 802.11 PTZ (pan/tilt/zoom) *cameras* to monitor secure areas throughout three locations. These cameras are on the one and only SSID in each location. Each SSID uses WPA2-PSK encryption. Due to location, these cameras must use 802.11 for communication. All cameras must be accessible not only in each location but also in headquarters. Your job as a consultant is to provide a list of actions the organization should take to harden these cameras. Here's a list of actions you should consider:

- Place all cameras in their own SSID.
- Put all the camera feeds on their own VLAN.
- Use a very long pre-shared key (PSK).
- Set up routine queries for camera firmware updates from the manufacturer.
- Use username ACLs to determine who may access the cameras.

NOTE   In high-security environments, many cameras will be wired, and isolated to a separate VLAN or network. Both IoT and closed-circuit TV (CCTV) can be networked cameras.

Heating, Ventilation, and Air Conditioning (HVAC) Sensors

Racks with servers, switches, routers, and such go into closets or server rooms and they dump heat. The environment within this space must be monitored and controlled for both temperature and humidity. Network components work better when cool rather than hot.

The placement of a rack should optimize the airflow in a server area. All racks should be placed so that components draw air in from a shared cool row and then exhaust the hot air into a hot row.

Heating, ventilation, and air conditioning (HVAC) sensors should be optimized to recirculate and purify the hot air into cool air in a continuous flow. What's the proper temperature and humidity level? The ideal for the room, regardless of size, is an average temperature of 68 degrees Fahrenheit and ~50% humidity.

These sensors make a big difference in server rooms and datacenters, where they are connected to alarm systems that notify administrators about issues. Some sensors have automation around server shutdowns, so if the temperature climbs above a certain level, secondary servers or services automatically shut down. In most cases, when cooling fails, shutting things down is better than risking the loss of the server.

Internet of Things (IoT)

The term *Internet of Things (IoT)* describes the huge variety of devices you can access and control via the Internet (discounting personal computers, routers, and servers) and devices that communicate directly with other devices. The term applies to lights you can turn on or off by using an app on your smartphone, air conditioning systems that you can monitor and control from a PC, devices that can query the Internet for information, and many other types of devices.

 ADDITIONAL RESOURCES   Listen to me talk on talk radio about Amazon Sidewalk's vulnerabilities at https://www.youtube.com/weissman52 in the Radio Cybersecurity Expert Playlist (video from 6/2/21, 13:09 duration). Amazon Sidewalk is a shared network designed to help devices work better. Read more about it at https://www.amazon.com/Amazon-Sidewalk/b?ie=UTF8&node=21328123011

IoT technologies enable you to integrate a surprising variety of devices into a home automation system that you can control. They're all called "smart" to distinguish them from their "dumb" unconnectable siblings.

Refrigerator

You can access a smart *refrigerator* on your drive home from the office to check levels of milk or bread from a smartphone app, which will show you pictures or a live view from a camera in the fridge itself. Alternatively, items can be placed on sensors, like those at a self-checkout, to detect levels of supply.

Smart Speakers

Many smart systems, like the Amazon Echo products, can connect to the music library of your choice, and you can sprinkle *smart speakers* throughout your home to give you a seamless soundtrack for your life. Integrated home audio systems used to require extensive wiring and power considerations for speakers, plus a central control area. Smart speakers handle voice commands and interconnect wirelessly.

Many IoT devices can connect directly to Internet resources to answer questions as well. By default, Amazon devices respond to the name "Alexa," similarly to how Google devices respond to "OK Google" and Apple devices to "Hey, Siri!"

 EXAM TIP The CompTIA Network+ objectives focus a lot on enterprise-level networking. The big exception to that is in IoT. Objective 2.1 lists a handful of personal IoT devices, like smart speakers. Expect a question or two on consumer-level IoT.

Smart Thermostats

Smart thermostats enable you to vary the temperature in your home. With app access, you can quickly and easily turn up the heat so that your abode is nice and cozy when you arrive.

Smart Doorbells

IoT makes setting up and monitoring a robust home security system very simple with *smart doorbells*. The Ring system from Amazon, for example, can be configured with any number of wireless cameras with motion sensors to automatically record movement—and can tell the difference between a squirrel and a person! You can add the Ring smart doorbell, which comes with a bell button, naturally, and a camera, microphone, and speaker. This enables you to "answer the door" and interact with visitors without being there in person.

Industrial Control Systems/Supervisory Control and Data Acquisition (SCADA)

Pretty much any industry that makes things, changes things, or moves things is filled with equipment to do the jobs that have to be done. From making mousetraps to ice cream, any given industrial plant, power grid, or pipeline is filled with stuff that needs to be monitored and stuff that needs to be controlled.

Here are some examples of things to monitor:

- Temperature
- Power levels
- Fill quantity
- Illumination
- Mass

And these are some examples of the things to control:

- Heaters
- Voltage
- Pumps
- Retractable roofs
- Valves

For a company, it's all about the robots that control the factory, the machines that help automate packing and shipping, and the air-conditioning controls for both buildings.

In the early days of automation, you might have a single person monitoring a machine that produced something. When the temperature hit a certain point, for example, that person—the operator—might open a valve or turn a knob to make changes and keep the machine functioning properly. As machines became more complex, the role of the operator likewise changed. The operator needed to monitor more functions and, sometimes, more machines. Eventually, computers were brought in to help manage the machines. The overall system that monitors and controls machines today is called an industrial control system (ICS).

The ICS isn't a new concept. *Industrial control systems* have been around for over 100 years using technology such as telescopes and horns to monitor and using mechanisms and pneumatics to control from a distance. But ICSs really started to take off when computers combined with digital monitors and controls. Over the last few years many ICSs have taken on more and more personal-computer aspects such as Windows- or Linux-based operating systems, Intel-style processors, and specialized PCs. Today, ICS is moving from stand-alone networks to interconnect with the Internet, bringing up serious issues for security. Competent network techs know the basic ICS variations and the components that make up those systems.

An ICS has three basic components: input/output (I/O) functions on the machine, a controller, and the interface for the operator. Input and output work through sensors and actuators. Sensors monitor things like temperature, for example, and the actuator makes changes that modify that temperature. The controller, some sort of computer, knows enough to manage the process, such as "keep the temperature between 50 and 55 degrees Fahrenheit." The operator watches some kind of monitor—the interface—and intervenes if necessary.

What if you have multiple machines that accomplish a big task, like in a factory that produces some finished product? For example, imagine a company that produces products in stages, with the machine at each stage needing monitoring and control. In the early days of computers, when computers were really expensive, the controller was a single computer. All the sensors from each of the machines had to provide feedback to that single controller. The controller would compute and then send signals to the various actuators to change things, managing the process.

As computing power increased and costs decreased, it made much more sense to put smaller controllers directly on each machine, to distribute the computing load. This is a distributed control system (DCS). In a modern DCS, each of the local controllers connects (eventually) to a centralized controller—called the ICS server—where global changes can be managed.

A *supervisory control and data acquisition (SCADA)* system is a subset of ICS. Generally, a SCADA system has the same basic components as a DCS, but differs in two very important ways. First, a SCADA system is designed for large-scale, distributed processes such as power grids, pipelines, and railroads. Second, due to the distance involved, a SCADA system must function with the idea that remote devices may or may not have ongoing communication with the central control.

In general, a SCADA system is going to be a DCS using servers, a human-machine interface (HMI), sensors, and actuators. The big difference is the replacement of controllers with devices called remote terminal units (RTUs). RTUs provide the same function as a controller but have two major differences. First, an RTU is designed to have some amount of autonomy in case it loses connection with the central control. Second, an RTU is designed to take advantage of some form of long-distance communication such as telephony, fiber optic, or cellular WANs.

All forms of ICS are by definition closed networks. A closed network is any network that strictly controls who and what may connect to it. However, there are two places where we begin to see connectivity. In many SCADA systems, it is very convenient to use public wireless networks to connect RTUs, and, in some cases, SCADA servers are connected to the Internet to provide intranet access. The biggest single line of defense for these two scenarios are virtual private network (VPN) connections. It's impossible to find any form of SCADA/ICS that doesn't use a VPN in the cases where it must be open to the public Internet.

REVIEW

Objective 2.1: Compare and contrast various devices, their features, and their appropriate placement on the network

- Obsolete devices, used by networks in the very distant past, include hubs and repeaters.

- Switches are Layer 2 devices that forward frames based on their destination MAC address, but also learn where hosts are, by mapping the source MAC address in a frame to the interface on which it was heard.

- A Layer 3 capable switch (also known as a multilayer switch) has the capability to create SVIs and physical routed ports, as well as the capability to route just like a traditional router.

- Routers are Layer 3 devices that forward packets based on their destination IP address.

- An access point (also known as a wireless access point, or WAP) is a device designed to interconnect wireless network nodes with wired networks.

- Wireless bridges are used to connect two wireless network segments together, two wired network segments together, or to join wireless and wired network segments together in the same way that wired switches do.

- Wireless LAN controllers are used to configure and control multiple WAPs simultaneously.
- Wireless repeaters pick up the Wi-Fi signal and repeat it into a wider space.
- Load balancers send requests to the servers in an efficient way that maximizes speed and capability, making sure that no single server is overburdened.
- A proxy server sits in between clients and external servers, essentially pocketing the requests from the clients for server resources and making those requests itself.
- DSL and cable modems connect customers to their ISP, and can use multiple protocols, depending on the ISP type.
- A voice gateway connects the VoIP PBX to the PSTN.
- A media converter interconnects different cabling standards.
- Firewalls are physical hardware devices or software that filter traffic based on rules.
- IDSs and IPSs detect malicious packets that were missed by the firewall, or malicious packets that originated from inside the network. IDSs are out-of-band and get copies of frames, while IPSs are inline and can stop traffic dead in its tracks. Both IDSs and IPSs can notify a firewall about adding rules to block certain packets.
- A VPN headend can be thought of as a router with special capabilities that can connect endpoints from multiple VPN tunnels simultaneously (thousands, in some cases) and manage those connections.
- A VoIP endpoint represents a location at which a call terminates, which could be a Voice over Internet Protocol (VoIP) phone, an application, and even a server.
- Printers, physical access control devices, and cameras are devices that can be networked.
- Heating, ventilation, and air conditioning (HVAC) sensors should be optimized to recirculate and purify the hot air into cool air in a continuous flow.
- Internet of Things (IoT) devices include refrigerators, smart speakers, smart thermostats, and smart doorbells.
- The overall system that monitors and controls machines today is called an industrial control system (ICS).
- A supervisory control and data acquisition (SCADA) system is a subset of ICS.

2.1 QUESTIONS

1. What do routers use to forward packets?
   A. Source IP address
   B. Destination IP address
   C. Source MAC address
   D. Destination MAC address

2. What do switches use to learn where hosts are?

    A. Source IP address

    B. Destination IP address

    C. Source MAC address

    D. Destination MAC address

3. What's the difference between ICS and SCADA?

    A. SCADA is a subset of ICS.

    B. ICS is a subset of SCADA.

    C. There is no difference between the two.

    D. ICS is designed for large-scale, distributed processes like power grids.

2.1 ANSWERS

1. **B** Routers match the destination IP address to a network in their routing table.

2. **C** This is the reason the table that maps MAC addresses to ports on a switch is called the source address table.

3. **A** An ICS is the overall system that monitors and controls machines and a SCADA system is a subset of ICS.

Objective 2.2   Compare and contrast routing technologies and bandwidth management concepts

Routing enables us to interconnect individual LANs into WANs. Routers, the magic boxes that act as the interconnection points, inspect incoming packets and forward them toward their eventual LAN destination. It's like one highway leading to others.

Bandwidth management, through traffic shaping and quality of service (QoS), allows certain packets to be prioritized over others, just like you'd pull over your car to let a first responder get through.

Routing

Routing begins as packets come into the router for handling. The router immediately strips off all of the Layer 2 information and drops the resulting IP packet into a queue. The router doesn't care where the packet originated. Everything is dropped into the same queue based on the time it arrived.

Routing Table Entry List

Destination LAN IP	Subnet Mask	Gateway	Interface
10.12.14.0	255.255.255.0	0.0.0.0	LAN
76.30.4.0	255.255.254.0	0.0.0.0	WAN
0.0.0.0	0.0.0.0	76.30.4.1	WAN

FIGURE 2.2-1   Routing table from a SOHO router

The router inspects each packet's destination IP address and then sends the IP packet out the correct port. To perform this inspection, every router comes with a routing table that tells the router exactly where to send the packets. This table is the key to understanding and controlling the process of forwarding packets to their proper destination. Figure 2.2-1 shows a very simple routing table for a typical SOHO router. Each row in this routing table defines a single route. Each column identifies one of two specific criteria. Some columns define which packets are for the route and other columns define which port to send them out. We'll break these down shortly.

The router in this example has only two ports internally: one port that connects to a service provider, labeled as WAN in the Interface column of the table, and another port that connects to the router's built-in switch, labeled LAN in the table. Due to the small number of ports, this little router table has only four routes. Wait a minute: four routes and only two ports? No worries, there is *not* a one-to-one correlation of routes to ports, as you will soon see. Let's inspect this routing table.

Reading Figure 2.2-1 from left to right shows the following:

- **Destination LAN IP**   A defined network ID. Every network ID directly connected to one of the router's ports is always listed here.
- **Subnet Mask**   Identifies which bits are network bits and which bits are host bits, described in Objective 1.4.

The router uses the combination of the destination LAN IP and subnet mask to see if a packet matches that route. For example, if you had a packet with the destination 10.12.14.26 coming into the router, the router would check the network ID and subnet mask. It would quickly determine that the packet matches the first route shown in Figure 2.2-1.

The other two columns in the routing table tell the router what to do with the packet:

- **Gateway**   The IP address for the *next hop* router; in other words, where the packet should go. If the outgoing packet is for a network ID that's not directly connected to the router, the Gateway column tells the router the IP address of a router to which to send this packet. That router then handles the packet, and your router is done. Well-configured routers ensure a packet will get to where it needs to go. If the network ID is directly connected to the router, then you don't need a gateway for that packet. If there is no gateway needed, most routing tables put either 0.0.0.0 or *On-link* in this column.

- **Interface**   Tells the router which of its ports to use. On this router, it uses the terms "LAN" and "WAN." Other routing tables use the port's IP address or some other description. Some routers, for example, use Gig0/0 (Gig is short for Gigabit Ethernet) or Gig0/1, and so on.

There's an assumption that the router will start at the top of the table and march down until it finds the correct route. That's not accurate. The router compares the destination IP address on a packet to every route listed in the routing table and only then sends the packet out. If a packet works for more than one route, the router will use the better route (we'll discuss this more in a moment).

The most important trick to reading a routing table is to remember that a zero (0) means "anything." For example, in Figure 2.2-1, the first route's destination LAN IP is 10.12.14.0. You can compare that to the subnet mask (255.255.255.0) to confirm that this is a /24 network. This tells you that any value (between 1 and 254) is acceptable for the last value in the 10.12.14.0/24 network.

A properly configured router must have a route for any packet it might encounter. Routing tables tell you a lot about the network connections. From just this single routing table, for example, the diagram in Figure 2.2-2 can be drawn.

Notice the last route. How can you tell that the 76.30.4.1 port connects to another network? The third line of the routing table shows the default route for this router. The way to read it is: for packets with any destination address (0.0.0.0), with any subnet mask (0.0.0.0), forward them to 76.30.4.1, using the WAN interface, as shown in Table 2.2-1.

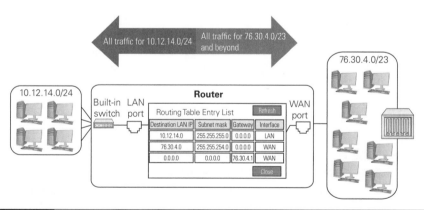

FIGURE 2.2-2   The network based on the routing table in Figure 2.2-1

TABLE 2.2-1   Default route

Destination LAN IP	Subnet Mask	Gateway	Interface
0.0.0.0	0.0.0.0	76.30.4.1	WAN

| TABLE 2.2-2 | LAN Route |

Destination LAN IP	Subnet Mask	Gateway	Interface
10.12.14.0	255.255.255.0	0.0.0.0	LAN

| TABLE 2.2-3 | LAN Route |

Destination LAN IP	Subnet Mask	Gateway	Interface
76.30.4.0	255.255.254.0	0.0.0.0	WAN

The default route is very important because this tells the router exactly what to do with every incoming packet *unless* another line in the routing table gives another route. Interpret the other two lines of the routing table in Figure 2.2-2 in the same fashion.

First, for any packets destined for the 10.12.14.0/24 network, don't use a gateway, just ARP on the LAN interface to get the MAC address (if it's not already in the router's ARP cache), and send it directly to the recipient, as shown in Table 2.2-2.

Next, for any packets destined for the 76.30.4.0/23 network, don't use a gateway, just ARP on the WAN interface to get the MAC address (if it's not already in the router's ARP cache) and send it directly to the recipient, as shown in Table 2.2-3.

Dynamic Routing

Based on what you've read up to this point, it would seem that routes in your routing tables come from two sources: either they are manually entered or they are detected at setup by the router. In either case, a route seems to be a static beast, just sitting there and never changing. And based on what you've seen so far, that is absolutely true. Routers have static routes, but routers also have the capability to update their routes dynamically with *dynamic routing* protocols (both IPv4 and IPv6).

What if your routers look like Figure 2.2-3?

Do you really want to try to set up all these routes statically? What happens when something changes? Can you imagine the administrative nightmare? Why not just give routers the brainpower to talk to each other so they know what's happening not only to the other directly connected routers but also to routers two or more routers/hops away? A hop is defined as a network/router that a packet passes through.

Protocols [Routing Internet Protocol (RIP), Open Shortest Path First (OSPF), Enhanced Interior Gateway Routing Protocol (EIGRP), Border Gateway Protocol (BGP)]

As the section title indicates, there are a handful of different routing protocols, and while their main goal is the same—to help routers advertise networks they know to other routers and learn about networks they didn't know about from other routers—they accomplish the goal in different ways.

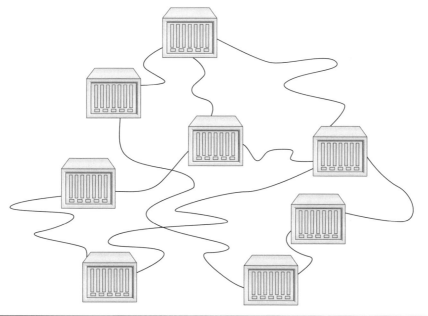

FIGURE 2.2-3   Lots of routers

EXAM TIP   CompTIA incorrectly identifies RIP as Routing *Internet* Protocol, instead of the correct Routing *Information* Protocol.

RIPv1   The granddaddy of all routing protocols is *Routing Information Protocol (RIP)*. The first version of RIP—called *RIPv1*—dates from the 1980s, although its predecessors go back all the way to the beginnings of the Internet in the 1960s.

RIP's metric, a value that helps a routing protocol determine the best path to a destination network, is hop count, which is simply the number of routers a packet has to pass through to get to a destination network. However, sometimes a path to a destination network with more hops over a path with fewer hops is actually preferred (which is how OSPF and EIGRP operate, coming up).

RIPv1 sent out an update every 30 seconds. This also turned into a big problem, because every router on the network would send its routing table at the same time, causing huge network overloads.

As if these issues weren't bad enough, RIPv1 didn't know how to use the concept of a *variable-length subnet masking (VLSM)*, where networks connected through the router use different subnet masks. Plus, RIPv1 routers had no authentication, leaving them open to cybercriminals sending false routing table information. RIP needed an update.

RIPv2   *RIPv2*, adopted in 1994 and still the current version, works the same way as RIPv1, but fixes many of the problems. RIPv2 supports VLSM, includes built-in authentication, swaps broadcasting for multicasting, and increases the time between updates from 30 seconds to 90 seconds.

Most routers still support RIPv2, but RIP's many problems, especially the time to convergence for large WANs, make it obsolete for all but small, private WANs that consist of a few routers. That doesn't mean RIP actually rests in peace! RIP is both easy to use and simple for manufacturers to implement in their routers, so most routers, even home routers, have the ability to use RIP.

OSPF   *Open Shortest Path First (OSPF)* is the most commonly used interior gateway protocol (IGP), a routing protocol used between routers of the same autonomous system to communicate and exchange routing information, in the world. OSPF converges dramatically faster and is much more efficient than RIP. Odds are good that if you are using dynamic routing protocols, you're using OSPF.

OSPF offers a number of improvements over RIP. When you first launch OSPF-capable routers, they send out Hello packets, looking for other OSPF routers. After two adjacent routers form a neighborship through the Hello packets, they exchange information about routers and networks through link state advertisement (LSA) packets. LSAs are sourced by each router and are flooded from router to router through each OSPF area.

Once all the routers communicate, they individually decide their own optimal routes, and convergence happens almost immediately. If a route goes down, OSPF routers quickly recompute a new route with stored LSAs.

OSPF's metric is *cost*, which is a function of bandwidth. All possible ways to get to a destination network are computed based on cost, which is proportional to bandwidth, which is in turn proportional to the interface type (Gigabit Ethernet, 10-Gigabit Ethernet, and so on). The routers choose the lowest total cost route to a destination network.

In other words, a packet could go through more routers (hops) to get to a destination when OSPF is used instead of RIP. However, more hops doesn't necessarily mean slower. If a packet goes through three hops where the routers are connected by fiber, for example, as opposed to a slow 56-Kbps link, the packet would get to its destination quicker. We make these decisions everyday as humans, too. Revisiting the street traffic analogy introduced in Objective 2.1, would you rather get to your destination quicker by driving more miles on the highway or get there slower by driving fewer miles on local streets where the speed limits are much lower and you have to contend with traffic lights and stop signs?

OSPF uses areas, administrative groupings of interconnected routers, to help control how routers reroute traffic (with the distribution of LSAs) if a link drops or comes up. All OSPF networks use areas, even if there is only one area. When you interconnect multiple areas, the central area—called the backbone area—gets assigned the Area ID of 0, which can also be expressed as 0.0.0.0. Note that a single area also gets Area ID 0. All traffic between areas has to go through the backbone.

OSPF also supports authentication, and the shortest-path-first method, by definition, prevents loops. Why would anyone use anything else?

EXAM TIP   OSPF corrects link failures and creates convergence almost immediately, making it the routing protocol of choice in most large enterprise networks. OSPF Version 2 is used for IPv4 networks, and OSPF Version 3 includes updates to support IPv6.

EIGRP   Cisco's proprietary *Enhanced Interior Gateway Routing Protocol (EIGRP)* was converted to an open standard in 2013. Back in the days when RIP was dominant, there was a huge outcry for an improved RIP, but OSPF wasn't yet out. Cisco, being the dominant router company in the world (a crown it still wears to this day, although not as dominantly anymore), came out with Interior Gateway Routing Protocol (IGRP), which was quickly replaced with EIGRP.

EIGRP uses bandwidth and delay as default metrics, but can also be configured to use other metrics (which are actually discouraged by Cisco) including load, reliability, and hop count. MTU (maximum transmission unit) was never used as part of the EIGRP metric calculation, but has been erroneously included as such many times in the past. EIGRP is calculated based on a route's slowest link as well as the cumulative delay of each interface between the source and destination.

BGP   The only EGP (exterior gateway protocol), a routing protocol used between routers of different autonomous systems, used on the backbone of the Internet since the mid 1990s has been *Border Gateway Protocol (BGP)*. BGP (specifically eBGP, Exterior Border Gateway Protocol) is the routing protocol used between different autonomous systems, although Internal BGP (iBGP) carries BGP information between peers of the same AS. Although BGP uses many metrics, policies, and configurations, the route with the shortest AS path is the first tie-breaker to determine the best route to a destination network.

ADDITIONAL RESOURCES   Read "Weissman's Way of Understanding the Facebook Outage" to understand inherent flaws that BGP has: https://www.linkedin .com/pulse/weissmans-way-understanding-facebook-outage-jonathan-s-weissman/.

Link State vs. Distance Vector vs. Hybrid

Link state routing protocols, including OSPF and IS-IS (Intermediate System to Intermediate System), require each router to graph out a map and individually calculate the best next hop, based on bandwidth, to send packets to for each destination network. Routers pass connection information among themselves with link state routing protocols.

Distance vector routing protocols, including RIP, involve routers sharing their actual routing tables, and determine the best route to destination networks by distance, the number of routers a packet passes through.

As mentioned earlier, going through the fewest number of routers is not always the best path. OSPF might choose a path to a destination network with eight routers, while RIP might choose a path to the same destination network with three routers. The OSPF route, with the better overall bandwidth, would get packets to the destination network quicker.

EIGRP, in the past, has been described as a hybrid routing protocol because it has characteristics of both link state and distance vector routing protocols. However, many years ago, Cisco reversed course and starting calling it an advanced distance vector routing protocol. EIGRP keeps track of just the distance to destination networks (not the path), which is pure distance vector. However, EIGRP allows routers to establish and maintain a state, which is link state.

BGP has its own unique classification, path vector, since it uses paths, network policies, and configured rule sets to make decisions on how to get to destination networks.

Static Routing

Static routing, manually configuring destination networks and how to get there, is a preferred option for stub networks, networks that have only one way in and out. Instead of using a dynamic routing protocol, which adds overhead to a router's processing and consumes bandwidth as well with updates, static routes keep the overhead and bandwidth consumption down. The fault tolerance and load balancing of a dynamic routing protocol are not needed for stub networks or a linear topology, so there's no point in running one.

Default Route

A *default route* on a router acts just like a default gateway IP address on an end device. When a router doesn't have knowledge of a destination network, the packet will be sent to the next hop IP address specified in the default route. Without this default route, packets not meeting any entry in a routing table will be dropped. The default route allows the packets to be sent to another router, which may know about the destination network and how to get there, or it might have a default route of its own.

Administrative Distance

Routers cannot use different routing protocols to communicate with each other, but many routers can speak multiple routing protocols simultaneously. When a router takes routes it has learned by one routing protocol, say, EIGRP or a statically configured route, and announces those routes over another protocol such as OSPF, this is called route redistribution. This feature can come in handy when you have a mix of equipment and protocols in your network, such as occurs when you switch vendors or merge with another organization.

When a router has two or more routing protocol possibilities to connect to the same destination network with, the router uses a value called *administrative distance* to determine which routing protocol's route to install in the routing table. For example, Cisco has the following ADs, among others: EIGRP 90, OSPF 110, RIP 120. Lower is better, so if a route to a destination network is learned by all three routing protocols, the EIGRP learned route will be installed in the routing table, since it has the lowest AD. Directly connected networks have an AD of 0, while statically configured routes have an AD of 1. Those two ADs have the lowest possible values, to supersede anything learned from a dynamic routing protocol.

You can think of administrative distance as the "order of trustworthiness," with the greatest trust being what the router is told to accept, what the network engineer saw and manually/ statically entered.

Exterior vs. Interior

Routing protocols can be *exterior vs. interior.*

The protocol used by routers of autonomous systems to communicate and exchange routing information with other autonomous systems is generically called an exterior gateway protocol (EGP). Networks within an autonomous system use an interior gateway protocol (IGP) to communicate and exchange routing information. Edge routers connect an AS to another AS.

The original EGP was actually known as EGP (Exterior Gateway Protocol), as was used between the middle of the 1980s through the middle of the 1990s, when it was replaced with BGP (Border Gateway Protocol). BGP has been the only EGP used ever since then, and is the glue that connects the different parts of the Internet together.

IGPs include RIP, OSPF, and EIGRP, and are used internally within each AS.

 EXAM TIP   Expect a question asking you to compare exterior vs. interior routing protocols. BGP is the exterior routing protocol used on the Internet. All the rest—RIP, OSPF, EIGRP, etc.—are interior protocols.

Time to Live

If a routing loop exists, sending packets back and forth (most likely an accidental configuration) between two or more routers with no end in sight, the *time to live* (TTL) field of the IP header will end a packet's traversal. As a router sends a packet out of an interface, it decrements the TTL field by 1. In the event that a router decrements a TTL to the value 0, it drops the packet and sends an ICMP time-to-live exceeded error message to the source.

Bandwidth Management

Just about any router you buy today has the capability to block packets based on port number or IP address, but these are simple mechanisms mainly designed to protect an internal network. What if you need to control how much of your bandwidth is used for certain devices or applications? *Bandwidth management* can make a big difference.

Quality of Service (QoS), Traffic Shaping

To manage bandwidth, you need *quality of service (QoS)* policies to prioritize traffic based on certain rules. These rules control how much bandwidth a protocol, PC, user, VLAN, or IP address may use.

On many advanced routers and switches, you can implement QoS through bandwidth management, such as *traffic shaping* where you control the flow of packets into or out of the network according to the type of packet or other rules.

 EXAM TIP The term bandwidth shaping is synonymous with traffic shaping. The routers and switches that can implement traffic shaping are commonly referred to as shapers.

Traffic shaping is very important when you must guarantee a device or application a certain amount of bandwidth and/or latency, such as with VoIP or video. Traffic shaping is also very popular in places such as schools, where IT professionals need to control user activities, such as limiting Web usage or blocking certain risky applications such as peer-to-peer file sharing.

Traffic shaping is also important for penalizing undesired network traffic you do not want on your network. For example, some ISPs filter/drop BitTorrent traffic, which can consume great amounts of bandwidth.

REVIEW

Objective 2.2: Compare and contrast routing technologies and bandwidth management concepts

- Routers use routing tables and select a next hop IP address based on the destination IP address.
- Link state routing protocols, including OSPF and IS-IS, require each router to graph out a map and individually calculate the best next hop, based on bandwidth, to send packets to for each destination network. Routers pass connection information among themselves with link state routing protocols.
- Distance vector routing protocols, including RIP, involve routers sharing their actual routing tables, and determine the best route to destination networks by distance, the number of routers a packet passes through.
- EIGRP, in the past, has been described as a hybrid routing protocol because it has characteristics of both link state and distance vector routing protocols. However, many years ago, Cisco reversed course and starting calling it an advanced distance vector routing protocol. The MTU defines the level of data that can be encapsulated in various protocols.

- BGP has its own unique classification, path vector, since it uses paths, network policies, and configured rule sets to make decisions on how to get to destination networks.

- Static routing, manually configuring destination networks and how to get there, is a preferred option for stub networks, networks that have only one way in and out.

- A default route on a router acts just like a default gateway IP address on an end device. When a router doesn't have knowledge of a destination network, the packet will be sent to the next hop IP address specified in the default route.

- When a router has two or more routing protocol possibilities to connect to the same destination network with, the router uses a value called administrative distance to determine which routing protocol's route to install in the routing table.

- The protocol used by autonomous systems to communicate with each other is generically called an exterior gateway protocol (EGP). Networks within an autonomous system use an interior gateway protocol (IGP). Edge routers connect an AS to another AS.

- IGPs include RIP, OSPF, and EIGRP.

- The only EGP used today is BGP.

- If a routing loop exists, sending packets back and forth (most likely an accidental configuration) between two or more routers with no end in sight, the time to live (TTL) field of the IP header will end a packet's traversal.

- Quality of service (QoS) policies prioritize traffic based on certain rules. These rules control how much bandwidth a protocol, PC, user, VLAN, or IP address may use.

- On many advanced routers and switches, you can implement QoS through bandwidth management, such as traffic shaping where you control the flow of packets into or out of the network according to the type of packet or other rules.

2.2 QUESTIONS

1. Which of the following is a link state routing protocol?

   A. RIP

   B. EIGRP

   C. OSPF

   D. BGP

2. Which of the following allows routers to pick one routing protocol's path over another routing protocol's path?

   A. Static routing

   B. Default route

   C. Administrative distance

   D. Time to live

3. What controls the flow of packets into or out of a network based on rules?
   A. Hybrid routing protocol
   B. IGP
   C. Time to live
   D. Traffic shaping

2.2 ANSWERS

1. **C** OSPF uses LSAs, as each router independently constructs the topology.
2. **C** The lower the AD, the more preferred a routing protocol is.
3. **D** QoS is implemented through traffic shaping.

Objective 2.3 Given a scenario, configure and deploy common Ethernet switching features

Ethernet switching features allow Ethernet frames to move around a LAN (device to device), just like you would move around parts of a city (homes, buildings, etc.) through the city's streets. Just like in an actual city, efficiency and security (which are inversely proportional) are top of mind in the world of Ethernet.

Data Virtual Local Area Network (VLAN)

All devices in a LAN are in the same broadcast domain. That means when one of them sends a broadcast frame, all other devices receive and process it. By default, all switch ports are in the same broadcast domain. If you wanted to create two broadcast domains, you could set up two different switches and put them on different networks. A *data virtual local area network (VLAN)* offers the capabilities to create broadcast domains within a single switch.

When a system in a VLAN sends a broadcast, that broadcast message does not go beyond the VLAN. Having fewer hosts receive and process broadcasts not meant for them improves efficiency, since there are less CPU processing requirements. It also improves security, since fewer hosts will see traffic that the switches flood from any single other host, whether the traffic is a multicast, broadcast, or unknown unicast (a destination unicast MAC address that's not in the MAC address table, discussed later in this objective). Furthermore, security policies can be configured for specific VLANs. Finally, using one or more switches with multiple VLANs allows for a more flexible network topology. Users and their devices can be logically grouped in switches, through VLANs, by department or by users that need to work together for a certain amount of time, instead of physically by actual locations.

VLANs are security boundaries and broadcast domains. Unless a Layer 3 device is used, only systems within a single VLAN and IP subnet will be able to communicate with one another, and not with systems in other VLANs or subnets. Furthermore, if two systems in the same IP subnet are configured for different VLANs (not following the best practice of putting each subnet in its own single VLAN), they will never be able to communicate under any circumstance, since Layer 3 devices only take traffic out of and bring traffic into a network/subnet/broadcast domain and have nothing to do with communication within a network/subnet/broadcast domain. There technically is a "hack" to allow two devices in the same subnet but different VLANs to communicate. It's done with a crossover cable connected to two ports of different VLANs, but you'll need physical access to the switch for that. If an attacker has physical access to a switch, there will probably be better things they'd like to do to it, though.

VLAN 1 is the default VLAN. This shows you that VLANs are always in effect on a switch. All ports by default are in VLAN 1, and that's a single broadcast domain. You configure VLANs on a switch, and then assign ports into the VLANs. Keep in mind that when thinking about "what is in a VLAN" or "what belongs to a VLAN," it's not PCs, protocols, or applications. They don't "belong" to a VLAN. In the most technical sense, Layer 2 frames belong to a VLAN.

 NOTE   The CompTIA Network+ exam objectives use the term *data virtual local area network (VLAN)* to describe the standard VLANs discussed here. This differentiates them from *voice* VLANs, discussed next. Although, if you have not optimized a custom VLAN for voice, it is technically still a data VLAN.

Voice VLAN

A VLAN optimized for voice data streams, a *Voice VLAN*, prioritizes voice traffic over data traffic to ensure smooth voice communication. A Voice VLAN can use MAC addresses to determine which devices on the network are phones or use VLAN-based tags in the received frame. The switch can prioritize the voice traffic and deprioritize data traffic as specified.

Port Configurations

A switch can have multiple *port configurations* for various reasons, as detailed in this section.

Port Tagging/802.1Q

When using just one switch, the VLAN configuration is as simplified as can be. However, when using multiple switches, it gets a little more involved. When using VLANs between multiple switches, VLAN trunking allows traffic from more than one VLAN (all by default, but VLANs can be pruned from trunk links automatically or manually) to traverse a link from one switch to another from a trunk port on one switch to a trunk port on another switch.

Broadcast traffic, multicast traffic, and unknown unicast traffic are sent only out of access ports that are associated with the same VLAN as the frame. Unicast traffic is sent out an access port associated with the same VLAN as the frame, where there is a matching entry in the SAT.

VLAN trunking is done through *port tagging/802.1Q*, which involves a switch inserting a 4-byte IEEE 802.1Q VLAN tag in the frame's Ethernet header. This tag, encapsulated in the Ethernet frame, contains multiple fields, with the one most relevant here being the VLAN ID field, which identifies frames coming in through certain ports to be in a specific VLAN. The tag is inserted by a switch before sending the frame out of a trunk port that leads to a trunk link to a trunk port of another switch. The other switch will now use this tag to decide which ports the frame should be sent out of. Tags are removed before frames are sent out of access ports, so devices connected to access ports never see tagged frames (with a couple of rare exceptions by certain VLAN-aware end devices). Tags are meant for adjacent switches, so they'll know how to forward the frames properly to the respective VLANs.

Port Aggregation

There are times when the data capacity of a connection between a switch and another device isn't enough to meet demand. Situations like these are encountered regularly in large data centers where tremendous amounts of data must be moved between racks of storage devices to vast numbers of users. Sometimes the solution is simple, like changing from a low-capacity standard like 100-megabit Ethernet to Gigabit Ethernet.

But there are other ways to achieve high-speed links between devices without having to upgrade the infrastructure. One of those ways is to join two or more connections' ports logically in a switch so that the resulting bandwidth is treated as a single connection and the throughput is multiplied by the number of linked connectors. All of the cables from the joined ports must go to the same device—another switch, a storage area network (SAN), a station, or whatever. That device must also support the logical joining of all of the involved ports. This is called *port aggregation* (as well as port bonding, link aggregation, NIC bonding, and NIC teaming).

Link Aggregation Control Protocol (LACP)

The Cisco protocol for accomplishing port aggregation is called Port Aggregation Protocol (PAgP). You may also run across it in a very common implementation called *Link Aggregation Control Protocol (LACP)*, which is an IEEE specification. LACP specifies a number of features and options to automate the negotiation, management, load balancing, and failure modes of aggregated ports.

Duplex

Modern switches enable you to provide manual support for older hardware in terms of controlling *duplex* settings. Some truly ancient wired devices operate at half duplex, meaning they can send or receive, but not both at the same time. (The latter is full duplex.) The default switch port setting is auto (which dynamically senses which setting should be used), but you can force a port to half duplex if necessary to support an old device.

Speed

A typical "Gigabit" switch, for example, automatically supports 1000 Gbps connections, the slower 100 Mbps "Fast Ethernet" connections, and the super slow 10 Mbps connections. In some rare circumstances, you might set a port manually to run at a specific *speed*, instead of leaving the default setting of auto (like duplex).

Flow Control

Flow control, disabled by default on all switch ports, allows a port to tell a sender to pause if the switch starts to get more traffic than it can handle. In this case, the switch port's buffers fill up quicker than the switch can send out traffic. Flow control prevents the port from dropping traffic for a short amount of time until the port is able to respond and process again.

Port Mirroring

When a PC sends a frame into a switch, the switch associates the source MAC address in the Ethernet frame with the port on which the frame arrived in its MAC address table (discussed later in this objective). If the switch then gets a frame with that MAC address as the destination MAC address in an Ethernet frame, the switch sends the frame just to the port that MAC address is associated with.

 NOTE   Don't confuse the table described here with an ARP cache. The MAC address table maps MAC addresses to ports, while the ARP cache maps IP addresses to MAC addresses.

A switch floods broadcasts, standard multicasts, and unknown unicasts (a destination unicast MAC address that's not in the SAT) out of all ports except the port on which the message originated. Let's say a company wants to implement an intrusion detection system (IDS) to inspect traffic flowing through a switch for security, or even for troubleshooting and debugging purposes. An IDS—for example, Snort—could be installed on a system and plugged into a switch. However, the switch will not send frames to the port that the IDS is connected to. *Port mirroring*, also known as port monitoring and SPAN (switched port analyzer), changes everything. A switch can be instructed to send transmitted frames, received frames, or both in relation to a certain switch port to another port, where an analyzer will be receiving them. Using a protocol analyzer, like Wireshark, these packets can be examined. You probably wouldn't want to send all traffic in both directions from a certain VLAN to a specific port, as that could overload the SPAN destination port. The general rule is to capture what you need to capture and try to capture as little of anything else. Local SPAN sends traffic from parts of a single switch to one or more ports on the same switch. Remote SPAN trunks the SPAN traffic to other switches, as the traffic will be sent to an analyzer not connected to the local switch.

Port Security

Ethernet switches learn where hosts are by analyzing the source MAC address field in Ethernet frames as the frames enter switch ports and by keeping mappings of MAC addresses to ports in a table in RAM called the MAC address table, source address table (SAT), or content addressable memory (CAM) table, as mentioned earlier.

The switch can keep a specific number of MAC addresses in this table. The size of the table and the number of entries each vary by switch. What would happen if an attacker connects a device to a port and runs a tool or script that sends thousands of Ethernet frames into the port with different, randomly generated MAC addresses? In this case, the switch would happily enter each MAC address into the MAC address table, associating each MAC address with the same physical port of the attacker. Eventually, the MAC address table will run out of space. At this point, the switch can't learn any new MAC addresses and will simply start flooding all traffic from all hosts out of all ports on the switch, except the originating port.

This CAM overflow attack, also known as a MAC flooding attack, essentially turns a switch into a hub, which always flooded traffic out of all ports except the port on which the message originated. The switch and its MAC address table put hubs out of business.

With this attack, the attacker is now able to sniff every single frame sent into the switch. The attacker could be an insider, physically on the premises, or an outsider with remote access to one of the organization's machines. Confidentiality is at great risk. macof, part of the dsniff suite of tools, can generate hundreds of thousands of random MAC addresses and flood them into a switch. From a cybersecurity perspective, this tests your switch's resistance to such an attack. To mitigate this attack, you can use a switch feature called *port security*.

First, you need to identify allowed MAC addresses so they can get access to the port. This can be done either statically or dynamically, as frames enter a port. The next step involves specifying the maximum number of MAC addresses that will have access to the port. By default, only one MAC address has access. In a switched environment, the main reason that more than one MAC address will be heard from on a single port is that the port is connected to a neighboring port. For example, all traffic coming into SwitchA, from hosts in SwitchB, will be heard through the port on SwitchA that connects to SwitchB. A second example of when multiple MAC addresses can be learned on a single port involves the use of virtual machines (VMs), where the VM sends frames with a source MAC address of its virtual NIC, which will be different from the MAC address of the physical NIC of the host. A third example of multiple MAC addresses being learned on a single port is when a VoIP (Voice over IP) phone is connected to a switch just with a PC, and that switch then connects upstream to another switch.

A violation occurs if a new MAC address is heard on a port after the maximum number of MAC addresses have been learned. On ports that are statically configured for certain MAC addresses, an unknown MAC address heard on that port would trigger a violation as well. When a violation occurs, the switch will enter one of three states and take appropriate action.

First, the shutdown mode is when the port is immediately shut down. No frames can enter or exit, and an SNMP (Simple Network Management Protocol) trap notification is sent.

The network engineer must re-enable the port manually, although the switch can be configured to have ports shut down because of errors and come back up again after a certain period of time has elapsed.

Second, the restrict mode is when the port doesn't shut down, but all frames from violating MAC addresses are discarded. The switch logs the number of violating frames and can send an SNMP trap, as well as a syslog message, if configured to do so.

Third, the protect mode is when the port doesn't shut down, but all frames from violating MAC addresses are discarded. So far, this state is exactly the same as restrict. The only difference is that in this state, no violations are logged. I've never heard of a valid use case—or even a contrived one—that works for this state. No sane administrator would want to stick their head in the sand like an ostrich and ignore violations!

As if a CAM overflow attack wasn't enough motivation for implementing port security, there are still other compelling reasons. First, imagine an organization dealing with sensitive, personally identifiable information (PII), like a healthcare organization or even the government. You would imagine that every device on that network would be tightly controlled and tracked, while personal devices would be forbidden. After a MAC address of a company device is learned on the port (which will happen instantly when it is set up for the first time), users would not be able to unplug it and plug in their own device. If someone tried that, the port would be shut down and an administrator would need to manually bring it up again.

Furthermore, port security also prevents users from plugging in unauthorized switches into ports, to allow multiple devices of theirs to connect to the network. In this case, the switch could just restrict and not completely shut down, to allow the user to keep working, while unauthorized devices will not be able to send traffic into the switch. In this case, too, the administrator will get alerts.

Finally, let's say there's a VoIP phone or a kiosk machine available for employees, or even visitors, to use. Port security will prevent someone from unplugging one of those devices and plugging in a personal device when the switch only allows the initial MAC address learned on the port to send frames into the port.

Jumbo Frames

iSCSI is built on top of TCP/IP, enabling devices that use the SCSI protocol to communicate across existing networks using cheap, readily available hardware. Because the existing networks and their hardware weren't built as a disk interface, performance can suffer. Part of this performance cost is time spent processing frame headers. We can ease some of the cost of moving large amounts of data around the network at standard frame size by configuring interfaces with MTU values above 1500 bytes, to support *jumbo frames*. Jumbo frames are usually 9000 bytes long—though technically anything over 1500 qualifies—and they reduce the total number of frames moving through the network. Using a Jumbo frame will reduce the overhead of the frame header, making a large transmission faster.

Auto-Medium-Dependent Interface Crossover (MDI-X)

Modern switches do not have a dedicated uplink port (as older devices had), but instead auto-sense, through the interfaces' physical *auto-medium-dependent interface crossover (MDI-X)* capability, when another switch is plugged in. You can plug a crossover cable going to another switch into any port on the other switch (and vice versa), but with MDI-X, ports don't even require a crossover cable, and can use a straight-through cable instead.

Media Access Control (MAC) Address Tables

Media access control (MAC) address tables, also known as source address tables (SATs) and content addressable memory (CAM) tables, allow a switch to make decisions on where frames should go to, as mentioned earlier. When a PC sends an Ethernet frame into a switch, the switch examines the destination MAC address in the frame and then checks to see if it knows which port a device with that destination MAC address is connected to. If the switch knows where the device with that MAC address is, the switch sends the frame out of just that corresponding port. If the switch doesn't know where the destination MAC address is, the switch floods the frame out of all ports, except the port on which the frame originated.

In Figure 2.3-1, if Host A sends a frame for Host B into Port 1 on Switch 1, the switch will associate the MAC address of Host A with the port on which it was heard through a table in memory known by various names, including the source address table (SAT), the content addressable memory (CAM) table, and the MAC address table.

Since the switch doesn't know where Host B is, it floods the frame out of all the ports, except the one the frame originated on. When Host B replies, the frame goes into the switch, and the

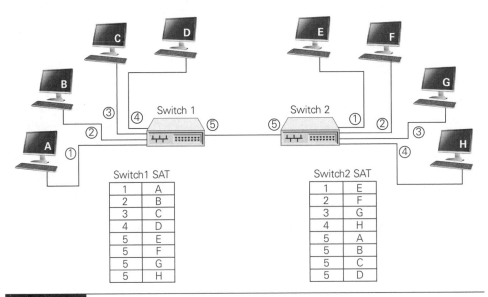

Switch1 SAT	
1	A
2	B
3	C
4	D
5	E
5	F
5	G
5	H

Switch2 SAT	
1	E
2	F
3	G
4	H
5	A
5	B
5	C
5	D

FIGURE 2.3-1   Two switches

switch learns that Host B can be found on Port 2. The switch then adds the MAC address of Host B and the port on which it was heard into its MAC address table as well.

The logic works the same for switches that are directly connected together. Each switch maintains its own MAC address table. You'll notice that Hosts E, F, G, and H are known to Switch 2 on Ports 1, 2, 3, and 4, respectively. However, as far as Switch 1 goes, Hosts E, F, G, and H are all accessible through Port 5, which connects to Switch 2.

Hosts A, B, C, and D are known to Switch 1 on Ports 1, 2, 3, and 4, respectively. However, as far as Switch 2 goes, Hosts A, B, C, and D are all accessible through Port 5, which connects to Switch 1.

So, if Host C sends a frame to Host E, it goes into Switch 1 on Port 3. Switch 1 consults its MAC address table and realizes Host E is accessible through Port 5. Therefore, Switch 1 sends the frame out of Port 5, where it's picked up by Switch 2. Switch 2 now looks at the destination MAC address in the frame, which is still the MAC address of Host E. Switches are transparent and don't change a single part of the frame. After consulting its MAC address table, Switch 2 sends the frame out of Port 1, and Host E gets it.

In addition to flooding unknown unicasts, which is when the switch doesn't know where a destination MAC address is, the switch will also flood multicasts and broadcasts out of all ports, except the port on which the frame originated. That means broadcast traffic, like ARP (Address Resolution Protocol) requests, is always flooded by switches. If there are 20 connected switches in a network with 20 PCs connected to each of those switches, a single ARP request by one of the PCs will be sent to and read by the other 399 PCs.

Power over Ethernet (PoE)/ Power over Ethernet Plus (PoE+)

Wireless access points need electrical power, but they're invariably placed in strange locations (like ceilings or high up on walls) where providing electrical power is not convenient. No worries! Many WAPs support one of the *Power over Ethernet (PoE)* standards that enables them to receive their power from the same Ethernet cables that transfer their data. The switch that connects the WAPs must support PoE, but as long as both the WAP and the switches to which they connect support PoE, you don't have to do anything other than just plug in Ethernet cables. PoE works automatically. As you might imagine, it costs extra to get WAPs and switches that support PoE, but the convenience of PoE for wireless networks makes it a popular option. Cameras also make great use of PoE.

The original PoE standard—802.3af—came out in 2003 with great response from the industry. PoE switches support a maximum of 15.4 watts of DC power per port. In 2009, 802.3af was revised to output as much as 25.5 watts per port. This PoE amendment to 802.3 is called 802.3at, *Power over Ethernet plus (PoE+)*. In 2018, the IEEE released upgraded PoE again with the 802.3bt standard. Switches that support PoE++ (or 4PPoE) can provide one of two power upgrades, with Type 3 supplying up to 51 watts per port and Type 4 supplying up to 71.3 watts per port.

Spanning Tree Protocol

Because you can connect switches together in any fashion, you can create redundant connections in a network. These are called bridging loops or switching loops, and in this unwanted state, frames simply loop around switches with no end in sight. There is no mechanism like the TTL in the IP header, as described in Objective 2.2, to stop this loop.

In the early days of switches, making a bridging loop in a network setup would bring the network crashing down. A frame could get caught in the loop, so to speak, and not reach its destination.

The Ethernet standards body adopted the *Spanning Tree Protocol* (STP) to eliminate the problem of accidental switching loops. For decades, switches have had STP enabled by default, and can detect potential loops before they happen. Using special STP frames known as bridge protocol data units (BPDUs), switches communicate with other switches to prevent loops from happening in the first place.

 NOTE While we say switching loops instead of bridging loops today (which was coined before the advent of switches), the term for the messages (which was also coined before the advent of switches), bridge protocol data units (BPDUs), remains.

Configuration BPDUs establish the topology, where one switch is elected root bridge and acts as the center of the STP universe. Each switch then uses the root bridge as a reference point to maintain a loop-free topology. There will be redundant links, for fault tolerance, that would ordinarily cause a bridging loop, but certain ports will be placed in a "blocking" state and will not send or receive data frames. Ports in the blocking state will still hear the configuration BPDUs, which are sourced by the root bridge and forwarded downstream to the other switches every 2 seconds.

When designing a switched network, STP (or RSTP, discussed shortly) is relied on as a way to provide fault-tolerant links on the network. Depending on the situation and hardware, link aggregation or STP/RSTP would be used.

If a link or device goes down, STP springs into action with another type of BPDU, called a topology change notification (TCN) BPDU, that enables the switches to rework themselves around the failed interface or device. The blocked ports, listening to the BPDUs, will realize they're needed and eventually move to a forwarding state.

Administrators can manually change STP settings for a switch. A switch port directly connected to a PC, for example, should never participate in STP, and could be configured with a setting called PortFast that enables the interface to come up right away, without the normal latency introduced by STP. Another reason to configure switch ports with PortFast is to prevent TCN BPDUs being sent out of that switch every time a PC is powered on and off, which has severe side effects, like causing all switches to flush their MAC address table, and relearn MAC addresses.

BPDU guard will move a port configured with PortFast into an errdisable state (i.e., error occurred, disabled) if a BPDU is received on that port. This requires an administrator to manually bring the port back up.

Ports configured with PortFast should never receive a BPDU, and if they do, it could start a bridging loop. Another mechanism, root guard, will move a port into a root-inconsistent state if BPDUs coming from a certain direction indicate another switch is trying to become the root bridge. The root-inconsistent port will automatically return to its forwarding state once these BPDUs stop. This helps define locations where the root bridge should never be located.

 NOTE The preceding terms used to describe functions within a switch apply specifically to Cisco switches. Other companies, notably Juniper, compete with Cisco and use different terms for the same actions.

The original Spanning Tree Protocol, introduced by the IEEE as 802.1d, was replaced a very long time ago, 2001 to be exact, by Rapid Spanning Tree Protocol (RSTP), 802.1w. RSTP offers significantly faster convergence time following some kind of network change. STP could take up to 52 seconds to get back to a steady state, for example, whereas an RSTP network could return to convergence in 6 seconds.

 NOTE Per-VLAN Spanning Tree+ (PVST+) is an enhancement and replacement of Per-VLAN Spanning Tree (PVST). PVST+ runs a separate instance of STP/RSTP for each VLAN for performance benefits and ease of configuration. A single instance of STP/RSTP, Common Spanning Tree (CST), is the alternative.

Carrier-Sense Multiple Access with Collision Detection (CSMA/CD)

One of the issues with bus communication was that devices essentially share the same cable. This applied to pure bus networks and hybrid star-bus networks as well. The NICs needed some way to determine which machine should send data at which time. Ethernet designers came up with a clever way to handle the issue of potential collisions.

Ethernet networks used a system called *carrier sense multiple access with collision detection (CSMA/CD)* to determine which computer should use a shared cable at a given moment. *Carrier sense* meant that each node using the network examined the cable before sending a data frame If another machine was using the network, the node detected traffic on the segment, waited a few milliseconds, and then rechecked. If it detected no traffic (i.e., the cable was "free"), the node sent out its frame.

Multiple access meant that all machines had equal access to the wire. If the line was free, any Ethernet node could send a frame. From Ethernet's point of view, it didn't matter what function the node performed: it could have been a desktop system or a file server running one of multiple operating systems. As far as Ethernet was concerned, a node was a node was a node and access to the cable was assigned strictly on a first-come, first-served basis.

So what happened if two machines, both listening to the cable, simultaneously decided that it was free and tried to send a frame? A collision occurred, and both of the transmissions were lost. A collision resembled the effect of two people talking at the same time: the listener hears a mixture of two voices and can't understand either one.

When two NICs transmitted at the same time, they'd sense the overlapping signals and immediately know that a collision occurred. When they detected a collision, both nodes stopped transmitting.

They then each generated a random number to determine how long to wait before trying again. If you imagine that each machine rolled its magic electronic dice and waited for that number of seconds, you wouldn't be too far from the truth, except that the amount of time an Ethernet node waited to retransmit was much shorter than one second. Whichever node generated the lowest random number began its retransmission first, winning the competition to use the wire. The losing node then saw traffic on the wire and waited for the wire to be free again before attempting to retransmit its data.

Collisions were a normal part of the operation of early Ethernet networks, because every device shared a bus. A group of nodes that have the capability of sending frames at the same time as each other, resulting in collisions, is called a collision domain.

As described earlier, the move from half-duplex to full-duplex disabled CSMA/CD and completely eliminated collisions.

Address Resolution Protocol (ARP)

Local communication is when a device sends traffic to another device on the same subnet. Remote communication is when a device sends traffic to another device on a different subnet.

Let's say Host A with IP address 10.10.1.1 wants to communicate with Host B, whose IP address is 10.10.1.2. The source of the traffic will take its IP address and its subnet mask and perform a Boolean/logical AND operation. All 32 bits of the IP address are lined up with the 32 bits of the subnet mask, which will be 255.255.255.0 or /24 for this example:

```
00001010.00001010.00000001.00000001 (10.10.1.1) Source IP address
11111111.11111111.11111111.00000000 (255.255.255.0) Subnet mask

===================================
00001010.00001010.00000001.00000000 (10.10.1.0) Network identifier
```

When the source logically ANDs each of the 32 columns, bringing down a 1 if both bits in the column are 1s and bringing down a 0 if the two bits in a column are not both 1s, what results is a network identifier. In this case, the source's network ID is 10.10.1.0.

Now the source needs to determine if the destination is on the same network or a different network by performing a second Boolean/logical AND operation. The source takes the destination IP address and logically ends it with the source's own subnet mask. The destination's subnet mask is unknown and it is never transmitted. The destination's IP address is either known by the source or resolved from its name with DNS. The source doesn't actually need the destination's mask because if they are on the same network their subnet masks will be the same anyway.

> 00001010.00001010.00000001.00000010 (10.10.1.2) Destination IP address
>
> 11111111.11111111.11111111.00000000 (255.255.255.0) Subnet mask
>
> ====================================
>
> 00001010.00001010.00000001.00000000 **(10.10.1.0) Network identifier**

After logically ANDing the destination IP address of 10.10.1.2 with the source mask of 255.255.255.0, the resultant network ID matches the network ID of the source 10.10.1.0. This lets the source know that the destination is on the same network and traffic can be delivered directly.

After determining that the traffic is local, the source needs the MAC address of the destination. The source puts the actual traffic on hold and sends out a broadcast message using *Address Resolution Protocol (ARP)*. ARP is meant to resolve a known IP address to the MAC address that it is bound to in software. The message in the ARP request explains that Host A (10.10.1.1) is looking for the MAC address of the device that has the IP address of 10.10.1.2. All devices on the network not only see this ARP request but they read it as well. Every device but the actual destination says "That's not for me" and discards it.

Host B (10.10.1.2) sends an ARP reply back to Host A 10.10.1.1. The ARP reply is unicast, which means it only goes to 10.10.1.1 (through the switch's MAC address table), and is not broadcast to every device on the network. In the ARP request, the source listed its MAC address so the destination didn't need to issue its own ARP request broadcast to find out the source's MAC address. Broadcasts on networks are bad. Hosts have to interrupt what they're doing and parse through the broadcast. In most cases, they realize that it's not even meant for them. It's like a professor e-mailing a 500-page PDF to the class with the subject line "Read this!" while the name of the single student who it was meant for appears on page 499 of the PDF.

Unfortunately, in the world of IPv4, there is no other way to do this. After the ARP reply comes back to Host A with Host B's MAC address, Host A can now fill in the destination's MAC address in the outgoing frame and send the traffic. The source MAC address and destination MAC address fields are found in the Layer 2 frame, while the source IP address and destination IP address fields are found in the Layer 3 packet.

When Host A gets the ARP reply, it adds an entry to its ARP cache, associating the IP address of Host B with the MAC address of Host B, so that if Host A needs to communicate with Host B again shortly, there's no need for the process to repeat itself. Different OSes have different lengths of time in which entries in the ARP cache stay, before being removed.

Furthermore, the target of the ARP request will also add the sender of the ARP request to its own ARP cache. It figures that if the sender wants to talk to it, then it probably will need to talk to the sender itself.

Now let's say Host A with IP address 10.10.1.1 wants to communicate with Host X, whose IP address is 10.10.4.1. Host A, the source, once again performs the Boolean/logical AND operation to determine that its network ID is 10.10.1.0 (same as previously shown). This time, the destination IP address is 10.10.4.1.

Here's how the second Boolean/logical AND operation looks with Host X's IP address:

00001010.00001010.00000100.00000001 (10.10.4.1) Destination IP address

11111111.11111111.11111111.00000000 (255.255.255.0) Subnet mask

====================================

00001010.00001010.00000100.00000000 **(10.10.4.0) Network identifier**

The two network IDs are not the same, and the source realizes it can't send traffic directly to the destination.

One of the golden rules of networking is that direct communication is only possible between devices on the same network. The source needs to get the traffic now to its default gateway, an interface on a router connected to its network. When a device is configured either statically or dynamically, in addition to an IP address and a subnet mask, that device also gets an IP address of a router interface on the network. That router interface is responsible for taking traffic off the network destined for other networks and bringing traffic from other networks back onto the network. The default gateway's IP address needs to be known by hosts on the network. You'll recall that routers are the devices that connect different networks together, and each interface of a router connects to a different network. Even though Host A, the source, determines that the traffic is remote, it will once again send an ARP request, which is once again broadcast to all devices on its network. This time, the ARP request is looking for the MAC address of Host A's default gateway, though, and not the actual destination.

Let's say the default gateway's IP address is 10.10.1.99. The default gateway will send its MAC address in a unicast ARP reply back to Host A. Host A now sends the traffic with a destination MAC address of the default gateway and the destination IP address of the actual destination, which could be two, five, ten, or more routers away. Incidentally, routers never forward broadcasts to other networks. Router interfaces will hear broadcasts on the networks they're connected to but will never forward broadcast traffic from one network out of another interface to a different network. If they did that, a simple broadcast could go around the world and back.

Now, Host A's default gateway has the actual traffic meant for the destination, and uses its routing table, as described in Objective 5.5, to get the packet to another router, to keep the packet flowing to its eventual destination.

In local communication (traffic for a device on the same subnet), the ARP request has the actual destination as the target IP address, while in remote communication (traffic for a device on a different network), the ARP request has the default gateway as the target IP address.

In local communication, the ARP reply has the actual destination's MAC address, as requested, while in remote communication, the ARP reply has the default gateway's MAC address, as requested.

After the ARP reply is received by the source of traffic, the MAC address answer (found in the Sender MAC address field in the ARP reply) is used for the outgoing frames as the destination MAC address. It's also used as the source MAC address in the incoming frames.

For local communication, the destination's MAC address is used in the frames and the destination's IP address is used in the packets. For remote communication, the default gateway's MAC address is used in the frames and the actual destination's IP address is used in the packets.

Neighbor Discovery Protocol

Neighbor Discovery Protocol (NDP) uses ICMPv6 (ICMP for IPv6, not the sixth version of ICMP) and consists of five control message types:

- Router Solicitation (RS, the IPv6 equivalent of a DHCP Discover)
- Router Advertisement (RA, the IPv6 equivalent of a DHCP Offer)
- Neighbor Solicitation (NS, the IPv6 equivalent of an ARP Request)
- Neighbor Advertisement (NA, the IPv6 equivalent of an ARP Reply)
- Redirect (how routers that are default gateways for PCs let the PCSs know if there is a more optimal router on the network to send traffic to for a specific destination)

When an IPv6 host has an interface enabled, it sends a router solicitation (RS) to the all-routers multicast address of ff02::2 (IPv6 multicast addresses were described in Objective 1.4) in hopes of receiving a router advertisement (RA) in response. (This RS can be sent to either the all-nodes multicast address of ff02::1, or it can be configured to be sent to the link-local unicast address of the host. The host's MAC address is included in the RS as well, so the router has all it needs.) Routers also send unsolicited router advertisements in regular time intervals. RA messages let hosts know how to go ahead with dynamic addressing and contain a prefix (the IPv6 term for network ID), prefix length (the IPv6 term for subnet mask, which should always be /64 to allow hosts to autoconfigure themselves—Stateless address autoconfiguration (SLAAC) was covered in Objective 1.4), default gateway, and other information for configuration. A router can also be configured to send IP addresses of DNS servers in an option in an RA.

Cross-Reference

NS, NA, RS, RA are detailed in Objective 1.4.

REVIEW

Objective 2.3: Given a scenario, configure and deploy common Ethernet switching features

- VLANs offer the capabilities of creating broadcast domains within a single switch.
- A VLAN optimized for voice data streams, a Voice VLAN, prioritizes voice traffic over data traffic to ensure smooth voice communication.
- Switch ports can be configured with port tagging/802.1Q, port aggregation (with LACP, for example), duplex, speed, flow control, port mirroring, port security, jumbo frames, and MDI-X.
- MAC address tables help switches send frames to the intended destinations.
- Many WAPs support one of the PoE standards that enables them to receive their power from the same Ethernet cables that transfer their data.
- STP prevents switching loops.
- CSMA/CD is disabled with full duplex.
- ARP is how a device associates a known IP address with an unknown MAC address.
- IPv6 uses five types of NDP messages for major functionality.

2.3 QUESTIONS

1. Which of the following is not a port configuration?
   - **A.** ARP
   - **B.** Duplex
   - **C.** Flow control
   - **D.** Port aggregation

2. Which of the following prevents switching loops?
   - **A.** ARP
   - **B.** STP
   - **C.** CSMA/CD
   - **D.** NDP

3. Which of the following NDP messages is the IPv6 equivalent of an ARP request?
   - **A.** RS
   - **B.** RA
   - **C.** NS
   - **D.** NA

2.3 ANSWERS

1. **A**   ARP is used to map a known IP address to an unknown MAC address.
2. **B**   STP prevents switching loops.
3. **C**   Neighbor solicitation is the IPv6 equivalent of an ARP request.

Objective 2.4   Given a scenario, install and configure the appropriate wireless standards and technologies

Like all technologies, wireless has improved over the years, and as a result, different versions of wireless standards and technologies exist. 802.11 standards, frequencies and range, channels, channel bonding, service set identifier (SSID), antenna types, encryption standards, cellular technologies, and multiple input, multiple output (MIMO) and multi-user MIMO (MU-MIMO) features all play a role in wireless networks today, affecting the experiences users have with them.

802.11 Standards

The *802.11 standards* define both how wireless devices communicate and how to secure that communication. The original 802.11 standard, now often referred to as 802.11-1997, is no longer used, but it established the baseline features common to all subsequent Wi-Fi standards.

The 802.11-1997 standard defined certain features, such as a wireless network adapters, special configuration software, and the capability to run in multiple styles of networks. In addition, 802.11-1997 defined how transmissions work, including frequencies of radio signals, transmission methods, and collision avoidance.

802.11a through 802.11ax, covered in the Network+ exam objectives, are variations of the original standard that feature improvements, enhancements, and new technologies.

a

The 802.11*a* standard differed from the other 802.11-based standards in significant ways. Foremost was that it operated in a different frequency range, 5.0 GHz. The 5.0 GHz range is much less crowded than the 2.4 GHz range, reducing the chance of interference from devices such as telephones and microwave ovens. Too much signal interference can increase latency, making the network sluggish and slow to respond. Running in the 5.0 GHz range greatly reduces this problem.

TABLE 2.4-1	802.11a Summary

Standard	Frequency	Spectrum	Speed	Range	Backward Compatibility
802.11a	5.0 GHz	Orthogonal frequency-division multiplexing (OFDM)	54 Mbps	~150′	n/a

 NOTE Despite the *a* designation for this extension to the 802.11 standard, 802.11a was available on the market *after* 802.11b.

The 802.11a standard also offered considerably greater throughput than 802.11b, with speeds up to 54 Mbps. Range, however, suffered somewhat and topped out at about 150 feet. Despite the superior speed of 802.11a, it never enjoyed the popularity of 802.11b. Table 2.4-1 summarizes 802.11a.

b

The first widely adopted Wi-Fi standard—802.11*b*—supported data throughput of up to 11 Mbps and a range of up to 300 feet under ideal conditions. The main downside to using 802.11b was its frequency. The 2.4 GHz frequency is a crowded place, so you were more likely to run into interference from other wireless devices. Table 2.4-2 summarizes 802.11b.

g

The 802.11*g* standard offered data transfer speeds equivalent to 802.11a—up to 54 Mbps—and the wider 300-foot range of 802.11b. More importantly, 802.11g was backward compatible with 802.11b (since both used the 2.4 GHz frequency band), so the same 802.11g WAP could service both 802.11b and 802.11g wireless nodes.

If an 802.11g network only had 802.11g devices connected, the network ran in *native mode*—at up to 54 Mbps—whereas when 802.11b devices connected, the network dropped down to *mixed mode*—all communication ran up to only 11 Mbps. Table 2.4-3 summarizes 802.11g.

TABLE 2.4-2	802.11b Summary

Standard	Frequency	Spectrum	Speed	Range	Backward Compatibility
802.11b	2.4 GHz	Direct-sequence spread spectrum (DSSS)	11 Mbps	~300′	n/a

| **TABLE 2.4-3** | 802.11g Summary |

Standard	Frequency	Spectrum	Speed	Range	Backward Compatibility
802.11g	2.4 GHz	OFDM	54 Mbps	~300'	802.11b

Later 802.11g manufacturers incorporated channel bonding into their devices, enabling the devices to use two channels for transmission. Channel bonding is not part of the 802.11g standard, but rather proprietary technology pushed by various companies to increase the throughput of their wireless networks. Starting with 802.11n, however, channel bonding was built into the standards. Both the NIC and WAP, therefore, had to be from the same company for channel bonding to work.

n (Wi-Fi 4)

The *802.11n (Wi-Fi 4)* standard brought several improvements to Wi-Fi networking, including faster speeds and new antenna technology implementations.

The 802.11n specification requires all but handheld devices to use multiple antennas to implement a feature called multiple input, multiple output (MIMO), which enables the devices to make multiple simultaneous connections called streams. With up to four antennas, 802.11n devices can achieve amazing speeds. They also implement channel bonding, combining two 20-MHz channels into a single 40-MHz channel to increase throughput even more. The official standard supports throughput of up to 600 Mbps, although practical implementation drops that down substantially.

Many 802.11n WAPs employ transmit beamforming, a multiple-antenna technology that helps get rid of dead spots—places where the radio signal just does not penetrate at all—or at least make them not so bad. The antennas adjust the signal once the access point discovers a client to optimize the radio signal.

Like 802.11g, 802.11n WAPs can support earlier, slower 802.11b/g devices. The problem with supporting these older types of 802.11 is that 802.11n WAPs need to encapsulate 802.11n frames into 802.11b or 802.11g frames. This adds some overhead to the process. Worse, if any 802.11b devices join the network, traffic speeds drop, although not all the way down to 802.11b speeds (as incorrectly thought by many). 802.11g devices don't cause this behavior on 802.11n networks.

To handle these issues, 802.11 WAPs transmit in three different modes: legacy, mixed, and greenfield. These modes are also sometimes known as connection types.

Legacy mode means the 802.11n WAP sends out separate packets just for legacy devices. This is a terrible way to utilize 802.11n, but was added as a stopgap measure if the other modes didn't work. In mixed mode, also often called high-throughput or 802.11a-ht/802.11g-ht, the access point sends special packets that support the older standards yet also improve the speed of those standards via 802.11n's wider bandwidth. Greenfield mode is exclusively for

TABLE 2.4-4   802.11n Summary

Standard	Frequency	Spectrum	Speed	Range	Backward Compatibility
802.11n	2.4 GHz[1]	OFDM (QAM)	100+ Mbps	~300'	802.11a/b/g

[1]Dual-band 802.11n devices can function simultaneously at both 2.4 and 5.0 GHz bands.

802.11n-only wireless networks. The access point processes only 802.11n frames. Dropping support for older devices gives greenfield mode the best goodput.

Table 2.4-4 summarizes 802.11n.

ac (Wi-Fi 5)

802.11*ac (Wi-Fi 5)* is a natural expansion of the 802.11n standard, incorporating even more streams, 80-MHz and 160-MHz channels, and higher speed. To avoid device density issues in the 2.4 GHz band, 802.11ac only uses the 5.0 GHz band.

Table 2.4-5 summarizes 802.11ac.

Current versions of 802.11ac include a version of MIMO called multiuser MIMO (MU-MIMO, discussed later in this objective). MU-MIMO gives an access point the capability to transmit to multiple users simultaneously.

NOTE   For a transmitting method, the 802.11n and 802.11ac devices use a version of OFDM called *quadruple-amplitude modulated (QAM)*.

ax (Wi-Fi 6)

In 2021, the IEEE released the 802.11*ax (Wi-Fi 6)* standard that brings improvements in high-density areas, like stadiums and conference halls. Marketed as Wi-Fi 6 (operating at the 2.4 GHz and 5-GHz bands) and Wi-Fi 6E (operating at the 6-GHz band), 802.11ax implements orthogonal frequency-division multiple access (OFDMA) to increase overall network throughput by as much as 400 percent and decrease latency by 75 percent compared to 802.11ac.

TABLE 2.4-5   802.11ac Summary

Standard	Frequency	Spectrum	Speed	Range	Backward Compatibility
802.11ac	5.0 GHz	OFDM (QAM)	Up to 1 Gbps	~300'	802.11a

TABLE 2.4-6   802.11ax Summary

Standard	Frequencies	Spectrum	Speed	Range	Backward Compatibility
802.11ax	2.4 GHz, 5 GHz, 6 GHz	OFDMA (1024-QAM)	Up to 10 Gbps	~300′	802.11a/b/g/n/ac

Table 2.4-6 summarizes 802.11ax.

The range of 802.11ax hits similar distances to previous Wi-Fi standards of ~300 feet because of limitations on power by the Federal Communications Commission (FCC) in the United States. That doesn't tell the whole story. Improvements in the standard means the throughput at that range is vastly superior to its predecessors.

NOTE   Wi-Fi Alliance President and CEO Edgar Figueroa made a major announcement on October 3, 2018: "For nearly two decades, Wi-Fi users have had to sort through technical naming conventions to determine if their devices support the latest Wi-Fi. Wi-Fi Alliance is excited to introduce Wi-Fi 6, and present a new naming scheme to help industry and Wi-Fi users easily understand the Wi-Fi generation supported by their device or connection." New names were given to previous standards as well (802.11a became Wi-Fi 1, 802.11b became Wi-Fi 2, 802.11g became Wi-Fi 3, 802.11n became Wi-Fi 4, and 802.11ac became Wi-Fi 5).

Frequencies and Range

Related to the wireless spectrum, the terms *frequencies* and *range* often come up.

One of the biggest issues with wireless communication is the potential for interference from other wireless devices. To solve this, different wireless devices must operate in specific transmission frequencies. Knowing about these wireless frequencies will assist you in troubleshooting interference issues from other devices operating in the same wireless band. 802.11 standards use the 2.4-GHz or 5.0-GHz radio frequencies.

NOTE   The Network+ exam objectives read 2.4GHz and 5GHz, but aside from those section headers and initial mention, this book will use the more widely used notation of 2.4 GHz and 5.0 GHz (with spaces after the numbers and .0 after 5).

NOTE   Some specialized 802.11 standards use the 6 GHz or 60 GHz frequencies, but those standards and frequencies are not covered in the Network+ exam objectives.

Wireless networking range is hard to define. You'll see most descriptions listed with quali-fiers such as "*around* 150 feet" and "*about* 300 feet." Wireless range is greatly affected by envi-ronmental factors. Interference from other wireless devices and solid objects affects range.

The maximum ranges listed in the tables for the different 802.11 standards, above, are those presented by wireless manufacturers as the *theoretical* maximum ranges. In the real world, you'll achieve these ranges only under the most ideal circumstances. Cutting the manufac-turer's listed range in half is often a better estimate of the true effective range.

2.4 GHz

Every Wi-Fi network communicates on a channel, a portion of the available spectrum. For the *2.4 GHz* band, the 802.11 standard defines 14 channels of 20 MHz each (that's the chan-nel bandwidth), but different countries limit exactly which channels may be used. In the United States, for example, an access point using the 2.4 GHz band may only use channels 1 through 11. These channels have some overlap, so two nearby WAPs should not use close channels like 6 and 7. Many WAPs use channels 1, 6, or 11 because they don't overlap. You can fine-tune a network by changing the channels on WAPs to avoid overlap with other nearby WAPs. This capability is especially important in environments with many wireless networks sharing the same physical space. A 2.4 GHz connection can travel farther than a 5.0 GHz connection, but at lower speeds 2.4 GHz devices can use a longer range from an access point than 5.0 GHz devices.

5.0 GHz

The *5 GHz* and 6 GHz bands offer many more channels than the 2.4 GHz band. In general, there are around 40 different channels in the spectrums, and different countries have wildly different rules for which channels may or may not be used. The versions of 802.11 that use the 5 GHz and 6 GHz bands use automatic channel switching, so from a setup standpoint we don't worry about channels when we talk about 5 GHz and 6 GHz 802.11 standards. A 5 GHz connection is faster than a 2.4 GHz connection, but 5 GHz devices have to be in a shorter range with the access point.

Channels

The *channels* mentioned in the previous section are regulated. It is important to note that these frequencies are actually a range of frequencies, and each frequency range is known as a channel. If you want, you can change the channel that your wireless devices use, which will change the frequency being used by your wireless network. This is important because you may have a wireless network running on the same channel (frequency) as some of your household devices (such as a cordless phone), which will cause them to interfere with one another. In this case, you can change the channel of the wireless network to prevent the interference from occurring.

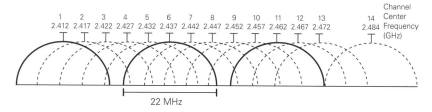

Figure 2.4-1 shows the breakdown of channels in the 2.4 GHz frequency range. You'll notice in Figure 2.4-1 that the frequencies overlap in the 2.4-GHz frequency band from one channel to another. In fact, in the United States (where channels 12–14 are not used), only channels 1, 6, and 11 don't overlap, and that's why they're the only channels that are in fact used. For example, if you are running on channel 6 and you are experiencing problems, try changing to channel 1 or 11. The overlap is caused because the channels in the 2.4-GHz frequency band are separated by 5.0 MHz but have a bandwidth of 22 MHz.

Regulatory Impacts

The *regulatory impacts* on Wi-Fi channels apply rather specifically to the channels in the 2.4 GHz range and more generally to the other ranges. The bottom line is that governments strictly regulate which bands, and which channels within each band, Wi-Fi systems can use.

 ADDITIONAL RESOURCE   Read the article "How Does Wi-Fi Work on Airplanes?," from marthastewart.com, in which I explain the issues with accessing certain Web sites on certain channels, while flying over certain countries: https://www.marthastewart.com/7989513/how-extend-wifi-range-outside.

Channel Bonding

When two adjacent channels in a frequency band are combined, throughput increases. Wi-Fi uses this concept of *channel bonding*, starting with 802.11n and extending to 802.11ac and 802.11ax, since greater throughput allows for more functionality.

Service Set Identifier (SSID)

The *service set identifier (SSID)*—sometimes called a network name—is an identification string (up to 32 bits) that's inserted into the header of each frame processed by an access point. Every Wi-Fi device must share the same SSID to communicate in a single network. By default, an access point advertises its existence by sending out a continuous SSID broadcast. It's the SSID broadcast that lets you see the wireless networks that are available on your wireless devices.

Basic Service Set

Wireless devices connected together into a network, whether ad hoc or infrastructure, require some way to identify that network. Frames bound for computers within the network need to go where they're supposed to go, even when you have overlapping Wi-Fi networks.

The basic service set identifier (BSSID) defines the most basic infrastructure mode network—a *basic service set* (BSS) of one WAP and one or more wireless clients. With such a simple network, the Wi-Fi folks didn't see any reason to create some new numbering or naming scheme, so they made the BSSID the same as the MAC address for the access point. Simple!

Ah, but what do you do about ad hoc networks that don't have an access point?

Independent Basic Service Set (Ad-hoc)

Two or more wireless nodes communicating in ad hoc mode form an IBSS, an *independent basic service set (ad-hoc)*. This is a basic unit of organization in wireless networks. If you think of an IBSS as a wireless workgroup, you won't be far off the mark.

Ad hoc mode networks work well for small groups of computers (fewer than a dozen or so) that need to transfer files or share printers. Ad hoc networks are also good for temporary networks, such as study groups or business meetings.

Hardly anyone uses ad hoc networks for day-to-day work, however, simply because you can't use an ad hoc network to connect to other networks (unless one of the machines is running Internet Connection Sharing [ICS] or some equivalent).

In the event of an actual ad hoc network, the nodes that connect in an IBSS randomly generate a 48-bit string of numbers that looks and functions just like a MAC address, and that BSSID goes in every frame.

You could, if required, discover the MAC address for the access point in a BSS and manually type that into the network name field when setting up a wireless computer. But that causes two problems. First, people don't want to remember strings of 48 binary digits, even if translated out as six hexadecimal octets, like A9–45–F2–3E–CA–12. People want names. Second, how do you connect two or more computers together into an IBSS when the BSSID has to be randomly generated?

To help the connection happen, the Wi-Fi folks created the previously described SSID, a standard name applied to the BSS or IBSS.

Extended Service Set

To really see the power of 802.11 in action, let's take it one step further into a Wi-Fi network that has multiple WAPs: an *extended service set* (ESS). How do you determine the network name at this level? You use the SSID, but you apply it to the ESS as an extended service set identifier (ESSID). In an ESS, every WAP connects to a central switch or switches to become part of a single broadcast domain.

Most Wi-Fi manufacturers just use the term SSID, by the way, and not ESSID. When you configure a wireless device to connect to an ESS, you're technically using the ESSID rather than just the SSID, but the manufacturer often tries to make it simple for you by using only the letters SSID.

Roaming

With multiple WAPs in an ESS, clients will connect to whichever WAP has the strongest signal. As clients move through the space covered by the broadcast area, they will change WAP connections seamlessly, a process called *roaming*.

Antenna Types

There are three *antenna types* common in 802.11 networks: omnidirectional, unidirectional, and patch. Each offers different solutions for coverage of specific wireless network setups. Plus, the signals emanating from the antennas have a feature called polarization that needs to be considered.

Omni

In general, an *omni*, also known as an omnidirectional antenna, radiates signal outward from the access point in all directions. For a typical network, you want blanket coverage and would place an access point with an omnidirectional antenna in the center of the area. This has the advantage of ease of use—anything within the signal radius can potentially access the network. The standard straight-wire antennas that provide the most omnidirectional function are called dipole antennas.

The famous little black antennas seen on older WAPs are all dipoles. A dipole antenna has two radiating elements that point in opposite directions. But if you look at an access point antenna, it looks like it only points in one direction. If you open up one of these antennas, however, you'll see that it has two opposing radiating elements.

A dipole antenna doesn't radiate in a perfect ball. It actually is more of a doughnut shape, which is great for outdoors or a single floor, but it doesn't send much signal above or below the access point.

The omnidirectional and centered approach does not work for every network, for three reasons:

- If the signal exceeds the size of the network space, that signal bleeds out. The signal can bleed out a lot in some cases, particularly if your specific space doesn't allow you to put the WAP in the center, but rather off-center. This presents a security risk as well, because someone outside your network space could lurk, pick up the signal, and do unpleasant things to your network.
- If your network space exceeds the signal of your WAP, you'll need to get some sort of signal booster.
- Any obstacles will produce glaring dead spots in network coverage. Too many dead spots make a less-than-ideal solution. To address these issues, you might need to turn to other solutions.

An antenna strengthens and focuses the radio frequency (RF) output from an access point. The ratio of increase—what's called gain—is measured in decibels (dB). The gain from a typical WAP is 2 dB, enough to cover a reasonable area, but not a very large room. Increasing the signal requires a bigger device antenna. Some WAPs have removable device antennas. To increase the signal in an omnidirectional and centered setup, simply replace the factory device antennas with one or more bigger device antennas.

Directional

When you don't necessarily want to broadcast to the world, you can use one or more *directional* antennas to create a nicely focused network. A directional antenna, also known as a unidirectional antenna, as the name implies, focuses a radio wave into a beam of sorts. Unidirectional antennas come in a variety of flavors, such as parabolic, dish, and Yagi, to name a just a few. A parabolic antenna looks like a satellite dish. A Yagi antenna (named for one of its Japanese inventors) is often called a beam antenna and can enable a focused radio wave to travel a long way, even miles! If you need to connect in a narrow beam (down a hallway or from one faraway point to another), unidirectional antennas are the way to go.

 NOTE The CompTIA Network+ exam objectives do not include patch antennas, but as a network tech you should know that they are flat, plate-shaped antennas that generate a half-sphere beam. Patch antennas are always placed on walls. The half-sphere is perfect for indoor offices where you want to fill the room with a strong signal but not broadcast to the room behind the patch.

Encryption Standards

Encrypting data packets enables wireless network security. *Encryption standards* allow for the electronic scrambling of data packets, locking them with an encryption key before transmitting them onto the wireless network. The receiving network device must possess the decryption key to unscramble the packet and process the data. Thus, a hacker who grabs any data frames out of the air can't read those frames unless the hacker has the decryption key. Enabling wireless encryption through WPA2 or WPA3 provides a good level of security to data packets in transit.

Wi-Fi Protected Access (WPA)/WPA2 Personal [Advanced Encryption Standard (AES)/Temporal Key Integrity Protocol (TKIP)]

Over the years there have been a number of encryption methods for wireless. The granddaddy of wireless security, Wired Equivalent Privacy (WEP), uses a 64- or 128-bit encryption key to scramble data frames. But even with the strongest encryption enabled, WEP isn't a particularly robust security solution. In fact, WEP can be cracked in under a minute with just a regular laptop and open source software. The bottom line with WEP? Don't ever use it today.

WiFi Protected Access (WPA)

The IEEE 802.11i standard was designed to address the problems with WEP and to provide proper authentication. However, the full standard took a while to complete, so the wireless industry implemented an intermediate fix. They invented a sales term called *Wi-Fi Protected Access (WPA)* that adopted most (not all) of the 802.11i standard, fixing some of the weaknesses of WEP. WPA offers security enhancements such as dynamic encryption key generation (keys are issued on a per-user and per-session basis) and an encryption key integrity-checking feature.

Temporal Key Integrity Protocol (TKIP)

WPA works by using an extra layer of security, called the *Temporal Key Integrity Protocol (TKIP)*, around the WEP encryption scheme. It's not, therefore, a complete replacement protocol for WEP and still uses RC4 for cipher initialization—hence the name TKIP-RC4. TKIP added a 128-bit encryption key that seemed unbreakable when first introduced. Within four years of introduction, however, researchers showed methods by which hackers could waltz through WPA security almost as quickly as through WEP security. Another solution had to be found.

WPA2 Personal

The IEEE 802.11i standard amended the 802.11 standard to add much-needed security features. The 802.1X (not used with PSK) authentication measure using EAP provides secure access to Wi-Fi networks.

Cross-Reference

802.1X, a port-based authentication mechanism, is covered in Objective 4.1.

Advanced Encryption Standard (AES)

802.11i also replaced TKIP-RC4 with the much more robust CCMP-AES, which uses *Advanced Encryption Standard (AES)*, a 128-bit block cipher that's much tougher to crack.

 KEY TERM   CCMP stands for Counter Mode Cipher Block Chaining Message Authentication Code Protocol. Whew! That's why we commonly just use the initials, CCMP.

Implementing the full 802.11i standard took time because most of the installed Wi-Fi hardware couldn't be updated to handle AES encryption. WPA held the title of "most secure wireless mechanism" for a number of years.

Eventually, enough devices were made that could support AES that the full 802.11i standard was implemented under the sales term *Wi-Fi Protected Access 2 (WPA2)*. A "WPA2-compliant device" is really just a marketing term for a device that fully supports the 802.11i standard. WPA2 is the current top security standard used on 802.11 networks. WPA2 is not hack-proof, but it definitely offers a much tougher encryption standard that stops the casual hacker cold.

The most common way to set up WPA or WPA2 encryption is to use a simple version called WPA (or WPA2) Pre-shared key (PSK). Basically, with these PSK versions, you create a secret key that must be added to any device that is going to be on that SSID. There is no authentication with WPA-PSK or WPA2-PSK. Wireless routers haven't shipped with WPA as an option for over a decade. This mode is also known as *Personal*.

WPA2 attacks can happen (like WPA attacks of the past), especially with wireless networks using WPA2-Personal passphrases. The attacks take place by using sophisticated methods that make assumptions about the passphrase, and the fact that certain passphrases are used quite often. The most important thing to do to prevent these attacks from succeeding is to use long passphrases (16 or more characters), thus making the network hard to crack. Otherwise, you need authentication.

WPA/WPA2 Enterprise (AES/TKIP)

If you want authentication you move into what most wireless folks call an enterprise setup. For example, when you use a RADIUS server for authentication with WPA2 (or WPA in the past) to create an amazingly secure wireless network, it gets a fancy name: *WPA/WPA2-Enterprise*.

WPA2 Enterprise has the same two encryption options (AES, TKIP) that WPA2 Personal has. TKIP is not considered secure today and is actually deprecated. WPA3 addresses weakness in WPA2's direct use of the Wi-Fi password to encrypt network traffic. WPA3 uses Simultaneous Authentication of Equals (SAE), a key exchange based on Diffie-Hellman that generates unique encryption keys between each client and WAP. This makes it difficult for an attacker to break the encryption key and capture Wi-Fi traffic right out of the air. The Wi-Fi Alliance announced and started certifying devices that use WPA3, the replacement for WPA2 in 2018, although industry adoption has been surprisingly slow. WPA3 does not appear in the CompTIA Network+ exam objectives.

Cellular Technologies

Anyone with a smartphone these days can enjoy the convenience of using wireless *cellular technologies*. Who doesn't love firing up an Android phone or an iPhone and cruising the Internet from anywhere? As cell-phone technology converges with Internet access technologies, competent techs need to understand what's happening behind the scenes. That means tackling an alphabet soup of standards.

Regardless of the standard, the voice and data used on smartphones (unless you have 802.11 wireless turned on) moves through a cellular wireless network with towers that cover the world.

Mobile data services started in the mid-1980s and, as you might imagine, have gone through a dizzying number of standards and protocols, all of which have been revised, improved, abandoned, and reworked. Instead of trying to advertise these fairly complex and intimidating technologies, the industry instead came up with the marketing term *generations*, abbreviated by a number followed by the letter *G*: 2G, 3G, 4G, and 5G.

Salespeople and TV commercials use these terms to push mobile cellular services. The generation terms aren't generally used within the industry, and certainly not at a deeply technical level.

Global System for Mobile Communications (GSM)

The *Global System for Mobile Communications (GSM)*, the first group of networking technologies widely applied to mobile devices, relied on a type of time-division multiplexing called time-division multiple access (TDMA). TDMA enabled multiple users to share the same channel more or less at the same time; and in this scenario, the switching from one user to another happened so quickly no one noticed.

 NOTE There's no "C" on the end of GSM because it originally came from a French term, Groupe Spécial Mobile.

GSM introduced the handy subscriber identity module (SIM) card that is now ubiquitous in smartphones. The SIM card identifies the phone, enabling access to the cellular networks, and stores some other information (contents differ according to many factors, none relevant for this discussion).

The GSM standard was considered a 2G technology. The standard continued to improve over the years, getting new names and better data speeds. One of the last of these was Enhanced Data rates for GSM Evolution (EDGE), which offered data speeds up to 384 Kbps.

Code-Division Multiple Access (CDMA)

Code-division multiple access (CDMA) came out not long after GSM, but used a spread-spectrum form of transmission that was totally incompatible with GSM's TDMA. Rather than enabling multiple users to share a single channel by splitting the channel into time slices, spread-spectrum transmission changed the frequencies used by each user.

CDMA was considered superior to GSM, and U.S. carriers adopted CDMA *en masse*, which created some problems later since the rest of the world went GSM. Plus, CDMA lacked some key features, such as SIM cards. The original CDMA was considered a 2G technology.

Long-Term Evolution (LTE)

Devices and networks using *Long Term Evolution (LTE)* technology rolled out world-wide in the early 2010s and now dominate wireless services. Marketed as and now generally accepted as a true 4G technology, LTE networks feature speeds of up to 300 Mbps download and 75 Mbps upload. All LTE services use SIM cards.

Smartphones have LTE radios built in, but it's easy to add LTE to almost any device. Need LTE on a laptop or a desktop? No problem, get an LTE NIC and just plug it into a convenient USB port.

3G, 4G, 5G

In the late 1990s the International Telecommunication Union (ITU) forwarded a standard called International Mobile Telecommunications-2000 (IMT-2000) to address shortcomings in mobile technology. IMT-2000 defined higher speeds, support for full-time Internet connections, and other critical functions. The standard pushed support for multimedia messaging system (MMS) (so you can send cat pictures in your text messages) and IP-based telephony.

Both GSM and CDMA improved during the late 1990s to the mid-2000s to address IMT-2000: all these improvements were marketed under probably the most confusing marketing term ever used: *3G*. Ideally, 3G meant a technology that supported IMT-2000, although the industry was very lax in how companies used this term. (This time period is so confusing that many technologies in this period were given decimal generations to clarify the situation. One example is GSM EDGE being called 2.9G due to its lack of full IMT-2000 support.)

Evolved High-Speed Packet Access (HSPA+) was the final 3G data standard, providing theoretical speeds up to 168 Mbps, although most HSPA+ implementations rarely exceeded 10 Mbps.

The successor to LTE, which is a true *4G* technology, called *5G* (for fifth generation), offers substantially upgraded technology and dramatically increased speeds over its predecessor. Cellular companies started rolling out 5G in 2019.

5G operates at three bands, low, medium, and high. Clever, huh? All three use a range of frequencies, with low-band running 600–800 MHz (similar to 4G), medium-band at 2.5–3.7 GHz, and high-band at 25–39 GHz. The higher the frequency, the faster the possible throughput speeds and the shorter the range. Depending on the radios installed in 5G towers and devices, expected speeds can range from 30 Mbps up to 1 Gbps.

The high-band 5G implementation will require dense saturation of transmitters/receivers and antennas, so will work best in dense settings, such as stadiums. Additionally, the exceptional speeds offered by 5G makes the technology a viable replacement for other technologies for mobile devices such as laptops and tablets, as well as smoking-fast speeds in the latest smartphones.

Multiple Input, Multiple Output (MIMO) and Multi-user MIMO (MU-MIMO)

You'll recall that MIMO enables the devices to make multiple simultaneous connections called streams and MU-MIMO gives an access point the capability to transmit to multiple users simultaneously. These features are absolutely amazing in their ability to overcome dead spots and similar issues that on earlier versions of 802.11 can only be fixed with aggressive tweaking of WAP locations and antenna types. While *multiple input, multiple output (MIMO) and multi-user MIMO (MU-MIMO)* aren't only to optimize and increase data speed, reduce the number of errors, and improve capacity, it's almost certain you'll see a scenario where simply updating WAPs to 802.11ac or 802.11ax will automatically fix otherwise tricky problems.

REVIEW

Objective 2.4: Given a scenario, install and configure the appropriate wireless standards and technologies

- 802.11 standards include a, b, g, n, ac, and ax. They differ in terms of frequency, spectrum, speed, range, and backward compatibility.
- 802.11 standards use the 2.4-GHz or 5.0-GHz radio frequencies.
- Wireless range is greatly affected by environmental factors. Interference from other wireless devices and solid objects affects range.
- Regulatory impacts by governments affect bands and channels for Wi-Fi.
- Channel bonding combines adjacent channels to increase throughput.
- Wi-Fi networks can be described as a basic service set, extended service set, and independent basic service set.
- The *service set identifier (SSID)*—sometimes called a network name—is an identification string (up to 32 bits) that's inserted into the header of each frame processed by an access point. Every Wi-Fi device must share the same SSID to communicate in a single network.
- When wireless clients roam in an ESS, they'll connect to the access point with the strongest signal.
- Two types of antennas used in Wi-Fi networks are omni and directional.
- Encryption standards include WPA and WPA2, with the encryption being performed by either AES or TKIP.
- Cellular technologies include CDMA, GSM, and LTE.
- Generations of cellular technologies are 3G, 4G, and 5G.
- MIMO and MU-MIMO allow for the overcoming of dead spots, increasing signal distance, and more.

2.4 QUESTIONS

1. Which of the following 802.11 standards is the latest?
   - **A.** n
   - **B.** ax
   - **C.** ac
   - **D.** g

2. Which of the following represents the most geography in a Wi-Fi setup?

    A. ESS

    B. BSS

    C. IBSS

    D. SSID

3. Which of the following encryption standards is likely running in your home?

    A. WPA Enterprise

    B. WPA2 Enterprise

    C. WPA Personal

    D. WPA2 Personal

2.4 ANSWERS

1. **B**   802.11ax is the latest.

2. **A**   An ESS is multiple BSSs.

3. **D**   WPA2 Personal. WPA is deprecated and 802.1X authentication is not found in homes.

Network Operations

DOMAIN 3.0

Domain Objectives

- **3.1** Given a scenario, use the appropriate statistics and sensors to ensure network availability.

- **3.2** Explain the purpose of organizational documents and policies.

- **3.3** Explain high availability and disaster recovery concepts and summarize which is the best solution.

Given a scenario, use the appropriate statistics and sensors to ensure network availability

It's important that information is able to be accessed in a timely and reliable fashion by those who are authorized to access it. That's availability, the "A" in the CIA triad discussed in detail in Objective 4.1. Here, Objective 3.1 explores the use of statistics and sensors for ensuring network availability.

Performance Metrics/Sensors

Various *performance/metrics sensors* can monitor performance and environmental factors to ensure that network operations are performing optimally.

Device/Chassis

Device/chassis sensors, for example, can show multiple performance metrics. Those metrics include temperature, central processing unit (CPU) usage, and memory.

Temperature

The *temperature* shown can reflect thresholds, as shown in sample output from a Cisco switch at https://www.cisco.com/c/en/us/td/docs/switches/lan/catalyst4500/12-2/54sg/configuration/guide/config/pwr_envr.html:

```
Switch# show environment
no alarm

Chassis Temperature = 35 degrees Celsius
Chassis Over Temperature Threshold = 75 degrees Celsius
Chassis Critical Temperature Threshold = 95 degrees Celsius

Power Fan Inline
Supply Model No Type Status Sensor Status
------ ---------------- --------- ----------- ------ ------
PS1 PWR-C45-2800AC AC 2800W good good good
PS2 PWR-C45-1000AC AC 1000W err-disable good n.a.
```

Central Processing Unit (CPU) Usage

Central processing unit (CPU) usage can show how active the CPU was in various units of time, as shown in this sample output from https://www.cisco.com/c/en/us/td/docs/switches/lan/catalyst3750/software/troubleshooting/cpu_util.html:

```
Switch# show processes cpu sorted
CPU utilization for five seconds: 5%/0%; one minute: 6%; five minutes: 5%
```

```
PID Runtime(ms) Invoked uSecs 5Sec 1Min 5Min TTY Process
1 4539 89782 50 0.00% 0.00% 0.00% 0 Chunk Manager
2 1042 1533829 0 0.00% 0.00% 0.00% 0 Load Meter
3 0 1 0 0.00% 0.00% 0.00% 0 DiagCard3/-1
4 14470573 1165502 12415 0.00% 0.13% 0.16% 0 Check heaps
5 7596 212393 35 0.00% 0.00% 0.00% 0 Pool Manager
6 0 2 0 0.00% 0.00% 0.00% 0 Timers
7 0 1 0 0.00% 0.00% 0.00% 0 Image Licensing
8 0 2 0 0.00% 0.00% 0.00% 0 License Client N
9 1442263 25601 56336 0.00% 0.08% 0.02% 0 Licensing Auto U
10 0 1 0 0.00% 0.00% 0.00% 0 Crash writer
11 979720 2315501 423 0.00% 0.00% 0.00% 0 ARP Input
12 0 1 0 0.00% 0.00% 0.00% 0 CEF MIB API
<output truncated>
```

Memory

Memory information can be displayed, as shown in sample output from a Cisco switch at https://www.cisco.com/c/en/us/support/docs/switches/nexus-3000-series-switches/213683-nexus-3000-average-memory-utilization.html:

```
N3K-3548.42# sh system resources | egrep "used"
Memory usage:   4117860K total,   2250220K used,   1867640K free

N3K-3548.42# sh system internal kernel memory global | be NAME |
cut -c 1-42
NAME           |TOTAL                            |
mtc_usd        |  462744   231212   223972 |
fwm            |  277132    97788    84907 |
afm            |  218180    53060    40829 |
netstack       |  380252    45592    38952 |
clis           |  219208    41924    32060 |
m2rib          |  182944    35812    31502 |
--More--
```

Network Metrics

Network metrics that sensors can monitor include bandwidth, latency, and jitter.

Bandwidth

Bandwidth refers to how quickly packets are being moved in and out of interfaces. This is important information that can be used for baseline measurements and troubleshooting/debugging purposes. NetFlow (coming up later in this objective) and Cacti are two software tools that can monitor the bandwidth of routers and switches.

Latency

On a network, *latency* is a delay between the time the sending machine sends a message and the time the receiving machine can start processing that message. Latency can be caused by processing or bandwidth issues. You can troubleshoot latency directly from a managed switch.

Jitter

While a certain amount of latency is expected between connections, when the latency and response rate start to vary, and become inconsistent, this is known as *jitter*. Usually jitter is noticeable in streaming applications, and can be directly attributed to the bandwidth. Jitter is one of the biggest problems with VoIP. You can troubleshoot jitter directly from a managed switch.

SNMP

SNMP (Simple Network Management Protocol) is the de facto network management protocol for TCP/IP networks.

SNMP has had three major versions. SNMP version 1 (SNMPv1) appeared in three RFC (Request for Comments) documents all the way back in 1988. SNMPv2c was a relatively minor tweak to version 1. SNMPv3 added additional security with support for encryption and robust authentication, plus it provided features to make administering a large number of devices easier.

SNMP consists of three components.

An SNMP manager, also known as a network management system (NMS), is software that collects and monitors traffic. Most of the processing and memory resources are provided by this software, which polls network devices at intervals to collect information related to network connectivity, activity, and events.

A managed device, including routers, switches, servers, and more, is what the NMS is polling. For example, a router interface might be polled to see if traffic is too high or low, which could be indicative of a cyberattack.

An agent is software that's running on the devices that are polled that uses SNMP to report to the NMS.

Management Information Bases (MIBs)

The kind of information the SNMP manager can monitor from managed devices varies a lot, primarily because SNMP is an extensible protocol, meaning it can be adapted to accommodate different needs. Developers can create software that queries pretty much any aspect of a managed device, from current CPU load on a server to how much paper is left in a printer. SNMP uses *management information bases (MIBs)* to categorize the data that can be queried and subsequently analyzed. A MIB is a hierarchical format, based on a tree structure, that stores SNMP data.

Object Identifiers (OIDs)

Object identifiers (OIDs) uniquely number individual data pieces within a MIB. Each variable read or set by SNMP is identified by an OID.

Traps

Once set up properly, an SNMP managed network runs regular queries to managed devices and then gathers that information in a format usable by SNMP operators. We need to add a little more jargon to go through the steps of the process.

An SNMP system has up to eight core functions (depending on the version of SNMP), of which four merit discussion here: Get, Response, Set, and Trap. The common term for each of these functions is protocol data unit (PDU).

 NOTE An SNMP PDU is not related to the PDU discussed in Objective 1.1 in the context of the OSI model. It's the typical tech sector practice of repurposing an excellent term. Although traps are the only type of PDU listed in the CompTIA Network+ exam objectives, the others in this section really need to be included for completness purposes.

When an SNMP manager wants to query an agent, it sends a Get request, such as GetRequest or GetNextRequest. An agent then sends a Response with the requested information. Figure 3.1-1 illustrates the typical SNMP process.

An NMS can tell an agent to make changes to the information it queries and sends, called variables, through a Set PDU, specifically SetRequest.

An agent can solicit information from an NMS with *Traps* from the Trap PDU. An agent can send a Trap with or without prior action from the SNMP manager.

You've just had a lot of jargon dropped on you, so here's a scenario that will make the process and terms a little more understandable. The CSCPROF Art Department has a high-end color laser printer for producing brochures. Their CompTIA Network+ certified technicians maintain that laser printer, meaning they replace toner cartridges, change paper, and install the printer maintenance kits. (They're also CompTIA A+ certified, naturally.)

To manage this printer, nicknamed "Anakin," the techs use an SNMP network management system. At regular intervals, the NMS sends a GetRequest to the printer agent about the number of pages printed. According to the Response sent from the printer agent to the NMS, the techs can determine if the printer needs maintenance (that is, if it's at the point in its usage cycle where the printer maintenance kit parts need to be replaced).

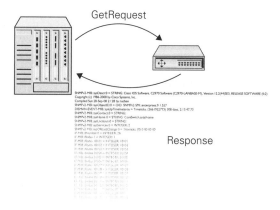

FIGURE 3.1-1 Simple SNMP process

At irregular intervals, the printer agent has to tell the techs that the printer is out of toner or out of paper. Although this information could come from the Get/Response interaction, it makes more sense that it come from the printer agent without a query. Anakin needs to yell "Help!" when he's out of toner. Otherwise the techs have to deal with irate artists, and that's just never going to be pretty. Anakin yells for help by sending a Trap to the NMS.

 NOTE   SNMP systems can use many additional utilities developed over the years. Some can automate various tasks. The snmpwalk utility, for example, tells the SNMP manager to perform a series of Get commands.

The CSCPROF network techs don't sit at the SNMP manager, waiting for Anakin the printer to send messages about toner or ink. Instead, the manager software has the event management capability to send alerts: notifications directly sent to the techs when their intervention is required. These notifications can have a variety of forms, such as text messages via SMS alerts to techs' smartphones or e-mail alerts.

Network Device Logs

Network device logs can provide a lot of information useful in troubleshooting. Devices can log traffic, SSH connections, and more, assuming they're set up to do so. Part of device configuration is to set up the device logging—local logging—to capture the data you'll need. The worst time to discover that logging wasn't set up properly is when devices go down and you're troubleshooting.

Any system that generates electronic log files has two issues. The first is security. Log files are important for the information they provide. The second is maintenance. Log files are going to continue to grow until they fill the mass storage they are stored on. The job of providing proper security and maintenance for log files is called log management.

Logs often contain private or sensitive data and thus must be protected. Access to active logs must be carefully controlled. It's very common to give read access rights only to specific users, to make sure only the correct users have access to the log files. In many cases it's not uncommon for the logging application to have only write access to the files—it's not a good idea to give root access to critical log files.

Generally, log files by default simply grow until they fill the space they are stored on. To prevent this, it's common to make log files *cyclical*—when a file grows to a certain size, it begins to cycle. *Cycling* just means that as a new record appears in the file, the oldest record in the file is deleted. It's also common for log files to be recreated on a time basis. Depending on the utility, you can set a new log file to be created daily, weekly, hourly—whatever is most convenient for the administrators. These files can then be backed up.

There are many laws today that require retention of log files for a certain period of time. It's important to check with your legal department to see if any files need to be kept longer than your standard backup time frames.

Log Reviews

Log reviews of important logs, like traffic logs, audit logs, and syslog, is necessary to be able to know what's happening on a network, especially if there are problems of any type.

Using a tool that can consolidate log data, as well as generate alerts on logs, is important. Splunk is a popular tool for this purpose. If you don't regularly review your logs, you're not getting value from even collecting them, especially at the highest logging level. You should regularly perform log consolidation and log review.

Traffic Logs

Traffic logs contain session information. Entries include date, time, source and destination MAC addresses, IP addresses, ports, application/service names, security rules, rule actions (allow, deny, drop), the interface that the traffic came in and went out on, byte counts, how the session ended, and more.

Audit Logs

Audit logs, also known as audit trails, store events and changes. These include the name of the user that performed an activity, information about the activity, and what the system did in response. Audit logs record system changes, enabling administrators to see what happened related to suspicious activity. Audit logs can even help them troubleshoot and debug. Both successes and failures are in these logs.

Syslog

Syslog, system message logging, enables the collection of messages from many devices, including routers and switches, and transmits them to a syslog server. Syslog servers listen on UDP port 514, logging messages coming from clients.

While syslog can run on computers, it is often used for networking devices, especially those that don't retain logs after a reboot. This is a big aid for troubleshooting a device that may be periodically rebooting or even tracking activity of an attacker who is trying to delete log data from exploited devices.

Logging Levels/Severity Levels

Syslog can automatically tag messages according to *logging levels/severity levels*, according to how it's set up. Severity levels range from 0 Emergency, which means "time to panic," to 7 Debug. The levels in between vary in usage by application, but follow the pattern where each successive level is more benign than the previous one.

0 Emergency

1 Alert

2 Critical

3 Error

4 Warning

5 Notice

6 Informational

7 Debug

Interface Statistics/Status

Cisco routers and switches have a `show interfaces` IOS command that provides *interface statistics/status* information including link state (up/down), speed/duplex, send/receive traffic, cyclic redundancy checks (CRCs), and protocol packet and byte counts.

Link State (Up/Down)

Link state (up/down) is a description of a specific switch or router interface status. The best state to be in is up/up. The first word describes the line status (Layer 1) and the second word describes the protocol status (Layer 2, in most, but not all, cases).

Here's what it looks like on a Cisco switch:

```
GigabitEthernet1/0/1 is up, line protocol is up (connected)
```

If you see down/down, likely causes are the lack of a cable, an incorrect cable, a bad cable, a speed mismatch (for example, one side is configured for 100 Mbps and the other side is configured for 1000 Mbps), the other device is not on, the interface on the other device that this device connects to is in the shutdown state, or the interface on the other device that this device connects to is error disabled.

If you see down/down (err-disabled), the interface was disabled by port security (covered in Objective 4.3). This state only applies to switches, since that's where port security is configured.

If you see administratively down/down, that means the interface was configured with the `shutdown` command and is in the shutdown state.

There is no possible way that up/down would be seen as a link state on a switch. However, on a router, a status of up/down usually indicates a Layer 2 issue, in most cases related to configuration, such as encapsulation errors (coming up shortly in this objective).

Speed/Duplex

Speed/duplex information describes the speed (for example, 100 Mbps, 1 Gbps, etc.) and duplex (half-duplex, which was obsoleted decades ago, or full-duplex, used since then) status of an interface. Here's what speed/duplex information looks like on a Cisco switch:

```
Full-duplex, 1000Mb/s
```

Seeing half-duplex or an unexpected speed could indicate an interface configuration error on the device or on the other device that this device is connected to. Duplex mismatches won't bring an interface down, and are hard to troubleshoot. Speed mismatches will bring an interface down and, therefore, are easier to troubleshoot.

Keeping the default setting of auto for duplex and speed is a best practice for avoiding mismatches.

Send/Receive Traffic

Send/receive traffic information reports on packets sent and received. Here's what it looks like on a Cisco switch:

```
5 minute input rate 0 bits/sec, 0 packets/sec
5 minute output rate 0 bits/sec, 0 packets/sec
956 packets input, 193351 bytes, 0 no buffer
Received 956 broadcasts, 0 runts, 0 giants, 0 throttles
0 input errors, 0 CRC, 0 frame, 0 overrun, 0 ignored, 0 abort
0 watchdog, 0 multicast, 0 pause input
0 input packets with dribble condition detected
2357 packets output, 263570 bytes, 0 underruns
0 output errors, 0 collisions, 2 interface resets
0 babbles, 0 late collision, 0 deferred
0 lost carrier, 0 no carrier
0 output buffer failures, 0 output buffers swapped out
```

Cyclic Redundancy Checks (CRCs)

Cyclic redundancy checks (CRCs) information reports on frames whose computed FCS (frame check sequence) trailer value did not match the value in the Ethernet trailer and, as a result, failed the integrity check. This information can be seen in the output in the preceding section.

Protocol Packet and Byte Counts

Protocol packet and byte counts can also be seen in the previously shown sent/receive traffic output. Values of 0 would indicate a problem with connectivity or configuration. Excessively high values could imply a possible distributed denial of service (DDoS) attack.

Interface Errors or Alerts

The show interfaces command on routers and switches can also display *interface errors or alerts*, including CRC errors, giants, and runts. Encapsulation errors can be seen if debugging is enabled on the routers involved.

CRC Errors

CRC errors in this section is a duplicate in the objectives, and appears in the previous section. They occur when packets contain invalid values, and possible causes include a faulty port, poor wiring, and even electromagnetic interference (EMI).

Giants

Giants are frames that exceed the maximum size of 1518 bytes (14 bytes for the Ethernet header, 1500 bytes for the Ethernet payload, and 4 bytes for the Ethernet trailer).

Here's what output that reports giants looks like on a Cisco switch:

```
Received 956 broadcasts, 0 runts, 0 giants, 0 throttles
```

Giants can be caused by a host configured with a maximum transmission unit (MTU) greater than 1500 bytes or a malfunctioning network interface card (NIC).

Runts

Runts are frames that didn't meet the minimum size of 64 bytes (14 bytes for the Ethernet header, 46 bytes for the Ethernet payload, and 4 bytes for the Ethernet trailer). This information can be seen in the output in the previous section.

In the past, collisions (which were eliminated with full-duplex Ethernet decades ago) were likely causes of runts. Nowadays, bad wiring and electrical interference are leading causes of runts.

Encapsulation Errors

Encapsulation errors occur when two sides of a WAN link are configured differently. WAN encapsulation protocols include PPP (Point-to-Point Protocol), HDLC (High-Level Data Link Control), Frame Relay, and ATM (Asynchronous Transfer Mode). These errors can be seen if debugging is enabled on the routers involved. As previously mentioned, an encapsulation error would cause an up/down state for a router interface.

Environmental Factors and Sensors: Temperature, Humidity, Electrical, Flooding

Environmental factors and sensors can show external *temperature* and *humidity* levels in the server room, issues with *electrical* load, and even information about *flooding*. Many of the available tools for monitoring sensor data are graphical. The popular Zabbix Dashboard, for example, will show all sorts of data about a switch or rack (see Figure 3.1-2). Even with a GUI tracking issues over time, it's a must to implement an altering system that notifies administrators when any sensor is tripped.

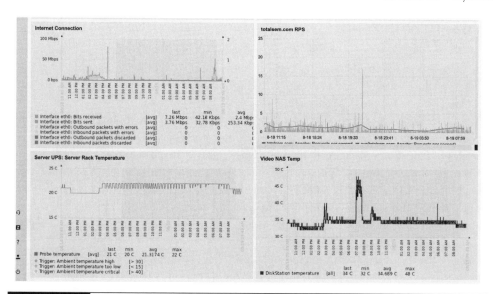

FIGURE 3.1-2   Zabbix reporting sensor data and other information

EXAM TIP   Flooding in a datacenter can occur if it is located in a basement, if a water line freezes and breaks, if the roof above it leaks (rain or melting snow), or if floors above the datacenter have similar issues.

Baselines

The only way to know when a problem is brewing on your network is to know how things perform when all's well with the network. Part of any proper performance monitor is the facility to create a baseline. *Baselines* include a log of performance indicators such as CPU usage, network utilization, and other values to give you a picture of your network and servers when they are working correctly. A major change in these values can point to problems on a server or the network as a whole.

A typical scenario for baselines is for techs and administrators to create and use appropriate documentation and diagrams for how the network optimally performs. They use this information to manage the network over time. CompTIA Network+ exam Objective 5.5 uses the phrase *network performance baselines* to describe the documentation and diagrams needed in this process.

All operating systems come with some form of baseline tools. Performance Monitor is the common tool used to create a baseline on Windows systems. Keep in mind that after major network or infrastructure changes, a new baseline should be generated to represent the new environment and configuration.

NetFlow Data

Packet flow monitoring, accomplished with a set of tools related to general packet sniffers and analyzers, tracks traffic flowing between specific source and destination devices. Cisco developed the concept of packet flow monitoring and subsequently included it in routers and switches. The primary tool is called NetFlow.

NetFlow has been around for quite a while and has evolved into a powerful tool that just about every owner of Cisco equipment uses. NetFlow is similar to SNMP. NetFlow is based on the idea of flows that you define to track the type of traffic you wish to see.

A single flow is a stream of packets from one specific place to another. Each of these flows is then cached in a flow cache. A single entry in a flow cache normally contains information such as destination and source addresses, destination and source ports, the source on the device running that flow, and total number of bytes of that flow. Keep in mind that actual data is not included in this information, just summary data/metadata about the communication.

Analyzing the flow data—CompTIA calls it *NetFlow data*—enables administrators to build a clear picture of the volume and flow of traffic on the network. This in turn enables them to optimize the network by adding capacity where needed or other options.

 NOTE   To use NetFlow you must enable NetFlow on that device. If the device doesn't support NetFlow, you can use stand-alone probes that can monitor maintenance ports on the unsupported device and send the information to the NetFlow collector.

Most of the heavy lifting of NetFlow is handled by the NetFlow collectors. NetFlow collectors store information from one or more devices' NetFlow caches, placing it into a table that can then be analyzed by NetFlow analyzers.

Cross-Reference

NetFlow analyzers are covered in Objective 5.3.

There are many different companies selling different NetFlow analyzers, and which tool you should choose is often a matter of features and cost. Figure 3.1-3 shows a screenshot of a popular tool called LiveAction.

Cisco's NetFlow started the idea of traffic flows that can then be collected and analyzed. Just about every other form of competing flow-monitoring concept (names like sFlow, NetStream, and IPFIX) builds on the idea of the flow.

Uptime/Downtime

Uptime/downtime represents the overall time a router or switch has been functional or dysfunctional.

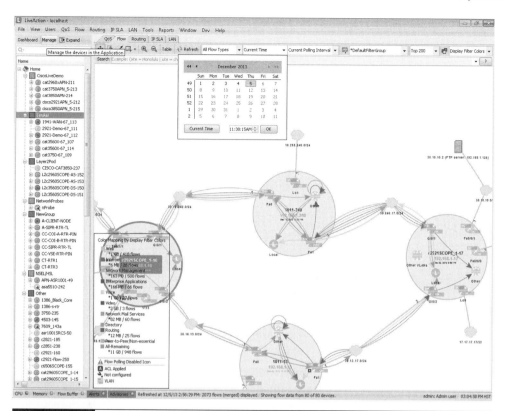

FIGURE 3.1-3   LiveAction in action!

REVIEW

Objective 3.1: Given a scenario, use the appropriate statistics and sensors to ensure network availability

- Various *performance/metrics sensors* can monitor performance and environmental factors. Device/chassis sensors, for example, can show multiple performance metrics. Those metrics include temperature, CPU usage, and memory.
- *Network metrics* that sensors can monitor include bandwidth, latency, and jitter.
- SNMP is the de facto network management protocol for TCP/IP networks.
- SNMP uses *management information bases (MIBs)* to categorize the data that can be queried and subsequently analyzed. A MIB is a hierarchical format, based on a tree structure, that stores SNMP data.
- *Object identifiers (OIDs)* uniquely number individual data pieces within a MIB. Each variable read or set by SNMP is identified by an OID.
- An agent can solicit information from an NMS with *Traps* from the Trap PDU.

- *Network device logs* can provide a lot of information useful in troubleshooting.
- *Log reviews* of important logs, like *traffic logs*, *audit logs*, and *syslog*, is necessary to be able to know what's happening on a network, especially if there are problems of any type.
- Syslog can automatically tag messages according to *logging levels/severity levels*, according to how it's set up. Severity levels range from 0 Emergency, which means "time to panic," to 7 Debug. The levels in between vary in usage by application, but follow the pattern where each successive level is more benign than the previous one.
- Cisco routers and switches have a `show interfaces` IOS command that provides *interface statistics/status* information, including link state (up/down), speed/duplex, send/receive traffic, cyclic redundancy checks (CRCs), and protocol packet and byte counts.
- The `show interfaces` command on routers and switches can also display *interface errors or alerts*, including CRC errors, giants, and runts. Encapsulation errors can be seen if debugging is enabled on the routers involved.
- *Environmental factors and sensors* that help ensure network availability include *temperature*, *humidity*, *electrical*, and *flooding*.
- *Baselines* include a log of performance indicators such as CPU usage, network utilization, and other values to give you a picture of your network and servers when they are working correctly. A major change in these values can point to problems on a server or the network as a whole.
- Analyzing *NetFlow data* enables administrators to build a clear picture of the volume and flow of traffic on the network. This in turn enables them to optimize the network (by adding capacity where needed or other options).
- *Uptime/downtime* represents the overall time a router or switch has been functional or dysfunctional.

3.1 QUESTIONS

1. What's the difference between latency and jitter?
   A. Latency is when jitter and response rate vary.
   B. Jitter is when latency and response rate vary.
   C. Jitter is a measure for LANs, while latency is a measure for WANs.
   D. There is no difference between the two.

2. Which of the following is not an SNMP component?
   A. Managed devices
   B. Agents
   C. Management systems
   D. All of the above are SNMP components.

3. Which of the following is the same thing as FCS errors?

A. CRC errors

B. Giants

C. Runts

D. Encapsulation errors

3.1 ANSWERS

1. **B**   While a certain amount of latency is expected between connections, when the latency and response rate start to vary, and become inconsistent, this is known as *jitter*. Usually this is noticeable in streaming applications, and can be directly attributed to the bandwidth. Jitter is one of the biggest problems with VoIP.

2. **D**   An SNMP system—which creates a managed network—consists of at least three components: managed devices (routers, switches, servers, clients, and more), agents, and management systems. Agents are found on managed devices, which collect and store network information that's sent to management systems.

3. **A**   Cyclic redundancy checks (CRCs) information reports on frames whose computed FCS (frame check sequence) trailer value did not match the value in the Ethernet trailer and, as a result, failed the integrity check.

Objective 3.2 # Explain the purpose of organizational documents and policies

There are hundreds of different organizational documents and policies, including some very common ones that are found in almost every level of organization and specifically identified in exam Objective 3.2, including plans and procedures, hardening and security policies, common documentation, and common agreements. Each has its own specific motivation, but when all of these documents and policies are used together, an organization and its employees can benefit by being efficient, secure, and staying on the right side of the law.

Plans and Procedures

Companies need to manage risk, to minimize the dangers posed by internal and external threats. They need policies in place for expected dangers and they need procedures for things that will happen eventually. This is contingency planning.

Change Management

An IT infrastructure is an ever-changing thing. Applications are updated, operating systems change, server configurations adjust; change is a tricky part of managing an infrastructure. Change needs to happen, but not at the cost of losing security or downtime (which can directly lead to loss of income). The process of creating change in your infrastructure in an organized, controlled, safe way is called *change management*.

Change management usually begins with a change management team. This team, consisting of people from across your organization, is tasked with the job of investigating, testing, and authorizing all but the simplest changes to your network.

Changes tend to be initiated at two levels: strategic-level changes, typically initiated by management (for example, we're going to switch some servers from Windows to Linux); and infrastructure-level changes, typically initiated by someone in IT on behalf of a department. A request needs to be made to the change management team. Strategic changes are larger in scope. For example, there will need to be firewall changes on interior firewalls, IP address information will need to be configured, and if the outgoing server contains business data, it will need to be backed up. In fact, adding it to the backup system may be a separate change request itself. The change management process documents what is going on with the IT infrastructure (often large enough changes are also added to an IT calendar), and they allow you to answer the question that is asked when things go wrong, "What has changed recently?"

The CompTIA Network+ exam objectives stress the latter type of change, where you are the person who will go before the change management team. Change management documents and policies include who can make the change, the reason why a change must occur, the request itself, who will make a decision on that request and how it will be decided, the timeframe needed to fulfil the request and what effect it might have on systems that might need to go down, how the affected parties need to be notified that the change is complete, and how each step is to be documented.

Incident Response Plan

The cornerstone of incident response is the incident response team—usually one or more trained, preassigned first responders with policies in place for what to do. Depending on the type of event, the team may be responsible for things like deciding whether it qualifies as an incident the team should address, ignore, or escalate; evaluating the scope and cause of the issue; preventing further disruption; resolving the cause; restoring order to affected systems; and identifying ways to prevent a recurrence. Most incidents are handled at this level. Organizations should have detailed incident response policies and a detailed *incident response plan* that will guide the actions of the team in various incident scenarios. However, if an incident is so vast that the incident response team cannot stop, contain, or remediate it, disaster recovery comes into play. It's possible that multiple related incidents (the event) will escalate into a problem (the source). In these cases, help desk tracking software apps will assist, as they are part of the Information Technology Infrastructure Library (ITIL) structure.

Disaster Recovery Plan

Disaster recovery (DR) is a critical part of contingency planning that deals directly with recovering your primary infrastructure from a disaster. A disaster is an event that disables or destroys substantial amounts of infrastructure, including natural disasters like hurricanes and floods, as well as attacks like ransomware and sabotage.

Disaster recovery starts before a disaster occurs, with an organization developing a *disaster recovery plan*. An organization considers likely disasters and creates plans for how to deal with them. The actual plans vary by the type of disaster. In many cases an organization has a disaster recovery team, whose goal is to get the IT infrastructure up and running at the primary business location(s). One of the big jobs here is figuring out what kind of system and data backups—copies of essential information that can be restored—your organization will need to get up and running, how often backups should be made, and making sure those backups are available quickly in the face of any negative event.

Business Continuity Plan

When a disaster disables, wipes out, floods, or in some other way prevents the primary infrastructure from operating, the organization should have a plan of action to keep the business going at remote sites. The planning and processes necessary to make this happen are known as business continuity (BC). Organizations plan for this with business continuity planning (BCP). As you might expect, the goal of the team doing BCP is to produce a worthwhile *business continuity plan* that details risks to critical systems, cost to replace or repair such systems, and how to make those replacements or repairs happen in a timely fashion. Good BCP will deal with many issues, but one of the more important ones—and one that must be planned well in advance of a major disaster—is the concept of backup sites. Four types of backup sites will be explored in Objective 3.3.

BCP can even kick in even without a disaster. It can be an onsite generator, which can be used during a potential extended power outage. BCP is meant to keep an organization operational, while DR looks to restore it to full operations. For example, with a main site and a hot standby site in operation, equipment level at the standby site could be 25 percent of what's at the main site. This will provide enough resources to continue business, but at a reduced level. DR will bring the company back to 100 percent level of operations.

 EXAM TIP   Although the terms are sometimes blurred, disaster recovery deals with recovering your primary infrastructure from disaster, and business continuity seeks to keep your business going at alternate locations if the primary location cannot be used. So both a business continuity plan (BCP) and a disaster recovery plan (DRP) should be in place, detailing the steps necessary in those cases.

System Life Cycle

New corporate resources will have a finite lifespan. Generally, you'll plan to purchase a new resource, then purchase it, implement it, and, eventually, decommission it. If a customer organization is caught off guard—for example, if an OS or device goes EOL (end of life) and is no longer supported—the organization might complain that it had no warning. However, when the OS or device was released, the customer knew it would be EOL at some point and, in fact, knew what that exact point was. That customer should have started the decommissioning process the day the new OS or device was installed. That is a way to be proactive in preventing the use of a device that goes EOL, before that EOL moment is reached.

Legacy systems are systems that are no longer supported by the OS maker and are no longer patched. In that case you need to consider the function of the system and either update if possible, or if not possible, isolate the legacy system on a locked-down network segment with robust firewall rules that give the system the support it needs (and protects the rest of the network if the system does get compromised). Equally, you need to be extremely careful about adding any software or hardware to a legacy system, as doing so might create even more vulnerabilities.

Most companies and institutions have policies and best practices in place for dealing with legacy systems. Every computing device has a *system life cycle*, from shiny and new, to patched and secure, to "you're still using that old junk?", to safely decommissioned.

System life cycle policies address asset disposal with the concept of reuse, repurpose, recycle. You shouldn't just throw old gear in the trash. Your old switches and routers might be perfect for a hungry nonprofit's network. Donate and take a tax write-off. Repurpose older access points as simple bridges for devices that don't need high speed, for example, printers and multifunction devices. Deal with anything that stored data by putting it through a shredder and tossing the remains in metal recycling.

Standard Operating Procedures

Organizations have *standard operating procedures* that detail how to do most tasks within the organization. Any changes to procedures made during the change management process should be reflected in an updated standard operating procedures document. Ideally, these should be like process guides to new staff, who should not have to rely on institutional knowledge. What they need to know should all be in the operating procedures.

Hardening and Security Policies

Hardening is a process that tries to eliminate certain attacks by patching any vulnerabilities and shutting down services that are not essential. *Security policies*, documents that define how an organization will protect its IT infrastructure, certainly help in the hardening process. There are hundreds of different security policies, but for the scope of the CompTIA Network+ certification exam you only need to identify just a few of the most common ones. These policies include internal and external ones that affect just about every organization.

Some policies are enforced through technology, while others are "paper policies." Technology doesn't manage everything.

Password Policy

The *password policy* should be based on recommendations that came down from NIST (National Institute of Standards and Technology) in 2017.

In May 2017, NIST drafted guidelines that dealt a big blow to well-established password policies. NIST recommended to remove periodic password change requirements and to remove the need for required character groups of uppercase letters, lowercase letters, numbers, and symbols. NIST instead recommended to add the screening of possible passwords against password lists and known compromised passwords. NIST also recommended multifactor authentication (MFA), which is discussed in Objective 4.1.

NIST's belief is that overly complex passwords and passwords that change too frequently are too hard for users to remember, which will cause these users to write them down and store them insecurely. Furthermore, keystroke logging, phishing, and social engineering attacks work just as well on complex passwords as they do on simpler ones.

Finally, keep in mind that length beats anything else against brute-force and dictionary password attacks, which are discussed in Objective 4.2. In other words, a long password using one character set is stronger and more secure than a shorter password that uses multiple character sets!

Acceptable Use Policy

An *acceptable use policy* (AUP) defines what is and what is not acceptable to do on an organization's computing devices, systems, services, networks, and other resources. It's arguably the most famous of all security policies because it is the one document that pretty much everyone who works for any organization is required to read and, in many cases, sign before they can start work. The following are some provisions contained in a typical acceptable use policy:

- **Ownership**   Equipment and any proprietary information stored on the organization's systems are the property of the organization.
- **Network access**   Users will access only information they are authorized to access.
- **Privacy/consent to monitoring**   Anything users do on the organization's systems is not private. The organization will monitor what is being done on computers at any time.
- **Illegal use**   No one may use an organization's resources for anything that breaks a law. This is usually broken down into many subheadings, such as introducing malware, hacking, scanning, spamming, and so forth.

 NOTE   Many organizations require employees to sign an acceptable use policy, especially if it includes a consent to monitoring clause.

Bring Your Own Device (BYOD) Policy

A *bring your own device (BYOD) policy*/deployment allows users to use their personal mobile devices and laptops for company work. The company installs their applications on employees' devices. Employees install their corporate e-mail accounts on their personal devices. BYOD requires tight controls and separation of employee personal data from corporate data.

BYOD deployments have benefits and challenges. The benefits are fairly obvious. The organization saves money because employees pay for their own devices. Employees get the devices they prefer, which can increase employee happiness and productivity. The flip side of this, BYOD challenges, revolve around security, end-user support, and privacy. If a user's device gets lost or stolen, that puts at risk both company information and private information. Does the support staff know how to provide help with every device? What if it's a later model than they've worked with in the past? What do they do then? What about monitoring software installed on the mobile device? Does it stay active during employee non-work time? How do you make that call? What about users who unwittingly bring in devices that are already compromised, putting the security of other devices—not to mention the organization's data—at risk?

Often, if a user uses a personal device to access company data, the device must be enrolled in the company device management solution. For example, during the setup of a company e-mail account on a device, the device needs to be set to be fully or partially managed by the company. From the company perspective, that device needs to meet a minimum standard to store corporate data, including e-mail. While this is very common, new features allow for the separation of business and personal profiles, so that when an employee loses their device or leaves the company, just the business data can be deleted, and not any personal data.

Remote Access Policy

A *remote access policy* enforces rules on how, when, and from what device users can access company resources from remote locations. A typical restriction might be to not allow access from an open wireless portal, for example.

Onboarding and Offboarding Policy

An *onboarding policy* includes the setup of employees in all IT systems and the issuing of devices. An *offboarding policy* includes the proper removal of user accounts, access, and return of devices.

Onboarding and offboarding can also apply to devices. Onboarding of devices takes place in several ways, but one common practice is to require any previously unfamiliar mobile device accessing an internal Wi-Fi network to go through a series of checks and scans. While exactly which checks and scans take place varies depending on the deployment model, a typical BYOD onboarding process may include the following:

* A sign-on page requiring a username and password
* An authorization page describing all applicable policies to which the user must agree

- A malware scan of the device
- An application scan of the device

Offboarding of devices is important, too. Mobile devices move out of organizations just as often as they move in, for various reasons. A person quits and intends to take their phone with them. Mobile devices get old and are due for replacement. A device that uses tablets for controls switches from iPads to Android tablets. Whatever the case, it's important that every outgoing device goes through an inspection (sometimes manual, sometimes automatic) that deletes proprietary applications as well as any data that the organization doesn't want out in the wild. The same applies to laptops.

Security Policy

Although all policies covered in this section are, in fact, examples of security policies, a specific *security policy* could be a high-level overview that identifies potential threats and protection mechanisms, both of which will be defined in greater detail in other policies. A security policy could cover other aspects, including the use of passcards and the need to adhere to physical security. For example, a company might have a policy that every employee entering a building must "badge in," so that in the event of an emergency, the locations of all employees are known. Another example would be requiring guests to sign in and, in some cases, have their picture taken.

Data Loss Prevention

Data loss prevention (DLP) can mean a lot of things, from redundant hardware and backups, to access levels to data. A *data loss prevention* policy takes into consideration many of these factors and helps minimize the risk of loss or theft of essential company data. This policy usually deals with use of data on portable devices (laptops or removable drives) and sending of data through e-mail or other communication platforms. Data loss prevention in retail locations, though, usually deals with external and internal theft.

Common Documentation

Common documentation includes a physical network diagram, logical network diagram, wiring diagram, site survey report, audit and assessment report, and baseline configurations.

Physical Network Diagram

A *physical network diagram* maps out physical aspects of the datacenter. One or more physical network diagrams can include floor plans, rack diagrams, and documents describing the physical components and connectivity in the centralized wiring rooms on each floor.

Physical network diagrams rely on a few standard tools for layout, such as Microsoft Visio, Wondershare EdrawMax, and diagrams.net.

Floor Plan

A datacenter *floor plan* includes the dimensions and locations of rooms, but expands dramatically to include details. Floor plans include locations of—and detailed information about—racks, hot and cold aisles, raised floors, ceiling heights, air conditioning units, ductwork, and so on. Floor plan documentation can take many pages, illustrations, and discussion.

A full office floor plan is used for fire safety, as well as a reference for something like a network locations spreadsheet to know where, for example, office GOL 2707 is.

A datacenter plan could include the wiring and switching in the temperature-controlled server room and a NOC (network operations center) room. There would be easy restroom access, and everything would be behind the safety of a reception area.

Intermediate Distribution Frame (IDF)/Main Distribution Frame (MDF) Documentation

The main distribution frame and intermediate distribution frames provide connectivity to the outside world (MDF) and network connectivity within each floor (IDF). The *intermediate distribution frame (IDF)/main distribution frame (MDF) documentation* require unique and detailed documentation of the overall layout and connections, plus specific rack diagrams (covered in the next section) for their various components. Figure 3.2-1 shows the MDF documentation. The figure provides details about the demarc connection and the rack holding the

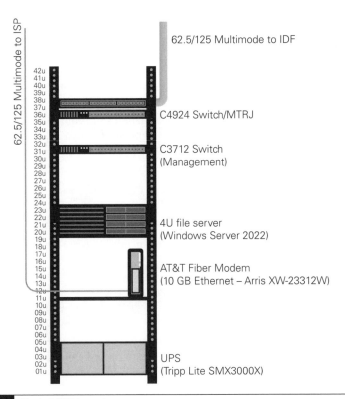

FIGURE 3.2-1 Basic MDF layout

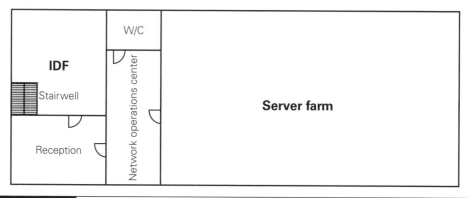

FIGURE 3.2-2   Basic layout of a datacenter lower floor

patch panels and switches that provide further connectivity within the datacenter, and the uninterruptible power supply (UPS) providing clean power to the rack components. The make and model of each component are clearly labeled.

Further documentation accompanies the MDF racks that details firmware versions, service and upgrade records, assigned technicians, vendor contacts, and so on.

Figure 3.2-2 shows the basic layout of the lower level of a datacenter. Note the three major sections. There is a wiring room in the west (left), a network operations center in the center, and the server farm in the east (right).

The wiring room is the IDF that serves as the wiring focal point for all the devices on that floor. This is also called a telecommunications room. The network operations center houses network engineers and technicians who maintain the applications housed in the datacenter, such as databases, Web servers, and more. The vast majority of the lower level is the server farm, with row upon row of racks holding stacks of servers. Each rack is topped with two switches.

Figure 3.2-3 drills down further into the server farm area, showing the hot aisles—where heat can go away from the servers—and cold aisles—where the air conditioning vents pump cold air for thirsty servers.

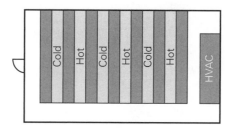

FIGURE 3.2-3   Floor plan details of the server farm

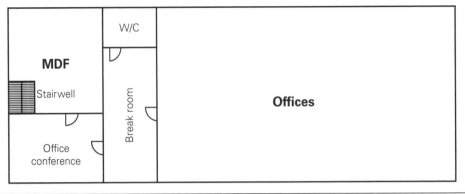

FIGURE 3.2-4 Upper level floor plan of a datacenter

Figure 3.2-4 shows the upper-floor layout—although without individual offices mapped—with both a telecommunications room for the floor and an MDF that holds all the equipment that enables a company's connection to the outside world.

Rack Diagram

Drilling down for more details, each rack (in the server farm and the IDFs and MDF) has a detailed *rack diagram* with many details. Figure 3.2-5 shows one such rack. Note that the

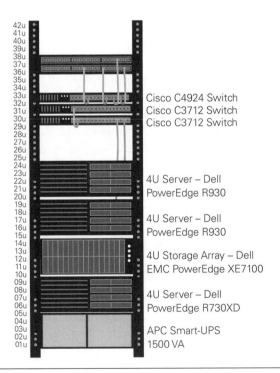

FIGURE 3.2-5 Rack diagram

location and make and model of each component on the rack is labeled. Appended to this illustration is further documentation that has the current firmware version, date of purchase, upgrade history, service history, technician in charge of servicing, vendor contact, licensing information, and more.

Logical Network Diagram

Essential network documentation includes a *logical network diagram*, a line drawing that shows the connectivity among the many devices in the network. Figure 3.2-6 shows the server farm portion of a datacenter. Accompanying the logical drawing would be pages of additional documentation, including specific wiring standards used, vendor information, and so on.

Wiring Diagram

A *wiring diagram* can show any number of types of wiring, from the full electrical map in Figure 3.2-7 to a detailed layout of the physical space with drops to each workstation and full cable runs. Wiring diagrams and the detailed additional documents provide absolutely essential network documentation for the datacenter.

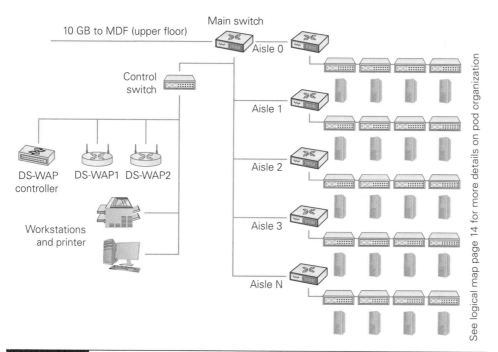

FIGURE 3.2-6 Logical network diagram showing a datacenter server farm

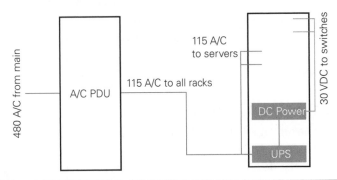

FIGURE 3.2-7   Wiring diagram showing the electrical components and connections in the server farm of a datacenter

Site Survey Report

A periodic site survey queries everything about the datacenter. Information learned from the site survey is the basis for a *site survey report*. This starts with an overall assessment and then drills down into each of the following categories:

- Layout and space utilization
- Infrastructure installed
- Expectations for the organization
- Future requirements
- Concerns about current performance

Drilling down, inspections should cover exhaustive details. For layout and space utilization, for example, examiners should inspect, and create detailed reports that include, at least the following:

- General layout
- Space utilization
- Thermal management
- Electrical distribution
- Cabling types and paths
- Racks, cabinets, server locations
- Labeling compliance with ANSI/TIA 606-C

Every category examined by the site survey team would get equally granular into aspects pertaining to that category.

The site survey final documentation, the site survey report, provides not only a picture of the current state of the datacenter, but also recommendations for improvements in any number of areas. The site survey report is an essential piece of datacenter maintenance and development.

Audit and Assessment Report

Annually at least, a datacenter should have a thorough audit that assesses compliance with every applicable law and regulation for the industry. This audit should be made by an outside organization that specializes in auditing to avoid any potential conflict of interest or bias. The laws and regulations that almost certainly apply include the following:

- **ISO/IEC 27001** Standard (jointly published by the International Organization for Standardization and International Electrotechnical Commission) that helps organizations manage and secure assets by making and implementing an information security management system (ISMS). An ISMS enables organizations to categorize and organize their many security controls—measures put in place to lock down the many systems employed.
- **ISO/IEC 27002** Standard that helps organizations manage security policies on every level.
- **HIPAA (Health Insurance Portability and Accountability Act)** U.S. federal law that regulates how organizations manage health information data to protect the privacy of individuals and other entities.
- **PCI DSS (Payment Card Industry Data Security Standard)** Standard for protecting credit card and other financial information exchanged between the organization and outside entities. The datacenter absolutely needs to be PCI DSS compliant.
- **GDPR (General Data Protection Regulation)** Standard that allows individuals to better control their personal data, which affects any business collecting information on European citizens, especially if that company conducts business in the EU. Many U.S. companies had to update their data collection and usage policies as a result of the GDPR.

The standards mentioned here are the tip of the iceberg when it comes to the laws and regulations governing organizations such as datacenters. The highly detailed and technical nature of each of these laws and regulations make yet another compelling case for using an outside firm to do the audit. At the end of an audit, the auditing firm produces an *audit and assessment report* that details all findings and recommendations for upgrades, fixes for compliance, and so on.

Baseline Configurations

Once the datacenter is up and running and efficiently humming along, the *baseline configurations* of all the components of the datacenter are documented. Note that this is a network baseline rather than a performance baseline—the latter examines throughput, bandwidth, and the like. A baseline configuration describes all the pieces, including portable computers, servers, switches, routers, and so on; plus, all the software packages installed on everything. The baseline configuration also includes network topology and placement of devices in the organization.

The baseline configuration provides the foundation for future upgrades. When any upgrades happen, organizations should update the baseline configuration documentation to the new baseline.

 NOTE This definition of baseline configuration reflects the best practices outlined in NIST Special Publication 800-128, Guide for Security-Focused Configuration Management of Information Systems.

Common Agreements

Dealing with third-party vendors is an ongoing part of any organization. When you are dealing with third parties, you must have common agreements that define the relationship between you and the third party.

Non-Disclosure Agreement (NDA)

Any company with substantial intellectual property will require new employees—and occasionally even potential candidates—to sign a *non-disclosure agreement (NDA)*, a legal document that prohibits the signer from disclosing any company information learned as part of his or her job.

An NDA will be signed by any person or organization coming into contact with any confidential business intellectual property (even in cases where the business doesn't have much). Viewing non-released versions of a program will often include an NDA as well.

Service-Level Agreement (SLA)

A *service-level agreement (SLA)* is a document between a customer and a service provider that defines the scope, quality, and terms of the service to be provided. In CompTIA terminology, SLA requirements are a common part of business continuity and disaster recovery.

SLAs are common in IT, given the large number of services provided. Some of the more common SLAs in IT are provided by ISPs to customers. A typical SLA from an ISP defines the following:

- **Service provided** Defines the minimum and/or maximum bandwidth and describes any recompense for degraded services or downtime.
- **Equipment** Defines what equipment, if any, the ISP provides. It also specifies the type of connections to be provided.
- **Technical support** Defines the level of technical support that will be given, such as phone support, Web support, and in-person support. This also defines costs for that support.

Furthermore, companies today have internal SLAs. For example, IT is often the provider of services to other departments, and they need to meet their own internal service delivery targets.

Memorandum of Understanding (MOU)

A *memorandum of understanding (MOU)* is a document that defines an agreement that is often a precursor to a contract. Oftentimes a CEO will write an MOU before having lawyers of both sides draft a contract. It is the first step in the formal process to work together. Such a document is also used to define an agreement between two parties in situations where a legal contract wouldn't be appropriate. This type of an MOU can define the duties the parties commit to perform for each other and a time frame for the MOU and is common between companies that have only occasional business relations with each other. For example, all of the hospitals in a city might generate an MOU to accept each other's patients in case of a disaster such as a fire or tornado. This MOU would define costs, contacts, logistics, and so forth.

REVIEW

Objective 3.2: Explain the purpose of organizational documents and policies

- Companies need to manage risk, to minimize the dangers posed by internal and external threats. They need policies in place for expected dangers and they need procedures for things that will happen eventually. This is contingency planning.

- The process of creating change in your infrastructure in an organized, controlled, safe way is called *change management.*

- Organizations should have detailed incident response policies and a detailed *incident response plan* that will guide the actions of the team in various incident scenarios.

- Disaster recovery starts before a disaster occurs, with an organization developing a *disaster recovery plan.* An organization considers likely disasters and creates plans for how to deal with them.

- The goal of the team doing BCP is to produce a worthwhile *business continuity plan* that details risks to critical systems, cost to replace or repair such systems, and how to make those replacements or repairs happen in a timely fashion.

- Every computing device has a *system life cycle*, from shiny and new, to patched and secure, to "you're still using that old junk?", to safely decommissioned.

- Organizations have *standard operating procedures* that detail how to do most tasks within the organization. Any changes to procedures made during the change management process should be reflected in an updated standard operating procedures document.

- *Hardening* is a process that tries to eliminate certain attacks by patching any vulnerabilities and shutting down services that are not essential. *Security policies*, documents that define how an organization will protect its IT infrastructure, certainly help in the hardening process.

- The *password policy* should be based on recommendations that came down from NIST (National Institute of Standards and Technology) in 2017.

- An *acceptable use policy* defines what is and what is not acceptable to do on an organization's computing devices, systems, services, networks, and other resources.

- A *bring your own device (BYOD) policy*/deployment allows users to use their personal mobile devices and laptops for company work.

- A *remote access policy* enforces rules on how, when, and from what device users can access company resources from remote locations.

- An *onboarding policy* and *offboarding policy* can refer to employees of a company as well as their devices.

- Although all policies in this objective are, in fact, examples of security policies, a specific *security policy* could be a high-level overview that identifies potential threats and protection mechanisms, both of which will be defined in greater detail in other policies.

- A *data loss prevention* policy takes into consideration many of these factors and helps minimize the risk of loss or theft of essential company data.

- A *physical network diagram* maps out physical aspects of the datacenter. One or more physical network diagrams can include floor plans, rack diagrams, and documents describing the physical components and connectivity in the centralized wiring rooms on each floor.

- A datacenter *floor plan* includes the dimensions and locations of rooms, but expands dramatically to include details.

- Each rack (in the server farm and the IDFs and MDF) has a detailed *rack diagram* with many details.

- Essential network documentation includes a *logical network diagram*, a line drawing that shows the connectivity among the many devices in the network.

- A *wiring diagram* can show any number of types of wiring, from a full electrical map to a detailed layout of the physical space with drops to each workstation and full cable runs.

- A periodic site survey queries everything about the datacenter. Information learned from the site survey is the basis for a *site survey report*.

- At the end of an audit, the auditing firm produces an *audit and assessment report* that details all findings and recommendations for upgrades, fixes for compliance, and so on.

- Once the datacenter is up and running and efficiently humming along, the *baseline configurations* of all the components of the datacenter are documented.

- Dealing with third-party vendors is an ongoing part of any organization. When you are dealing with third parties, you must have *common agreements* that define the relationship between you and the third party.

- Any company with substantial intellectual property will require new employees—and occasionally even potential candidates—to sign a *non-disclosure agreement (NDA)*, a legal document that prohibits the signer from disclosing any company information learned as part of his or her job.

- A *service-level agreement (SLA)* is a document between a customer and a service provider that defines the scope, quality, and terms of the service to be provided.

- A *memorandum of understanding (MOU)* is a document that either defines an agreement that is often a precursor to a contract or defines an agreement between two parties in situations where a legal contract wouldn't be appropriate.

3.2 QUESTIONS

1. Which of the following deals with how an organization will get the original site operational again if it becomes unusable?
    A. Remote access policy
    B. System life cycle
    C. Business continuity plan
    D. Disaster recovery plan

2. Which of the following policies deals with what users can do on an organization's resources?
    A. Remote access policy
    B. Acceptable use policy
    C. Password policy
    D. Onboarding and offboarding policy

3. Which of the follow agreements is used where a legal contract wouldn't be appropriate?
    A. Non-disclosure agreement (NDA)
    B. Service-level agreement (SLA)
    C. Memorandum of understanding (MOU)
    D. Audit and assessment report

3.2 ANSWERS

1. **D**   The disaster recovery plan deals with recovering the primary infrastructure.

2. **B**   The AUP defines what is and what is not acceptable to do on an organization's resources and is arguably the most famous of all security policies.

3. **C**   A memorandum of understanding (MOU) can be used in lieu of a legal contract.

Objective 3.3 Explain high availability and disaster recovery concepts and summarize which is the best solution

As previously covered in Objective 3.2, disaster recovery is a critical part of contingency planning that deals directly with recovering all or part of your primary infrastructure from a disaster. A disaster is an event such as a hurricane or flood that disables or destroys substantial amounts of infrastructure. While natural disasters are often considered foremost in this context, a powerful cyberattack could also qualify as a disaster, especially if done to critical infrastructure.

Disaster recovery starts before a disaster occurs, with an organization developing a disaster recovery plan, discussed in Objective 3.2. An organization considers likely disasters and creates plans for how to deal with them. The actual plans vary by the type of disaster, but there are a few concepts you'll find in just about every situation. It's important that the disaster recovery plan contains high availability and disaster recovery concepts, with different solutions specified for different scenarios. These include load balancing, multipathing, network interface card (NIC) teaming, redundant hardware/clusters, facilities and infrastructure support, redundancy and high availability (HA) concepts, and network device backup/restore plans.

Load Balancing

As a concept, *load balancing* means to share among two or more systems the effort to enable some process to work. One such example is using multiple servers as a server cluster that manifests as a single entity. Special-purpose load balancers help apportion the work among the various servers. For example, spine and leaf datacenters rely on protocols like Equal-Cost Multipath (ECPM) to balance the work among the various switches so that no single connection gets swamped. Load balancing in its many forms is one pillar of high availability. Network load balancers, like BIG-IP from F5, are frontend load balancers for pools of servers or services, like Web servers.

Multipathing

As explained in Objective 1.7 (in regard to iSCSI), *multipathing* involves creating and using multiple paths or connections between resources. At a minimum, an OS needs drivers that support multipathing, as multipathing is managed at the OS or driver level. Furthermore, multipathing requires at least two special NICs or two host bus adapters (HBAs), or a dual-port HBA.

This provides the host OS two paths to the storage controller. A typical layout would have two HBAs connected to two different switches, with each switch having two connections, one to each storage controller, providing four paths from the server to storage. The storage controllers are usually active/active, but often limit a server to one active path to the storage.

Network Interface Card (NIC) Teaming

Grouping up to 32 physical Ethernet network interface cards (also known as network adapters) into one or more virtual network adapters, implemented through software, is known as *network interface card (NIC) teaming*. This allows for fault tolerance, load balancing, and improved performance.

 NOTE   NIC teaming is also known as NIC bonding, port bonding, port aggregation, and link aggregation

Redundant Hardware/Clusters

Clustering, in the traditional sense, means to have multiple pieces of equipment, such as servers, connected in a manner that appears to the user and the network as one logical device, providing data and services to the organization. Clusters usually share high-speed networking connections as well as data stores and applications and are configured to provide redundancy if a single member of the cluster fails.

Even when talking about clustering, such as Microsoft clustering solutions, services like IIS (Internet Information Services, a Web server) can be load balanced through network cluster components (network load balancing), which is different from server or service clustering. Few clustering solutions are active-active (where all members of the cluster are active at the same time, discussed later in this objective), but there are more instances for load balancing.

Redundancy ensures high availability on many levels through the use of additional equipment and connection options. If one goes down, another takes its place.

With *redundant hardware/clusters*, you put into place primary switches, routers, firewalls, and other network gear, then have at the ready backup machines to step up in case the primary machine fails. Core to building high availability into a network is failover, the ability for backup systems to detect when a master has failed and then to take over.

If you're going to use multiple devices to do one job, there must be a way to make multiple devices look like a single device to the rest of the devices. This is commonly done by having multiple devices share a single external MAC address or IP address while using their own internal MAC addresses and IP addresses to communicate to each other.

Redundant hardware inside of devices, such as power supplies, also fits into this category. Redundant hardware is separate from clusters. Two redundant switches (for example, at the distribution layer or in spine and leaf) are not clustered; they are just redundant and provide a backup for each other in the event that one device fails. The same is true of a pool of Web frontend servers, where there can be several servers serving up Web pages for a domain. There are multiple servers, but no cluster. The way they're selected could be through a DNS round robin algorithm or through the decision of a network load balancer in front of them.

Switches

Switches can be placed in a stack. Stackable switches appear as a single switch but have the port capacity of all the combined switch capacities. A single IP address of the stack is used for remote administration. Cisco EtherSwitch service modules or Catalyst 9500 switches connect through special Cisco StackWise ports, and the Cisco StackWise technology allows them to act together and appear as a single switch.

Switches can be non-stacked and redundant. Stacking them gives them one configuration that is shared, and the manager of the stack will fail over to another switch if one fails. In that case, it becomes much like a small cluster of switches. It is a good idea to have redundant paths out of that stack of switches, not all on the same switch.

Routers

Routers support both redundancy and clustering. You can have redundant routers (non-clustered) that route packets out of a network, with redundant equal or different cost routes or managed via a dynamic routing protocol. There can also be redundant service providers for those routers, with one router supporting two ISPs or each router handling one ISP. Clustering is supported through a first hop redundancy protocol (FHRP), discussed later in this objective.

Firewalls

Firewalls can also be deployed with redundancy and clustering. Multiple firewalls can be independent but allow for possible manual failover (by updating clients or routers). Also, an organization that implements defense-in-depth philosophy will have network perimeter firewalls, internal firewalls, and device-level (host) firewalls that provide redundancy. In fact, many firewall products allow for load balancing or failover, where failover can be considered clustering.

Facilities and Infrastructure Support

Facilities and infrastructure support requires many different elements for equipment rooms, including an uninterruptible power supply (UPS), power distribution units (PDUs), a generator, HVAC, and fire suppression.

Uninterruptible Power Supply (UPS)

You can mount almost any network hardware component into a rack. All manufacturers make rack-mounted switches that mount into a rack with a few screws. These switches are available with a wide assortment of ports and capabilities. There are even rack-mounted servers, complete with slide-out keyboards, and rack-mounted uninterruptible power supplies (UPSs) to power the equipment (see Figure 3.3-1).

All those boxes in the rack need good-quality power. Even the smallest rack should run off of a good *uninterruptible power supply (UPS)*, a battery backup that plugs into the wall. Make sure you get one that can handle the amount of wattage used by all the equipment in the rack.

A UPS provides several benefits. First, it acts as an inverter. It stores power as direct current in its battery, then inverts that power to alternating current as needed by the servers and other boxes in the rack. A good UPS acts as a power monitoring tool so it can report problems when there's any fluctuation in the electrical supply. All UPS boxes can provide security from power spikes and sags.

A UPS enables you to shut down in an orderly fashion. It does not provide enough power for you to continue working (generators, which do, are covered shortly). The orderly shutdown of servers ensures availability during the disaster recovery phase, when the servers need to be brought back up again, without corruption.

 NOTE A datacenter UPS can power a whole server room. An example of one is the Eaton Power Xpert 9395C UPS: https://www.eaton.com/us/en-us/catalog/backup-power-ups-surge-it-power-distribution/power-xpert-9395c-ups.html?utm-source=SwitchOn&utm-medium=301.

FIGURE 3.3-1 A rack-mounted UPS

Power Distribution Units (PDUs)

Bigger installations will incorporate *power distribution units (PDUs)* for centralized power management (see Figure 3.3-2). PDUs enable remote connectivity and management for monitoring power levels. On the surface, a PDU works like a power strip, providing multiple outlets for components, drawing electricity directly from a wall socket or indirectly from a UPS. Better PDUs enable remote connectivity and management for monitoring power levels.

Generator

The more-demanding equipment room also demands more robust power and battery backup. A single, decent UPS might adequately handle brief power fluctuations for a single rack, for example, but won't be able to deal with a serious power outage. For that kind of power redundancy—keeping the lights on and the servers rolling—you'd need to connect to the equipment room a power *generator*, a device that burns some petroleum product to produce electricity when the main grid goes dark.

Important considerations include sizing, location, and gas supply. Gas, diesel, or propane need a form of onsite storage, but natural gas will be on-demand.

HVAC

Racks with servers, switches, routers, and such go into closets or server rooms and they dump heat. The environment within this space must be monitored and controlled for both temperature and humidity. Network components and servers work better when cool rather than hot.

FIGURE 3.3-2   PDU in server rack

The placement of a rack should optimize the airflow in a server area. All racks should be placed so that components draw air in from a shared cool row and then exhaust the hot air into a hot row (shown previously in Figure 3.2-3).

Known simply as *HVAC*, the heating, ventilation, and air conditioning system should be optimized to recirculate and purify the hot air into cool air in a continuous flow. What's the proper temperature and humidity level? The ideal for the room, regardless of size, is an average temperature of 68 degrees Fahrenheit and around 50 percent humidity.

Fire Suppression

A proper *fire suppression* system—one that can do things like detect fire, cut power to protect sensitive equipment, displace oxygen with fire-suppressing gasses, alert relevant staff, and activate sprinklers in a pinch—is an absolute must for any server closet or room. You need to get any electrical spark out quickly to minimize server or data loss.

Redundancy and High Availability (HA) Concepts

Redundancy and high availability (HA) concepts help ensure that resources offered are available when clients request them.

Cold Site

A *cold site* is a location that consists of a building, facilities, desks, toilets, parking—everything that a business needs…except computers. A cold site generally takes more than a few days to bring online.

Warm Site

A *warm site* has everything found in cold site, but adds computers loaded with software and functioning servers—a complete hardware infrastructure. A warm site lacks current data and may not have functioning Internet/network links. Bringing this site up to speed may start with activating your network links, and it most certainly requires loading data from recent backups. A warm site should only take a day or two to bring online.

Hot Site

A *hot site* has everything a warm site does, but also includes very recent backups. It might need just a little data restored from a backup to be current, but in many cases a hot site is a complete duplicate of the primary site. A proper hot site should only take a few hours to bring online.

Cloud Site

As organizations increasingly migrate servers and services to the cloud, a cloud-site backup becomes a viable alternative to any of the traditional options. With a *cloud site* backup "location," everything of note is stored in the cloud, including servers, clients, applications, and data. If some disaster hits, an organization can quickly move to a new location unaffected by the disaster and access its resources as soon as it has Internet connectivity. In the increasingly decentralized workplace today, having a cloud-based system makes disaster "recovery" almost a moot point.

Active-Active vs. Active-Passive

Clustering solutions are commonly *active-active* examples of high availability in that all members of the cluster are active at the same time. One example of an active-active clustering solution is Gateway Load Balancing Protocol (GLBP), the discussion of which is coming up shortly.

Virtual Router Redundancy Protocol (VRRP) and Hot Standby Router Protocol (HSRP), both coming up shortly, are examples of *active-passive* high availability in that only one router is active at a time. All other routers are passive until the active router fails.

Multiple Internet Service Providers (ISPs)/Diverse Paths

Redundancy applies to connections as well as systems. What's an absolutely critical connection point for a datacenter? A connection to the Internet should never be a single point of failure for a datacenter (or for any organization, for that matter). It's common for a datacenter to use *multiple Internet service providers (ISPs)*, so that if one goes down, the other ISP either takes over to maintain (failover) or continues to work (a measure of fault tolerance).

It's very common for ISPs to share common lines and such, especially when they are servicing the same physical location. It's therefore critically important to ensure path diversity, where the lines out of your ISP follow *diverse paths* to other routers. A common method for path diversity in smaller centers, for example, uses a fiber connection for the primary path and a very fast cellular connection as a failover. Use of both a fiber ISP and a different cable ISP can also lead to path diversity.

Virtual Router Redundancy Protocol (VRRP)/First Hop Redundancy Protocol (FHRP)

Building with high availability in mind extends to more than just servers; a default gateway, for example, is a critical node that can be protected by adding redundant backups. Protocols that support HA and redundancy are known as a *first hop redundancy protocol (FHRP)* and include the open standard Virtual Router Redundancy Protocol (VRRP) and the Cisco-proprietary Hot Standby Router Protocol (HSRP) and Gateway Load Balancing Protocol (GLBP). The nice thing about VRRP, HSRP, and GLBP is that, conceptually, they perform the same function.

They take multiple routers and gang them together into a single virtual router with a single virtual IP (VIP) address that clients use as a default gateway. This includes making redundant firewalls on the redundant routers! GLBP takes things a step further, providing full load balancing as well

 NOTE   GLBP allows for true load balancing, while the other two can be configured to perform a (not perfect) form of load balancing. VRRP and HSRP are examples of active-passive high availability in that only one router is active at a time. All other routers are passive until the active router fails.

Mean Time to Repair (MTTR)

The *mean time to repair (MTTR)* is the amount of time it takes to fix a system after it fails. That includes time to replace components, repair parts, and restore the system to its fully functional state. When devices have a low MTTR, they can be placed back into production quicker, which is a direct contributor to high availability.

Mean Time Between Failure (MTBF)

The *mean time between failure (MTBF)*, which typically applies to hardware components, represents the manufacturer's best guess (based on historical data) regarding how much time will pass between major failures of that component. This assumes that more than one failure will occur, which means that the component will be repaired rather than replaced. Organizations take this risk factor into account because it may affect likelihood and impact of the risks associated with critical systems.

Recovery Time Objective (RTO)

The *recovery time objective (RTO)* sets an upper limit to how long the organization can tolerate an outage before full functionality must be restored. It's the amount of time needed to restore a business process after an incident or disaster. An RTO of 4 hours, for example, requires a company to ensure a lot of preparation and a high budget so that systems can be covered quickly. If systems are not restored in that timeframe, consequences can result. An RTO of a week, on the other hand, requires less preparation and a smaller budget.

Recovery Point Objective (RPO)

The *recovery point objective (RPO)* sets an upper limit to how much lost data the organization can tolerate if it must restore from a backup, effectively dictating how frequently backups must be taken. It's a time measurement of the maximum amount of data that can be lost after recovering from an incident or disaster, before which the loss of data will exceed an organization's threshold. An RPO of 4 hours, for example, requires an organization to perform a backup every 4 hours. In that case, a business process recovery could succeed within 4 hours of a failure. Anything more than that would hinder the recovery process.

 NOTE   SQL servers offer great examples for RPO and RTO. Database systems, like Microsoft SQL Server, have active logs stored separately from data files. The logs have all data transactions, which are committed to the logs prior to being written to the data files. This gives SQL a great RPO, assuming the logs are protected. SQL allows for backups to be written to remote storage, and the logs are often backed up (since each is small) as often as every 5 minutes. Therefore, if you only lose the data drive in a server, you can back up the current log and lose no data. Alternatively, if you lose an entire server, you can recover all data from remote backups, and only lose the data since the last log backup, from perhaps 5 minutes prior. SQL recovery solutions often include a spare SQL server, which then just needs backups to be restored, keeping the RTO and RPO fairly low. At the same time, SQL Log Shipping (sending transaction log backups from primary databases on primary servers to secondary databases on secondary servers) adds automatic backup and restore to the spare server, so the RTO is very low, while the RPO is the last 5-minute backup, or less if the active log was recoverable.

Network Device Backup/Restore

The *network device backup/restore* ability is very important as far as state data and configuration data go.

Configuration

Configuration data includes all the customized settings for a router, switch, load balancer, IDS/IPS, firewall, or other network device. Having a solid backup of what is essentially a text file enables network professionals to replace and restore settings to a failed device quickly.

State

State data is a different animal. Replacing a router and updating its configuration to match its predecessor is great, but the router still needs to interact with other routers to get into convergence—its state. State can also refer to a router's position in an active-passive cluster. If an active router fails, the passive node becomes active. After the failed device is repaired or replaced, it will be added back into the cluster, and you may then want to promote it back to the active state.

REVIEW

Objective 3.3: Explain high availability and disaster recovery concepts and summarize which is the best solution

- As a concept, *load balancing* means to share among two or more systems the effort to enable some process to work.
- In general, implementing multiple paths or connections between resources is called *multipathing*.
- Grouping up to 32 physical Ethernet network interface cards (also known as network adapters) into one or more virtual network adapters, implemented through software, is known as *network interface card (NIC) teaming*. This allows for fault tolerance, load balancing, and improved performance.
- With *redundant hardware/clusters*, you put into place primary switches, routers, firewalls, and other network gear, then have at the ready backup machines to step up in case the primary machine fails.
- *Facilities and infrastructure support* requires many different elements like UPSs, PDUs, generators, HVAC, and fire suppression.
- *Redundancy and high availability (HA) concepts* help ensure that resources offered are available when clients request them. Examples include cold sites, warm sites, hot sites, and cloud sites.
- Clustering solutions are commonly *active-active* examples of high availability in that all members of the cluster are active at the same time.
- It's common for a datacenter to use *multiple Internet service providers (ISPs)*, so that if one goes down, the other ISP either takes over to maintain (failover) or continues to work (a measure of fault tolerance).
- It's very common for ISPs to share common lines and such, especially when they are servicing the same physical location. It's therefore critically important to ensure path diversity, where the lines out of your ISP follow *diverse paths* to other routers.
- *Virtual Router Redundancy Protocol (VRRP)* is an *first hop redundancy protocol (FHRP)* that takes multiple routers and gangs them together into a single virtual router with a single virtual IP (VIP) address that clients use as a default gateway.
- The *mean time to repair (MTTR)* is the amount of time it takes to fix a system after it fails. That includes time to replace components, repair parts, and restore the system to its fully functional state.
- The *mean time between failure (MTBF)*, which typically applies to hardware components, represents the manufacturer's best guess (based on historical data) regarding how much time will pass between major failures of that component.

- The *recovery time objective (RTO)* sets an upper limit to how long the organization can tolerate an outage before full functionality must be restored.
- The *recovery point objective (RPO)* sets an upper limit to how much lost data the organization can tolerate if it must restore from a backup, effectively dictating how frequently backups must be taken.
- The *network device backup/restore* ability is very important as far as state data and configuration data go.

3.3 QUESTIONS

1. Which of the following is not an FHRP?
   A. GLBP
   B. VRRP
   C. HSRP
   D. NIC teaming

2. What is the difference between a UPS and a generator?
   A. The generator is only for keeping systems up long enough to be properly shut down, while the UPS is meant to keep power for an extended period of time.
   B. The UPS is only for keeping systems up long enough to be properly shut down, while the generator is meant to keep power for an extended period of time.
   C. There is no difference between the two devices.
   D. Generators replace UPSs in modern enterprises.

3. What is the difference between RTO and RPO?
   A. RPO is used for large organizations, while RTO is used for smaller organizations.
   B. RTO is used for large organizations, while RPO is used for smaller organizations.
   C. RPO deals with systems, while RTO deals with data.
   D. RTO deals with systems, while RPO deals with data.

3.3 ANSWERS

1. **D** NIC teaming combines up to 32 physical Ethernet NICs together. Gateway Load Balancing Protocol, Virtual Router Redundancy Protocol, and Hot Standby Router Protocol are all first hop redundancy protocols.

2. **B** A UPS is only meant to keep systems up long enough to be properly shut down. Extended periods of time without electricity require the use of a generator.

3. **D** RTO represents time that passes between a system's failure and availability, while RPO represents time between the loss of data and a previous backup.

Network Security

Domain Objectives

- **4.1** Explain common security concepts.
- **4.2** Compare and contrast common types of attacks.
- **4.3** Given a scenario, apply network hardening techniques.
- **4.4** Compare and contrast remote access methods and security implications.
- **4.5** Explain the importance of physical security.

Objective 4.1 Explain common security concepts

Networking education starts with the OSI model, covered in Objective 1.1. In a similar fashion, security education starts with the CIA (confidentiality, integrity, availability) triad. Once you understand each of those models, you can pivot in many different directions to learn about and implement different technologies. In the case of Objective 4.1, after you understand the CIA triad, you'll be able to learn about common network security concepts, including threats, vulnerabilities, exploits, least privilege, role-based access, zero trust, defense in depth, authentication methods, risk management, and security information and event management (SIEM). Each of those concepts falls under one or more of the CIA triad components.

Confidentiality, Integrity, Availability (CIA)

Confidentiality, integrity, and availability (CIA) are the components of the CIA triad (also known as the CIA model) as well as the tenets of information security. Every breach, every cyberattack, every vulnerability, and every exploit will deal with at least one of these components. Every cybersecurity mechanism and mitigation technique will deal with at least one of them as well.

NOTE The CIA triad is put into practice through various security mechanisms and controls. Every security technique, practice, and mechanism put into place to protect systems and data relates in some fashion to ensuring confidentiality, integrity, and availability.

Confidentiality deals with keeping unauthorized people from seeing data, messages, and files. Confidentiality is a characteristic met by keeping data secret from people who aren't allowed to see it or interact with it in any way, while making sure that only those people who do have the right to access it can do so. Systems enforce confidentiality through various means, including encryption and permissions.

Integrity deals with making sure that part of a message or file hasn't changed, either accidentally or maliciously. Meeting the goal of integrity requires maintaining data and systems in a pristine, unaltered state when they are stored, transmitted, processed, and received, unless the alteration is intended due to normal processing. In other words, there should be no unauthorized modification, alteration, creation, or deletion of data. Any changes to data must be done only as part of authorized transformations in normal use and processing. Integrity is enforced by the use of hashing.

EXAM TIP   Hashing enforces integrity at the file/message level. Other options for enforcing integrity are done at various layers of the OSI model. As discussed in Objective 1.1, a CRC is used for Ethernet and 802.11 frames, while a checksum is used for ICMP packets, TCP segments, and UDP datagrams. Furthermore, there are differences between a CRC/checksum and hashing. A CRC or checksum is meant to detect accidental changes and is not always guaranteed to be accurate. Hashing is meant to detect malicious changes and is always guaranteed to be accurate.

Availability deals with systems and networks staying online, so that authorized users can access them. Maintaining availability means ensuring that systems and data are available for authorized users to perform authorized tasks, whenever they need them. Availability bridges security and functionality, because it ensures that users have a secure, functional system at their immediate disposal. An extremely secure system that's not functional is not available in practice. Availability is enforced in various ways, including fault tolerance, load balancing, system redundancy, data backups, business continuity, and disaster recovery.

ADDITIONAL RESOURCES   Listen to me talk on TV news about attacks on availability at https://www.youtube.com/weissman52 in the TV News Cybersecurity Expert Playlist (videos from 4/3/20, 6/25/21, 8/30/21, and 12/8/21).

Threats

From a cybersecurity perspective, you are looking to protect assets—things that have value to an organization. Assets could be physical hardware, logical software, data, information, company trade secrets, and even employees. A *threat* is a looming danger that has the potential to cause change or cause damage to your assets, operations (including image, reputation, functions, and mission), and even individuals through violations of confidentiality, integrity, or availability.

Internal

We often fear the unknown cybercriminals from the outside, but insiders performing actions (ranging from infiltrating or exfiltrating data to falling for a phishing e-mail), *internal* threats, can do far greater damage. Insiders already have some level of access, means, and opportunity.

External

External threats come from the outside, for example, fires, floods, attackers getting into your network, malware infecting your systems, your server crashing without backups to go to, or even a cleaner accidentally pulling out the plug to an important server.

Threat agents or actors are the ones carrying out the threats. Yes, cybercriminals are the first examples that come to mind, including a person, organization, or even a nation state. However, Mother Nature, through earthquakes, tornadoes, fires, and floods, is also a threat agent.

ADDITIONAL RESOURCES   Another example of a threat agent is…squirrels:
https://theweek.com/articles/452311/forget-hackers-squirrels-are-bigger-threat-americas-power-grid
https://arstechnica.com/information-technology/2017/01/whos-winning-the-cyber-war-the-squirrels-of-course/

Vulnerabilities

Vulnerabilities are weaknesses, flaws, gaps in an operating system, program, device, network, and even a person that provide a way into a system or network for the cybercriminals. Weak authentication checks, default username/password combinations, incorrectly configured firewalls, susceptibility to buffer overflows, susceptibility to SQL injection attacks, and even a gullible or naive employee are all vulnerabilities. Some vulnerabilities are obvious, such as connecting to the Internet without an edge firewall or not using any form of account control for user files. Other vulnerabilities are unknown or missed, and that makes the study of vulnerabilities very important for a network tech.

Common Vulnerabilities and Exposures (CVE)

The *Common Vulnerabilities and Exposures (CVE)* database hosted by MITRE Corporation at https://cve.mitre.org/ is a public reference of identified vulnerabilities and exposures. Each vulnerability is assigned a CVE ID, which is included in security advisories issued by researchers and vendors and helps cybersecurity specialists synchronize on vulnerabilities that need to be addressed immediately.

Zero-Day

How do vulnerabilities come to light? Who discovers them? From the black hat camp, malicious evil attackers do. From the white hat camp, security researchers do. Both sides spend day in and day out poking and prodding operating systems, software, and hardware. Black hat hackers, in the event that they're caught, go to prison. White hat hackers, who do the same things that black hat hackers do but with explicit permission from system/network owners, get paid, have thrilling careers, and are held in high regard in the cybersecurity community. White hat hackers, also known as penetration testers (or pentesters) and ethical hackers, are hired by companies to find and exploit vulnerabilities so that the vulnerabilities can be identified and fixed before they are discovered by black hat hackers.

Some vulnerabilities are labeled *zero-day*. These are vulnerabilities that are discovered but not publicly announced before being exploited. Therefore, the companies and individuals who would normally patch the vulnerabilities now have zero days to fix the problems or suggest mitigation techniques. Zero-day exploits (also known as zero-day attacks) aren't used against a large number of targets because an increase in usage will trigger discovery and subsequent detection signatures (by anti-malware programs and IDS/IPS devices) and patches by vendors. A zero-day won't be a zero-day if used too often! Therefore, attackers stockpile them and use them in certain "emergency" situations. Governments can stockpile them, too, instead of notifying vendors whose devices and software protect their own citizens. Such a stockpile of zero-days would be very valuable for reconnaissance and cyber-attacks against nation-state cybercriminals. However, bad things, like ransomware attacks, can happen as a result.

 ADDITIONAL RESOURCES   Read this article about zero-day vulnerabilities, in which I'm featured: https://cybernews.com/editorial/governments-pay-millions-for-0days-more-harm-than-good/.

Exploits

Exploits are tools or methods used to penetrate systems through vulnerabilities. In that sense, exploit is a noun. Exploit can also be a verb, meaning the actual act of penetrating a system. When threat actors carry out the threat, they exploit the vulnerability.

Interestingly enough, exploits are usually named after the vulnerability they exploit. For example, MS08-067 is a famous exploit from 2008 that allowed cybercriminals to gain control of a Windows XP or a Windows Server 2003 system. More recently, in 2021, the Hafnium cyber espionage group unleashed multiple zero-day exploits attacking Microsoft Exchange Server, leading to the publication of the following CVEs: CVE-2021-26855, CVE-2021-26857, CVE-2021-26858, and CVE-2021-27065.

Pentesting and cyberattacks follow the same algorithm.

1. Find systems.
2. Find programs or services on those systems.
3. Find vulnerabilities in those programs or services on those systems.
4. Find ways that those vulnerabilities can be exploited.
5. Go ahead and actually exploit those vulnerabilities.
6. Now that you've compromised systems, you can use them to pivot to other systems on the same network as well as systems on different networks.

Payload is the actual code that allows attackers to control systems after they've been exploited. Imagine two burglars driving in a van. The driver rams the van into a storefront. The other guy jumps out and starts looting the store. The van would be the exploit, and the burglar filling his bags would be the payload. As another example, think of a missile: the rocket, fuel, and everything else in the rocket is the exploit. The warhead is what does the actual damage—that's the payload. Take out the warhead, and the missile doesn't have a strong impact. Furthermore, a warhead without being delivered by a rocket won't do much either.

Least Privilege

On any system, it's important that you implement the principle of *least privilege*. Users should have only the permissions they need to perform their jobs, and not a drop more. Any additional permissions could result in accidental or even malicious compromise of confidentiality, integrity, and availability.

Role-Based Access

Security permissions to resources should be assigned to group account objects, not user account objects, with *role-based access*. Think of the groups as roles that users fill. If security permissions to resources were assigned to user objects, it would be an administrative nightmare. If a user were being moved out of a department in the organization that has access to 100 resources and into a different department that has access to 100 other resources, you'd have to make 200 changes if permissions were assigned to user account objects. If groups are implemented, and permissions to resources are tied to group account objects, all you'd have to do is remove the user's membership from the original group and add the user as a member to the new group. That would be two changes instead of 200. Furthermore, as is the practice today, users can serve in multiple roles, and as such, they need to have the cumulative permissions of multiple groups. Giving permissions to groups and assigning users to groups is the way to go.

Zero Trust

Trust is a big deal when it comes to IT security. Who do you trust? How do you establish trust relationships between systems, organizations, and people? This is a massive conversation, but a great place to start is by starting with no trust at all, a concept called *zero trust*. Quoting NIST Special Publication (SP) 800-207: "Zero trust is a cybersecurity paradigm focused on resource protection and the premise that trust is never granted implicitly but must be continually evaluated."

Areas in which zero trust is implemented include verifying users and their devices, verifying applications that communicate with other applications, and verifying infrastructure components, including routers, switches, cloud components, IoT devices, and more.

Traditionally, many organizations have assumed that if you are in the perimeter of the network, then you can be trusted to a certain degree. Zero trust starts off by not trusting any user on any device until there is confidence that the user is who they claim to be and the device is validated to be secure. The multifactor authentication (coming up in this objective) effort can be reduced based on device used, verification of device safety, location (office, home, another country, etc.), and level of access needed. Essentially, start from a position of not trusting users or devices at all, and if a check is failed, either ask for proof or deny access altogether.

Defense in Depth

Defense in depth is the usage of multiple layers of security to protect against known threats. This strategy provides protection, for example, when a security mechanism fails or a network component is exploited, where another layer will pick up the slack and implement the security needed. Different layers of defense in depth include people (education, training), procedures (hiring practices, treatment of data, security steps), technical security (encryption, hashing, multifactor authentication), physical security (fence, guard, CCTV, dogs), and more. In the following sections, network segmentation enforcement, screened subnet [previously known as demilitarized zone (DMZ)], separation of duties, network access control, and honeypot topics are explored in relation to defense in depth.

Network Segmentation Enforcement

Network segmentation enforcement is the blocking or allowing traffic to enforce your segmentation policy. Network segmentation itself separates an organization's infrastructure into multiple segments, implemented through subnets in most cases (there are other ways, like isolated VLANs, for example). Through network segmentation enforcement, traffic flow can be controlled between subnets through detailed policies. Network segmentation enforcement makes monitoring easier, improves performance, simplifies troubleshooting and debugging issues, and, most importantly, improves security.

Screened Subnet [Previously Known as Demilitarized Zone (DMZ)]

The use of a single firewall between the network and the ISP is just one approach to firewall placement. That configuration works well in simple networks or when you want strong isolation between all clients on the inside of the firewall. But what happens when we have servers, like a Web server, that need less restricted access to the Internet? That's where the concepts of the screened subnet and internal/external firewalls come in.

A *screened subnet [previously known as demilitarized zone (DMZ)]* is a network segment carved out by firewalls to provide a special place (a zone) on the network for any servers that need to be publicly accessible from the Internet. By definition, a screened subnet uses network segmentation as a mitigation technique against attacks on the network.

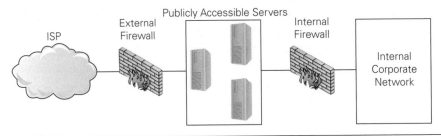

FIGURE 4.1-1   Screened subnet

A bastion host is a system in a screened subnet that is directly exposed or connected to the unfiltered Internet. As such, it requires extra hardening and securing, as well as extra effort to ensure its ongoing safety. The term bastion host refers to the bastion structure, which is extra strong, projecting from a protected perimeter. Think of a bastion on the wall of a castle that has to stick out, and therefore needs to be extra strong and well manned.

No, bastion hosts are not the corporate file servers or corporate application servers. The public has no business accessing those systems. Instead, think of a company's DNS servers, Web servers, and mail servers. Those are great examples of bastion hosts. You want, by definition, the public to access those resources. In fact, they could even be proxies for the actual servers that directly communicate with the actual servers, providing another layer of defense. In this fashion, the actual servers have an additional filter, and no one can communicate with them directly except for the proxies.

The most common screened subnet design is to use two routers with firewalls to create a perimeter network, as shown in Figure 4.1-1. With a perimeter network, the two firewalls carve out areas with different levels of trust. The external firewall that sits between the perimeter network and the Internet protects the public servers from known Internet attacks, but still allows plenty of traffic through to the public-facing servers.

These servers are still publicly accessible, though, and are still more vulnerable to attack and takeover. That's acceptable for the public-facing servers, but the light protection afforded by the external firewall is unacceptable for internal systems. That's where the internal firewall comes in; it sits between the perimeter network and the trusted network that houses all the organization's private servers and clients. The internal firewall provides extremely strong ACLs to protect internal servers that should only be accessed by employees, unlike the bastion hosts. Having the screened subnet, with the public-facing servers segmented from the internal devices, limits a potential breach to an individual server, thereby protecting the other servers in the screened subnet or any internal device.

Separation of Duties

Separation of duties means to separate a responsibility in such a way that it requires the input of two or more users. With this checks-and-balances implementation, no single person has enough privileges and access to breach or damage a system to perform fraud, theft, sabotage, or other unauthorized activity alone. This would force a nefarious user to find a willing accomplice, which is unlikely given that it would have to be the coworker assigned by the organization to perform the other duties required to accomplish the activity. As an example of separation of duties, one employee might do purchasing for a department, while a separate employee would log all information about the transaction, including vendor, price, and date.

Network Access Control

Network access control (NAC) is a standardized approach to verify that a node meets certain criteria before it is allowed to connect to a network. Many product vendors implement NAC in different ways, including 802.1X and EAP, both of which are covered later in this objective.

Network Admission Control (also known as NAC) is Cisco's version of network access control. Cisco's NAC can dictate that specific criteria must be met before allowing a node to connect to a secure network. Devices that do not meet the required criteria can be shunted with no connection or made to connect to another network. The types of criteria that can be checked (for example, an OS or update versions) are broad ranging and can be tested for in a number of ways. The biggest concern is verifying that a device attempting to connect is not a threat to network security.

Honeypot

Imagine a server with lots of PII (personally identifiable information), including passwords stored in plaintext, credit card numbers, addresses, and even healthcare-related information. Imagine the administrators deliberately not putting any strong form of cybersecurity on the server. What is this, a bad dream? No, this is by design, and the PII is fake. A server like this is called a *honeypot*. A network of these machines is called a honeynet.

Decoy systems are deployed on networks designed to lure potential attackers away from critical systems. This also allows security specialists to collect information about attackers' activities. Typically, these honeypots encourage attackers to stay on the system long enough for administrators to document and respond to the attack. It also allows administrators to refine the firewall rules based on observed attacker behaviors.

Honeypots need to be protected to the point that a cybercriminal thinks that they are real. The level of protection should take some time to exploit and present some form of a challenge. Without any protection at all, cybercriminals would easily identify them simply as honeypots.

 NOTE   Deception software is the new wave of honeypots. These decoys can be centrally managed, made to work with other security software, and run through virtualization. Intruders can be fooled at many layers, such as network, endpoint, application, and data. They can be fooled with decoy workstations, fake browser credentials, phony files, fabricated datasets, and more. An endpoint might be set up to look like it runs a particular version of Windows when it is really a Linux machine. This will deceive malware into attacking vulnerabilities the system doesn't have. A decoy document can be made to look like it contains new product designs or be embedded with a tracking capability that will let the company know when and from where it was opened.

Authentication Methods

Authentication methods serve the purpose of positively validating the identification of users trying to gain access to a system, network, or some data. The first exposure to authentication for most users is local authentication, coming across a login screen prompting you to enter a username and password, to sign in to a computer. However, there are many other ways to authenticate, especially when networking is added into the mix. A network technician should understand not only how different authentication methods control usernames and passwords, but also some of the authentication standards used in today's TCP/IP networks.

But you can't stop with usernames and passwords. What if someone obtains your username and password? To defeat those types of threat actors, some systems require a second form of authentication. These second forms of authentication include items you carry (like a hardware token) or something physical that uniquely identifies you (such as your retinal patterns or fingerprints—biometrics).

Multifactor

Multifactor authentication (MFA) means using two or more distinctly different methods for authentication. When only two authentication methods are used, you might see the term two-factor authentication (2FA). These methods fall into one of three categories. The CompTIA Network+ exam objectives do not list specific factors, but it's a good idea to be able to recognize examples of all of them:

- Something you know (a knowledge factor) is a password, a passphrase, or a personal identification number (PIN).
- Something you have (a possession factor) is either a hardware token (YubiKey, for example) which you'd plug into a USB port or a smartphone app (Google Authenticator, for example) that sends you a code to enter. MFA through SMS text messages, though, is discouraged because it can be hacked.
- Something you are (an inherent or inherence factor) indicates some distinguishing, unique characteristic, like the biometrics just mentioned.

Conditional access policies in Microsoft Azure can accept identification and authentication with just a username and password only if you are in the corporate offices. From registered offsite locations (based on your IP address), multifactor authentication would be required. Access from other countries can be denied altogether.

 ADDITIONAL RESOURCES   Listen to me talk on TV news about MFA at https://www.youtube.com/weissman52, in the TV News Cybersecurity Expert Playlist (videos from 1/5/22, 1/7/22, and 3/3/22.)

Terminal Access Controller Access-Control System Plus (TACACS+)

Routers and switches need administration. In a simple network, you can access the administration screen for each router and switch by entering a username and password for each device. When an infrastructure becomes complex, with many routers and switches, logging into each device separately starts to become administratively messy. The answer is to make a centralized server store the credentials for all the devices in the network. To make this secure, you need to follow the AAA (authentication, authorization, and accounting) model. As previously mentioned, authentication is proving you are who you say you are. Once you do that, you are authorized for certain actions and accessing certain data, but not all (discussed earlier in this objective—least privilege). Keeping track of what users do or try to do (through logs and alerts), both successfully and unsuccessfully, is accounting.

Terminal Access Controller Access Control System Plus (TACACS+) is a protocol developed by Cisco to support administration of networking devices, allowing administrators to authenticate, gain authorization, and be logged through accounting. TACACS+ is very similar to RADIUS (coming up next) in function, but uses TCP port 49 by default and separates authorization, authentication, and accounting into different parts. Unlike RADIUS, TACACS+ encrypts the entire packet.

Remote Authentication Dial-in User Service (RADIUS)

Remote Authentication Dial-In User Service (RADIUS) is an Internet Engineering Task Force (IETF) standard/protocol and, as its name implies, was created to support ISPs with hundreds or thousands of modems in hundreds of computers to connect to a single central database. While originally designed for dial-up connections, RADIUS still works hard in a huge number of different types of networks, both wired and wireless, and is the protocol of choice for implementing AAA related to network access—in contrast to TACACS+, which is the authentication protocol of choice for allowing remote management of routers and switches.

Unlike TACACS+, RADIUS combines authentication and authorization, encrypts just the password field, and uses UDP ports 1812 (authentication) and 1813 (accounting) defined by the IETF or UDP ports 1645 (authentication) and 1646 (accounting) implemented by access servers. RADIUS works in conjunction with 802.1X, coming up shortly.

Single Sign-On (SSO)

Single sign-on (SSO) is a process whereby a client performs a one-time login to an authenticating system. That system, in turn, takes care of the client's authentication to any other connected systems the client is authorized to access. When used with federated authentication, users from one organization can use their credentials for another organization's resources, which mitigates risk, since credentials are stored locally to the users' organization. SSO also cuts down on overwhelming users with an inordinate number of username/password combinations, which ultimately leads to security since users won't perform bad password management (by writing them down, for example). Also minimized is the time needed to reenter passwords. Having better administrative control, with a single entry for users in a database of credentials, adds to productivity for administrators and help desk workers, who won't have to deal with as many password calls.

LDAP

Programs use *LDAP* (Lightweight Directory Access Protocol) to store, query, and change database information used by the network. These databases track aspects of networks, such as username/password hash combinations, computers connected to a domain, signed-in users, or the location of printers.

One of the most complex and also most used databases is Active Directory, found on Microsoft Windows domain controllers. Active Directory is the power behind single sign-on and network information. Every Windows domain controller stores a copy of the Active Directory database.

LDAP can talk to Active Directory and other directory service providers to query and modify items. You will probably never use LDAP manually. Your domain controllers will use it automatically and transparently in the background to keep your databases in good order. LDAP uses port 389 (TCP and UDP) by default.

The now-deprecated secure version of LDAP, Lightweight Directory Access Protocol over SSL (LDAPS), used TCP port 636. You'll see it on the CompTIA Network+ exam objectives, but LDAP version 3 made it obsolete.

Kerberos

Kerberos, a cross-platform authentication protocol, has been the default authentication protocol for Windows domain controllers for over two decades. A client authenticates once to the authentication server, and gets a Ticket-Granting Ticket (TGT). From that point, the client can pass the TGT to the Ticket-Granting Service/Server (TGS), to request a ticket to a specific resource. The authentication server and the TGS are part of the key distribution center. Symmetric-key encryption is used to protect the confidentiality of messages.

In fact, the "password checking" is actually done by the client decrypting a message with its secret key, consisting of its password hash, the result of running the password and salt through a hash function. The message was encrypted with the client's key, and if the user enters the password correctly, the password and appended salt will be hashed, and the hash, acting as the secret key, will be able to decrypt a message sent from the ticket granting server.

On Windows domain controllers running Active Directory, password hashes are stored in the C:\Windows\NTDS\ntds.dit file.

ADDITIONAL RESOURCES   The following two links give you an in-depth look at the Kerberos process:
https://youtu.be/kp5d8Yv3-0c
https://www.roguelynn.com/words/explain-like-im-5-kerberos/

Local Authentication

A user can use *local authentication* to authenticate to a computer, router, or switch without that device having to consult an external, centralized database.

On Linux systems, password hashes are stored in the /etc/shadow file. Most Linux distributions use a modified version of SHA-512 called sha512crypt with salt. However, the 2021.1 release of Kali Linux changed to a new hash function for passwords, called yescrypt. On Windows systems, password hashes are stored in the SAM (expanded as both Security Account Manager and Security Accounts Manager) database file, located in C:\Windows\System32\config.

Routers and switches have a local database. On Cisco routers and switches, a password for privileged EXEC mode can be configured without a username, or a local database can contain username/password pairs. As mentioned earlier in this objective, TACACS+ is an even better choice.

Extensible Authentication Protocol (EAP)

One of the great challenges to authentication is getting the two ends of the authentication process to handle the many different types of authentication options. Even though PPP for a time pretty much owned the username/password authentication business, proprietary forms of authentication using smart cards/tokens, certificates, and so on, began to show up on the market, threatening to drop practical authentication into a huge mess of competing standards.

Extensible Authentication Protocol (EAP) was developed to create a single standard to allow two devices to authenticate. Despite the name, EAP is not a protocol in the classic sense, but rather it is inside a PPP wrapper that EAP-compliant applications can use to accept one of many types of authentication. Although EAP is a general-purpose authentication wrapper, its only substantial use is in wireless networks. EAP comes in various types, but currently only seven types are in common use:

- **EAP-PSK**   EAP-PSK (Pre-Shared key) is nothing more than a shared secret value that's stored on both the wireless access point and the wireless client, encrypted using the powerful AES encryption. This is easily the most popular form of authentication used on SOHO wireless networks today.

- **PEAPv0/EAP-MSCHAPv2**   PEAP (Protected EAP)v0/EAP-MSCHAPv2 (Microsoft Challenge-Handshake Authentication Protocol), more commonly and simply known as PEAP (Protected EAP), uses a password function based on MS-CHAPv2 with the addition of an encrypted TLS tunnel similar to EAP-TLS. The inner authentication protocol is Microsoft's Challenge Handshake Authentication Protocol, meaning it allows authentication to databases that support the MS-CHAPv2 format, including the ubiquitous Active Directory. This is easily the most common implementation of EAP on enterprise wireless networks.

- **EAP-TLS** EAP-TLS (Transport Layer Security) defines the use of a RADIUS server as well as mutual authentication, requiring certificates on both the server and every client. On the client side, a smart card may be used in lieu of a certificate. EAP-TLS is very robust, but the client-side certificate requirement is an administrative challenge. Even though it's a challenge, the most secure wireless networks all use EAP-TLS. EAP-TLS is only used on wireless networks, but TLS is used heavily on secure Web sites.

- **EAP-TTLS** EAP-TTLS (Tunneled TLS) is similar to EAP-TLS but only uses a single server-side certificate (although the client can also be authenticated by a certificate as well). After the server authenticates to the client, the server uses that secure connection, known as a tunnel, for the client authentication. EAP-TTLS is very common for more secure wireless networks.

- **EAP-MD5** EAP-MD5 (Message Digest version 5) is a very simple version of EAP that uses only MD5 hashes for transfer of authentication credentials. It's weak and the least used of all the versions of EAP described.

- **LEAP** LEAP (Lightweight EAP) is a proprietary EAP authentication used almost exclusively by Cisco wireless products. LEAP is an interesting combination of MSCHAP authentication between a wireless client and a RADIUS server. Due to the lack of protection of user credentials, which can easily be compromised, Cisco recommends moving on to LEAP's replacement, EAP-FAST.

- **EAP-FAST** EAP-FAST (Flexible Authentication via Secure Tunneling) is Cisco's replacement for LEAP that includes optional server certificates and a Protected Access Credential (PAC) that establishes a TLS tunnel to verify client credentials, at the same time as keeping a lightweight implementation. All current operating systems support EAP-FAST (assuming the right software is installed).

802.1X

EAP was a huge success and almost overnight gave those who needed point-to-point authentication a one-stop-shop methodology to do so. EAP was so successful that there was a cry to develop an EAP solution for wired (Ethernet) and wireless networks. This solution is *802.1X*. Whereas traditional EAP is nothing more than an authentication method wrapped in PPP, 802.1X gets rid of the PPP (Ethernet is not a point-to-point protocol) and instead puts the EAP information inside an Ethernet frame.

802.1X is a port-based authentication network access control mechanism for networks. In other words, it's a complete authentication standard designed to force devices to go through a full AAA process to get anywhere past the interface on a gateway system. Before 802.1X, a system on a wired network could always access another system's port. Granted, attackers wouldn't be able to do much until providing a username/password or certificate, but they could still send packets to any computer on the network. This wasn't good, because it enabled attackers to get to the systems to try to do evil things. 802.1X prevented them from even getting in the door until they were authenticated and authorized.

802.1X manages the communication between an end device (computer) and a network device (switch in wired networks, access point in wireless networks). The network device uses a RADIUS client to communicate with a RADIUS server. Instead of creating a separate database for AAA, often an existing Microsoft Active Directory (AD) domain controller (DC) LDAP database is used. The supplicant (computer), using EAP over LAN (EAPoL) or EAP over Wireless (EAPoW), makes a request to the authenticator (switch or access point). The authenticator passes the request to the authentication server (AD) with encrypted RADIUS. Using the same channels and protocols, the authentication server sends the response to the authenticator and the authenticator sends the response to the supplicant.

802.1X combines the RADIUS-style AAA with EAP versions to make a complete authentication solution. The folks who developed 802.1X saw it as a total replacement for every other form of authentication (even Kerberos). 802.1X is greatly used in secured wired and wireless infrastructures.

Risk Management

Risk management is the never-ending process of assessing risks to resources and data and ensuring that proper security countermeasures are implemented on systems and networks.

The entire field of security is based on the premise that somewhere, at some time, something will attack some part of your network. The attack may take as many forms as your paranoia allows: intentional, unintentional, earthquake, accident, war, meteor impact...whatever.

 ADDITIONAL RESOURCES Read this article about cyber risk, in which I'm featured: https://advisorsmith.com/cyber-liability-insurance/?expert=jonathan-weissman.

Security Risk Assessments

Security risk assessments help organizations deal with many types of potential attacks. You can't afford to build up a defense for every possible attack—nor should you need to, for a number of reasons. First, different attacks have different probabilities of taking place. The probability of a meteor taking out your server room is very low. There is, however, a pretty good chance that some clueless user will eventually load malware on his or her company-issued laptop. Second, different attacks/potential problems have different impacts. If a meteor hits your server room, you're going to have a big, expensive problem. If a user forgets his or her password, it's not a big deal and is easily dealt with.

Threat Assessment

As defined earlier in this objective, a threat is a looming danger that has the potential to change or damage your assets, operations (including image, reputation, functions, and mission), and even individuals through violations of confidentiality, integrity, or availability. A *threat assessment*, therefore, is the process of evaluating various threats that could come to fruition and affect an organization.

Consider, for example, a factory that makes widgets. The factory and all of its control systems are extremely important assets for an organization. A proprietary technology that makes that organization's products the best in the world is also a key corporate asset. What are the threats?

A threat actor—a person, organization, or even a nation state that has both the capability and intent to harm, steal, copy, or otherwise diminish an asset—could infiltrate the corporate network and steal the proprietary technology details. That's a threat. A disgruntled employee could change key programming details in the factory system right before quitting just to derail the production line. That's a threat too. Security-conscious organizations assess threats and rate them according to both the likelihood they might happen and the amount of damage they would cause if they do.

Vulnerability Assessment

Every asset has some weakness that makes it potentially susceptible to a threat—a vulnerability. Imagine an organization where factory technicians control a lot of the systems remotely, for example, across the Internet. That Internet connection presents a potential weak spot in keeping out threat actors. If security controls aren't sufficient to stop the latest attack, then that connection is a clear vulnerability. Assigning a monetary or intrinsic value to an asset helps the organization prioritize its security.

Given the huge number of potential vulnerabilities out there, it's impossible for even the most highly skilled technician to find them by manually inspecting an organization's infrastructure. The best way to know the infrastructure's vulnerabilities is to run some form of program—a vulnerability scanner—that will inspect a huge number of potential vulnerabilities and create a report that can be used as part of a *vulnerability assessment* for the organization to then act upon. The vulnerability assessment can include other discoveries of security specialists, independent of a vulnerability scanner, as well.

When you need to perform serious vulnerability testing, it's common to turn to aggressive and powerful comprehensive testers. There are plenty out there, but two dominate the field: Nessus and OpenVAS. Nessus, from Tenable Network Security, is arguably the first truly comprehensive vulnerability testing tool and has been around for almost two decades. Nessus is an excellent, well-known tool. Once free to everyone, Nessus is still free for home users, but commercial users must purchase a subscription.

OpenVAS is an open source fork of Nessus that is also extremely popular and, in the opinion of many security professionals, superior to Nessus.

Penetration Testing

Once you've run your vulnerability tools and hardened your infrastructure, it's time to see if your network can stand up to an actual attack. The problem with this is that you don't want real threat actors making these attacks. You want to be attacked by a white hat hacker, who will find the existing vulnerabilities and exploit them to gain access. Instead of hurting your infrastructure or stealing your secrets, this hacker reports findings so that you can further harden your network. This is called *penetration testing* (pentesting).

 NOTE   A legal pentest requires lots of careful documentation that defines what the pentester is to test, the level of testing, time frames, and documentation.

Unlike vulnerability testing, a good pentest requires a skilled operator who understands the target and knows potential vulnerabilities. To that end, there are a number of tools that make this job easier. Two examples are Aircrack-ng and Metasploit.

Aircrack-ng is an open source tool for pentesting pretty much every aspect of wireless networks. It's powerful, relatively easy to use (assuming you understand 802.11 wireless networks in great detail), and completely free.

Metasploit is a unique, open source tool that enables the pentester to use a massive library of exploits and payloads as well as tweak those attacks for unique penetrations. Metasploit is a command-line tool, but there is a GUI front end to it called Armitage.

Kali Linux is a great Linux distribution for pentesting, since it incorporates many tools used by pentesters.

Posture Assessment

Cybersecurity professionals use the term risk posture to describe the overall risk for an organization. A company's risk posture, for example, includes threats from threat actors to vulnerable assets, like factory systems and intellectual property. Other risk factors need to be included as well, such as the potential for changes in laws or regulations that could negatively affect the company, natural disasters that could take out physical plants, and personal disasters such as the death or disablement of key corporate personnel.

A *posture assessment* covers it all—all the various threats and risks to which the company is exposed. And such an assessment includes the cost of negative events in both money and time. A proper risk assessment details how the company is vulnerable and can protect against potential negative events.

Business Risk Assessments

Business risk assessments include a subset of risk assessment focused on operations in the organization, such as process assessment and vendor assessment. A business risk assessment looks at other aspects of overall risks facing an organization.

Process Assessment

A *process assessment* examines various actions performed by an organization to produce desired results. For a manufacturing company, for example, one essential process is producing its main products, so that the company can grow and provide livelihoods for its employees. Another essential process is the research and development into making new and improved products in the future. A third essential process is the procurement of the materials used to create the final product. Another process is the sales force that interacts with other companies to sell its products.

Within each of these broad-stroke processes are many subprocesses. An essential subprocess in sales, for example, is recruiting the best salespeople the company can find. A corollary to that is the subprocess of all the support people and equipment that go into a making a sales force effective.

In a risk management scenario, a process assessment codifies and ranks essential processes, then examines the likelihood of weakness in the process. A sales force in New York, for example, would have a much lower likelihood of weakness than a brand-new team that just started in the first branch office in a different state. The same kind of assessment would apply all across the board to all essential processes.

Vendor Assessment

Many organizations rely on third parties to provide important pieces that make up their final product. Proper risk assessment—or in this case, business risk assessment—takes into consideration any potential problems outside of the control of the organization. A *vendor assessment* examines all aspects of a third party's security controls, processes, procurement, labor policies, and more to see what risks that vendor poses to the organization.

Security Information and Event Management (SIEM)

An approach called *security information and event management (SIEM)* is used to monitor and manage an organization's network. SIEM is an industry-standard term, but there are many products of various types that are marketed as SIEM solutions. SIEM is a mashup of two processes: security event management (SEM) and security information management (SIM).

As the name implies, SIEM is a two-part process that begins with the security event monitoring component. SEM is based on real-time monitoring of security events. The SEM framework calls for monitoring the entire enterprise, often through edge devices at monitor points, then saving the logged events to a location that supports single viewpoint review and analysis of the events. In addition to active event monitoring, another task of SEM is to collect and centralize otherwise disparately located security and event logs.

Once logs are created and saved, the second part of SIEM, security information management, kicks in: here, the log files are reviewed and analyzed by automated and human interpreters.

One place SIEM comes into play is with file integrity monitoring (FIM), checking for changes in all sorts of aspects of files. These include attributes and file size, configuration values, content, credentials, hash values, and privileges and security settings.

Any changes discovered could indicate that an attack has occurred or is happening right now. The verification process compares a baseline or known good copy of the file with the current file, checking for differences.

SIEM systems are complex solution suites that are found in large, enterprise environments. Depending on the organization, they may be self-implemented and managed or may be administered under contract by a vendor in the form of a managed security service provider (MSSP).

REVIEW

Objective 4.1: Explain common security concepts

- *Confidentiality, integrity, and availability* (CIA) are the components of the CIA triad (aka the CIA model) as well as the tenets of information security.

- A threat is a looming danger that has the potential to cause change or cause damage to your assets, operations (including image, reputation, functions, and mission), and even individuals through violations of confidentiality, integrity, or availability.

- We often fear the unknown cybercriminals from the outside, but insiders doing something, *internal* threats, can do far greater damage.

- Think of *external* threats as the actual actions like fires, floods, attackers getting into your network, malware infecting your systems, your server crashing without backups to go to, or even a cleaner accidentally pulling out the plug to an important server.

- *Vulnerabilities* are weaknesses, flaws, gaps in an operating system, program, device, network, and even a person that provide a way into a system or network for the cybercriminals.

- The *Common Vulnerabilities and Exposures (CVE)* database hosted by MITRE Corporation at https://cve.mitre.org/ is a public reference of identified vulnerabilities and exposures.

- Vulnerabilities labeled *zero-day* are vulnerabilities that are discovered but not publicly announced before being exploited.

- *Exploits* (noun) are tools or methods used to penetrate systems through vulnerabilities. Exploit (verb) can also mean the actual act of penetrating a system.

- On any system, it's important that you implement the principle of *least privilege*. Users should have only the permissions they need to perform their jobs, and not a drop more.

- Security permissions to resources should be assigned to group account objects, not user account objects, with *role-based access*.

- Quoting NIST SP 800-207: "*Zero trust* is a cybersecurity paradigm focused on resource protection and the premise that trust is never granted implicitly but must be continually evaluated."

- *Defense in depth* is the usage of multiple layers of security to protect against known threats.
- *Network segmentation enforcement* separates an organization's infrastructure into multiple segments, implemented through subnets in most cases (there are other ways, like isolated VLANs, for example).
- A *screened subnet [previously known as demilitarized zone (DMZ)]* is a network segment carved out by normally two routers—with firewalls—to provide a special place (a zone) on the network for any servers that need to be publicly accessible from the Internet.
- *Separation of duties* means to separate a responsibility in such a way that it requires the input of two or more users.
- *Network access control* (NAC) is a standardized approach to verify that a node meets certain criteria before it is allowed to connect to a network.
- A *honeypot* is a server with lots of fake PII, including passwords stored in plaintext, credit card numbers, addresses, and even healthcare-related information without any strong form of cybersecurity on the server.
- *Authentication methods* serve the purpose of positively validating the identification of users trying to gain access to a system, network, or some data.
- *Multifactor* authentication (MFA) means using two or more distinctly different methods for authentication.
- *Terminal Access Controller Access Control System Plus (TACACS+)* is a protocol developed by Cisco to support authentication, authorization, and accounting (AAA) in a network with many routers and switches.
- *Remote Authentication Dial-In User Service (RADIUS)* is the protocol of choice for implementing AAA related to network access, in contrast to TACACS+, which is the protocol of choice for remote management of routers and switches.
- *Single sign-on (SSO)* is a process whereby a client performs a one-time login to an authenticating system, which in turn takes care of the client's authentication to any other connected systems the client is authorized to access.
- Programs use *LDAP* (Lightweight Directory Access Protocol) to store, query, and change database information used by the network.
- *Kerberos*, a cross-platform authentication protocol, has been the default authentication protocol for Windows domain controllers for over two decades.
- A user can use *local authentication* to authenticate to a computer, router, or switch, without that device having to consult an external, centralized database.
- *Extensible Authentication Protocol (EAP)* was developed to create a single standard to allow two devices to authenticate.
- *802.1X* is an EAP solution for wired (Ethernet) and wireless networks.

- *Risk management* is the never-ending process of assessing risks to resources and data, so proper security implementations can be added to systems and networks.
- *Security risk assessments* help organizations deal with many types of potential attacks.
- A *threat assessment* is the process of evaluating various threats that could come to fruition and affect an organization.
- A *vulnerability assessment* includes reports from vulnerability scanners and other discoveries of security specialists and provides direction for the organization to then act upon.
- *Penetration testing* involves "white hat" hackers, finding existing vulnerabilities and exploiting them to gain access.
- A *posture assessment* covers all the various threats and risks to which the company is exposed.
- *Business risk assessments* include a subset of risk assessment focused on operations in the organization, such as process assessment and vendor assessment.
- A *process assessment* examines various actions performed by an organization to produce desired results.
- A *vendor assessment* examines all aspects of a third party's security controls, processes, procurement, labor policies, and more to see what risks that vendor poses to the organization.
- An approach called *security information and event management (SIEM)* is used to monitor and manage an organization's network.

4.1 QUESTIONS

1. Seeing the answers to an exam prior to taking the exam would be a breach of what?
   A. Confidentiality
   B. Integrity
   C. Availability
   D. SIEM

2. Which of the following is true?
   A. TACACS+ is used for authenticating remote users, while RADIUS is used for allowing administration of routers and switches.
   B. TACACS+ is used for allowing administration of a router, while RADIUS is used for allowing administration of a switch.
   C. RADIUS is used for allowing administration of a switch, while RADIUS is used for allowing administration of a server.
   D. RADIUS is used for authenticating remote users, while TACACS+ is used for allowing administration of routers and switches.

3. Which of the following is never used in a domain environment?

   A. LDAP

   B. Kerberos

   C. Local authentication

   D. 802.1X

4.1 ANSWERS

1. **A**   Seeing something you shouldn't see is a breach of confidentiality.

2. **D**   TACACS+ is a Cisco proprietary protocol, while RADIUS is an open protocol.

3. **C**   LDAP and Kerberos are used on domain controllers. 802.1X can be used on a domain. However, local authentication never occurs with a domain setup.

Objective 4.2   Compare and contrast common types of attacks

It's never been a fair fight, and it never will be. As a cybersecurity defender, you'll have to protect each and every single one of your company's vulnerabilities. Cybercriminals, on the other hand, need to be able to exploit just one vulnerability. Attackers can choose from many different technology-based attacks, but often they find great success from human and environmental attacks that don't involve technology, but rather the ability to prey on gullible and naive humans.

Technology-Based

There are many types of *technology-based* attacks. Some require great knowledge on the part of the attackers, while others require very little knowledge. All of the attacks described in this section can also be used by pentesters to see if an infrastructure can withstand these attacks, if carried out by cybercriminals.

Denial-of-Service (DoS)/Distributed Denial-of-Service (DDoS)

Denial-of-service (DoS)/distributed denial-of-service (DDoS) attacks attempt to compromise the availability of systems and networks. Internet-based servers are robust devices, designed to handle a massive number of requests per second. These robust servers make it tricky for a single attacker at a single computer to send enough requests to even slow them down, let alone bringing them down with a Denial-of-service (DoS) attack. Far more menacing, and far more common, than a simple DoS attack are DDoS attacks. A DDoS attack uses hundreds, thousands, or even millions of infected computers under the command and control of a single operator to launch a coordinated attack. DDoS operators usually don't own these computers, but instead use malware (discussed later in this objective) to take control of computers.

The security and robustness of a public-facing server (accessible through the Internet) depends on the organization hosting that server as well as the group within that organization that is responsible for the server. Using a college as an example, both the main college Web site and the course enrollment Web site would have higher-capacity servers than the servers of individual departments. Even so, they may still fall victim to a DDoS attack. However, a specific department that runs its own servers through faculty-acquired funding and technology might be dealing with less secure and less robust servers. Protecting these vulnerable servers often is overlooked, but they really need to be defended from DDoS attacks. Similarly, in business, some departments with shoestring budgets use discarded devices and equipment for critical business services, without considering DDoS defense mechanisms for them.

For mitigation, there are DDoS protection services that will detect abnormal traffic flows, and redirect such traffic away from your network.

ADDITIONAL RESOURCES   Listen to me talk on TV news about a DDoS attack at https://www.youtube.com/weissman52, in the TV News Cybersecurity Expert Playlist (videos from 8/17/20 and 9/29/20).

Botnet/Command and Control

A single computer under the control of an operator is called a zombie or bot. A group of computers under the control of one operator is called a *botnet*. *Command and control* (known as both C&C and C2) indicates "hands-on keyboard" by the adversary. Botnets are used in mass attacks, compromising as many hosts as possible (millions in many cases) to make an enormous network of zombies, which are then used to perform DDoS attacks or proliferate malware.

EXAM TIP   A remote access Trojan (RAT) is malware that also allows for command and control. However, RATs control fewer hosts than botnets. RATs are controlled one at a time as opposed to botnets, which are controlled all at once, and RATs are used in attacks that are targeted, while botnets are used for mass attacks.

For mitigation, practice good cyber hygiene, including user education, password management, and malware protection.

On-Path Attack (Previously Known as Man-in-the-Middle Attack)

In an *on-path attack (previously known as man-in-the-middle attack)*, an attacker taps into communications between two systems, covertly intercepting traffic thought to be only between those systems, reading or in some cases even changing the data and then sending the data on. A classic on-path attack would be a person using special software on a wireless network to make all the clients think his laptop is an access point. He could then listen in on that wireless network, gathering up all the conversations and gaining access to passwords, shared keys, or other sensitive information. On-path attacks are commonly perpetrated using ARP spoofing, as described next.

ARP Spoofing

A specific type of on-path attack, an *ARP spoofing* attack, involves an attacker forging ARP messages. (ARP was explained in Objective 2.3.) The attacker intercepts, relays, and possibly alters the communication, while the two parties believe they are directly communicating with each other.

As an example of how ARP spoofing is accomplished, let's say we've got five hosts plugged into a switch, A, B, C, D, and E, as well as their default gateway. When Host A has remote traffic to send, it knows the traffic goes through the default gateway, so it has to send a broadcast ARP request looking for the MAC address of the gateway.

In its unicast ARP reply, the gateway sends its MAC address to Host A, which caches it, and then uses it in subsequent frames as the destination MAC address for remote traffic. A gateway's MAC address should be constantly present in a host's ARP cache, since most (if not all) traffic sent is for devices on different networks, including corporate servers located on different subnets.

So, suppose that Host A's ARP cache knows that the MAC address of its default gateway, 10.0.0.99, is AAA (instead of using the full 12-hex-digit MAC address form, we'll use three characters for simplicity here). We're now going to discuss an attack known as *ARP spoofing*, also known as ARP cache poisoning. Enter the on-path attacker, represented by Host C. Host C sends out an ARP, which can be either a request or a reply, saying that the MAC address of 10.0.0.99 is CCC. Host A looks at this ARP and says, "Hmm, it was AAA. I guess they put a new NIC in that device. I'll update my ARP cache accordingly." Host A now overwrites the correct MAC address it has on file for its default gateway with the MAC address of the attacker's machine.

Shortly thereafter, the guy sitting in front of Host A wants to go to a Web site. Host A gets the IP address of the Web server from its local DNS server and puts that IP address as the destination IP address in the outgoing IP header.

After determining that the destination is not on the same network, Host A realizes that it needs the MAC address of its gateway, 10.0.0.99. Lo and behold, there is an entry in Host A's ARP cache for the gateway's MAC address, and Host A uses this for the destination MAC address field in the outgoing Ethernet frame, which encapsulates the outgoing IP packet.

However, instead of the switch sending the traffic to the gateway, the switch now sends the traffic to Host C, because Host C is connected to the interface associated with the destination MAC address in the switch's MAC address table. The attacker will be using a program like Cain and Abel, Ettercap, or arpspoof to continue this attack. Host C will now remove the frame, and in the IP packet, change the source IP address to its own IP address.

Now, Host C will reframe the packet. The new source MAC address is that of Host C, and the new destination MAC address is the real gateway MAC address. The normal IP routing process gets the packet to the Web server, which will send return traffic back to the attacker. The attacker can modify the traffic or leave it as is, and will then send it back to the victim.

For mitigation of ARP spoofing, use dynamic ARP inspection, as explained in Objective 4.3.

DNS Poisoning

A common attack on DNS (Domain Name System) today involves poisoning DNS caches. (DNS was explained in Objective 1.6.) In *DNS poisoning*, also known as DNS cache poisoning and DNS spoofing, an attacker sends unsolicited DNS answers to caching DNS servers. For example, if the cache on the RIT DNS server were changed to associate www.flcc.edu with an IP address different from the legitimate one (a malicious Web site, for example), any downstream RIT client would be given that incorrect IP address upon request, and would be led to a site under control of an attacker.

This site could be a phishing site or could contain a drive-by-download exploit kit. If that happened to an ISP's DNS server cache, all ISP customers would be affected. If that happened to a root server, or an authoritative TLD DNS server, all ISPs and customers downstream would be affected.

The false DNS resource records will even make their way to DNS caches on user machines. Furthermore, cybercriminals could change the TTLs to really high values to keep those false entries in cache for a long time.

China's great firewall blocks at the DNS level. For example, a Web site blocked in China, such as www.twitter.com, will have an incorrect IP address associated with it on the Chinese DNS servers. It's an intentional, self-inflicted DNS cache poisoning attack.

In 2010, a non-Chinese ISP configured its DNS servers incorrectly to fetch information from DNS servers in China and cached them locally. Other ISPs got their DNS information from that ISP and used it on their DNS servers. The poisoned DNS entries spread quickly, and people in the United States were blocked from accessing sites including Twitter, Facebook, and YouTube.

For mitigation of DNS poisoning, make sure that the DNS responses are actually coming from the authoritative DNS servers. This is done through DNSSEC, a protocol designed to secure DNS from DNS cache poisoning attacks.

VLAN Hopping

An older form of attack that still comes up from time to time is called *VLAN hopping*, which comes in two forms. The first, switch spoofing, is when an attacker sends traffic to the switch, convincing the switch to change the attacker's port from an access port to a trunk port. After this happens, the attacker can now read traffic from and inject traffic to other VLANs.

The second form, a VLAN double-tagging attack, injects traffic from one VLAN into a different one by sending two 802.1Q tags, one of which is removed by the switch. In this attack, the attacker sends both an outer 802.1Q tag that matches the attacker's access port VLAN and an inner tag that matches the VLAN the traffic will be injected into. The attacker's access port will read in the frame, because the outer tag's VLAN ID matches the attacker's access port VLAN. If it didn't, the switch would drop the frame. The key to this attack is that the trunk link from the attacker's switch to another switch must use a native VLAN that is the same VLAN of the attacker's access port. If this is the case, the trunk port on the attacker's switch will strip off the outer tag and send the frame, still with the inner tag, to the switch at the other end of the trunk link. Now that second switch will send the traffic to access ports in the VLAN specified by the inner tag (as well as to any trunk ports). The attacker has now sent traffic (which could be malicious or part of a DoS) to a VLAN other than his own. VLAN hopping is almost never seen anymore because modern switches are all designed to prevent this.

Switches used to accept 802.1Q tagged frames on access ports if the VLAN in the tag matched the VLAN configured for that port. Modern switches don't, so if the attacker sends a double-tagged frame, or even a single-tagged one, it will simply be dropped without exception on modern switches.

Rogue DHCP

Dynamic Host Configuration Protocol (DHCP), discussed in Objective 1.6, allows clients to automatically get leases on IP addresses, and other configuration parameters, without having to be manually configured. Most DHCP servers in a company are on a subnet with other servers, such as DNS servers. In other words, clients are not going to be on the same subnet as their servers. In the world of DHCP, relay agents take the DHCP Discover broadcasts, turn them into unicasts, and send them to the DHCP servers, which send the DHCP Offers back to the relay agents, which in turn relay them back to the clients. If a client gets multiple DHCP Offers, as there should be more than one DHCP server (or any server for that matter) for fault tolerance and load balancing, it usually accepts the first offer.

As you can imagine, if there is a DHCP server on a client's subnet that hears the DHCP Discover broadcast, it would send a DHCP Offer in response a lot quicker than the actual DHCP servers, which have to wait for the relay agent's traffic to be routed across multiple hops and then back again. Therefore, an attacker can place a nefarious, insidious *rogue DHCP* server on a subnet to respond to DHCP Discover messages. The rogue DHCP server will answer a DHCP Discover with a DHCP Offer containing the normal information given out to the clients in that autonomous system, with one small difference: it lists itself as the default gateway! When clients need to send traffic off their network, and need the MAC address of their default gateway, they will now ARP for the MAC address of the attacker, thinking that the attacker IP address is the gateway IP address. All remote traffic will be sent directly to the attacker, who can sniff the packets, perform an on-path attack, and perform reconnaissance.

There are a bunch of programs to detect the presence of a rogue DHCP server, and they all follow the same algorithm: send a DHCP Discover message and check if any DHCP Offers come back from IP addresses that are not in an authorized DHCP servers list.

For mitigation, enable DHCP snooping, a security mechanism at the Layer 2 switch, as covered in Objective 4.3.

Rogue Access Point (AP)

A *rogue access point (AP)* is simply an unauthorized access point. Rogue access points have tortured every wireless network since the day Linksys came out with the first cheap wireless router back in the early 2000s. Most rogue APs are evil, but some are installed by authorized users seeking to connect to the wired network from a location that doesn't have decent Wi-Fi coverage available from existing authorized APs. Evil rogue APs are far more nefarious, acting as a backdoor to a network or an on-path attack, grabbing usernames and passwords, among other items.

For mitigation, use wireless intrusion prevention systems (WIPSs) or wireless LAN controllers (like the ones from Cisco) that have rogue AP detection built into the devices themselves.

Evil Twin

The most infamous form of a rogue AP is called an *evil twin*, which intentionally mimics an existing SSID (service set identifier, the name of a Wi-Fi network) in order to get people to connect to it instead of the proper WAP. Evil twins work best in unsecured networks such as those you see in airports and hotels.

It's easy to access the wrong SSID. Some 802.11 devices are notorious for moving their list of discovered SSIDs in such a way that you think you are clicking one SSID when you are actually accidentally clicking the wrong one. For mitigation, practice diligence when connecting to a new SSID. For example, who hasn't seen SSIDs such as the infamous "attwifi"? This SSID is AT&T's attempt to use all of its devices as hotspots. Sadly, it's a simple process to create an evil twin SSID to mimic the attwifi SSID and get otherwise unsuspecting people to connect to it.

Manually entering an SSID can obviously result in a typo. Luckily, in these cases your typo won't accidentally land you onto another SSID. You'll just get an error.

Ransomware

A 2016 study by PhishMe (acquired by and incorporated into Cofense in 2018) found that 97 percent of phishing e-mails were specifically designed to deliver *ransomware*, which locks and encrypts a device until a user pays a ransom fee. More recent studies have similar conclusions. Scare tactics include threatening the user or company: if they don't pay within a certain amount of time, files will start to be deleted. The general recommendation is not to pay the ransom because doing so encourages the adversaries to continue this type of extortion. It also funds their future activities and doesn't guarantee that you will get a decryption key or, if you do, that it will actually work.

For mitigation, educate users on refraining from clicking any unknown links and downloading and running any unknown attachments. Also, keep a good set of backups that can be used to restore a damaged system.

ADDITIONAL RESOURCES   Listen to me talk on TV news and talk radio about ransomware attacks at https://www.youtube.com/weissman52, in the TV News Cybersecurity Expert Playlist (videos from 2/2/21, 2/3/21), and in the Radio Cybersecurity Expert Playlist (two videos from 2/4/21 and one from 5/10/21).
Read this article about ransomware, in which I'm featured: https://www.mpnnow.com/story/news/2021/02/08/victor-ny-schools-ransomware-attack-revealed-vulnerabilities-how-to-protect-against-malware/4432616001/.

Password Attacks

One of the biggest takeaways from Verizon's 2020 Data Breach Investigations Report (DBIR) was that over 80 percent of hacking-related breaches involve brute force or the use of stolen credentials.

ADDITIONAL RESOURCES   Go to https://enterprise.verizon.com and search for "DBIR." Various versions and sections will be listed in the search results, which, when clicked, will lead to many links, including one to download the full report. Googling "Verizon DBIR" will do the trick as well.

Although they're not the best choice for authentication and gaining remote access to systems and networks, passwords (something you know) are still more heavily used than security tokens, key fobs, or smart cards (something you have) and biometrics (something you are).

Attackers can use a technique called password guessing in which they manually enter passwords at a login prompt to gain access to an account when they have a valid username. In fact, this is exactly what happened with two Major League Baseball teams in 2013, when a St. Louis Cardinals executive guessed the password of a former coworker who used to work for the Cardinals but moved on to the Houston Astros. This led to lots of confidential information about players, potential trades, and scouting reports getting into the hands of a rival executive. The information was publicly dumped and wound up embarrassing numerous players and teams.

ADDITIONAL RESOURCES   Read about the MLB incident at these links:
www.npr.org/sections/thetwo-way/2016/07/18/486538276/former-cardinals-official-gets-nearly-4-years-in-prison-over-astros-hack
www.vice.com/en/article/d7mkvx/did-a-houston-astros-executive-use-david-eckstein-as-his-password

There are tools to automate this password-guessing process, a type of online attack, including Medusa, Ncrack, and THC-Hydra (also known just as Hydra). These tools were built to help companies secure their networks, as security specialists can test hosts and networking devices for poor passwords. These tools are used to audit devices as well. Password-guessing online attacks can also be used to check that your firewalls, intrusion detection systems (IDSs), and intrusion prevention systems (IPSs) detect when a server gets bombarded with unsuccessful login attempts, and that accounts automatically get locked when this happens. Password guessing through manual or automated means is obviously very noisy, so attackers perform *password attacks* on their own time and resources, after stealing a password database.

Passwords should never be stored in plaintext in databases, which allows them to be used immediately after they're stolen. Passwords should be stored in hashed format, because hashing is a one-way function.

In many of the data breaches of years past, stolen password databases contained passwords that were either stored in plaintext or hashed with weak functions, like MD5 and SHA-1.

The Local Authentication section in Objective 4.1, discussed local password databases. The LDAP section in Objective 4.1 discussed a domain controller's password database.

The Windows NTLM (New Technology LAN Manager) suite actually uses the MD4 hash function, without a salt, for storing Windows password hashes.

Web sites that have logins store passwords in a backend database, likely using the MySQL or MariaDB relational database management system (RDBMS). If an attacker enters the stolen hash into the password field, the hash itself would be hashed, so the attacker won't enter a hash into a password field.

Attackers have three attack options after they steal the hashed password database: a brute-force attack, a dictionary attack, and a rainbow table attack (which is not covered in the CompTIA Network+ exam objectives).

 ADDITIONAL RESOURCES   Listen to me talk on talk radio about a Facebook breach at https://www.youtube.com/weissman52, in the Radio Cybersecurity Expert Playlist (video from 4/5/21).

Dictionary

A *dictionary* attack involves a file called a wordlist, containing words like those found in a dictionary. These words are possible passwords. The dictionary file uses likely possibilities for passwords and, unlike a regular dictionary, includes alternate spellings and additional letters, numbers, and symbols in variations of the words.

Unfortunately, there are lots of people who choose short passwords that are common words with simple variations. Attackers will make wordlists containing commonly used passwords. This is why substituting 0 for the letter *o* or $ for the letter *s* is not any form of security.

After an attacker steals a password database, on the attacker's own machine and time, the words in the wordlist are hashed and compared to the stolen password hashes. If a hash from

Possible plaintext password	Computed hash		Stolen hashes
123456	ba32...		4fcb...
123456789	d9e6...		59a3...
picture1	83fe...		1c03...
password	b109...		b8b3...
qwerty	0dd3...		b109...

FIGURE 4.2-1 Dictionary attack

the stolen database matches a computed hash of a word from the wordlist, the attacker can simply associate the matching computed hash with its plaintext input, which would be the actual plaintext password, as shown in Figure 4.2-1.

The hash function used in this attack must be the same one used by the organization from which the password hashes were stolen. Hash functions (like encryption algorithms) are never secret (which ones are used and how they work). In fact, the length of a hash is enough to reveal which hash function is being used. Furthermore, the type of hash function used for the database will be stored alongside the hash with the username and other data in the password database, in plaintext form. Since a username is always stored in the same record as its corresponding hash, attackers can choose to attack specific accounts and their hashes instead of all accounts.

It's even possible to precompute the hashes for all entries in a wordlist, so the words in a wordlist (possible plaintext passwords) don't need to be hashed with each attempt to crack a password. The most renowned such password file, rockyou.txt, contains over 14 million words.

Brute-Force

A *brute-force* attack is similar to a dictionary attack. However, instead of using a set of words in a wordlist file, which might be potential passwords, a brute-force attack involves iterating through all possible lowercase letters, uppercase letters, numbers, and symbols (whitespace can be included, too, for passphrases) for all lengths, to produce every possible password. These produced words are dynamically hashed and compared to the stolen hashes, as done in a dictionary attack with a wordlist, as shown in Figure 4.2-2.

If a password is not in a wordlist used in a dictionary attack, the attack will fail. With a brute-force attack, there is no possibility of failure because all potential passwords will come up at some point. It's a guarantee! The con is that you might not be alive to see it. Long passwords render such an attack useless because attackers don't want to tie up so many resources in cracking passwords for hours, days, weeks, months, or years. This is a great example of how length beats anything else for passwords.

To speed things up, you can restrict the iterations to a minimum length and maximum length of characters. Another restriction for speed involves the character sets, which could be

Possible plaintext password	Computed hash		Stolen hashes
abcdef	e32e…		4fcb…
abcdeg	ab32…		59a3…
abcdeh	7c2d…		e32e…
abcdei	0d60…		1c03…
abcdej	1aec…		b8b3…

FIGURE 4.2-2 Brute-force attack

just letters, just lowercase letters, just uppercase letters, just numbers, just symbols, or some combination of different character sets.

You could even use a program like crunch, which uses all the previously mentioned restrictions but also gives you more control over specifics. Examples include allowing just certain characters from a single character set or multiple character sets, as well as including a known string, like a birthdate.

The wordlist generated by crunch can be dynamically passed to a program that attempts to crack the passwords, like John the Ripper. The crunch wordlist can also be saved to a wordlist file and later passed to a password-cracking program, like John the Ripper. John the Ripper, as mentioned earlier, can do a brute-force attack on its own, without any input file.

Since random characters are generated, even with restrictions and possibly an output wordlist as well, this can still be considered a brute-force attack. A dictionary attack wordlist uses predetermined characters that are meaningful rather than assembling random characters together.

Mitigation to password attacks includes using long passwords, as described in Objective 4.3.

MAC Spoofing

MAC spoofing, spoofing a MAC address, can bypass blacklists and MAC address filters. This allows an attacker to send traffic on a network they ordinarily wouldn't be able to on. MAC spoofing can be done through software and drivers.

Mitigation includes port security and private VLANs, both of which are discussed in Objective 4.3.

IP Spoofing

IP spoofing, spoofing an IP address, is used to perform DDoS attacks. Attackers randomly generate spoofed IP addresses for packets in a DDoS attack, so that filters can't simply block the IP addresses of the attacking systems, since they're all going to be very different. Spoofing IP addresses also masks the identity and location of the attackers.

Mitigation includes BCP38 (Best Current Practice), detailed in RFC 2827 (https://data-tracker.ietf.org/doc/html/rfc2827), which looks at the source IP address of packets and filters them if they are coming from a direction contrary to what's listed in a router's routing table. For example, a spoofed IP address that enters a router on one interface (like a packet with a source IP address of 192.168.1.52 appearing on the interface connecting to the ISP), while that network ID is connected to another interface (like the network of 192.168.1.0/24 being connected to the LAN interface), indicates maliciousness.

Other mitigation techniques include DHCP snooping and Dynamic ARP inspection, both of which are discussed in Objective 4.3.

Deauthentication

WEP (Wired Equivalent Privacy), established as the first encryption standard for 802.11 wireless networks and ratified in 1997, was a poor attempt at preventing attackers from sniffing wireless traffic sent between wireless clients and APs. It was in no way equivalent to the privacy that wired (Ethernet) networks have with cables.

WPA (Wi-Fi Protected Access) debuted in 2003 as an intermediate step between WEP and WPA2 (Wi-Fi Protected Access 2), which debuted itself in 2004. There were so many problems with WEP that a temporary upgrade (WPA) was immediately needed, until a better long-term solution (WPA2) could be designed.

WPA2 has had its share of problems and vulnerabilities, but has been the only choice for wireless security since 2004. It is now slowly being phased out in favor of WPA3, which was introduced in 2018. WPA3 prevents dictionary attacks and replay attacks, which are possible with WPA2. Whereas you could crack a WPA2 password and decrypt packets, both are simply not possible with WPA3!

WPA2 (all of the following applies to WPA as well) has two modes: Personal mode, also known as Pre-Shared key (PSK), and Enterprise mode. Personal mode simply uses a PSK in the form of a password, while Enterprise mode uses a username/password pair, which is used with 802.1X (port-based authentication) and a RADIUS server (in most cases, also using an Active Directory database). Cracking Enterprise mode is significantly harder than cracking Personal mode.

Each client on a WPA2-PSK infrastructure has its own handshake. Therefore, by default, you won't be able to monitor any traffic except your own on an encrypted network. However, if you know the Pre-Shared key and capture the handshakes of other clients with the AP, you can decrypt their entire sessions.

In order for Wireshark to decrypt WPA2 traffic, it must capture an EAPoL (Extensible Authentication Protocol over LAN) 802.1X handshake, which is a four-way handshake that contains values used by WPA2 to set up keys used for encrypting traffic between the client and the AP. This happens each time a client connects to an AP, and the values and keys are different for each session.

Using packet injector tools, you can type a simple command to send a *deauthentication* frame (only if 802.11w-2009, discussed shortly, is not enabled) to clients associated with the AP, causing them to immediately reauthenticate. This is more effective when sent to the unicast addresses of the clients, as opposed to the broadcast address. Wireshark can then capture the EAPoL four-way handshake. Once this is done, and you've cracked the WPA2 password, you can put the password in Wireshark with the SSID, which will allow you to decrypt packets. You'll be able to see every packet sent to and received by each client whose EAPoL handshake you captured. Cracking the Pre-Shared key and forcing the victims to reconnect is all that's needed!

The latest standard, WPA3, limits active attacks, where unlimited password attempts are flooded to the AP in a dictionary attack or brute-force attack, through a new key exchange protocol called Simultaneous Authentication of Equals (SAE), which replaces WPA2's PSK. WPA3 also eliminates passive attacks, preventing users from sniffing traffic from other devices, even with the Wi-Fi password and a successful connection. WPA3 also prevents the passive capturing of an exchange to determine session keys and the decrypting of data captured earlier (perfect forward secrecy). WPA3 actually eliminates the problem of open networks not using encryption, like the ones found in coffee shops, hotels, and the like. However, it leaves them unauthenticated through unauthenticated encryption with Opportunistic Wireless Encryption (OWE), which encrypts the messages and creates a MAC for each message using a key that the client and AP generate under OWE. The keys used are unique and individualized for each client, so other devices can't decrypt this traffic.

Laptops and phones that support WPA3 will fall back to WPA2, if that's the highest level of security offered by the AP. Upgrading a home router can be a swift action, but for organizations as well as public Wi-Fi hotspots, the changeover could take a much longer time. Therefore, expect to still see WPA2, and the vulnerabilities introduced in this chapter, for quite some time.

IEEE 802.11w-2009, which was introduced in 2009 but hasn't been supported in client device chipsets until recently, added wireless security features. While frames can't be protected before the four-way handshake, management frames sent after the key establishment can be protected. These frames include deauthentication frames, which, based on this standard, will be encrypted between the client and the AP. If a client gets an unencrypted deauthentication frame, it will not be accepted. 802.11w-2009 is not enabled on most wireless networks and client devices, though.

WPA3 requires 802.11w-2009, but as of this writing, most home routers don't yet ship with WPA3, and most NICs on client devices don't support it.

Wi-Fi 5 (802.11ac) operates just in the 5GHz range. The newest standard, Wi-Fi 6 (802.11ax), operates in both the 5GHz and 2.4GHz ranges, as did Wi-Fi 4 (802.11n), and will eventually replace Wi-Fi 5 (802.11ac) in stadiums, conference halls, and many other high-demand public locations. Change doesn't come quickly, so public Wi-Fi networks could still be using Wi-Fi 5 (802.11ac) and WPA2 for many years to come.

For mitigation of deauthentication attacks, use a long and strong WPA2 password. WPA3 does, in fact, eliminate deauthentication attacks.

Malware

Malware, short for malicious software, is intended to damage or break a computer system or network without user knowledge or approval. There are many different types of malware but the two most often confused ones are viruses and worms.

 EXAM TIP Although the CompTIA Network+ exam objectives do not list specific types of malware, you will be expected to know about the specific types of malware in this section for the exam.

 NOTE Most malware propagates via phishing, unsecured ports, and stolen credentials.

Let's start off by defining what a computer program is. A computer program, also known as software or an application, is a collection of instructions following algorithms to solve problems or accomplish tasks. These instructions are executed by the CPU, central processing unit, the brain of the computer. With that in mind, let's explore the differences between a virus and a worm.

Viruses and Worms

Difference number one between a virus and a worm is that a virus injects itself into a program's instructions, so that the CPU will execute the malicious instructions when they are reached in the original program. Just like a biological virus, a computer virus needs a host file to infect and that file has to be run for the virus to start running. The infected host file, in addition to a program, could be a data file or even the boot sector of a hard drive. The malicious instructions, whenever read, are executed. However, the malware known as a worm does not infect host files. It stands alone in its own file.

Difference number two between a virus and a worm is that viruses can spread and replicate by themselves to other files on the same machine. However, in order to spread and replicate to other machines on the network and other networks across the world, some human intervention is required. One common way this happens is when someone forwards an e-mail attachment. Worms can propagate all by themselves across networks all around the world. They exploit vulnerabilities in protocols, networks, and configurations. Worms can get into your e-mail lists, compose an e-mail, attach themselves to e-mails, and even make the subject and body of the e-mail sound like it came from a trusted human.

Difference number three between a virus and a worm is that a virus always has a malicious payload that is meant to execute. A worm doesn't need to have any malicious payload. Think about this, if Harry the hacker sends a picture of a tiger to an important Web server, nothing will happen. If Harry the hacker sends 10, 100, or even 1000 pictures to an important Web server, nothing will happen. However, if Harry the hacker puts a program on 10,000 user machines and they each are instructed to place the program on thousands of other machines, when the time comes, Harry the hacker will give the kill signal and all machines known as zombies in this botnet will be sending traffic to a poor victim's server that will come to a grinding halt. This is a DDoS attack, covered in Objective 4.2. Interestingly enough, a DDoS doesn't go after the confidentiality or integrity of the CIA model. It's meant to go after the A, the availability of a system or a network.

Macro Virus   A macro virus is any type of virus that exploits application macros to replicate and activate. A macro is programming within an application that enables you to control aspects of the application. Macros exist in any application that has a built-in macro language, such as Microsoft Excel, that users can program to handle repetitive tasks among other things.

Logic Bomb

A logic bomb is another type of malware, and its distinction is that it introduces latency to when it executes. Either a certain date, time, or event will trigger this type of malware to run. From a malware author's perspective, the more time that goes by before a new malware specimen is detected, the better. This allows the malware to silently spread so that anti-malware companies don't detect it. Then after a period of time, boom, the malware on all infected systems will run.

One famous story involves a software engineer who thought he was going to get fired. He wrote into the company's software that if human resources generated payroll and his name was not on the list, do x, y, and z to the company. He knew that if he was going to be fired, his computer rights would be revoked first, so this was his way of getting revenge before the fact. He knew that if he was wrong, nothing would happen and all would be hunky-dory. Turns out though, he was right. He got fired and his logic bomb did a lot of bad things to the company and its data. He got caught and was handed a stiff fine and prison sentence. Another programmer wrote a logic bomb into his company's software before resigning. He was hoping to be rehired at a big premium to save the company from the malware that he launched. Yet another programmer wrote logic bombs in company sites all around the world. To fix these issues, the company sent him on trips worldwide and he gained fame and fortune fixing these problems… until he got caught.

Trojan Horse

Malware known as a Trojan horse is named after the famous story about Greek troops hiding inside a big wooden horse. The Trojans thought the Greeks were gone and took this horse as a conquest into their city. At night, the Greeks hiding in the horse jumped out, opened the gates, and in came the rest of the Greek troops. They destroyed Troy and ended the war.

The malware Trojan horse is really the same thing. Think about a program that has one advertised use but also has another hidden ability used by an attacker. There is definitely a social engineering component involved. The user must download and install it. Trojan horses do not replicate either on the local machine or across a network. You've seen these free screensavers, free ringtones, free WeatherBug links. Well, users have clicked on them. They got the screensavers. They got the ringtones. They got the WeatherBugs. But also, in the process, they installed, unknown to them, some other programs which were malicious. These hidden malicious programs could damage the computers, spread malware, spy on user activities, and use the computer as part of a botnet.

RAT

A RAT, remote administration tool, is a piece of software used to remotely access or control a computer. This tool can be used legitimately by systems administrators for accessing client computers or even servers. A RAT, when used for malicious purposes, is known as a remote access Trojan. It can be used by a malicious user to control a system without the knowledge of users of that system. Remote access Trojans are malicious pieces of software that infect victim machines to gain administrative access. They are often included in pirated software through patches as a form of a cracked game or even via e-mail attachments. Most of the popular RATs are capable of performing keystroke logging, packet capture, screen capture, camera capture, file access, code execution, registry management, password sniffing, and more. After the infection, they may perform unauthorized operations and hide their presence in the infected system.

Rootkit

A rootkit is a set of programs and code that allows a persistent or permanent undetectable presence on a computer. A rootkit can sanitize logs and repair timestamps, hiding actions of the cybercriminals. A rootkit can also mask files, processes, and network connections and enable privileged access to the computer. It also conceals installed malware. For instance, when anti-malware software checks a location where malware is resident, the rootkit will respond, "You checked it already and it's clean. Move on to somewhere else." Rootkits also install another piece of malware called a backdoor. After cybercriminals exploit vulnerabilities to get into your system or network, they want to come back later with less effort. Backdoors allow cybercriminals to do so, bypassing the normal authentication process through software left after the initial penetration. It's like breaking into a physical location and propping open an unmonitored back window or a back door to get back in another time.

Adware

There are two types of programs that are similar to malware in that they try to hide themselves to an extent: adware and spyware. Adware is a program that monitors the types of Web sites you frequent and uses that information to generate targeted advertisements, usually pop-up windows. Adware automatically plays or displays advertisements or downloads promotional material. It's often bundled with a product or package and it's common in shareware, free software that might require subsequent payment after a trial run. Adware isn't, by definition, evil, but many adware makers use sneaky methods to get you to use adware, such as using deceptive-looking Web pages ("Your computer is infected with a virus—click here to scan NOW!"). As a result, adware is often considered malware. Some of the computer-infected ads actually install malware when you click them, so avoid them.

Spyware

Spyware covertly monitors user's activities and reports personal user data to a third party that expects financial gain. Spyware also includes the sale of personal data, the redirecting of Web activity to ad sites, and the presentation of targeted ads and pop-ups through a related piece of malware called adware.

Spyware is a function of any program that sends information about your system or your actions over the Internet. The type of information sent depends on the program. A spyware program will include your browsing history. A more aggressive form of spyware may send keystrokes or all of the contacts in your e-mail. Some spyware makers bundle their product with ads to make them look innocuous. Adware, therefore, can contain spyware.

For mitigation, use a good anti-malware program, as well as the Windows Security real-time protection feature.

 ADDITIONAL RESOURCES   Listen to me talk on TV news about how Facebook tracks you at https://www.youtube.com/weissman52, in the TV News Cybersecurity Expert Playlist (video from 10/8/21).

Human and Environmental

Human and environmental attacks do not rely on technology, but rather how humans behave in certain environments. Humans are, have been, and will always be the weakest link in any security implementation. Any hardware or software implementation of security can easily be undone extremely quickly by a gullible or naive human.

Social Engineering

Social engineering is an art and science that is used by cybercriminals to convince people to grant the attackers' requests—often things they normally wouldn't and shouldn't do. Social engineering cybercriminals use psychological tricks to get people to reveal information the criminals need regarding systems, networks, and infrastructures. It's much easier to ask someone for a password than it is to break into a system and get it. The following are some examples of social engineering tactics:

"Hello, this is tech support. We need your help to fix a problem with your account. Can you help us out today? Okay, great. What's your password?"

"Hi, I'm from corporate. Today I'm just doing a security assessment, and I need you to check out a few things for me."

"I'm here to fix the heating in the datacenter. See the logo on my polo shirt?"

"Hold the door please, I forgot my badge."

How about an employee who finds a flash drive in the parking lot with a label that reads "Corporate finances, top secret information," or something enticing like that? The employee will then plug the flash drive into a company machine and start spreading malware, maybe even ransomware, across all corporate devices.

The above example are all scary examples of the only threats to cybersecurity that doesn't involve any technology. Social engineering involves preying on humans who are gullible and naive, and will always be the weakest link in cybersecurity system.

You can patch a computer, but you can't patch people. You can teach them the signs of social engineering, but they forget and make mistakes. As computer vulnerabilities get more difficult for cybercriminals to exploit, people become their most obvious targets. Skilled social engineers fool victims with their body language, body posture, gestures, facial expressions, eye movements, voice sounds, inflection, size, word choices, context, and framework.

"I really need you to help me right now! Time is of the essence!"

"This is Bob Jones. We met last year at the company picnic. You know me."

"Alice told me that you're a great worker, willing to help out whenever you can."

"If you don't give me the information, I'm going to complain to your manager."

"I'm actually the one who signs your checks. You don't want me on your bad side."

"Actually, the other guy in the office did this for me last week."

Using social engineering, cybercriminals can commit fraud, network intrusion, industrial espionage, identity theft, and simply disrupt systems and networks. Potential targets include telephone companies, answering services, big name corporations, financial institutions, military and governmental agencies, hospitals, and even…you.

The process starts with information gathering. Social engineers do their homework to figure out what the victims like and don't like. They find any potential weaknesses and vulnerabilities of the victims that can be exploited. Public information online is a great resource. In certain cases, companies don't even realize how much public-facing information can be used against them in a social engineering attack. Names of employees, titles, phone numbers, and more are waiting to be gleaned. Dumpster diving is another technique used during this information gathering step. Yes, attackers will dive into corporate dumpsters and sift through trash cans looking for any information that can be used. They're not really looking for passwords that were written down and thrown out. In fact, phone directories, calendars, company memos, and more can prove to be even more valuable. Suppose an attacker finds a discarded invoice from an HVAC company or a computer contractor. All the attacker needs to do is make a knockoff polo shirt with a logo and show up for some "maintenance repairs."

The next step is exploitation. Social engineers develop relationships, rapport, trust, and credibility with their victims. Alternatively, they threaten, intimidate, impersonate, use scare tactics, and make things seem very urgent. In this step the attackers get what they want by any means necessary.

Why is social engineering so effective? People want to help others. People don't want to get in the way, especially if someone is carrying a clipboard and glancing it as if they are fulfilling an assignment. Just look and act like you belong there and people won't ask questions. People don't like conflict. People don't like to question authority. For the users who give out usernames, passwords, or other information to participate in some random survey for gifts in return, it's because people like free stuff. That chocolate bar could prove to be very expensive in the long run, though.

Mitigation of social engineering involves teaching users right from wrong. Make them read policies and test them to make sure that they follow them. Throwing legitimate rewards and incentives their way is not a bad idea, either.

Phishing, tailgating, piggybacking, and shoulder surfing are the specific forms of social engineering covered in the CompTIA Network+ exam objectives.

 ADDITIONAL RESOURCES   Listen to me talk on TV news about social engineering at https://www.youtube.com/weissman52, in the TV News Cybersecurity Expert Playlist (video from 3/5/22).

Phishing

The digital form of social engineering is *phishing*. Phishing involves sending out "bait," mostly through e-mail. It can also be done through *smishing* via SMS (Short Message Service) text messages, over live phone calls, and via recorded messages; or through *vishing* via voicemail to a large number of people, in hopes that some users will take the bait by revealing usernames, passwords, and other items, such as credit card information. When a user clicks a link in a phishing e-mail, for example, a Web page opens that looks and feels like a real banking site, the real PayPal site, the real eBay site, the real Facebook site, the real LinkedIn site, and much more. Therefore, the user feels safe and secure in entering sensitive information, which goes directly to the attacker.

Furthermore, simply visiting these sites could install malware on a victim's machine. After the user clicks the link to open the site, the page could use a drive-by download exploit kit, which collects information from a victim's machine, finds vulnerabilities in operating systems, browsers, and other software such as video players, determines the appropriate exploit, delivers the exploit, and executes malware. All of this happens automatically, just by a victim visiting the attacker's site.

In addition, if you fail to apply operating system or software security updates, you're very vulnerable to exploit kits. These are usually hosted on a legitimate Web site that's been hacked or are delivered through a legitimate Web site's third-party advertisements.

In another scenario, users could be asked to click a link to view content or install a program that will enable them to view content. Clicking these links, however, installs malware. This could include *scareware*, pop-up windows from the visited site asking users to click to remove a virus or to scan for a virus. Clicking these links actually installs the malware. The pop-ups could include phone numbers for users to call to continue the social engineering attack over the phone. Victims then give the attackers their credit card numbers and enable the attackers to control their machines remotely to "fix" the supposed problems.

Phishing also involves e-mail attachments that users are asked to open, such as a ZIP file. This offers the attacker three advantages: it bundles multiple files into one, compresses them, and can bypass malware scanners. Alternatively, an e-mail attachment may be a Microsoft Word document or an Excel spreadsheet with a macro. Users are convinced to believe that the file is secure, and they can only view it by enabling macros. Of course, when a user clicks the button to enable macros, that triggers the installation of malware. In fact, that's exactly how the 2015 Ukraine power grid cyberattack started.

Phishing often involves sending e-mails to random e-mail addresses that may or may not be valid—for example, bob1@gmail.com, bob2@gmail.com, bob3@gmail.com, and so on. *Spear phishing* takes phishing to a whole new level by targeting specific users in a specific company—for example, alice@company.org, eve@company.org, harry@company.org, and so on. When attackers go after the "big fish" of a company, such as a senior executive, they're taking spear phishing to an even higher level; this is called *whaling*—for example, ceo@company.org, daboss@company.org, ciso@company.org, and so on.

There are many ways to spot phishing e-mails and fake sites. When you hover over a link, before you click it, you can see the real Web address you'll be sent to. This is impossible on mobile devices, however, so make it a practice never to click these links, but instead to open up a new browser window or tab and go to the site manually. Pressing on a link and holding is the mobile device equivalent of previewing a link, but that's way too risky to consider.

 ADDITIONAL RESOURCES   This tip of hovering over a link is starting to lose steam. Check out this article from August 2021, which explains why: https://www.microsoft.com/security/blog/2021/08/26/widespread-credential-phishing-campaign-abuses-open-redirector-links/.

A generic greeting instead of your actual name is another sign of something amiss. The e-mail address can be spoofed to appear legitimate, or it can be noticeably off. URLs that have the actual domain name, but are in the wrong location of the web address (for example, linkedin.attackersite.com) are also malicious. Seeing "HTTP" instead of "HTTPS" in the URL can be another indicator, and so is the fact that you're asked to fill in way too much information that should not be required.

Phishing e-mails often include a desperate story that asks the user to act urgently, and in some cases, they actually threaten the user. The formatting and appearance of the e-mail or Web site, including the quality of images, is another giveaway. Images of text, instead of text, are suspicious, as they can't be keyword scanned by phishing filters. An e-mail consisting of just a single image or a single Web link is, therefore, highly suspicious.

Users should look for poor spelling and grammar, since most phishing campaigns originate from non-English-speaking countries. However, there are a number of theories that poor spelling and grammar in phishing e-mails is deliberate. First, phishers want to only spend their time interacting with those who will yield them great benefits. To eliminate all but the most gullible of people, phishers introduce spelling and grammar errors so that they are left with likely people they can successfully scam and, ultimately, collect money from. Second, when certain words are misspelled, the e-mails can evade filters and reach more people. Third, people can relate to making minor spelling errors and may perceive an e-mail to be authentic if it has a few minor errors.

A phishing e-mail often includes a generic signature without contact information. Attachments and mentions of scripts are the icing on the cake.

Mitigation techniques should include never clicking any links in any e-mail. Don't take any chances. Open up a new browser or tab and go to a site manually. Never download and run any attachments without verifying that they are legitimate by sending an e-mail to a company or person (a new e-mail, not by clicking a link or replying to the e-mail you got), or by picking up the phone and calling them.

ADDITIONAL RESOURCES   Listen to me talk on TV news and talk radio about phishing at https://www.youtube.com/weissman52, in the TV News Cybersecurity Expert Playlist (videos from 4/19/20 and 2/24/22) and in the Radio Cybersecurity Expert Playlist (videos from 5/10/21 and 2/24/22), and at https://www.wxxinews.org/connections/2021-09-23/connections-how-to-recognize-and-avoid-online-scams.

Tailgating

A locked front door can be opened by an authorized person, and an unauthorized person can attempt to enter through that already opened door, in a process called *tailgating*. While it is possible to prevent tailgating with policies, it is only human nature to "hold the door" for that person coming in behind you. Tailgating is especially easy to do when dealing with large organizations in which people don't know everyone else. If the tailgater dresses like everyone else and maybe has a badge that looks right, he or she probably won't be challenged. Add an armload of gear, and who could blame you for helping that person by holding the door?

There are a couple of techniques available to foil a tailgater. The first is a security guard. Guards are great. They get to know everyone's faces. They are there to protect assets and can lend a helping hand to the overloaded, but authorized, person who needs in. They are multipurpose in that they can secure building access, secure individual room and office access, and perform facility patrols. The guard station can serve as central control of security systems such as video surveillance and key control. Like all humans, security guards are subject to attacks such as social engineering, but for flexibility, common sense, and a way to take the edge off of high security, you can't beat a professional security guard or two.

Another option to prevent tailgating is the use of turnstiles (https://www.controlledaccess .com/), which can be connected to the badge access system, allowing only one person through at a time, unlike badged or fob access doors that allow multiple people through at a time.

Alternatively, an access control vestibule (aka mantrap), a small room with two doors, can be used. People need to scan through the two doors, but only door can be open one at a time. See Objective 4.5 for a full description of an access control vestibule.

Piggybacking

Piggybacking is very similar to tailgating. The only difference is that while tailgating is done without the authorized person's consent or even realization, piggybacking means the authorized person is aware of the unauthorized person's attempt.

Shoulder Surfing

Shoulder surfing is the process of surreptitiously monitoring people when they are accessing any kind of system, trying to ascertain passwords, personal identification numbers (PINs), or personal information. The term shoulder surfing comes from the classic "looking over someone's shoulder" as the bad guy tries to get your password or PIN by watching which keys you press. Shoulder surfing is an old but still very common method of social engineering.

REVIEW

Objective 4.2: Compare and contrast common types of attacks

- There are many types of *technology-based* attacks. Some require great knowledge on the part of the attackers, while others do not.
- *Denial-of-service (DoS)/distributed denial-of-service (DDoS)* attacks attempt to compromise the availability of systems and networks. A DoS attack is conducted by one attacker one computer, whereas a DDoS attack is a simultaneous coordinated effort from many systems infected and under control of the attacker.
- A group of computers under the control of one operator is called a *botnet. Command and control* (known as both C&C and C2) indicates "hands-on keyboard" by the adversary.

- In an *on-path attack (previously known as man-in-the-middle attack)*, an attacker taps into communications between two systems, covertly intercepting traffic thought to be only between those systems, reading or in some cases even changing the data and then sending the data on.

- A specific type of on-path attack, an *ARP spoofing* attack, involves an attacker forging ARP messages.

- In *DNS poisoning*, also known as DNS cache poisoning and DNS spoofing, an attacker sends unsolicited DNS answers to caching DNS servers.

- An older form of attack that still comes up from time to time is called *VLAN hopping*, which comes in two forms, switch spoofing and double-tagging attack.

- An attacker can place a nefarious, insidious *rogue DHCP* server on a subnet to respond to DHCP Discover messages.

- A *rogue access point (AP)* is an unauthorized access point that can be set up either by attackers for evil purposes or authorized network users for convenience purposes.

- The most infamous form of a rogue AP is called an *evil twin*, which intentionally mimics an existing SSID to get people to connect to it instead of the proper WAP.

- *Ransomware* locks and encrypts a device until a user pays a ransom fee.

- Password guessing through manual or automated means is obviously very noisy, so attackers perform *password attacks* on their own time and resources, after stealing a password database.

- A *dictionary* attack involves a file called a wordlist, containing words like those found in a dictionary.

- A *brute-force* attack is similar to a dictionary attack. However, instead of using a set of words in a wordlist file, which might be potential passwords, a brute-force attack involves iterating through all possible lowercase letters, uppercase letters, numbers, and symbols (whitespace can be included, too, for passphrases) for all lengths, to produce every possible password.

- *MAC spoofing*, spoofing a MAC address, can bypass blacklists and MAC address filters.

- *IP spoofing*, spoofing an IP address, is used to perform DDoS attacks.

- Using packet injector tools, you can type a simple command to send a *deauthentication* frame (only if 802.11w-2009 is not enabled) to clients associated with the AP, causing them to immediately reauthenticate.

- *Malware*, short for malicious software, is intended to damage or break a computer system or network without user knowledge or approval.

- *Human and environmental* attacks do not rely on technology, but rather how humans behave in certain environments.

- *Social engineering* is an art and science that is used by cybercriminals to convince people to grant the attackers' requests—often things they normally wouldn't and shouldn't do.

- The digital form of social engineering is *phishing*, which involves sending out "bait," mostly through e-mail but also through other mediums, to a large number of people, in hopes that some users will take the bait by revealing usernames, passwords, and other items, such as credit card information.
- A locked front door can be opened by an authorized person, and an unauthorized person can attempt to enter through that already opened door, in a process called *tailgating.*
- *Piggybacking* is very similar to tailgating. The only difference is that while tailgating is done without the authorized person's consent or even realization, piggybacking means the authorized person is aware of the unauthorized person's attempt.
- *Shoulder surfing* is the process of surreptitiously monitoring people when they are accessing any kind of system, trying to ascertain password, PIN codes or personal information.

4.2 QUESTIONS

1. Which of the following attacks is a botnet associated with?
   A. Dictionary attack
   B. Deauthentication
   C. VLAN hopping
   D. DDoS

2. Which of the following is under attack with a brute-force attack?
   A. IP addresses
   B. Passwords
   C. MAC addresses
   D. DHCP servers

3. Which of the following is not a human and environmental attack?
   A. On-path attack
   B. Tailgating
   C. Piggybacking
   D. Shoulder surfing

4.2 ANSWERS

1. **D**   Distributed denial of service attacks are carried out by botnets.
2. **B**   A brute-force attack tries to crack a password.
3. **A**   An on-path attack (aka man-in-the-middle attack) uses technology, unlike the others.

Objective 4.3   Given a scenario, apply network hardening techniques

The National Institute of Standards and Technology (NIST) defines hardening at https:// csrc.nist.gov/glossary/term/Hardening as follows:

> *A process intended to eliminate a means of attack by patching vulnerabilities and turning off nonessential services.*

Hardening eliminates needless functionality and involves the deployment of configurations and settings that are secure. This reduces the risk of the exploitation of vulnerabilities and also helps to ensure that an infrastructure is compliant with regulations.

Best Practices

Objective 4.3 includes a lengthy list of *best practices* for implementing network hardening techniques that you need to be familiar with.

Secure SNMP

SNMP, previously discussed in Objective 3.1, has three major versions. SNMP version 1 (SNMPv1) appeared in three requests for proposals (RFP) all the way back in 1988. SNMPv2c was a relatively minor tweak to version 1. Neither version provided encryption. SNMPv3 allows for *secure SNMP* since it has additional security with support for encryption and robust authentication. It also has features to make administering a large number of devices easier.

Router Advertisement (RA) Guard

As discussed in Objective 1.4, IPv6 hosts can use stateless address autoconfiguration (SLAAC) to self-configure their own IPv6 address. When an IPv6 host has an interface enabled, it sends a router solicitation (RS) to the all-routers multicast address of ff02::2 in hopes of receiving a router advertisement (RA) in response. The RA can be sent either the all-hosts multicast address of ff02::1, or it can be configured to be sent to the link-local unicast address of the host. The host's MAC address is included in the RS as well, so the router has all it needs. Routers also send unsolicited RAs in regular time intervals.

RA messages let hosts know how to go ahead with dynamic addressing and contain a prefix (the IPv6 term for network ID), prefix length (the IPv6 term for subnet mask, which should always be /64 to allow hosts to autoconfigure themselves), default gateway, and other information for configuration. A router can also be configured to send IP addresses of DNS servers in an option in an RA.

Hosts don't perform any validation of these RAs, allowing an attacker to send fake RAs. Clients could be configured with a default gateway IP address of an attacker machine, and could be victim to an on-path attack. Alternatively, many RAs sent by a rogue device could cause a denial of service (DoS) attack.

Router Advertisement (RA) Guard is configured on switches to filter bogus RAs and keep a network safe from the previously mentioned attacks. All RAs can be filtered from interfaces in which they are not expected (from directions and interfaces where routers are not found), or highly sophisticated policies can permit certain RAs matching certain conditions, including VLAN ID, hop limit, RA flags, source IPv6 address, and source MAC address.

Port Security

As discussed in Objective 2.3, Ethernet switches learn where hosts are by analyzing the source MAC address field in Ethernet frames as the frames enter switch ports and by keeping mappings of MAC addresses to ports in the MAC address table.

The switch can keep a specific number of MAC addresses in this table. The size of the table and the number of entries each vary by switch. If an attacker connects a device to a port and runs a tool or script that sends thousands of Ethernet frames into the port with different, randomly generated MAC addresses, the switch enters each MAC address into the MAC address table, associating each with the same physical port of the attacker. Eventually, the MAC address table will run out of space. At this point, the switch can't learn any new MAC addresses and will simply start flooding all traffic from all hosts out of all ports on the switch, except the originating port.

This CAM overflow attack (using one of the other names of the MAC address table, as explained earlier), also known as a MAC flooding attack, essentially turns a switch into an old, obsolete networking device called a hub, which always flooded traffic out of all ports except the port on which the message originated. The switch and its MAC address table put hubs out of business.

With this attack, the attacker is now able to sniff every single frame sent into the switch. The attacker could be an insider, physically on the premises, or an outsider with remote access to one of the organization's machines. Confidentiality is at great risk. macof, part of the dsniff suite of tools, can generate hundreds of thousands of random MAC addresses and flood them into a switch. From a cybersecurity perspective, this tests your switch's resistance to such an attack. To mitigate this attack, you can use a switch feature called *port security*.

First, you need to identify allowed MAC addresses so they can gain access to the port. This can be done either statically or dynamically, as frames enter a port. The next step involves specifying the maximum number of MAC addresses that will have access to the port. By default, only one MAC address has access. In a switched environment, the main reason that more than one MAC address will be heard from on a single port is that the port is connected to a neighboring port. For example, all traffic coming into Switch A, from hosts in Switch B, will be heard through the port on Switch A that connects to Switch B. A second example of when multiple

MAC addresses can be learned on a single port involves the use of virtual machines, where the VM sends frames with a source MAC address of its virtual NIC, which will be different from the MAC address of the physical NIC of the host. A third example of multiple MAC addresses being learned on a single port is when a VoIP phone is connected to a switch just with a PC, and that switch then connects upstream to another switch.

A violation occurs if a new MAC address is heard on a port after the maximum number of MAC addresses have been learned. On ports that are statically configured for certain MAC addresses, an unknown MAC address heard on that port would trigger a violation as well. When a violation occurs, the switch will enter one of three states and take appropriate action.

- **Shutdown mode**   The port is immediately shut down. No frames can enter or exit, and an SNMP trap notification is sent. The network engineer must re-enable the port manually, although the switch can be configured to have ports shut down because of errors come back up again after a certain period of time has elapsed.
- **Restrict mode**   The port doesn't shut down, but all frames from violating MAC addresses are discarded. The switch logs the number of violating frames and can send an SNMP trap, as well as a syslog message, if configured to do so.
- **Protect mode**   The port doesn't shut down, but all frames from violating MAC addresses are discarded. So far, this state is exactly the same as restrict. The only difference is that in this state, no violations are logged. I've never heard of a valid use case—or even a contrived one—that works for this state. No sane administrator would want to stick their head in the sand like an ostrich and ignore violations!

As if a CAM overflow attack wasn't enough motivation for implementing port security, there are still other compelling reasons. First, imagine an organization dealing with sensitive PII, like a healthcare organization or even the government. You would imagine that every device on that network would be tightly controlled and tracked, while personal devices would be forbidden. After a MAC address of a company device is learned on the port (which will happen instantly when it is set up for the first time), users would not be able to unplug it and plug in their own device. If someone tried that, the port would be shut down and an administrator would need to manually bring it up again.

Furthermore, port security also prevents users from plugging in unauthorized switches into ports, to allow multiple devices of theirs to connect to the network. In this case, the switch could just restrict and not completely shut down, to allow the user to keep working, while unauthorized devices will not be able to send traffic into the switch. In this case, too, the administrator will get alerts.

Finally, let's say there's a VoIP phone or a kiosk machine available for employees, or even visitors, to use. Port security will prevent someone from unplugging one of those devices and plugging in a personal device when the switch only allows the initial MAC address learned on the port to send frames into the port

Dynamic ARP Inspection

The way to mitigate ARP spoofing, described in Objective 4.2, is through *dynamic ARP inspection*. ARP replies are checked against a database, and if they contain invalid or conflicting values, they are dropped. Therefore, they won't be sent by switches to hosts, whose ARP caches would subsequently be poisoned.

ARP replies coming from trusted switch ports, like ports connected to other switches, will not be checked or filtered. The logic is that the other switch is also inspecting on its other ports. Switch ports connected to router interfaces will be trusted, too.

ARP replies coming from untrusted switch ports will be checked against manually configured entries (for servers and router interfaces whose IP addresses were statically configured) or dynamically generated entries in the DHCP snooping database (coming up soon) for clients using DHCP.

Control Plane Policing

Devices like routers and switches have different planes, abstractions of locations for certain functions:

- The management plane is used to access the device, for instance, through SSH or a console port.
- The data plane, also known as the forwarding plane, forwards packets within the device and out of specific ports.
- The control plane is responsible for how the forwarding of packets is done. For example, router routing tables, discussed in Objective 5.5, are created with work from the control plane. Switch MAC address tables, Spanning Tree Protocol, and ARP caches, all covered in Objective 2.3, are also created within the control plane.

Think of the data plane consisting of cars driving on roads and the control plane as the traffic lights and signs that dictate how the cars should obey the rules of the road. *Control plane policing* is a security mechanism that filters needless traffic from the CPU, protects traffic on the control plane and management plane from being dropped because of large amounts of lower-priority traffic, and prevents DoS attacks. These are all achieved through grouping common criteria together, assigning them to a CPU queue, and configuring policers in hardware.

Private VLANs

Private VLANs involve a primary VLAN and secondary VLANs. Devices on secondary VLANs can't communicate with other secondary VLANs, but can communicate with a port on the primary VLAN, which will be connected to their default gateway. The following are some use cases for private VLANs:

- Servers of the same organization on the same VLAN need to be able to communicate with the default gateway but do not need to receive each other's broadcast traffic.

- Servers of different organizations, in the same server farm and VLAN, need to be able to communicate with the default gateway, but not with each other.
- An ISP infrastructure where a single VLAN connects to multiple customer networks. Each customer network must communicate with the ISP's gateway on the VLAN, but the customer networks do not need to communicate with each other.

Logically associating a primary VLAN with multiple secondary VLANs accomplishes this task. A secondary VLAN can be configured as isolated, allowing devices to reach the primary VLAN but not secondary VLANs. Hosts in an isolated VLAN can't even communicate with each other. If you need hosts in a secondary VLAN to communicate with each other, the secondary VLAN should be configured as community instead of isolated.

Physical switch ports of primary VLANs are configured to be promiscuous if they connect to a router, allowing communication to anything on the primary VLAN or any secondary VLAN. Physical switch ports of secondary VLANs are configured to be hosts, which allows communication to just a promiscuous port or host ports in a community VLAN configuration.

Disable Unneeded Switchports

A good way to make sure that no one can plug unauthorized cables and devices into switches, and in turn inject or capture traffic, is to *disable unneeded switchports* by issuing the `shutdown` command for each individual interface.

Disable Unneeded Network Services

From a security standpoint, it's important to *disable unneeded network services*. Any unneeded service that is running expands the attack surface and makes your network more vulnerable to attacks.

A port scanner like nmap, covered in Objective 5.3, can identify open ports that could represent unneeded network services.

Change Default Passwords

Every configurable device, like a router or switch, has a default password and default settings, all of which can create an inadvertent insider threat if not addressed. People sometimes can't help but be curious. A user might note the IP address of a device on the user's network, for example, and run SSH "just to see." Because it's so easy to get the default passwords/settings for devices with a simple Google search, that information is available to the user. One unauthorized change on that device might mean a whole lot of pain for the network tech or administrator who has to fix things.

Dealing with such authentication issues is straightforward. Before bringing any system online, *change default passwords*. This is particularly true for administrative accounts. Also, disable or delete any "guest" accounts (make sure you have another account created first!).

NOTE Insecam, at www.insecam.org, allows you to view various webcams around the world that haven't had their default credentials changed, specifically any password set. According to the site, the way to remove your camera from their directory is simply to set a password!

Password Complexity/Length

As detailed in Objective 3.2, overly complex passwords and passwords that change too frequently are too hard for users to remember, which will cause these users to write them down and store them insecurely. Furthermore, keystroke logging, phishing, and social engineering attacks work just as well on complex passwords as they do on simple ones. A long password using one character set is stronger and more secure than a shorter password that uses multiple character sets! Simply stated, length beats complexity for security of passwords.

Enable DHCP Snooping

To mitigate rogue DHCP server attacks, described in Objective 4.2, you can *enable DHCP snooping* at the Layer 2 switch. When DHCP snooping is enabled, switch ports are put into one of two categories, trusted or untrusted. It's really very simple, the switch ports that DHCP servers connect to, both directly and indirectly, including switch ports that routers are connected to, are labeled as trusted ports. Every other switch port connected to a host is labeled "untrusted." Recall Objective 1.6 DHCP's DORA: Discover, Offer, Request, and ACK. Clients send DHCP Discover broadcast messages into the switch, which floods any broadcast out of all ports, except the port on which the message originated. Now, here's the kicker: DHCP Offers coming from an untrusted port are dropped, since there should be no legitimate DHCP servers connected to that port. Furthermore, the switch port automatically shuts down.

DHCP Offers coming from a trusted port are treated as they always are, sent in most cases as unicast messages to the systems that sent the DHCP Discovers. DHCP snooping also keeps track of the completed DHCP bindings, when DORA completes. Included in this database are client MAC addresses, client IP addresses, lease time, interface, and more.

Change Default VLAN

By default, ports are associated with VLAN 1, which is the management VLAN. Since VLAN 1 is the default VLAN that carries traffic that's used to remotely manage, control, monitor, and troubleshoot devices, like SSH, SNMP, and more, it's a best practice to *change* the *default VLAN* so that non-administrative devices won't be able to see important management traffic.

Patch and Firmware Management

Best practices with *patch and firmware management* require both aggressive updates when manufacturers release patches and research to know when patches might cause problems. Patching and updating software and firmware is of critical importance in hardening networks.

Firmware updates are far less common than software updates and usually aren't as automated. In general, firmware patching is a manual process and is done in response to a known problem or issue, new features, optimization purposes, and more. Keep in mind that firmware updates are inherently risky, because in many cases it's difficult to recover from a bad patch.

Unpatched systems—including operating systems and firmware—and legacy systems present a glaring security threat. You need to deal with such problems on live systems on your network. When it comes to unpatched OSs, well, patch or isolate them!

Unpatched firmware presents a little more of a challenge. Many people only patch firmware if there is a known issue, but firmware should be kept up to date on all devices. Many vendors have even improved the firmware upgrade process. For example, some enterprise networking equipment, SAN equipment, and even SOHO routers have two firmware slots, which are used in an alternating fashion when patching. This allows the quick and easy rollback and recovery from the other slot, if necessary.

 EXAM TIP   Look for questions on hardening network systems that discuss disabling unnecessary systems, patching and upgrades for software, and upgrading firmware.

The process of patching device firmware varies from device to device, so you'll need to do some research on each. In general, you'll download a patch from the manufacturer and run it on the device. Make sure you have good power before you start the patch. If something goes wrong in the update, you'll brick whatever device you're trying to patch. There's no undo or patch rollback with firmware, so patch only when necessary.

Legacy systems are a different issue altogether. "Legacy" means systems that are no longer supported by the OS maker and are no longer patched. In that case you need to consider the function of the system and either update if possible or, if not possible, isolate the legacy system on a locked-down network segment with robust firewall rules that give the system the support it needs (and protects the rest of the network if the system does get compromised). Equally, you need to be extremely careful about adding any software or hardware to a legacy system, as doing so might create even more vulnerabilities.

Backing up configurations is critical, especially when backing up firmware. The process of backing up a configuration varies from platform to platform, but almost all PCs can back up their system setups, and switches and routers have well-known backup commands. Backing up firmware of routers, switches, and PCs should be done as well. When dealing with systems that you know no longer have the current firmware, back up the firmware prior to upgrading. Since vendors usually allow you to download just the latest version of the firmware (or maybe the latest and the one that preceded it), if you need to restore what's currently running, your backups will be your only option.

A single system may have many patches over time. When necessary, you might find yourself having to perform a downgrade or rollback of the patch, returning to a patch that is one or two versions old. This is usually pretty easy on PCs because OSs track each update. With firmware, the best way to handle this is to track each upgrade and keep a separate copy for each patch in case a downgrade/rollback is needed.

Access Control List

Let's say you have some hosts on a particular subnet that should have access to other subnets in your autonomous system, with the exception of a specific subnet where servers are storing sensitive data. Maybe one specific host from a subnet should be allowed to access a specific service on a certain machine, but not others. There could even be government privacy regulations that require you to prevent or allow packets from reaching certain servers.

Enter the stateless packet filter, which, through a set of rules, either lets packets in or denies their entrance to a network as well as lets packets out or denies their exit from a network.

The best example of a stateless packet filter is an IP *access control list* (ACL), which will permit or deny packets from entering inbound or exiting outbound the network, based on criteria such as source IP address, destination IP address, protocol, and port (a logical port, representing a connection endpoint). The terms inbound and outbound are flipped with ACLs compared to networks, and are used in relation to the router and not the network. Inbound to a network means outbound from a router, and outbound from a network means inbound to a router.

IP ACLs filter by Layer 3 and Layer 4 information of the OSI model, so they don't use MAC addresses as a criteria, since MAC addresses are found in Layer 2 frames. If you did want to filter at Layer 2, you would use a MAC ACL. Other types of ACLs include a VLAN ACL and a port ACL.

IP ACLs can be configured on a router or on a stand-alone firewall like Cisco's Adaptive Security Appliance (ASA). An ACL has multiple lines of instructions that are processed in a sequential order. In fact, order does matter, unlike a shopping list. When my wife gives me a shopping list, the order in which I get the items doesn't matter. I could get the milk, bread, eggs, cereal, ice cream, taco kit, and pancake mix in any order I want. However, the order of instructions in an ACL is crucial. Ordering the instructions incorrectly could actually do the opposite of what you intended to do. Certain packets that should be denied will be permitted. Certain packets that should be permitted will be denied. In the world of cybersecurity, that sets you up to be breached or to be the victim of a possible DoS attack.

An ACL is a list of multiple instructions or statements. Some instructions permit traffic, while others deny traffic. As soon as a packet is matched to a statement based on source IP address, destination IP address, protocol, or port, the packet is either permitted or denied, regardless of what comes later in the ACL.

ACLs are processed from the first line, and then all the subsequent lines sequentially down, until a match is found. If a general statement in one of the first few lines of an ACL denies a specific packet, it's denied, even if there's a more specific statement later in the ACL that would permit the packet. The packet will never reach the later line because as soon as a match is made, the packet is dealt with at the earlier line. There's no branching or looping. There's no comparing general statements to more specific ones.

Firewall Rules

Firewall rules permit certain types of traffic and deny others. When traffic is denied, it's filtered, which means blocked and dropped.

Explicit Deny

An *explicit deny* statement drops packets meeting certain criteria, including source IP address, destination IP address, protocol, and port. Packets could be permitted on the same criteria with an explicit permit statement.

Implicit Deny

If no statements in the configured ACL match a packet, the packet will meet an *implicit deny* statement at the end of every ACL that just discards the packet. After all, if we have no instruction that deals with the packet in our configured statements, from a cybersecurity perspective, it makes sense to just drop the packet instead of letting it into or out of a network.

Role-Based Access

Role-based access was covered in Objective 4.1. CompTIA lists it for a second time in Domain 4, here.

 EXAM TIP   Look for a scenario question on network hardening techniques that involve specific access to resources. Implementing role-based access is considered best practice for hardening networks.

Wireless Security

One of the biggest problems with wireless networking devices is that right out of the box, some provide little to no security. Vendors go out of their way to make setting up their devices easy, so usually the only thing that you have to do to join a wireless network is turn on your wireless devices and let them find each other. Setting up an open Wi-Fi network is relatively simple. Once you decide to add security, on the other hand, you need to decide how you plan to share access with others. In the past couple of years, though, this trend has started to change. Some newer wireless devices won't activate or be able to be used until updates are installed, a secured Wi-Fi network is set up, and an admin password is set.

We need to use a number of techniques to implement *wireless security*, to harden it from malicious actions and people. Wireless security is a form of network hardening.

 NOTE   All the methods used in wireless network security—authentication, encryption, MAC address filtering—can be considered network hardening techniques.

You also need to consider that your network's data frames float through the air on radio waves instead of zipping safely along wrapped up inside network cabling. What's to stop an unscrupulous network tech with the right equipment from grabbing those frames out of the air and reading that data?

MAC Filtering

Most WAPs (wireless access points) support *MAC filtering*, a method that enables you to limit access to your network based on the physical MAC addresses of wireless NICs. MAC address filtering creates a type of "accepted users" list—an access control list (ACL)—to restrict access to your wireless network. A table stored in the WAP lists the MAC addresses that are permitted to participate in the wireless network, called a whitelist. Any network frames that don't contain the MAC address of a node listed in the table are rejected.

 EXAM TIP WAPs use an access control list (ACL) to enable or deny specific MAC addresses. Note that a WAP's ACL has nothing to do with ACL in NTFS or a router IP ACL; it's just the same term used for different things.

Many WAPs also enable you to deny specific MAC addresses from logging onto the network, creating a blacklist. This works great in close quarters, such as apartments or office buildings, where your wireless network signal goes beyond your perimeter. You can check the WAP and see the MAC addresses of every node that connects to your network. Check that list against the list of your computers, and you can readily spot any unwanted interloper. Putting an offending MAC address in the "deny" column effectively blocks that system from piggybacking onto your wireless connection.

 EXAM TIP MAC filtering with a whitelist means you allow only specific computers to join the network. When you deny specific computers, you create a blacklist. Whitelisting and blacklisting are labor-intensive processes, with whitelisting requiring far more work.

Although MAC address filtering sounds good, an attacker can very easily spoof a MAC address—make the NIC report a legitimate address rather than its own—and access the network.

Whitelisting requires an admin to collect and enter all MAC addresses for all wireless devices, which is impossible on a transient network and hard to do on a more stable one. As such, MAC address filtering (whitelisting or blacklisting) is not really a viable security measure.

Antenna Placement

The location of the WAPs is also very important. WAP antennas come in many shapes and sizes. In the early days it was common to see WAPs with two antennas. Some WAPs have only one antenna, and some (802.11n, 802.11ac, and 802.11ax) have more than two. A WAP that doesn't seem to have antennas is simply hiding them inside the case.

Optimal *antenna placement* varies according to the space to fill and security concerns. You can use a site survey (covered in Objective 5.4) and wireless analyzer tools (covered in Objective 5.2) to find dead spots, odd corners, and so on. Use the right kind of antenna on each WAP to fill in the space.

Also, look for incorrect antenna placement, where moving a few inches away from an obstacle can make big changes in performance. Antenna placement related to security involves moving access points away from outside walls, directing signals toward the interior, and testing the signal strength to verify if it leaks out of walls and windows.

Power Levels

802.11 is a low-power radio and has a limited range. If the WAP doesn't have enough power, you'll have signal attenuation and your device won't be able to access the wireless network. All of the 802.11 standards have distance limitations; exceeding those limitations will reduce performance. Certainly a quick answer is to move closer to the WAP, but there are a number of issues that cause power levels to drop too low to connect beyond the obvious "you're too far away" from the WAP.

To measure *power levels*, manufacturers use scales called received signal strength indication (RSSI) to show the signal between a WAP and a receiver. Every manufacturer uses different numbers, but they usually show as "how many bars" you have.

If your WAP lacks enough signal power, you have a few choices: get closer to the WAP, avoid physical issues, turn up the power, use a better antenna, or upgrade to a newer 802.11 version (like 802.11ac or 802.11ax) with features that enable the WAP to use the power it has more efficiently.

A physical issue is what it sounds like: something physical in the way keeps the signal from reaching its destination. When installing a network, you must watch out for concrete walls, metal (especially metal studs), and the use of special RF-blocking window film. The solution is more careful planning of WAP placement and realizing that even in the best-planned environment it is not at all uncommon to move WAPs based on the need to clear dead spots.

Some wireless devices make it easy to increase the power. It's tempting to think "cranking it up to 11" (for all you *This Is Spinal Tap* fans) will fix all your Wi-Fi problems, but the unfortunate reality is more complex. If you have one WAP and live in the country, go ahead and crank the transmit power as high as it will legally go. But in a crowded urban environment, this can make Wi-Fi worse. Nearby WAPs will see your stronger signal and turn their own power up to compensate.

It's like being in a crowded restaurant. If everyone is talking at a moderate to low volume, everyone can converse without problems. But if one table starts to get boisterous, the table next to them has to get louder to be heard over the din. This cascades until everyone in the restaurant is practically shouting just so someone a few feet away can hear them.

From a security perspective, this involves not turning the signal strength too high, since it will increase the chances of unauthorized connections from outside the building.

Wireless Client Isolation

Wireless client isolation prevents wireless clients of the same wireless network from sending and receiving traffic to and from each other, through configuration options. For example, at an airport or coffee house, you don't want a stranger's wireless client to communicate with yours.

Guest Network Isolation

Guest network isolation involves configuring a separate wireless network that's isolated from the primary wireless network that a home or company uses. Any device connected to a guest network will not be able to access anything on your primary network or whatever your primary network is connected to but will still have Internet access.

Preshared Keys (PSKs)

The most common way to set up WPA2 encryption is to use a version called WPA2 Pre-Shared key (PSK). This also existed for WPA. Using *preshared keys (PSKs)*, you create a secret key that must be added to any device that is going to connect to the corresponding service set identifier (SSID). There is no user-level authentication with WPA-PSK or WPA2-PSK.

 EXAM TIP Objective 4.3 lists "Preshared keys" (without the hyphen) but the Acronym List identifies PSK as "Pre-Shared Key," so either form might appear on the exam.

EAP

EAP, a wired (Ethernet) and wireless network hardening technique, was discussed in this context, in Objective 4.1. Please refer to the "Extensible Authentication Protocol (EAP)" section there.

Geofencing

Geofencing is the process of using a mobile device's built-in GPS capabilities and mobile networking capabilities to set geographical constraints on where the mobile device can be used.

Geofencing works in several ways, and Objective 4.3 uses "given a scenario" language, so keep geofencing in mind as a wireless network security option.

An example scenario is that an organization uses very high-security mobile devices that must never be taken outside the large campus. The organization installs a geofencing application on each device. If any device goes outside very specific GPS ranges, the device will notify the administrator via one or more methods.

Geofencing can also be enforced with IP address ranges. Corporate or user devices that are not in the IP subnet/network segment they should be in are considered out of range. Streaming services use IP ranges to determine if you are in a specific country that should be receiving specific content.

Geofencing is often used in anti-theft applications that will also silently turn on cameras and microphones as well as lock the system.

Before users can join networks, they have to provide a username (identification), and then prove they are who they say they are (authentication). After being authenticated, they will have limits on what they can do and what they can access (authorization). Furthermore, the relatively new concept of geofencing uses GPS capabilities to control where devices can be used.

WEP networks used shared or open authentication. WPA networks, for authentication, used PSKs and RADIUS servers, as do current WPA2 networks. Devices can be authorized by their MAC address, while geofencing authorizes devices based on where they are located geographically.

Captive Portal

Many public facilities, like airports, employ a *captive portal* to control access to their public Wi-Fi networks. An attempt to connect to the network opens a Web browser that insists you follow the AUP (acceptable use policy). Higher security standards in your Web browser can actually block this content and thus your access to the network.

The captive portal can verify users, authenticate users, and regulate the bandwidth of users. Furthermore, a legal warning can absolve the provider of responsibility if you do anything illegal. The captive portal can also prompt for logon credentials to verify that you are a registered guest, as is the case for many businesses. Hotels usually just confirm a name and room number.

IoT Access Considerations

As discussed in depth in Objective 2.1, the Internet of Things (IoT) represents nontraditional computing devices. *IoT access considerations* are easy to grasp when you explore Shodan, often labeled the world's scariest and most terrifying search engine. Google is usually the first thing that comes to mind when you hear the term search engine. However, what Shodan is looking for is completely different from what Google is looking for. Google's spider crawls the World Wide Web, a collection of information that can be accessed through Web pages, identified by URLs (Uniform Resource Locators), also known as Web addresses, typed into the address bar of a browser. Documents accessed from the Web are written in HTML and are accessed through HTTP or HTTPS, which uses HTTP over TLS for encryption and decryption. The Web is just one way that data and information are sent and received over the Internet, a global interconnection of networks and devices that use the TCP/IP protocol suite.

The Internet and the Web are not the same thing. The Internet represents the infrastructure connecting systems and networks worldwide. It's the hardware—computers, routers, switches, and more. It includes the client and server services and software running on these devices, as well as the TCP/IP suite that all devices use. It also includes the cables and wireless technologies connecting the devices.

The Internet itself is what Shodan searches. Shodan is looking for webcams, routers, servers, and lots of different types of devices connected to the Internet of Things (IoT).

IoT represents nontraditional computing devices that have sensors, software, and more that communicate with other devices. They can be found in smart homes, vehicles, and organizations including medical and healthcare, transportation, manufacturing, agriculture, maritime, infrastructure (city, energy, and environmental), military, and much more.

Many IoT devices have little to no security for various reasons. The financial cost of implementing security could make the device less profitable. Security is inversely proportional to convenience and usability (just like a seesaw, when one side goes up, the other goes down), so some manufacturers make their IoT devices as simple as possible for users, worrying that some customers won't buy a device they believe will be hard to use and configure. IoT devices don't have much RAM and CPU power, compared to other devices, and as such can't support certain security mechanisms. Many use default passwords that are a simple Web search away. Some were designed without a single thought toward security and have literally none! Some IoT devices need a human to initiate an upgrade or security patch (which is not a guarantee), while others don't even have the capability of updates.

Now consider that IoT devices are always connected to the Internet, are constantly collecting tons of data and information, and are running on networks with little to no security using insecure protocols.

One of my favorite stories is about a casino that got hacked through its Internet-connected fish tank thermometer. Read about it here: https://thehackernews.com/2018/04/iot-hacking-thermometer.html.

There is a famous meme, "The S in IoT Stands for Security," which should make complete sense now.

The greatest users of Shodan are not actually cybercriminals, but rather cybersecurity specialists, penetration testers, academic researchers, law enforcement, and governments.

Billions of devices are accessible online. These devices can be identified easily by banner information. These banners contain metadata about a device's software, including the version and options supported, as well as welcome messages, warning messages, and more. From the banners, Shodan is able to identify the specifics of these devices, including make and model. The banners could even indicate what authentication mechanisms are used or if authentication is disabled. Banners vary based on the person creating them and the type of the service the device provides. When this information is combined with geographic information, Internet service provider (ISP) information, and more gleaned from the IP address, a clear picture of a device can emerge. That clear picture can include device vulnerabilities that can be easily exploited, such as unchangeable hardcoded passwords and manufacturer-created backdoors. Shodan is a great tool that can help find these vulnerable devices, which will ultimately lead to securing them.

Shodan can even collect statistics and calculate measurements. For example, Shodan can indicate countries that are increasingly connecting with each other more, which version of Apache is used the most, and even how many devices are vulnerable to a new piece of malware.

Some of the IoT devices found by researcher Dan Tentler using Shodan in 2013, five years after its debut in 2008, included traffic light controls, traffic cameras, a swimming pool acid pump, a hydroelectric plant, a hotel wine cooler, a hospital heart rate monitor, a home security app, a gondola ride, and a car wash. In the case of traffic light controls, a warning message "DEATH MAY OCCUR !!!" was visible in the banner. If Tentler wanted to, he could have easily put the lights in "test" mode and caused unimaginable damage! Why? These controls, incredibly enough, required no login credentials.

 ADDITIONAL RESOURCES   You can read more about Tentler's discoveries at https://money.cnn.com/gallery/technology/security/2013/05/01/shodan-most-dangerous-internet-searches/index.html.

In further research, announced at the beginning of 2016, Tentler found webcams showing marijuana plantations, bank back rooms, rooms inside houses (including kitchens, living rooms, and garages), areas outside of houses (including front gardens and backyards), public locations such as ski slopes and swimming pools, students in colleges and schools, laboratories, and even cash registers inside of retail stores.

In 2013, another researcher, Shawn Merdinger, detailed what he found with Shodan, including Caterpillar trucks whose onboard monitoring systems had an easily guessable username/password combination, fetal heart monitors, and even the power switch that controlled a hospital's neurosurgery wing.

Also in 2013, researcher Billy Rios, who had already found close to 2000 building management systems that had no username or password configured on Shodan, found one such building management system without credentials belonging to…Google.

Anything that has a Web interface can be discovered by Shodan, including smart TVs, smart refrigerators, water treatment facilities, wind turbines, yachts, license plate readers, heating and security control systems for banks, condos, corporations, and universities, industrial control systems, SCADA systems (some controlling nuclear power plants), and electrical grids.

In his book *Complete Guide to Shodan*, Shodan founder John Matherly explains how the discovery process of Shodan works:

> The basic algorithm for the crawlers is:
>
> **1.** Generate a random IPv4 address.
>
> **2.** Generate a random port to test from the list of ports that Shodan understands.
>
> **3.** Check the random IPv4 address on the random port and grab a banner.
>
> **4.** Goto 1.
>
> This means that the crawlers don't scan incremental network ranges. The crawling is performed completely random to ensure a uniform coverage of the Internet and prevent bias in the data at any given time.

Remember, "The S in IoT Stands for Security."

IoT hardening starts with requiring device authentication and network authentication. Knowing what all of your IoT devices are and where they are is key. That way, implementing segmentation, where certain IoT devices in a specific category can reside on one segment with specific policies, becomes easier.

 ADDITIONAL RESOURCES   Listen to me talk on TV news and talk radio about IoT concerns at https://www.youtube.com/weissman52, in the TV News Cybersecurity Expert Playlist (video from 11/30/18) and the Radio Cybersecurity Expert Playlist (video from 6/2/21).

REVIEW

Objective 4.3: Given a scenario, apply network hardening techniques

- Exam objective 4.3 includes a lengthy list of *best practices* for implementing network hardening techniques that you need to be familiar with.
- SNMPv3 allows for *secure SNMP* since it has additional security with support for encryption and robust authentication. It also has features to make administering a large number of devices easier.
- *Router Advertisement (RA) Guard* is configured on switches to filter fake RAs and keep a network safe from an on-path attack and a denial of service (DoS) attack.
- *Port security* protects against a CAM overflow attack.
- The way to mitigate ARP spoofing, described in Objective 4.2, is through *dynamic ARP inspection.*
- *Control plane policing* is a security mechanism that filters needless traffic from the CPU, protects traffic on the control plane and management plane from being dropped because of large amounts of lower-priority traffic, and prevents DoS attacks.
- *Private VLANs* involve a primary VLAN and secondary VLANs. Devices on secondary VLANs can't communicate with other secondary VLANs, but can communicate with a port on the primary VLAN, which will be connected to their default gateway.
- A good way to make sure that no one can plug unauthorized cables and devices into switches, and in turn inject or capture traffic, is to *disable unneeded switchports* by issuing the `shutdown` command for each individual interface.
- From a security standpoint, it's important to *disable unneeded network services*, because any unneeded service that is running expands the attack surface and makes your network more vulnerable to attacks.

- Before bringing any system online, *change default passwords*.

- In May 2017, NIST drafted guidelines that dealt a big blow to well-established password policies, regarding *password complexity/length*. Simply stated, length beats complexity for security of passwords.

- To mitigate rogue DHCP server attacks, you can *enable DHCP snooping* at the Layer 2 switch.

- Since VLAN 1 is the default VLAN that carries traffic that's used to remotely manage, control, monitor, and troubleshoot devices, like SSH, SNMP, and more, it's a best practice to *change* the *default VLAN* so that non-administrative devices won't be able to see important management traffic.

- *Patch and firmware management* require both aggressive updates when manufacturers release patches and research to know when patches might cause problems. Patching and updating software and firmware is of critical importance in hardening networks.

- The best example of a stateless packet filter is an IP *access control list* (ACL), which will permit or deny packets from entering inbound or exiting outbound the network, based on criteria such as source IP address, destination IP address, protocol, and port (a logical port, representing a connection endpoint).

- *Firewall rules* permit certain types of traffic and deny others. When traffic is denied, it's filtered, which means blocked and dropped.

- An *explicit deny* statement drops packets meeting certain criteria, including source IP address, destination IP address, protocol, and port.

- If no statements in the configured ACL match a packet, the packet will meet an *implicit deny* statement at the end of every ACL that just discards the packet.

- In *role-based access*, security permissions to resources are assigned to group account objects, not user account objects.

- We need to use a number of techniques to implement *wireless security*, to harden it from malicious actions and people.

- Most WAPs support *MAC filtering*, a method that enables you to limit access to your network based on the physical MAC addresses of wireless NICs.

- Optimal *antenna placement* varies according to the space to fill and security concerns.

- To measure *power levels*, manufacturers use scales called received signal strength indication (RSSI) to show the signal between a WAP and a receiver.

- *Wireless client isolation* prevents wireless clients of the same wireless network from sending and receiving traffic to and from each other, through configuration options.

- *Guest network isolation* involves configuring a separate wireless network that's isolated from the primary wireless network that a home or company uses.

- Using *preshared keys (PSKs)*, you create a secret key that must be added to any device that is going to connect to the corresponding SSID.
- *Geofencing* is the process of using a mobile device's built-in GPS capabilities and mobile networking capabilities to set geographical constraints on where the mobile device can be used.
- Many public facilities, like airports, employ a *captive portal* to control access to their public Wi-Fi networks.
- *IoT access considerations* can be easy when you think about Shodan, which can easily allow users to find webcams, routers, servers, and lots of different types of devices.

4.3 QUESTIONS

1. On which type of device should you implement best practices such as port security, DHCP snooping, dynamic ARP inspection, private VLANs, disabling unneeded ports, and more?
   A. Switch
   B. Router
   C. WAP
   D. Server

2. On which type of device should you implement best practices such as RA guard, access control lists, firewall rules, and more?
   A. Switch
   B. Router
   C. WAP
   D. Server

3. Which of the following is the weakest form of wireless security?
   A. Wireless client isolation
   B. Guest network isolation
   C. MAC filtering
   D. Geofencing

4.3 ANSWERS

1. **A** These are all great ways to harden your network at the switch level.
2. **B** These are all great ways to harden your network at the router level.
3. **C** MAC addresses can be spoofed, foiling a blacklist. MAC addresses need to be collected, which could hinder the construction of a whitelist.

Compare and contrast remote access methods and security implications

Remote connections have been around for a long time, even before the Internet existed. The biggest drawback to remote connections was the cost to connect. If you were on one side of the continent and had to connect to your LAN on the other side of the continent, the only connection option was a telephone. Or, if you needed to connect two LANs across the continent, you ended up paying outrageous monthly charges for a private connection. The introduction of the Internet gave people wishing to connect to their home or work networks a very inexpensive connection option, but there was one problem—the whole Internet was (and is) open to the public. People wanted to stop using dial-up and expensive private connections and use the Internet instead, but they wanted to be able to do it securely.

Several standards use encrypted tunnels between a computer or a remote network and a private network through the Internet, resulting in a virtual private network (VPN). A VPN creates an encrypted tunnel between two networks over another, less secure, network.

An encrypted tunnel requires endpoints—the ends of the tunnel where the data is encrypted and decrypted. In the tunnels you've seen thus far, the client for the application sits on one end and the server sits on the other. VPNs do the same thing. Either some software running on a computer or, in some cases, a dedicated box must act as an endpoint for a VPN.

The key with the VPN is that the computers should be on the same network—and that means they must all have the same network ID. You would want the laptop that you use in the Rochester airport lounge, for example, to have the same network ID as the computers in the LAN back at the office. But there's no simple way to do this. If it's a single client trying to access a network, that client is going to take on the IP address from its local DHCP server. In the case of your laptop in the airport, your network ID and IP address come from the DHCP server in the airport, not the DHCP server back at the office.

To make the VPN work, you need VPN client software installed on your local machine— the laptop at the Rochester airport—and VPN server software or hardware at your office. You connect your laptop first to the Internet using the airport wireless network; it's just a normal Internet connection. Second, the VPN client software creates a virtual NIC (vNIC) on your laptop (endpoint 1), makes a connection with the VPN server at the office (endpoint 2), and then, in essence, creates a virtual direct cable from the virtual NIC to the office. That "virtual cable" is called a VPN tunnel. The laptop now has two IPv4 addresses. One is local from the airport DHCP server. The other is "local," but works with the office network. That second IP address goes with the virtual NIC.

Site-to-Site VPN

You can connect two VPN concentrators to connect two physically separate LANs permanently. This kind of connection enables two LANs to function as a single network, sharing files and services as if they were in the same building. This is called a *site-to-site VPN* connection.

Leased lines are secure but expensive and difficult to move between locations. Site-to-site VPNs are easy to set up, cost effective, and are easy to move between locations. This does involve a tradeoff of some security with flexibility, but site-to-site VPNs are still quite secure because of encryption and security exchange options. The endpoints are areas where attacks may be attempted. Furthermore the endpoints represent location where devices on the joined networks are set up.

Client-to-Site VPN

You can use client software to connect a single PC to VPN server. This creates a *client-to-site VPN* connection.

VPN clients, originally, were a hassle, since most companies forced employees to use IPSec (Internet Protocol Security) VPNs rather than PPTP (Point-to-Point Tunneling Protocol) or L2TP (Layer 2 Tunneling Protocol) VPNs when using a VPN client. Business travelers had problems, since the destination ports were typically blocked at client offices and hotels. Destination ports of 80 and 443 were not filtered by firewalls, but IPSec requires extra ports and protocols that would get blocked by firewalls. One option involved expensive tethering to your cellphone. Another option would be not using a VPN at all.

The company F5 released its SSL VPN client (SSL has since been replaced by TLS), and shortly thereafter, other vendors followed suit. An SSL VPN was client based, and it was a game changer. When the VPN client tried to connect to the VPN server on port 443, that outbound traffic was allowed out of most networks. Now VPNs worked wherever people went, and there was no extra networking configuration required.

Clientless VPN

A *clientless VPN* is a VPN run through a Web page or portal. An advantage of this type of VPN is that it doesn't require any special client software. All major vendors have a clientless option.

When F5 first started providing their VPN client, the client provided built-in Java apps to do all of the functions users needed (e-mail client, RDP/ICA client, file access client, etc.), and it included a Java-based "SSL VPN client," which allowed users a full tunnel, rather than just the apps. The Java-based VPN client, though technically clientless, was a poor substitute for a standalone client due to the limitations of Java.

Split Tunnel vs. Full Tunnel

A *split tunnel* VPN connection creates a secure connection to a remote network but leaves the rest of the Internet connection to the local connection. When you open a browser, in other words, and surf to www.google.com, you would go through the local connection, not the

VPN one. In a *full tunnel* VPN, in contrast, every connection goes through the remote connection. This offers security in exchange for performance; that is, full tunnel Internet connections are slower compared to split tunnel Internet connections.

Due to security concerns, many companies today scan and validate all Internet-bound traffic, and possibly all incoming Web content and file downloads, by enforcing full tunnels through proxy servers or Web filters. This introduces latency, since traffic now goes through the VPN that's shared at the concentrator with the other VPN clients, and Internet-bound traffic leaves the network on a connection that's shared with everyone else in the company. This means that on a 1 Gbps connection, connection speeds will only be the speed going to the office and then back out, which could be less than 1 Gbps leaving the company.

Remote Desktop Connection

You can use a terminal emulation program to create a remote terminal, a connection on a remote computer that enables you to control that computer as if you were sitting in front of it, logged in. Terminal emulation has been a part of TCP/IP from its earliest days, in the form of good-old Telnet. Because it dates from pre-GUI days, Telnet is a text-based utility; most modern operating systems are graphical, so there was a strong desire to come up with graphical remote terminal tools. Citrix Corporation made the first popular terminal emulation products—the WinFrame/MetaFrame products. Their current product is called Citrix Virtual Apps and Desktop.

Remote terminal programs all require a server and a client. The server is the computer to be controlled. The client is the computer from which you do the controlling. Citrix created a standard called Independent Computing Architecture (ICA) that defined how terminal information was passed between the server and the client. Citrix made a breakthrough product—so powerful that Microsoft licensed the Citrix code and created its own product called Windows Terminal Services. Not wanting to pay Citrix any more money, Microsoft then created its own standard called Remote Desktop Protocol (RDP) and unveiled a new remote terminal called *Remote Desktop Connection* (RDC), starting with Windows XP.

EXAM TIP   The CompTIA Network+ exam objectives list RDP as "Remote desktop connection," and you might see it with the lowercase *d* and *c* (and maybe even *v*) letters on the exam. However, it is referring to Microsoft's Remote Desktop Connection (all words starting with uppercase letters).

There are some security concerns with RDP. Best practices include implementing restrictions on who can use RDP, using strong passwords, and using multifactor authentication.

ADDITIONAL RESOURCES   Check out https://securityintelligence .com/articles/remote-desktop-protocol-rdp-security-2022/ and https://www .bleepingcomputer.com/news/security/logins-for-13-million-windows-rdp-servers- collected-from-hacker-market/ for more on RDP vulnerabilities.

Using data-heavy software over a VPN could be very slow. With RDP, however, the client software runs on the RDP/terminal server that's in the datacenter, right by the servers with the data. As such, the process becomes much quicker, and can make you feel like you're actually in the office. One small caveat is that without mapping drives through the client, you won't be able to access or save files on the local machine rather than through the RDP server. You can, however, access remote desktops and remote apps, which makes it seem like you're running the apps on your own machine.

Remote Desktop Gateway

Microsoft's *Remote Desktop Gateway* encapsulates and encrypts a Remote Desktop Protocol session with TLS. This tunneling mechanism can alleviate the need to use a VPN, since encryption is being used. Now, companies don't have to worry about the risks of putting RDP servers on the Internet (and being subsequently attacked), since this server takes care of the first level of authentication and multifactor authentication.

SSH

SSH (Secure Shell) allows an SSH client to remotely sign in to a system running an SSH server. During this session, SSH encrypts all traffic between the SSH client and the SSH server, thwarting on-path attacks including eavesdropping, connection hijacking, and more. SSH is used by systems administrators (and others) for remote management of systems and programs, software patch deployment, execution of commands, file management, and other tasks.

SSH debuted in 1995. Before then, and unfortunately in some cases since then, the notorious Telnet has served the same purpose, but with one big difference: Telnet doesn't do any encryption. That means client-to-server and server-to-client communications are in plaintext. Just think of all the juicy things an on-path attacker can do with those packets!

SSH uses the Diffie-Hellman key exchange (DHKE) the same way that TLS uses it. The SSH client on the PC and the SSH server on the switch agree on a shared secret with the DHKE. This shared secret is the symmetric key that encrypts communications in both directions, including the username and password that the client sends to the server for authentication. The SSH server's public key is transmitted to the client the first time the client connects to that server. Just like with TLS, during the DHKE, the SSH server hashes values and encrypts that hash with its private key, forming a digital signature. The client decrypts the encrypted hash with the server's public key and computes the hash on its own. If the computed hash matches the decrypted hash, the client can trust that the server really is the server and that the symmetric key (shared secret) is legitimate.

Instead of a password, a more secure method for client authentication involves a public/private key pair. The client can generate a public/private key pair and place its public key on the server. The server would then encrypt a random number with that public key and send the ciphertext to the client. If the client has the corresponding private key, it will decrypt the message. The decrypted message and the session key (the shared symmetric key that is established with DHKE before this phase) will then be hashed and sent to the server in response. The server uses the original number and the same session key to compute the hash value itself. If the computed hash matches the received hash, the client is authenticated. This provides greater security than a simple username/password pair that can be stolen and used by an attacker.

Furthermore, SSH keys can be thousands of bits long, making them a lot harder to crack, compared to passwords that consist of around 12 characters or so. Other advantages include that a private key isn't sent to the server the way a password is, the SSH connection can only originate from the machine that has the private key, and you can even add a password to your SSH key authentication for further security. The convenience of passwords shouldn't outweigh the security of keys. However, when SSH is used with routers, it's very common to see the password authentication method in place.

SSH is secure on its own, but it's still important to ensure security on the server endpoint. SSH allows for the setup and maintenance of a tunneled connection, for example, by forwarding ports through the SSH connection from a port on your machine to port 3389 on a remote server. Unfortunately, if you use SSH for remote access, so can cybercriminals, who can get access to tunnels.

Virtual Network Computing (VNC)

Virtual Network Computing (VNC) is a popular tool to remotely use the graphical user interface (GUI) of a remote system. It works nicely in Secure Shell (SSH) tunnels for great security, plus it comes, by default, with every copy of macOS and almost every Linux distro. It's also free.

 EXAM TIP   The CompTIA Network+ exam objectives list VNC as "Virtual network computing (VNC)," and you might see it with the lowercase *n* and *c* (and maybe even *v*) letters on the exam. However, it is referring to the GUI desktop sharing program (all words starting with uppercase letters).

Since VNC is a remote access solution, the security risk is high, like RDP, unless used over a VPN.

Virtual Desktop

Desktop virtualization replaces direct access to a system's local desktop environment with a client that can access a *virtual desktop* running on a virtual machine in the datacenter. You could technically run that VM on the same device, but benefits like flexible management come from centralizing the desktop VMs on a smaller number of servers—a pattern called virtual desktop infrastructure (VDI). The connections are securable with things like the VMware Horizon solution.

Authentication and Authorization Considerations

From a security standpoint, all remote connections have *authentication and authorization considerations.* Connecting via Telnet can require a username and password for authentication, but it lacks any real security because credentials are passed unencrypted. Most other remote connection types at least have encryption to make the authentication part more secure. Once logged into a remote system, the remote operating system handles authorization.

As discussed earlier in Objective 4.1, multifactor authentication ensures security, especially with remote access. The principle of least privilege should enforce authorization.

In-Band vs. Out-of-Band Management

As you might imagine, it would be scary to let unauthorized people have access to your switch management configuration interface. In cases where you configure the switch over the network, *in-band management*, anyone who knows the IP addresses of the managed devices will be able to access them if they can provide a valid username and password combination. In-band refers to using the switch's network to manage it.

To reduce exposure, it's common to dedicate one port on every managed device as a management port. You can do interface configuration only by directly connecting to that port. Then, connect all those dedicated ports into a switch that's totally separate from the rest of the network, which will prevent unauthorized access to those ports. The management port on each device is also considered in-band management, as it is still using a switch's or router's network interfaces, while in a more secure fashion. In most cases, this is done over a dedicated management VLAN.

Out-of-band management involves connecting to a console or serial port on the switch, which doesn't use the switch's network connection—it could be down. Terminal servers can provide out-of-band management to all of a network's devices through a serial connection. This would involve securely connecting to the terminal server, and then to the port (1–32 serial ports per device; RJ45 connections would be serial connections). This can also be done through network-connected PDUs for those same devices. Power could be individually killed to one port to force a device that's stuck to reboot. This kit often runs on a separate network to ensure security and availability.

In many cases a switch might be in a far-flung location, making it important to provide some method of remote management. Switches with Web management interfaces often provide a well-protected HTTPS/management URL that administrators can use to log into the switch via the Internet (another example of out-of-band management).

REVIEW

Objective 4.4: Compare and contrast remote access methods and security implications

- You can connect two VPN concentrators to connect two physically separate LANs permanently. This kind of connection enables two LANs to function as a single network, sharing files and services as if they were in the same building. This is called a *site-to-site VPN* connection.

- You can use client software to connect a single PC to VPN server. This creates a *client-to-site VPN* connection.

- A *clientless VPN* is a VPN run through a Web page or portal.

- A *split tunnel* VPN connection creates a secure connection to a remote network but leaves the rest of the Internet connection to the local connection. When you open a browser, in other words, and surf to www.google.com, you would go through the local connection. In a *full tunnel* VPN, in contrast, every connection goes through the remote connection.

- Microsoft's RDP standard defines how terminal information is passed between the server and the client. Microsoft's remote terminal is *Remote Desktop Connection* (RDC), introduced way back in Windows XP.

- *Remote Desktop Gateway* encapsulates and encrypts a Remote Desktop Protocol session through HTTPS.

- *SSH* allows an SSH client to remotely sign in to a system running an SSH server. During this session, SSH encrypts all traffic between the SSH client and the SSH server.

- *Virtual Network Computing (VNC)* is a popular tool to remotely use the GUI of a remote system.

- Desktop virtualization replaces direct access to a system's local desktop environment with a client that can access a *virtual desktop* running on a VM in the datacenter.

- *Authentication and authorization considerations* should reflect the fact that resources are being accessed remotely.

- *In-band management* allows anyone who knows the IP addresses of the managed devices to access them if they can provide a valid username and password combination.

- *Out-of-band management* involves connecting to a console or serial port on the switch, which doesn't use the switch's network connection (it could be down).

4.4 QUESTIONS

1. Which of the following technologies involves a split tunnel?
   A. Remote Desktop Connection
   B. Remote Desktop Gateway
   C. Site-to-site VPN
   D. Client-to-site VPN

2. Which of the following is proprietary?

   A. Remote Desktop Protocol

   B. Remote Terminal

   C. Site-to-site VPN

   D. SSH

3. What does VNC allow you to do that SSH, by itself, doesn't?

   A. Transmit information to a remote system

   B. Receive information from a remote system

   C. Access the terminal of a remote system

   D. Access the GUI of a remote system

4.4 ANSWERS

1. **D** Client-to-site VPNs allow for a split tunnel or a full tunnel.

2. **A** RDP is a Microsoft protocol.

3. **D** VNC allows access of a remote system through its GUI.

Objective 4.5 # Explain the importance of physical security

Physical security involves detection methods, prevention methods, and asset disposal. All three implementations are vital to maintaining the confidentiality, integrity, and availability of infrastructures.

Detection Methods

After you secure the physical assets of the network with guards, locks, passwords, eyeballs, and other technologies, the only people who have access to IT resources are those who have been carefully selected, screened, trained, and authorized. The network is safe, right? Maybe not. You see, here comes the old problem again: people are human. Humans make mistakes, humans can become disgruntled, and humans can be tempted. The only real solution is heavily armored robots with artificial intelligence and bad attitudes. Until that becomes practical, maybe what we need to do next is to ensure that those authorized people can be held accountable for what they do with the physical resources of the network. There are several such *detection methods*.

Camera

With video surveillance of facilities and assets, authorized staff can be monitored for mistakes or something more nefarious. Unauthorized people can be tracked and caught after they sneak into a building.

Video monitoring entails using remotely monitored visual systems. An IP *camera* setup is a specific implementations of video monitoring. IP video streams can be monitored by anyone who is authorized to do so and can access the network on which the cameras are installed. The stream can be saved to a hard drive or network storage device. Multiple workstations can simultaneously monitor video streams and multiple cameras with ease.

Motion Detection

Many small office/home office (SOHO) video surveillance systems rely on *motion detection* systems that start and stop recordings based on actions caught by the camera(s). This has the advantage of saving a lot of storage space, hopefully only catching the bad guys on film when they're breaking into your house or stealing your lawn gnomes. Furthermore, door sensors, window sensors, and glass break sensors add to the overall security implementation.

Asset Tags

Many organizations use *assets tags* to simplify inventory management of all their devices. This alleviates them from using a serial number as a main ID criteria in inventory systems. Items without serial numbers, in this fashion, can be tracked. Some systems track a number and barcode to make it easier to record inventory information.

Asset tags should be attached to a fixed portion of assets, because otherwise assets could get mixed up when technicians are working on multiple computers at the same time. The asset tags should also be tamperproof and difficult to remove, for integrity purposes. Some companies use labels, while others use small metal plates which use super-strong adhesive.

Tamper Detection

All modern server chassis come with *tamper detection* features that will log in the motherboard's nonvolatile RAM (NVRAM) if the chassis has been opened. The log will show chassis intrusion with a date and time. Some higher-value client desktops could also come with tamper detection mechanisms.

Many organizations use low-tech physical security tools like special stickers or zip ties for *tamper detection* in its most basic use of the term.

Prevention Methods

The first thing we have to do when it comes to protecting the physical security of the network is to make the network resources accessible only to personnel who have a legitimate need to access them, through multiple *prevention methods*.

Employee Training

Employee training involves educating users and letting them know what is expected of them, and should be done the day they are hired. Employee training also applies to organizations that are nonprofit and have other goals. The more they know, the better equipped they will be in responding to situations that could threaten the business's operational security (making sure the business runs efficiently and effectively) and organizational security (achieving the goal of the business: profit).

Without a plan, there will be confusion, mistakes, and possibly malicious acts (intentional or unintentional) by the users. The plan starts with published policies, high-level documents that explain the principles and guidelines of the organization, that are meant to instruct users on exactly what they must do to be in compliance.

Procedures are step-by-step instructions for actions to take in fulfilling policies. In the event of an incident or disaster, the policies and procedures should clearly guide the next steps so that all employees know exactly what their roles and responsibilities entail. Additionally, these procedure documents ensure that tasks are completed in consistent and reliable ways that are in accordance with policy requirements. Anything from a regular ticket entry procedure to a disaster recovery procedure needs to be documented and referenced.

It's important to make sure that users read the policies and procedures through education, training, and testing. Otherwise, these documents could easily go unseen and be completely worthless. That also means that employees may not be acting in accordance with company policies, which could result in negative security outcomes or even noncompliance.

Access Control Hardware

Access control hardware devices are designed to physically check users for credentials, to determine the level of access they are to receive. Two ways of doing this include badge readers and biometrics.

Badge Readers

Badge readers (also known as a proximity readers) read proximity cards and radio-frequency identification (RFID) cards for authentication and authorization.

Proximity cards are read only and run at just two radio frequencies. The ID of the card, on the outside, authorizes things like door control systems to open certain doors. RFID cards are read/write, hold more data than a proximity card, and run at a wide range of frequencies. Both proximity cards and RFID cards can be either active or passive.

The passive versions, usually the size of credit cards, have a metal coil in them, which when pressed up to the badge reader will get enough power from the reader through the coil to send their ID to the reader. Active devices have a battery in them and are able to be used from further distances (RFID cards have longer-distance capabilities than proximity cards).

NOTE RFID and a battery (active) are what make up the transponders used in cars for toll booths. The transponder is just a big RFID card. RFID readers can be set to a very short distance, like the tap for credit and debit card readers, which needs to be within contact range of the reader. Those cards are passive, so they need to be extremely close. Furthermore, you would not want them reading and charging your card from 10 feet away. The tap cards used by many transit systems could be either proximity or RFID, but many providers have standardized on RFID, for example, those in Toronto, London, and Hong Kong. New York is switching from a magnetic stripe card, used for MetroCard, to new RFID cards, which allows the electronic versions of the card to be loaded into a smartphone or watch.

Anti-passback prevents someone that badges into an area from entering again, until exiting first. This prevents someone from passing their badge to another person. This is implemented in both building security and parking garages. In another situation, if you don't badge out, you will have to visit security control in order to get back in. This is usually implemented in buildings with higher-security locations (for example, a server room or a money room). This even works in reverse, where if you don't badge into a room, you can't badge out. You have to wait for security to come and help.

Biometrics

The best way to prevent loss of access control is to build physical security around a key that cannot be shared or lost. *Biometrics* involves using unique physical characteristics of a person to permit access to a controlled IT resource. Doorways can be triggered to unlock using fingerprint readers, facial recognition cameras, voice analyzers, retinal blood vessel scanners, or other, more exotic characteristics. While not perfect, biometrics represent a giant leap in secure access. For even more effective access control, multifactor authentication can be used, where access is granted based on more than one access technique. For instance, in order to gain access to a secure server room, a user might have to pass a fingerprint scan and have an approved security badge. Biometrics can be used for device authentication as well. There's no password to steal when the logon is tied to fingerprints, and that form of authentication can't be shoulder surfed.

NOTE There are compelling reasons why biometrics might not be the only factor used in authentication, but rather a part of multifactor authentication. Biometric data can be hacked, stolen, and changed. However, you can't change your biometrics, like you can change your password, if your biometric data is hacked, stolen, or changed. Also, you can't share biometrics. Although not a best practice, there are instances where users share passwords with others, like a shared Facebook account between husband and wife, a shared Netflix account, etc. In those cases, you can't give someone your hand, face, or eyeball. In addition, biometric systems are expensive and introduce possible privacy issues. Finally, authentication can fail based on environment or changes like growing or shaving a beard, with false negatives (false positives can occur too).

Locking Racks, Locking Cabinets

If a room with devices and equipment cannot be secured, then the rack should be. If the room houses many types of equipment, then all of that equipment needs to be secured into separate racks. This allows a company to apply extra security to the rack housing the payroll server, or even their ERP system. Typically, in a colocation data center, a company's rack is locked (front and back) with keys that only that company would have (and the colocation staff, but only for emergency). This prevents people from other companies from messing with equipment that doesn't belong to them.

Start with the simplest approach: a lock. Locking the door to the network closet or equipment room that holds servers, switches, routers, and other network gear goes a long way in protecting the network. *Locking racks* and *locking cabinets* is vital. Key control is critical here and includes assigning keys to appropriate staff, tracking key assignments, and collecting the keys when they are no longer needed by individuals who move on. This type of access must be guarded against circumvention by ensuring policies are followed regarding who may have or use the keys. The administrator who assigns keys should never give one to an unauthorized person without completing the appropriate procedures and paperwork.

Access Control Vestibule (Previously Known as a Mantrap)

For areas where an entry guard is not practical, one solution is to use an *access control vestibule (previously known as a mantrap)*, which is an entryway with two successive locked doors and a small space between them providing one-way entry or exit. After entering the first door, the second door cannot be unlocked until the first door is closed and secured. Access to the second door may be a simple key badge or may require approval by someone else who watches the trap space on video. Unauthorized persons remain trapped until they are approved for entry, let out the first door, or held for the appropriate authorities.

 NOTE Some buildings use turnstiles (in the lobby before getting to the elevators) with badges, and then on the actual floors badges are used again to get into the main office doors. Other places use turnstiles (rotating doors) for staff with badges to enter, while guests enter through the security-manned vestibule. Some vestibules are also managed with badges, where you need to badge through, but only one door will be opened at a time.

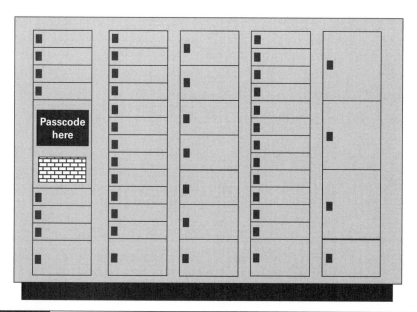

FIGURE 4.5-1 Typical smart locker

Smart Lockers

Smart lockers are lockers that an organization can control via wireless or wired networking to allow temporary access to a locker so users can access items (Figure 4.5-1). First popularized by Amazon as a delivery tool, smart lockers are common anywhere an organization needs to give users access to…whatever they can fit into a locker!

Asset Disposal

Most companies and institutions have policies and best practices in place for dealing with legacy systems. As discussed in Objective 3.2, every computing device has a system life cycle, from shiny and new, to patched and secure, to "you're still using that old junk?" System life cycle policies address *asset disposal* with the concept of reuse, repurpose, recycle. Donating older routers and switches to a nonprofit for a tax write-off is one option. Another option is to repurpose older WAPs as simple bridges for devices that don't have high speed requirements, for example, printers and multifunction devices. Shred anything that contained data and send what's left to metal recyling.

Factory Reset/Wipe Configuration

Prior to disposing routers, switches, and mobile devices, all configurations and data should be destroyed, especially if there is sensitive customer information on the devices. When you *factory reset* a device and *wipe configuration* that may be present, there could be data stored externally (for example, on a SIM card or a memory card) that must be properly disposed as well. Most mobile device management solutions feature a remote wipe feature that clears all of a device's data in the case of loss or theft.

Sanitize Devices for Disposal

Furthermore, you should *sanitize devices for disposal*, specifically computers, following government-grade erasure standards. Some companies use an accredited company that specializes in asset disposal, to ensure complete data destruction. Writing zeros to hard drives (sometimes random 1s and 0s are written too, in three or more passes) allows the devices to be used again, while degaussing (with a magnetic force) prevents storage media from being used again. Solid-state devices (SSDs), including USB devices, can't be degaussed. In some cases, hard drives (including SSD and USB devices) will be destroyed through shedding or other techniques.

After data is destroyed and prior to asset disposal, there should be a verification process to ensure that the data has been deleted and is completely unrecoverable.

Secure companies will donate computers, without hard drives, to charity.

REVIEW

Objective 4.5: Explain the importance of physical security

- Physical security needs to be thoroughly implemented and enforced; otherwise, hacking into systems, routers, and switches becomes trivial.
- An IP *camera* setup is a specific implementations of video monitoring.
- Many SOHO video surveillance systems rely on *motion detection* systems that start and stop recordings based on actions caught by the camera(s).
- Many organizations use *assets tags* to simplify inventory management of all their devices.
- All modern server chassis come with *tamper detection* features that will log in the motherboard's nonvolatile RAM (NVRAM) if the chassis has been opened.
- The first task when it comes to protecting the network is to make the network resources accessible only to personnel who have a legitimate need to access them, through multiple *prevention methods*.
- *Employee training* involves educating users and letting them know what is expected of them, and should be done the day they are hired.
- *Access control hardware* devices are meant to physically check users for credentials, to determine the level of access users are to receive. Two ways of doing this include badge readers and biometrics.
- *Badge readers* (also known as a proximity readers) read proximity cards and RFID cards for authentication and authorization.
- *Biometrics* involves using unique physical characteristics of a person to permit access to a controlled IT resource.

- *Locking racks* and *locking cabinets* is vital physical network security.
- For areas where an entry guard is not practical, a solution is to use an *access control vestibule (previously known as a mantrap)*, an entryway with two successive locked doors and a small space between them providing one-way entry or exit.
- *Smart lockers* are lockers that an organization can control via wireless or wired networking to allow temporary access to a locker so users can access items.
- System life cycle policies address *asset disposal* with the concept of reuse, repurpose, recycle.
- When you *factory reset* a device and *wipe configuration* that may be present, there could be data stored externally (for example, on a SIM card or a memory card) that must be properly disposed as well.
- You should *sanitize devices for disposal*, following government-grade erasure standards.

4.5 QUESTIONS

1. Which of the following is not a detection method?
    A. Camera
    B. Badge reader
    C. Motion
    D. Tamper

2. Which of the following is not a prevention method?
    A. Training
    B. Biometrics
    C. Asset tags
    D. Smart lockers

3. Which of the following is not done for asset disposal?
    A. Factory reset
    B. Wipe configuration
    C. Sanitize devices
    D. Access control vestibule

4.5 ANSWERS

1. **B**   A badge reader is used for prevention, not detection.
2. **C**   Asset tags are used for detection, not prevention.
3. **D**   An access control vestibule is a prevention method, not an asset disposal method.

Network Troubleshooting

Domain Objectives

- **5.1** Explain the network troubleshooting methodology.
- **5.2** Given a scenario, troubleshoot common cable connectivity issues and select the appropriate tools.
- **5.3** Given a scenario, use the appropriate network software tools and commands.
- **5.4** Given a scenario, troubleshoot common wireless connectivity issues.
- **5.5** Given a scenario, troubleshoot general networking issues.

Objective 5.1 # Explain the network troubleshooting methodology

Have you ever seen a network tech walk up to a network and seem to know all the answers, effortlessly typing in a few commands and magically making the system or network work? They tend to follow the same steps for similar problems—looking in the same places, typing the same commands, following the same algorithms.

When someone performs a task the same way every time, they're probably following a plan. They understand what tools they have to work with, and they know where to start and what to do second and third and fourth until they find the problem. Primary troubleshooting tools help you formulate a troubleshooting process, enabling you to learn where to look for different sorts of problems. I will admit, though, that sometimes when I'm helping my students troubleshoot issues in the labs at RIT (Rochester Institute of Technology) and FLCC (Finger Lakes Community College), all I have to do is walk over and watch them execute the same commands they've been executing for the 10 minutes prior to when they called me over. Somehow, someway, when I look, it just…works. As much as I'd like to think I could do Jedi mind tricks on technology, the students obviously are doing something different, or they made a change or two before calling me over.

The CompTIA Network+ exam objectives include the following seven steps, describing the network troubleshooting methodology: identify the problem; establish a theory of probable cause; test the theory to determine the cause; establish a plan of action to resolve the problem and identify potential effects; implement the solution or escalate as necessary; verify full system functionality and, if applicable, implement preventive measures; and document findings, actions, outcomes, and lessons learned. Let's dig into them now.

Identify the Problem

First off when troubleshooting, you need to *identify the problem*. That means grasping the true problem, rather than what someone tells you. A user might call in and complain that she can't access the Internet from her system, for example, which could be the only problem. However, the problem could also be that the entire wing of the office just went down and you've got a much bigger problem on your hands. How do you identify the problem? You need to gather information, question users, identify symptoms, determine if anything has changed, duplicate the problem, if possible, and approach multiple problems individually. Following these steps will help you get to the root of the problem. Keep in mind that in larger corporate environments, identifying changes includes consulting change management documentation to determine if anything has changed on the network.

Gather Information

Gather information about the problem. Just like Lieutenant Columbo (from the classic TV series *Columbo*), assembling bits and pieces of information, and then putting them together, could lead to you identifying the problem. You can gather information can by talking to people or by using software tools. With some tools, you can generate information to analyze, but you'll also be able to examine logs, which might have the information you're looking for already.

Question Users

If you're troubleshooting in person or even over the telephone, you will need to *question users*. These questions can be close-ended, which is to say there can only be a yes-or-no-type answer, such as "Can you see a light on the front of the monitor?" You can also ask open-ended questions, such as "What have you already tried in attempting to fix the problem?"

The type of question you ask at any given moment depends on what information you need and on the user's knowledge level. If, for example, the user seems to be technically oriented, you will probably be able to ask more close-ended questions because the user will know what you are talking about. If, on the other hand, the user seems to be confused about what's happening, open-ended questions will allow him or her to explain in his or her own words what is going on.

Identify Symptoms

One of the first steps in trying to determine the cause of a problem is to understand the extent of the problem. Is it specific to one user or is it network-wide? Sometimes this entails trying the task yourself, both from the user's machine and from your own or another machine.

If you are working directly on an affected system and not relying on somebody on the other end of a telephone to guide you, you will *identify symptoms* through your observation of what is (or isn't) happening. Are the symptoms indicative of a problem for one user, multiple users, or everyone? There's a difference if an Internet outage is limited to one user, spread across multiple users, or affecting everyone in the company. What about a system slowdown? Is one machine possibly infected with malware, or has it spread to multiple machines? Is it just a PC? A switch somewhere? A router? A firewall?

Determine if Anything Has Changed

Determine if anything has changed on a system or on the network recently that might have caused the problem. You may not have to ask many questions before the person using the problem system can tell you what has changed, but, in some cases, establishing if anything has changed can take quite a bit of time and involve further work behind the scenes. Here are some examples of questions to ask:

- "What exactly was happening when the problem occurred?"
- "Has anything been changed on the system recently?"
- "Has the system been moved recently?"

Notice the way I've tactfully avoided the word *you*, as in "Have you changed anything on the system recently?" This is a deliberate tactic to avoid any implied blame on the part of the user. Being nice never hurts, and it makes the whole troubleshooting process friendlier.

You should also internally ask yourself some isolating questions, such as "Was that machine involved in the software push last night?" or "Didn't a tech visit that machine this morning?" Note you will only be able to answer these questions if your documentation is up to date. Sometimes, isolating a problem may require you to check system and hardware logs (such as those stored by some routers and other network devices), so make sure you know how to do this.

 EXAM TIP Avoid aggressive or accusatory questions when trying to get information from a user.

Duplicate the Problem, if Possible

If a user is experiencing problems going to a certain Web site, you might need to go to that user's machine and try to go to that Web site from that machine yourself. In other words, try to *duplicate the problem, if possible*. Doing this tells you whether the problem is a user error of some kind, as well as enables you to see the symptoms of the problem yourself. Next, you probably want to try the same thing from a different machine.

In some cases, you can ask other users in the area if they are experiencing the same problem to see if the issue is affecting more than one user. Depending on the size of your network, you should find out whether the problem is occurring in only one part of your company or across the entire network.

What does all of this tell you? Essentially, it tells you how big the problem is. Using another example, if nobody in an entire remote office can log in, you may be able to assume that the problem is the network link or router connecting that office to the server. If nobody in any office can log in, you may be able to assume the server is down or not accepting logins. If only that one user in that one location can't log in, the problem may be with that user, that machine, or that user's account.

Once you've identified the problem and verified that it is really the problem by duplicating it, you can now remediate the problem to ensure it doesn't happen again.

Approach Multiple Problems Individually

If you encounter a complicated scenario, with various machines off the network and potential server room or wiring problems, break it down. *Approach multiple problems individually* to sort out root causes. Methodically tackle them and you'll eventually have a list of one or more problems identified. Then you can move on to the next step. If you try to solve multiple problems at once, it will be hard to determine what each unique problem is and its solution.

Establish a Theory of Probable Cause

Once you've identified one or more problems, try to figure out what could have happened. In other words, *establish a theory of probable cause*, which requires you to question the obvious and consider multiple approaches. Just keep in mind that a theory is not a fact. You might need to dismiss the theory later in the process and establish a revised theory.

This step comes down to experience—or good use of the support tools at your disposal, such as your knowledge base. You need to select the most probable cause from all the possible causes, so the solution you choose fixes the problem the first time. This may not always happen, but whenever possible, you want to avoid spending a whole day stabbing in the dark while the problem snores softly to itself in some cozy, neglected corner of your network.

Question the Obvious

When establishing a theory of probable cause, first *question the obvious*. If Bob can't print to the networked printer, for example, check to see that the printer is plugged in and turned on. It may be hard to believe, but the obvious causes are sometimes the actual causes.

Consider Multiple Approaches

Consider multiple approaches when establishing a theory of probably cause. This will keep you from locking your imagination into a single train of thought. Two possible approaches are discussed next.

Top-to-Bottom/Bottom-to-Top OSI Model

You can use the OSI seven-layer model as a troubleshooting tool in several ways to help with this process. Here's a scenario to work through.

Caitlin can't access the database server to start her workday. The problem manifests this way: She opens the database client on her computer, then clicks on recent documents, one of which is the current project that management has assigned to her team. Nothing happens. Normally, the database client connects to the database that resides on the server on the other side of the network.

Try a *top-to-bottom/bottom-to-top OSI model* approach to the problem. Sometimes it pays to try both. Table 5.1-1 provides some ideas on how starting at the top might help.

You might imagine the reverse model in some situations. If the network was newly installed, for example, running through some of the basic connectivity at Layers 1 and 2 (see Table 5.1-1) might be a good first approach.

Divide and Conquer

Another option for tackling multiple options is to use the *divide and conquer* approach. On its face, divide and conquer appears to be a compromise between the top-to-bottom/ bottom-to-top OSI model. However, it's better than a compromise. If we arbitrarily always

TABLE 5.1-1   Top-to-Bottom/Bottom-to-Top OSI Model Example

7	Application	Could there be a problem with the API that enables the client database application to connect to the database server service?
6	Presentation	Could there be a problem with encryption between the application and the database server? Maybe, but Caitlin would probably see an error message rather than nothing.
5	Session	Could the fact that a socket can't be established be the cause?
4	Transport	Maybe an incorrect port is specified. Maybe there's something keeping the TCP three-way handshake from completing.
3	Network	Maybe an IP access control list is incorrectly configured. Maybe an incorrect IP address is manually specified or returned by DNS.
2	Data Link	Maybe an incorrectly (and ill-advised) MAC address filter is configured. As explained in Objective 4.3, MAC filtering with a blacklist can be thwarted by an attacker spoofing their MAC address, while MAC filtering with a whitelist requires a human to collect all MAC addresses, which is impossible on a transient network. Furthermore, since the human element is involved, whitelisting can even result in errors in the collection/recording of the addresses or configuration of the whitelist itself.
1	Physical	Maybe a cable is disconnected. Maybe a NIC is faulty.

perform top-to-bottom troubleshooting, we'll waste a lot of time at Layers 7 through 3 if the issue is in the Data Link layer or Physical layer.

Divide and conquer is a time saver that comes into play as part of developing a theory of probable cause. As you gather information for troubleshooting, a general sense of where the problem lies should manifest. Place this likely cause at the appropriate layer of the OSI model and begin to test the theory and related theories at that layer. If the theory bears out, follow the appropriate troubleshooting steps. If the theory is wrong, move up or down the OSI model with new theories of probable causes. For example, executing `ipconfig` (Windows), `ip a` (Linux), or `ifconfig` (Mac) could reveal valuable information. A ping of the default gateway could also be very telling.

Test the Theory to Determine the Cause

After you identify the problem and establish a theory of probable cause, you need to *test the theory to determine the cause*. Be sure to do so without changing anything or risking any repercussions.

If the Theory Is Confirmed, Determine the Next Steps to Resolve the Problem

If you have determined that the probable cause for Bob not being able to print is that the printer is turned off, go look. If that's the case, then you should plan out your next step to resolve the problem. Do not act yet! That comes next.

Regardless of how many times you need to go through this process, you'll eventually reach a theory that seems right. *If the theory is confirmed, determine the next steps to resolve the problem.*

If the Theory Is Not Confirmed, Reestablish a New Theory or Escalate

If the theory is not confirmed, reestablish a new theory or escalate the problem. Go back to step two and determine a new probable cause. Once you have another idea, test it.

The reason you should hesitate to act at this third step (*test the theory to determine the cause*) is that you might not have permission to make the fix or the fix might cause repercussions you don't fully understand yet. For example, if you walk over to the print server room to see if the printer is powered up and online and find the door padlocked, that's a whole different level of problem. Sure, the printer is turned off, but management has done it for a reason. In this sort of situation, you need to escalate the problem.

Trying solutions as simple as rebooting the print server could also pose problems. For example, you may not be aware that the machine the print server is running on is also running a database server.

To "escalate" has two meanings: either to inform other parties about a problem for guidance or to pass the job off to another authority who has control over the device/issue that's most probably causing the problem. Let's say you have a server with a bad NIC. This server is used heavily by the accounting department, and taking it down may cause problems you don't even know about. You need to consult with the accounting manager. Alternatively, you'll come across problems over which you have no control or authority. A badly acting server across the country is the responsibility of another person (hopefully) to whom you need to hand over the job.

Escalating could also be to someone outside of your organization. For example, you might need to call the vendor support line or open a support case or ticket with the applicable vendor, such as Cisco or VMware.

Establish a Plan of Action to Resolve the Problem and Identify Potential Effects

By this point, you should have some ideas as to what the problem might be. It's time to "look before you leap" and *establish a plan of action to resolve the problem and identify potential effects.* An action plan defines how you are going to fix this problem. Most problems are simple, but if the problem is complex, you need to write down the steps. As you do this, think about what else might happen as you go about the repair. Identify the potential effects of the actions you're about to take, especially the unintended ones. If you take out a switch without a replacement switch at hand, the users might experience excessive downtime while you hunt for a new switch and move them over. If you replace a router, can you restore all the old router's settings to the new one or will you have to rebuild from scratch?

Implement the Solution or Escalate As Necessary

Once you think you have isolated the cause of the problem, you should decide what you think is the best way to fix it and then *implement the solution*, whether that's giving advice over the phone to a user, installing a replacement part, or adding a software patch. Or, if the solution you propose requires either more skill than you possess at the moment or falls into someone else's purview, *escalate as necessary* to get the fix implemented.

If you're the implementer, follow these guidelines. All the way through implementation, try only one likely solution at a time. There's no point in installing several patches at once, because then you can't tell which one fixed the problem. Similarly, there's no point in replacing several items of hardware (such as a hard disk and its controller cable) at the same time, because then you can't tell which part (or parts) was faulty.

As you try each possibility, always document what you do and what results you get. This isn't just for a future problem either—during a lengthy troubleshooting process, it's easy to forget exactly what you tried two hours before or which thing you tried produced a particular result. Although being methodical may take longer, it will save time the next time—and it may enable you to pinpoint what needs to be done to stop the problem from recurring at all, thereby reducing future call volume to your support team—and as any support person will tell you, that's definitely worth the effort!

Then you need to test the solution. This is the part everybody hates. Once you think you've fixed a problem, you should try to make it happen again. If you can't, great! But sometimes you will be able to re-create the problem, and then you know you haven't finished the job at hand. Many techs want to slide away quietly as soon as everything seems to be fine, but trust me on this, it won't impress your customer when her problem flares up again 30 seconds after you've left the building—not to mention that you get the joy of another two-hour car trip the next day to fix the same problem, for an even more unhappy client!

Verify Full System Functionality and, if Applicable, Implement Preventive Measures

Okay, now that you have changed something on the system in the process of solving one problem, you must think about the wider repercussions of what you have done. If you've replaced a faulty NIC in a server, for instance, will the fact that the MAC address has changed (remember, it's built into the NIC) affect anything else, such as the logon security controls or your network management and inventory software? If you've installed a patch on a client PC, will this change the default protocol or any other default settings that may affect other functionality? If you've changed a user's security settings, will this affect his or her ability to access other network resources? This is part of testing your solution to make sure it works properly, but it also makes you think about the impact of your work on the system as a whole.

Make sure you *verify full system functionality*. If you think you fixed the problem between Caitlin's workstation and the database server, have her open the database while you're still there. That way you don't have to make a second tech call to resolve an outstanding issue. This saves time and money and helps your customer do his or her job better. Everybody wins.

In the scenario where you are providing support to someone else rather than working directly on the problem, you should have them try to re-create the problem. This tells you whether they understand what you have been telling them and educates them at the same time, lessening the chance that they'll call you back later and ask, "Can we just go through that one more time?"

 EXAM TIP   Always test a solution before you walk away from the job!

 ADDITIONAL RESOURCES   Here's a funny video that illustrates this objective very well (Medieval helpdesk with English subtitles): https://youtu.be/pQHX-SjgQvQ.

Also at this time, *if applicable, implement preventive measures*, steps taken through software, hardware, or human interaction, to avoid a repeat of the problem. Automation, with scheduled tasks, is a good idea. Consider installing software to patch a system, as well. Deploying a new router, switch, or PC might be required. You might even need to educate users to do or not do something, but be sure to teach them tactfully.

Document Findings, Actions, Outcomes, and Lessons Learned

It is vital that you *document findings, actions, outcomes, and lessons learned* of all support calls, for two reasons: First, you're creating a support database to serve as a knowledge base for future reference, enabling everyone on the support team to identify new problems as they arise and know how to deal with them quickly, without having to duplicate someone else's research efforts. Second, documentation enables you to track problem trends and anticipate future workloads, or even to identify a particular brand or model of an item, such as a printer or a NIC, that seems to be less reliable or that creates more work for you than others. Don't skip this step—it really is essential! The unofficial repository for documentation, though, for almost every problem, cause, and solution, of course, is…Google. If you're having a problem, it's almost a guarantee that someone else had that exact or similar problem, posted to a forum, and got an answer.

 EXAM TIP The CompTIA Network+ exam will likely ask you about some of the soft skills in this objective. A network tech needs soft skills in addition to technical skills.

REVIEW

Objective 5.1: Explain the network troubleshooting methodology

- There are multiple steps involved to identify a problem when troubleshooting. You need to gather information, question users, identify symptoms, determine if anything has changed, duplicate the problem, if possible, and approach multiple problems individually. Following these steps will help you get to the root of the problem.
- Once you've identified one or more problems, try to figure out what could have happened. In other words, establish a theory of probable cause, which requires you to question the obvious and consider multiple approaches.
- After you identify the problem and establish a theory of probable cause, you need to test the theory to determine the cause.
- The next step is to establish a plan of action to resolve the problem and identify potential effects.
- After that, you need to implement the solution or escalate as necessary.
- Next, verify full system functionality and, if applicable, implement preventive measures.
- Finally, document findings, actions, outcomes, and lessons learned.

5.1 QUESTIONS

1. What is the first step in the troubleshooting model?
   - **A.** Establish a plan of action to resolve the problem and identify potential effects.
   - **B.** Test the theory to determine the cause.
   - **C.** Identify the problem.
   - **D.** Establish a theory of probable cause.

2. Which of the following is not a recommended troubleshooting approach?
   - **A.** Top-to-bottom OSI model
   - **B.** Bottom-to-top OSI model
   - **C.** Side-to-side OSI model
   - **D.** Divide and conquer

3. What is the last step in the troubleshooting model?
   A. Establish a plan of action to resolve the problem and identify potential effects.
   B. Document findings, actions, outcomes, and lessons learned.
   C. Implement the solution or escalate as necessary.
   D. Verify full system functionality and, if applicable, implement preventive measures.

5.1 ANSWERS

1. **C** The first step when troubleshooting a problem is to identify the problem.

2. **C** There is no side-to-side OSI model, nor does that even make sense as far as the OSI model is concerned.

3. **B** Documentation should always come last. Future troubleshooting can involve using the final documentation as a repository for solving problems.

Objective 5.2 Given a scenario, troubleshoot common cable connectivity issues and select the appropriate tools

While working through the process of finding a problem's cause, sometimes you need to use one or more tools. If the problem is related to cable connectivity issues, there are many hardware tools that can provide information to help you troubleshoot. The trick is knowing when and how to use these tools to solve your cable connectivity issues.

Specifications and Limitations

Before the troubleshooting begins, you need to understand *specifications and limitations* in regard to throughput, speed, and distance. Cables and devices come with both specifications and limitations, and going above or below each of them could result in issues that need troubleshooting.

Throughput

Throughput represents the amount of actual data transmitted in a certain timeframe and is measured in bits per second (bps), megabits per second (Mbps), and gigabits per second (Gbps). In certain cases, throughput is measured in packets per second. Throughput is often confused with bandwidth, which represents how much data can theoretically be transmitted at a time, and is also measured in bits, megabits, and gigabits per second.

As an analogy, the New York State Thruway could be the bandwidth, while the cars driving on it could be the throughput. With many lanes and a high speed limit, many cars can start their drive from Rochester, NY, headed eastbound to Staten Island, NY. However, if there are too many cars attempting to travel at the same time, causing congestion on the highway, or if lanes are closed due to construction, the cars won't be able to use the bandwidth to its fullest capability. On a country road with one lane in each direction and traffic lights, the bandwidth is not as great as the New York State Thruway, so the throughput of the cars will not be as great, either. Increasing the bandwidth doesn't increase the speed. If a person who doesn't drive quickly in general gets on a highway with a great bandwidth, that bandwidth doesn't make the car go faster. It allows for greater potential of that car, and other cars as well.

This analogy and concept of throughput applies to both throughput from ISPs and within a corporate infrastructure.

Speed

As mentioned above, when talking about *speed*, although most sources will use the term bandwidth incorrectly, but the term throughput is actually the technically correct term. Throughput and speed are synonyms. Some ISPs, as shown in this link, https://www.greenlightnetworks.com/, will simply use the term speed. However, the speeds shown, 500 Mbps, 750 Mbps, 1 Gbps, and 2 Gbps, are not actually what customers will be getting, since the ISP has other customers (like many cars on a highway in the previous analogy) and there are other factors that will slow down traffic as well, like device capabilities, attenuation (coming up in this objective), and more (like traffic lights slow down cars).

EXAM TIP   Throughput is a real-world value that represents how much data was actually transferred and is dependent on latency, while bandwidth is a theoretical value that represents the maximum potential amount of data that can be transferred at any point in time that is not dependent on latency. Whenever you hear the term "speed," it's referring to throughput.

Speed, in relation to network switches, deals with the limitation of slower ports, switches, or NICs/devices, which need to have speed settings set to something other than auto or they can't negotiate full speed.

ADDITIONAL RESOURCES   Listen to me talk on talk radio about these concepts at https://www.youtube.com/weissman52, in the Radio Cybersecurity Expert Playlist (video from 4/16/21).

Distance

Cables, as detailed in Objective 1.3, have certain *distance* limitations. For example, twisted pair cabling standards limit the distance for twisted pair cable segments to 100 meters (a tad more than 328 feet). Cable segments longer than 100 meters could work, but are not guaranteed as they would not be adhering to the distance standard.

From the ISP perspective, DSL has limitations of cable distance (18,000 feet for data transmission without a repeater, with data rates decreasing as you go further from the ISP). Furthermore, some companies could have offices outside of ISP high-speed coverage areas, so distance would limit those businesses.

Cable Considerations

Cable considerations include choosing between shielded and unshielded cable as well as choosing between plenum and riser-rated cable.

Shielded and Unshielded

The most common type of cabling used in networks consists of twisted pairs of wires, bundled together into a common jacket. Each pair in the cable works as a team either transmitting or receiving data. Using a pair of twisted wires rather than a single wire to send a signal reduces a specific type of interference, called crosstalk, which is when signals from one pair bleed into other pairs. The more twists per square foot, the less crosstalk. Two types of twisted-pair cabling are manufactured: *shielded and unshielded.*

Shielded Twisted Pair

Shielded twisted pair (STP) cable consists of twisted pairs of wires surrounded by shielding to protect them from EMI (electromagnetic interference). There are six types, differentiated by which part gets shielding, such as the whole cable or individual pairs within the cable. The typical scenario in which you'd deploy STP over UTP is in high-EMI environments that have things like fluorescent lights, motors, power lines, and air conditioners.

Unshielded Twisted Pair

Unshielded twisted pair (UTP) cable consists of twisted pairs of wires surrounded by a plastic jacket that does not provide any protection from EMI. When installing UTP cabling, you must be careful to avoid interference from EMI sources or use STP instead. UTP costs much less than STP but, in most environments, performs just as well.

Twisted-pair cabling has been around since the 1970s and evolving technologies demanded higher speeds. Over the years, manufacturers increased the number of twists per foot, used higher gauge cable, and added shielding to make twisted pair able to handle higher data speeds. To help network installers get the right cable for the right network technology, the cabling industry developed a variety of grades called category (Cat) ratings, covered in Objective 1.3. Cat ratings are officially rated in megahertz (MHz), indicating the highest frequency the cable can handle.

UTP cables handle a certain frequency or cycles per second, such as 100 MHz or 1000 MHz. You could take the frequency number in the early days of networking and translate that into the maximum throughput for a cable. Each cycle per second (or hertz) basically accounted for one bit of data per second. A 10 million cycle per second (10 MHz) cable, for example, could handle 10 million bits per second (10 Mbps). The maximum amount of data that can go through the cable per second is called bandwidth (similar to the capacity of bandwidth mentioned earlier in this objective).

Because most networks can run at speeds of up to 1000 MHz, some new cabling installations use Category 6 (Cat 6) cabling, although a large number of installations use Cat 6A to future-proof the network.

Make sure you can look at twisted pair and know its Cat rating. There are two places to look. First, twisted pair is typically sold in boxed reels, and the manufacturer will clearly mark the Cat level both on the box and on the cable itself.

Plenum and Riser-Rated

To reduce the risk of your network cables burning and creating noxious fumes and smoke, Underwriters Laboratories (UL) and the National Electrical Code (NEC) joined forces to develop cabling fire ratings. The two most common fire ratings are PVC and *plenum*. Cable with a polyvinyl chloride (PVC) rating has no significant fire protection. If you burn a PVC-rated cable, it creates lots of smoke and noxious fumes. Burning plenum-rated cable creates much less smoke and fumes, but plenum-rated cable costs about three to five times as much as PVC-rated cable. Most city ordinances require the use of plenum cable for network installations. The bottom line in such scenarios? Get plenum!

The space between the acoustical tile ceiling in an office building and the actual concrete ceiling above is called the plenum—hence the name for the proper fire rating of cabling to use in that space.

A third type of fire rating, known as riser, designates the proper cabling to use for vertical runs between floors of a building. *Riser-rated* cable provides less protection than plenum cable, though, so most installations today use plenum for runs between floors.

 EXAM TIP   Look for a troubleshooting scenario question on the CompTIA Network+ exam that asks you to compare plenum versus PVC cable best use. If it goes in the wall, make it plenum!

Cable Application

Cable application, choosing the right cable for the right situation, is also important.

Rollover Cable/Console Cable

A *rollover cable/console cable* (also known as a Yost cable) is used to connect a PC to a router or switch console (not Ethernet) port for management purposes, not for data transfer. See Figure 5.2-1.

 NOTE   The term *Yost cable* comes from its creator's name, Dave Yost. For more information visit http://yost.com/computers/RJ45-serial.

The RJ45 (8P8C) side goes into the port on the back of the router or switch marked Console, and the other side, USB, or serial (if so, you'll need a serial-to-USB dongle), goes into a port on the PC.

Once you've made this connection, you need to use a terminal emulation program to talk to the router. One of the most popular programs is PuTTY (https://www.chiark.greenend .org.uk/~sgtatham/putty/).

Crossover Cable

When crimping a UTP cable, you can create two types of cables—a straight-through cable or a *crossover cable*. Straight-through cables used for Fast Ethernet (100 Mbps) and Ethernet (10 Mbps) use only four wires—wires 1, 2, 3, and 6. With a straight-through cable, pin 1 of the RJ45 connector on one end follows the wire to pin 1 on the other end, and as a result, pin 1 on both ends of the wire are connected.

 EXAM TIP   Even though the CompTIA Network+ Exam Objectives do not explicitly list the straight-through cable type, you can't understand how a crossover cable works or why it's needed without understanding the straight-through cable first. As such, a discussion on the straight-through cable type is included in this section.

FIGURE 5.2-1   Console cable

This straight-through cable works great for connecting a PC to a switch because the network interface card on the PC uses pins 1 and 2 as the transmit pins, while pins 3 and 6 are the receive pins. On the switch, pins 1 and 2 are the receive pins, while pins 3 and 6 are the transmit pins. When you use straight-through cable, the transmit pins of the PC will connect to the receive pins on the switch (via the straight-through cable), allowing data to be sent. Likewise, the receive pins on the PC are connected to the transmit pins on the switch via the straight-through cable, allowing the PC to receive data. Router interfaces have the same NIC configuration as PCs: they transmit on 1 and 2 and receive on 3 and 6. As a result, when connecting a switch to a router, once again, the cable should be straight-through.

If you try to connect two computers directly (NIC to NIC) with a straight-through cable, the systems will not be able to communicate because the transmit pins (pins 1 and 2) on one system will be connected to the transmit pins on the second system, so neither system can receive data. The transmit pins have to be connected to the receive pins at the other end, which is what the *crossover cable* creates. With a crossover cable, wires 1 and 2 (transmit) from one end of the cable are switched to the receive wire placeholders (pins 3 and 6) at the other end of the cable (shown in Figure 5.2-2a).

When you use a crossover cable to connect two PCs, two routers, or two switches, the crossover cable connects the transmit pins on one device to the receive pins on the second device using wires 1 and 2 in the cable. Gigabit Ethernet and above, however, uses a modified scheme. Because cables that support Gigabit Ethernet (Cat 5, Cat 6, and Cat 6a) use all eight wires, in addition to wires 1 & 3 and 2 & 6 being crossed, wires 4 & 7 and 5 & 8 are crossed (shown in Figure 5.2-2b). Furthermore, because all Gigabit Ethernet devices have an automatic crossover detection feature (covered in Objective 2.3) called auto-medium-dependent interface crossover (MDI-X), which automatically detects signals and determines how to send them down the wires (straight or crossed), the Gigabit Ethernet crossover cable is not necessary.

Devices using Fast Ethernet, though, need to be wired with the correct cable or the interface will not come up. This is a very easy troubleshooting step, and should be one of the first things to check when troubleshooting a device having a connection problem.

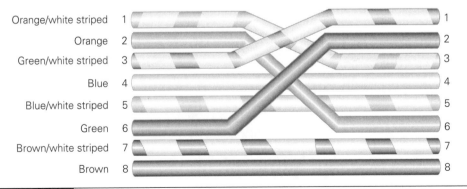

Orange/white striped	1
Orange	2
Green/white striped	3
Blue	4
Blue/white striped	5
Green	6
Brown/white striped	7
Brown	8

FIGURE 5.2-2a Crossover cable for Fast Ethernet and below

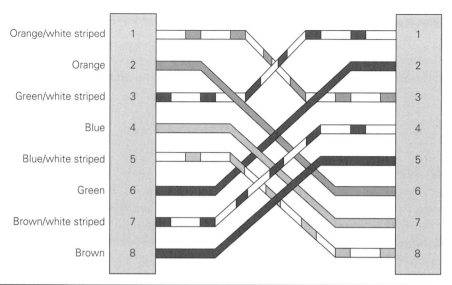

Orange/white striped — 1
Orange — 2
Green/white striped — 3
Blue — 4
Blue/white striped — 5
Green — 6
Brown/white striped — 7
Brown — 8

FIGURE 5.2-2b   Crossover cable for Gigabit Ethernet and above

Power over Ethernet

Wireless access points need electrical power, but they're invariably placed in strange locations (like ceilings or high up on walls) where providing electrical power is not convenient. No worries! Many WAPs support one of the *Power over Ethernet* (PoE) standards that enables them to receive their power from the same Ethernet cables that transfer their data. The switch that connects the WAPs must support PoE, but as long as both the WAP and the switches to which they connect support PoE, you don't have to do anything other than just plug in Ethernet cables. PoE works automatically. As you might imagine, it costs extra to get WAPs and switches that support PoE, but the convenience of PoE for wireless networks makes it a popular option.

The original PoE standard—802.3af—came out in 2003 with great response from the industry. PoE switches support a maximum of 15.4 watts of DC power per port. In 2009, 802.3af was revised to output as much as 25.5 watts per port. This PoE amendment to 802.3 is called 802.3at, PoE plus, or PoE+. In 2018, the IEEE released upgraded PoE again with the 802.3bt standard. Switches that support PoE++ (or 4PPoE) can provide one of two power upgrades, with Type 3 supplying up to 51 watts per port and Type 4 supplying up to 71.3 watts per port.

Common Issues

Now that you understand specifications and limitations, cable considerations, and cable application, it's time to discuss *common issues* for cable connectivity, which include attenuation, interference, decibel (dB) loss, incorrect pinout, bad ports, open/short, Light-emitting diode (LED) status indicators, incorrect transceivers, duplexing issues, transmit and receive (TX/RX) reversed, and dirty optical cables.

Attenuation

Attenuation is the weakening of a signal as it travels long distances and is caused when wave signals travel too far without help. As a cable run gets longer, the attenuation increases, and the signal becomes weaker. Therefore, the signals need to be amplified before they become completely worthless. A signal from a cable is fed into a network/signal repeater, which processes the signal and sends out a stronger signal. Signal boosters (which are used for wireless signals as well) can be used for amplification of cable-bound attenuating signals.

Interference

Interference is when a cable's signal is disrupted or degraded and is usually caused by EMI or crosstalk. Sources of EMI, as previously mentioned in the discussion of twisted-pair cabling, are things like fluorescent lights, motors, power lines, and air conditioners.

As also mentioned in that discussion, crosstalk is when signals from one wire pair bleed into other pairs. The more twists per square foot, the less crosstalk. Every piece of UTP in existence generates crosstalk. Worse, when you crimp the end of a UTP cable to a jack or plugs, crosstalk increases. A poor-quality crimp creates so much crosstalk that a cable run won't operate at its designed speed. To detect crosstalk, a normal-strength signal is sent down one pair of wires in a cable. An electronic detector, connected on the same end of the cable as the end emanating the signal, listens on the other three pairs and measures the amount of interference, as shown in Figure 5.2-3. This is called near-end crosstalk (NEXT).

If you repeat this test, sending the signal down one pair of wires, but this time listening on the other pairs on the far end of the connection, you test for far-end crosstalk (FEXT), as shown in Figure 5.2-4.

A tester must send a signal down one end of a wire, test for NEXT and FEXT on the ends of every other pair, and then repeat this process for every pair in the UTP cable.

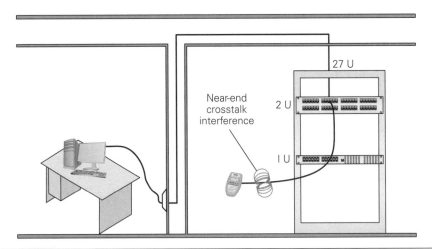

FIGURE 5.2-3 Near-end crosstalk

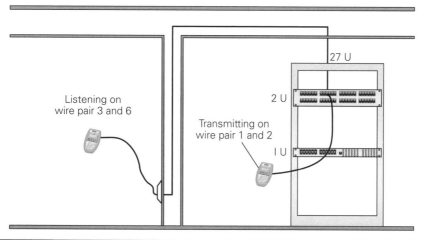

FIGURE 5.2-4   Far-end crosstalk

This process of verifying that every cable run meets the exacting TIA standards requires very powerful testing tools, generally known as cable certifiers or just certifiers. Cable certifiers can do the high-end testing as well as generate a report that a cable installer can print out and hand to a customer to prove that the installed cable runs pass TIA standards.

Cross-Reference

Objective 1.3 discusses the T568A and T568B standards.

If you want a device that fully tests a cable run to the very complex TIA standards, the price shoots up fast. These higher-end testers can detect things the lesser testers cannot, such as crosstalk and attenuation.

 NOTE   Both NEXT and FEXT are measured in decibels (dB).

Decibel (dB) Loss

Signal loss in networking is measured in a unit called a decibel (dB), and the problem itself is known as *decibel (dB) loss*. This applies to both electrical signals in copper cables and light signals in fiber cables.

When referring to a signal traveling from one end of a cable to another, you really care about how much information on that signal gets to the end. In a simple sense, if you have some interference, some imperfections in the cable or fiber, you'll get some loss from beginning to end. Most people think about that loss in terms of percentage or even in more common terms, like "a little" or "a lot of" loss.

The problem when you take that same concept to networking is that the percentages lost can be gigantic or really, really small. When you start talking about a 10,000% loss or a 0.00001% loss, most folks' eyes glaze over. The numbers are simply too big or small to make intuitive sense.

Technicians use the term decibel to describe those numbers in a more digestible format. When techs look at a signal loss of 3 dB, for example, they should be able to know that that number is a lot smaller than a signal loss of 10 dB.

Incorrect Pinout

An *incorrect pinout* scenario could involve copper cable wires not terminated in the right place in the plug or jack or each termination not matching the same standard.

Bad Ports

Bad ports on routers and switches, caused by hardware failure of the port itself or the hardware that the port is part of, can cause connectivity issues and should be replaced.

If a system is not connecting to the network, eliminate the possibility of a bad port, switch, or other larger problem by checking to make sure other people can access the network, and that other systems can access the shared resource (a server, for example) that the problem system can't see. Make a quick visual inspection of the cable running from the back of the PC to the port in the wall jack.

If you remove the cable from the wall jack and plug it into a known good jack, the system might be able to connect. If so, the problem could be the wall jack, the infrastructure cable to the patch panel (someone could have driven a nail or screw through a cable in the wall), the patch panel jacks, the patch panel patch cable, or even the switch port. The device can be ruled out as the problem, but there is still a lot of hardware between that device and the switch port. In fact, the problem could be the switch port itself.

Open/Short

When dealing with potentially bad copper cable, one of the first things to check is if any of the wires are broken or not connected in the crimp. If a wire is broken or a connection is *open*, it no longer has continuity (a complete, functioning connection). Are there bent pins on the RJ45 or in the jack? Is there any place where two bare wires touch? This creates a *short*. Shorts can occur when cables are damaged, but you can also get a short when improperly crimping two cables into the same place on a crimp.

Light-Emitting Diode (LED) Status Indicators

A hardware failure can certainly make a network device unreachable. Fall back on your CompTIA A+ training for troubleshooting. Check the link lights on the NIC and the switch. Try another NIC if the machine seems functional in every other aspect. Try another port on the switch. Try another cable.

Pay attention to link lights when you have a "hardware failure." The network *connection light-emitting diode (LED) status indicators*—link lights—can quickly point to a connectivity issue.

Incorrect Transceivers

Fiber networks have a relatively small number of connectors but offer a pretty wide variety of signal types that use those connectors. These variations come into play in several ways. First, just because you can connect to a particular small form-factor pluggable (SFP) or gigabit interface converter (GBIC), that doesn't mean the signal will work. Using *incorrect transceivers* in switches might work in a physical sense, but if the switch won't play with anything but Cisco technology, for example, you'll get a transceiver mismatch.

Duplexing Issues

If a switch port or NIC on one end of a cable connection is explicitly set to use specific speed and duplex settings, it will no longer auto-negotiate settings with its partner port at the other end. While newer high-speed Ethernet standards only support or default to full-duplex connections, much older/slower standards default to half-duplex connections.

If a switch port or NIC of a PC is manually configured for a speed of 10 or 100 Mbps and a duplex of full, and the switch port it's connected to is set to auto for both speed and duplex, there will be problems. The switch will try to sense the speed without auto-negotiation (since the other side is not set for auto). If that fails, the switch will use the IEEE default slowest supported speed of 10 Mbps. If the other side's speed is 10 or 100 Mbps, the switch will use half-duplex, but if the other side's speed is 1000 Mbps or greater, the switch will use full-duplex.

In the example at hand, the switch will sense the speed of 100 Mbps and use that speed, but the switch will choose half-duplex. This is a condition known as a duplex mismatch. Due to these *duplexing issues*, CSMA/CD will not be used by the device at the other side of the switch, since it will be using full-duplex. The switch port at the other end, configured for half-duplex, will use CSMA/CD and, incredibly enough, will believe that collisions are occurring. Objective 2.3 discussed CSMA/CD. Objective 3.1 discussed seeing speed/duplex settings. Objective 5.5 will continue this discussion on collisions.

Transmit and Receive (TX/RX) Reversed

When using a punchdown tool to connect UTP cables to a 110-block, make sure you insert the wires according to the same standard (T568A or TIA568B) on both ends of the cable. If you don't, you might end up swapping the sending and receiving wires, and with *transmit and receive (TX/RX) reversed*, you've inadvertently created a crossover cable, which might halt communication.

Dirty Optical Cables

Damaged cables or open connections obviously stop signals. The typical SFP or GBIC can have problems. When you're checking for a bad SFP/GBIC, you'll need to check both the connector and the cable going into that connector. Either or both could cause the signal loss.

A dirty connector can lead to *dirty optical cables*, which can cause pretty serious signal loss with fiber. It's important not to smudge the glass!

Common Tools

Now it's time to examine some *common tools* used to troubleshoot common cable connectivity issues. Selecting the appropriate tools for a problem is an important step in the troubleshooting process.

Cable Crimper

An RJ45 connector is usually called a crimp, and the act (some folks call it an art) of installing a crimp onto the end of a piece of UTP cable is called crimping. The tool used to secure a crimp onto the end of a cable is a *cable crimper* (see Figure 5.2-5). Each wire inside a UTP cable must connect to the proper pin inside the crimp. Make sure, of course, to test each cable that you make, because if a cable is bad, that could lead you down the road of troubleshooting.

Punchdown Tool

A *punchdown tool* (Figure 5.2-6) puts UTP wires into 66- and 110-blocks. The only time you would use a punchdown tool in a diagnostic environment is for a quick repunch of a connection, to make sure all the contacts are properly set.

Tone Generator

It would be nice to say that all cable installations are perfect and that over the years they won't tend to grow into horrific piles of spaghetti-like, unlabeled cables. In the real world, though, you might eventually find yourself having to locate or trace cables. Even in the best-planned

FIGURE 5.2-5   Cable crimper

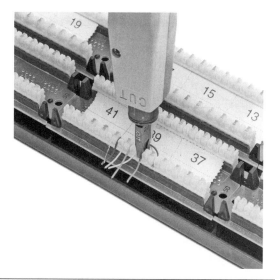

FIGURE 5.2-6   Punchdown tool

networks, labels fall off ports and outlets, mystery cables appear behind walls, new cable runs are added, and mistakes are made counting rows and columns on patch panels. Sooner or later, most network techs will have to be able to pick out one particular cable or port from a stack.

When the time comes to trace cables, network techs turn to a device called a toner for help. Toner is the generic term for two separate devices that are used together: a *tone generator* and a tone probe. The tone generator connects to the cable using alligator clips, tiny hooks, or a network jack, and it sends an electrical signal along the wire at a certain frequency. The tone probe emits a sound when it is placed near a cable connected to the tone generator. These two devices are often referred to by the brand-name Fox and Hound (Figure 5.2-7), a popular model of toner made by the Triplett Corporation.

To trace a cable, connect the tone generator to the known end of the cable in question, and then position the tone probe next to the other end of each of the cables that might be the right one. The tone probe makes a sound when it's placed next to the right cable. Some toners have one tone probe that works with multiple tone generators. Each generator emits a separate frequency, and the probe sounds a different tone for each one. Even good toners are relatively inexpensive ($75). Although inexpensive toners can cost less than $25, they don't tend to work well, so spending a little more is worthwhile. Just keep in mind that if you have to support a network, you'd do best to own a decent toner.

A good, medium-priced cable tester and a good toner are the most important tools for folks who must support, but not install, networks. A final tip: Be sure to bring along a few extra batteries—there's nothing worse than sitting on the top of a ladder holding a cable tester or toner that has just run out of juice!

FIGURE 5.2-7   Fox and Hound

Loopback Adapter

Be warned that a bad NIC can generate the "can't see the network" problem. Use the utility provided by your OS to verify that the NIC works. If you've got a NIC with diagnostic software, run it—this software will check the NIC's circuitry. The NIC's female connector is a common failure point, so NICs that come with diagnostic software often include a special test called a loopback test. A loopback test sends data out of the NIC and checks to see if it comes back. Some NICs perform only an internal loopback, which tests the circuitry that sends and receives, but not the actual connecting pins. A true external loopback requires a *loopback adapter* (also known as a loopback plug) inserted into the NIC's port (Figure 5.2-8). If a NIC is bad or has a bad port, replace it—preferably with an identical NIC so you don't have to reinstall drivers!

Don't confuse these hardware loopback adapters with software loopback adapters, which run diagnostic checks inside the machine, just through software. Also, keep in mind that a loopback adapter is totally unrelated to the loopback address, 127.0.0.1, covered in Objective 1.4, which has nothing to do with testing a NIC (disable all NICs, ping 127.0.0.1, and it will work!), but rather testing if TCP/IP is working correctly on the local machine.

FIGURE 5.2-8   Loopback adapter

Optical Time-Domain Reflectometer (OTDR)

A time-domain reflectometer (TDR) and *optical time-domain reflectometer (OTDR)* can tell you where a break is on a cable (Figure 5.2-9). A TDR works with twisted pair/copper cables and an OTDR works with fiber-optic cables, but otherwise they share the same function.

FIGURE 5.2-9   An EXFO AXS-100 OTDR (photo courtesy of EXFO)

If a problem shows itself as a disconnect and you've first checked easier issues that would manifest as disconnects, such as loss of permissions, an unplugged cable, or a server shut off, then think about using these tools.

Multimeter

A *multimeter* (Figure 5.2-10) tests current, voltage (both AC and DC), resistance, and continuity in copper cables. Multimeters are the unsung heroes of cabling infrastructures because no other tool can tell you how much voltage is on a line. They are also a great fallback for continuity testing when you don't have a cable tester handy.

Cable Tester

A *cable tester* can tell you if you have a continuity problem or if a wire map (coming up next) isn't correct (Figure 5.2-11).

Wire Map

Better testers can run a *wire map* test that goes beyond mere continuity, testing that all the wires on both ends of the cable connect to the right spot. A wire map test will pick up shorts, crossed wires, and more.

A *wire map* problem occurs when one or more of the wires in a cable don't connect to the proper location on the jack or plug. This can be caused by improperly crimping a cable.

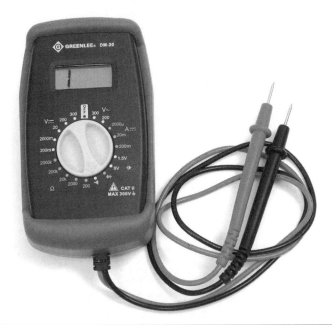

FIGURE 5.2-10 Multimeter

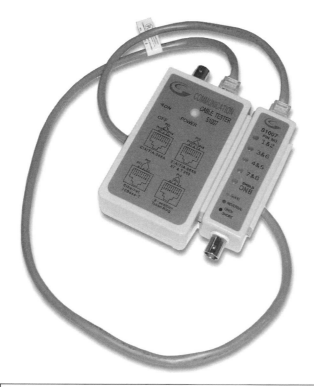

FIGURE 5.2-11 Cable tester

Tap

A *tap* connects multiple drop cables to a single distribution cable and splits the signal unevenly. This allows a tap to reduce the signal for a shorter cable run and increase the signal for a longer cable run, providing similar signal strength. A related device, a splitter, always splits the signal evenly, which wouldn't be good for runs of different lengths.

Fusion Splicers

Fusion splicers fuse/weld two optical fibers together.

Spectrum Analyzers

The fix to interference (other than avoiding RF reflective surfaces) is to scan for RF sources with *spectrum analyzers*. We measure RFI with the signal-to-noise ratio (SNR), essentially comparing the signal strength and the overall interference in the space. Figure 5.2-12 shows the popular AirMagnet Wi-Fi Analyzer Pro reporting SNR. Use a channel that's not overwhelmed.

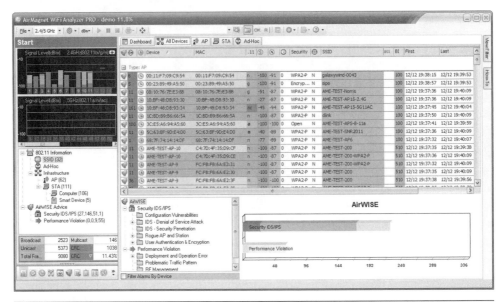

FIGURE 5.2-12 Spectrum analyzer

Snips/Cutters

Figure 5.2-13 shows a pair of wire *snips/cutters* that provides a nice clean snip/cut to the cable.

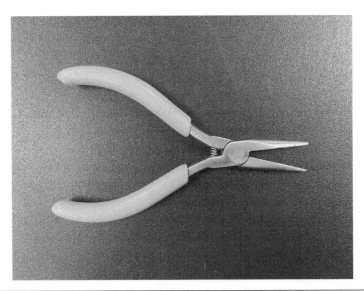

FIGURE 5.2-13 Snips/cutters

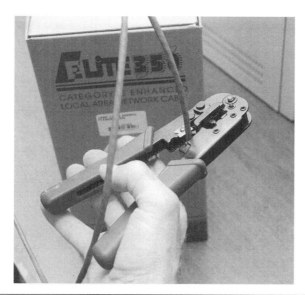

A crimper with built-in cable stripper

Cable Stripper

A *cable stripper* (shown as part of a crimper in Figure 5.2-14) is used to strip/remove the outside of a cable in order to gain access to the wires inside.

Fiber Light Meter

The extremely transparent fiber-optic cables allow light to shine but have some inherent impurities in the glass that can reduce light transmission. Dust, poor connections, and light leakage can also degrade the strength of light pulses as they travel through a fiber-optic run. To measure the amount of light loss, technicians use a *fiber light meter* (also known as an optical power meter). Figure 5.2-15 shows an example.

 EXAM TIP   The CompTIA Network+ exam objectives use the term *fiber light meter*. The more accurate term in this context is either *power meter* or *optical power meter*. You may see any of these terms on the exam.

FIGURE 5.2-15 FiberLink® 6650 Optical Power Meter (photo courtesy of Communications Specialties, Inc.)

REVIEW

Objective 5.2: Given a scenario, troubleshoot common cable connectivity issues and select the appropriate tools

- Before the troubleshooting begins, you need to understand *specifications and limitations* in regard to throughput, speed, and distance.

- *Throughput* represents the amount of actual data transmitted in a certain timeframe, and is measured in bits per second (bps), megabits per second (Mbps), and gigabits per second (Gbps). Therefore, when talking about *speed*, although most sources will incorrectly use the term bandwidth, the term throughput is actually the technically correct term.

- Cables, as detailed in Objective 1.3, have certain *distance* limitations.

- *Cable considerations* include choosing between *shielded and unshielded* cable as well as choosing between *plenum and riser-rated* cable.

- Shielded twisted pair (STP) cable consists of twisted pairs of wires surrounded by shielding to protect them from EMI (electromagnetic interference).

- Unshielded twisted pair (UTP) cable consists of twisted pairs of wires surrounded by a plastic jacket that does not provide any protection from EMI.

- Burning plenum-rated cable creates much less smoke and fumes than burning PVC-rated cable, but plenum-rated cable costs about three to five times as much as PVC-rated cable. A third type of fire rating, known as riser, designates the proper cabling to use for vertical runs between floors of a building. Riser-rated cable provides less protection than plenum cable, though, so most installations today use plenum for runs between floors.

- *Cable application*, choosing the right cable for the right situation, is also important.

- A *rollover cable/console cable* (also known as a Yost cable) is used to connect a PC to a router or switch console (not Ethernet) port for management purposes, not for data transfer.

- If you try to connect two computers directly (NIC to NIC) with a straight-through cable, the systems will not be able to communicate because the transmit pins (pins 1 and 2) on one system will be connected to the transmit pins on the second system, so neither system can receive data. The transmit pins have to be connected to the receive pins at the other end, which is what the *crossover cable* creates. With a crossover cable, wires 1 and 2 (transmit) from one end of the cable are switched to the receive wire placeholders (wires 3 and 6) at the other end of the cable.

- Many WAPs support one of the *Power over Ethernet* (PoE) standards that enables them to receive their power from the same Ethernet cables that transfer their data.

- *Common issues* for cable connectivity include attenuation, interference, decibel (dB) loss, incorrect pinout, bad ports, open/short, Light-emitting diode (LED) status indicators, incorrect transceivers, duplexing issues, transmit and receive (TX/RX) reversed, and dirty optical cables.

- *Attenuation* is the weakening of a signal as it travels long distances and is caused when wave signals travel too far without help.

- *Interference* is when a cable's signal is disrupted or degraded and is usually caused by EMI and crosstalk.

- Signal loss in networking is measured in a unit called a decibel (dB), and the problem itself is known as *decibel (dB) loss*.

- An incorrect pinout scenario could involve wires not terminated in the right place in the plug or jack or each termination not matching the same standard.

- *Bad ports* on routers and switches, caused by hardware failure of the port itself or the hardware that the port is part of, can cause connectivity issues and should be replaced.

- If a wire is broken or a connection is *open*, it no longer has continuity (a complete, functioning connection). A *short* can occur when cables are damaged, but you can also get a short when improperly crimping two cables into the same place on a crimp.

- The network connection *light-emitting diode (LED) status indicators*—link lights—can quickly point to a connectivity issue.

- Using *incorrect transceivers* in switches might work in a physical sense, but if the switch won't play with anything but Cisco technology, for example, you'll get a transceiver mismatch.

- Due to *duplexing issues*, CSMA/CD will not be used by a device at the side of a switch, using full-duplex, while the switch port at the other end, configured for half-duplex, will use CSMA/CD and, incredibly enough, will believe that collisions are occurring.

- When using a punchdown tool to connect UTP cables to a 110-block, make sure you insert the wires according to the same standard (T568A or TIA568B) on both ends of the cable. If you don't, you might end up swapping the sending and receiving wires, and with *transmit and receive (TX/RX) reversed*, you've inadvertently created a crossover cable, which might halt communication.

- A dirty connector can lead to *dirty optical cables*, which can cause pretty serious signal loss with fiber.

- *Common tools* are used to troubleshoot common cable connectivity issues. Selecting the appropriate tools for a problem is an important step in the troubleshooting process.

- The tool used to secure a crimp onto the end of a cable is a *cable crimper*. Each wire inside a UTP cable must connect to the proper pin inside the crimp.

- A *punchdown tool* puts UTP wires into 66- and 110-blocks.

- Toner is the generic term for two separate devices that are used together to trace cables: a *tone generator* and a tone probe. To trace a cable, the tone generator is connected to the known end of the cable in question and the tone probe is positioned next to the other end of each of the cables that might be the right one. The tone probe makes a sound when it's placed next to the right cable.

- A loopback test sends data out of the NIC and checks to see if it comes back. A true external loopback requires a *loopback adapter* (also known as loopback plug) inserted into the NIC's port.

- An *optical time-domain reflectometer (OTDR)* can tell you where a break is on a cable.

- A *multimeter* tests current, voltage (both AC and DC), resistance, and continuity in copper cables.

- A *cable tester* can tell you if you have a continuity problem or if a wire map isn't correct.

- Better testers can run a *wire map* test that goes beyond mere continuity, testing that all the wires on both ends of the cable connect to the right spot. A wire map test will pick up shorts, crossed wires, and more.

- A *tap* connects multiple drop cables to a single distribution cable and splits the signal unevenly.
- *Fusion splicers* fuse/weld two optical fibers together.
- The fix to interference (other than avoiding RF reflective surfaces) is to scan for RF sources with *spectrum analyzers*.
- The two main tools of the crimping trade are an RJ45 crimper with built-in cable stripper and a pair of wire *snips/cutters* that provides a nice clean snip/cut to the cable.
- A *cable stripper* is used to strip/remove the outside of a cable in order to gain access to the wires inside.
- To measure the amount of light loss, technicians use a *fiber light meter* (also known as an optical power meter).

5.2 QUESTIONS

1. What is the weakening of a signal over distances called?
   - **A.** Attenuation
   - **B.** Latency
   - **C.** Jitter
   - **D.** EMI
2. Which one of these scenarios is the least likely to cause an issue on a network today?
   - **A.** Bad ports
   - **B.** Open/short
   - **C.** Incorrect transceivers
   - **D.** Duplexing issues
3. Which of the following tools is used for twisted pair/copper cables?
   - **A.** Optical time-domain reflectometer (OTDR)
   - **B.** Multimeter
   - **C.** Fusion splicer
   - **D.** Spectrum analyzer

5.2 ANSWERS

1. **A**   Attenuation is the weakening of a signal over distances.
2. **D**   With modern devices defaulting to auto for full-duplex, duplexing issues are the least likely of the choices to be an actual issue today.
3. **B**   A multimeter tests current, voltage (both AC and DC), resistance, and continuity in copper cables. An OTDR and fusion splicers are used for fiber-optic cables, while a spectrum analyzer is used for RF.

Given a scenario, use the appropriate network software tools and commands

Software tools and command line tools are vital for network troubleshooting. The trick is knowing which tool(s) to use for specific scenarios.

Software Tools

Software tools for troubleshooting include the following: WiFi analyzer, protocol analyzer/ packet capture, bandwidth speed tester, port scanner, iPerf, NetFlow analyzers, TFTP server, terminal emulator, and IP scanner.

WiFi Analyzer

Discovering any wireless network signals other than your own in your space enables you to set both the SSID and channel to avoid networks that overlap. One part of any good site survey is a wireless analyzer. A *WiFi analyzer* (the CompTIA Network+ exam objectives omit the hyphen in Wi-Fi) is any device that looks for and documents all existing wireless networks in the area. Wireless analyzers are handy tools that are useful for diagnosing wireless network issues and conducting site surveys. You can get dedicated, hand-held wireless analyzer tools or you can run site survey software on a laptop or mobile wireless device. Wireless survey tools like AirMagnet Survey Pro always include an analyzer as well. Figure 5.3-1 shows a screenshot of Acrylic Wi-Fi, a free and popular wireless analyzer.

Protocol Analyzer/Packet Capture

IP packets, which exist at Layer 3 of the OSI model, are encapsulated inside of Layer 2 frames. On wired LANs, they are Ethernet frames. On wireless LANs, they are 802.11 frames. In the context of capturing and analyzing network traffic, though, even though the lowest unit to capture and analyze is the frame, it's still called packet sniffing.

Every single bit, all the 1s and 0s that go in and out of a network interface card (NIC), can be seen and analyzed. There is an option to see them in true binary, even hexadecimal, but as humans, we prefer a format that is more intuitive.

A *protocol analyzer/packet capture* program, also known as a packet sniffer, not only inter-cepts and logs all the 1s and 0s moving in and out of a NIC but also shows its capture in a human-readable format, in addition to binary and hexadecimal. All of the fields of every single frame, packet, segment, datagram, and upper-layer data protocols will be shown with their names, along with their corresponding data values. For example, in the IP packet, you'll see the

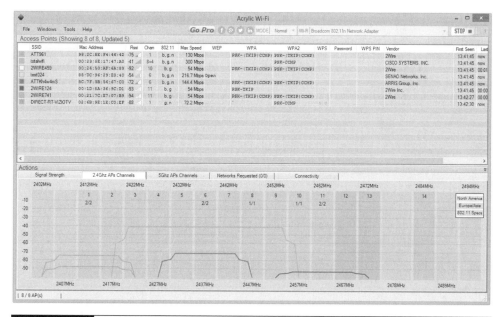

FIGURE 5.3-1   Acrylic Wi-Fi

source IP address with a value like 192.168.1.113 and the destination IP address with a value like 192.168.1.107. You'll see the content as it's listed in an RFC or other specifications.

A protocol analyzer/packet capture/packet sniffer can provide much insight into network traffic. This includes the following:

- Provide analysis for troubleshooting
- Provide information about cyberattack attempts
- Provide information about malicious insider and outsider activities.

It can be used to collect enough intelligence to carry out an actual cyberattack from both pentesting and cybercriminal perspectives. Items that can be seen include client/ server communications, actual data, network protocol implementation (including proprietary protocols), suspicious content, and login details or cookies (in the event of plaintext transmission).

It can help monitor and manage bandwidth, network usage, transmitted data, administration (items that have been added, removed, or changed), and security (effectiveness of firewalls, IDS/IPS implementations, filters, proxies).

It can collect information to generate a network statistics report.

It can even help with the process of documenting regulatory compliance by logging traffic at both the perimeter and endpoint levels.

FIGURE 5.3-2 Wireshark in action

While there are a few dozen packet sniffers, some with specialized purposes, Wireshark stands above the rest (see Figure 5.3-2). From Wireshark's Web site (https://www.wireshark.org/):

> Wireshark is the world's foremost and widely-used network protocol analyzer. It lets you see what's happening on your network at a microscopic level and is the de facto (and often de jure) standard across many commercial and non-profit enterprises, government agencies, and educational institutions. Wireshark development thrives thanks to the volunteer contributions of networking experts around the globe and is the continuation of a project started by Gerald Combs in 1998.

KEY TERM The terms **frame** and **packet** are often used interchangeably. However, this is incorrect. Frames are found at Layer 2 and encapsulate packets, while packets are found at Layer 3 and encapsulate ICMP packets, TCP segments, UDP datagrams, and more. You should use the proper terms!

Bandwidth Speed Tester

A *bandwidth speed tester* (also called a throughput tester) enables you to measure the data flow in a network. Which tool is appropriate depends on the type of network throughput you want to test. Most techs use one of several speed-test sites for checking an Internet connection's throughput like https://www.speedtest.net/. Try it out!

NOTE   Troubleshooting speeds at the WAN level (through an ISP) might call for a speed test from an Internet-based site. Troubleshooting speeds at the LAN level, within an organization, would call for a speed test from a local device.

Port Scanner

A *port scanner* is a tool that sends packets to a destination machine in order to identify the state of that machine's ports. The process of running such scans is called port scanning. From a cybersecurity perspective, port scanning helps you verify the security of systems under your control. From a cybercrime perspective, it allows attackers to find programs or services with vulnerabilities that can be exploited.

Many different types of scans can be sent. You'd just select an appropriate one, or a combination of different scan techniques, for the task at hand.

Cross-Reference

Port scanners identify the state of ports as open, closed, or filtered. Nmap scan classification states also include unfiltered, open|filtered (open or filtered), and closed|filtered (closed or filtered). Please refer to the Port States section in Objective 1.5 for more.

Port scanning can also potentially identify operating systems of target machines, as well as versions of programs running on machines.

Think of a burglar casing out the neighborhood. The burglar might walk up to a house and simply turn a doorknob or push a window to see if it's locked or unlocked. Technically, there's nothing illegal about that (trespassing notwithstanding). What about port scanning, then? Well, there are actually three well-known, but very rare, legal cases against people who performed port scans.

Is port scanning legal? Well, there's no conclusive answer, although precedent leads one to believe that intent to follow up the port scan with an attack is where the legal system might catch up to you.

While there are many port scanning tools, some with specialized purposes, Nmap stands above the rest. From Nmap's Web site (https://nmap.org/):

> Nmap ("Network Mapper") is a free and open source (license) tool for network discovery and security auditing. Many systems and network administrators also find it useful for tasks such as network inventory, managing service upgrade schedules, and monitoring host or service uptime. Nmap uses raw IP packets in novel ways to determine what hosts are available on the network, what services (application name and version) those hosts are offering, what operating systems (and OS versions) they are running, what type of packet filters/firewalls are in use, and dozens of other characteristics. It was designed to rapidly scan large networks, but works fine against single hosts. Nmap runs on all major computer operating systems, and official

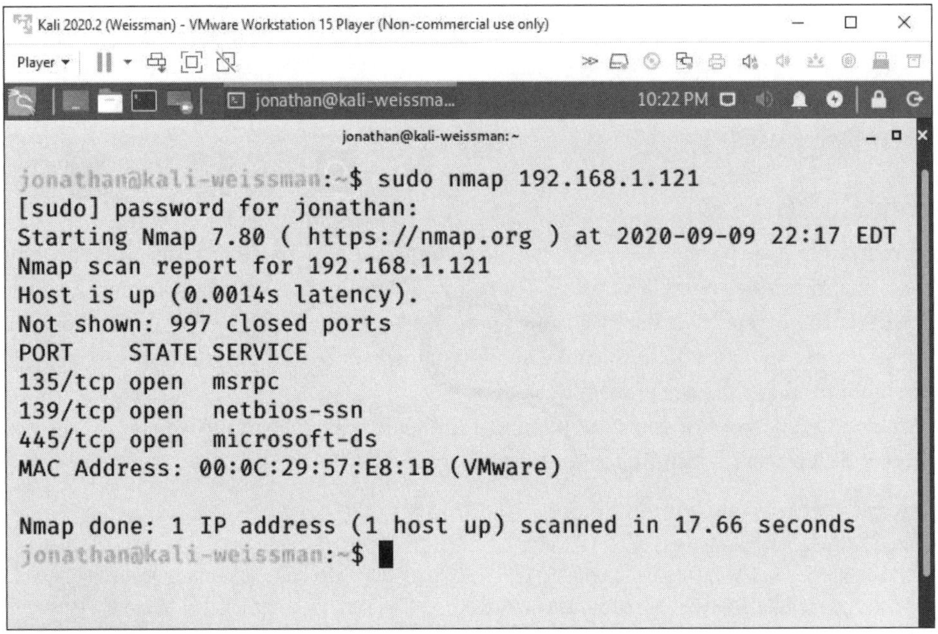

FIGURE 5.3-3 Nmap in action

binary packages are available for Linux, Windows, and Mac OS X. In addition to the classic command-line Nmap executable, the Nmap suite includes an advanced GUI and results viewer (Zenmap), a flexible data transfer, redirection, and debugging tool (Ncat), a tool for comparing scan results (Ndiff), and a packet generation and response analysis tool (Nping).

Check out Nmap in action in Figure 5.3-3.

iperf

A tool like *iPerf* (the current version is iPerf3) can actively measure the available and maximum bandwidth on a network. iPerf works with TCP, UDP, and SCTP. Check out https://iperf.fr for more details.

NetFlow Analyzers

NetFlow Analyzers were discussed in the NetFlow Data section in Objective 3.1.

Trivial File Transfer Protocol (TFTP) Server

A *Trivial File Transfer Protocol (TFTP) server* uses UDP at Layer 4 and enables you to transfer files from one machine to another. TFTP, since it uses UDP, doesn't have any authentication, so you would never use TFTP between computers across the Internet. TFTP only has five messages, and none of them allows you to see directory contents. The typical scenario for using TFTP is updating software and configurations on routers, switches, VoIP phones, and the like on a LAN, where the chances of losing packets and security risk are very small.

Terminal Emulator

A *terminal emulator* program like PuTTY (https://www.putty.org/) allows you to send commands through keystrokes from your machine to a remote router or switch and allows the router or switch to send its output to your monitor.

IP Scanner

An *IP scanner* is a tool that scans a network for IP addresses, MAC addresses, hostname, manufacturer, operating system, ports, and other information. This can help you identify both legitimate and rogue devices on a network. Angry IP Scanner (https://angryip.org/) is a popular one.

Command Line Tool

Selecting and using the right *command line tool* is a skill that aids greatly in network troubleshooting. These tools include ping, ipconfig/ifconfig/ip, nslookup/dig, traceroute/tracert, arp, netstat, hostname, route, telnet (ssh should be used instead of this CompTIA listed tool), tcpdump, and nmap.

ping

The *ping* tool is a commonly used test to see if you can communicate with another device. The ping tool uses ICMP, sending ICMP Echo requests, hoping to elicit ICMP Echo replies. By default, Windows sends four ICMP Echo requests, so you should see four replies in the output, as shown in Figure 5.3-4 (first resolving, by default, to an IPv6 address, and then being forced to resolve to an IPv4 address). The `ping` command can be followed by either an IP address (IPv4 or IPv6) or an FQDN.

However, the ping tool is not perfect. Sometimes ICMP will be filtered by the destination machine itself or a router or firewall before the destination. If you get a "Request Timed Out" message instead of ICMP Echo replies, that doesn't necessarily mean you can't communicate with the destination machine. It could be that just these probes are being blocked for security (a weak form of hindering the ability of attackers to quickly and easily discover devices) or efficiency (taking devices away from what they're normally doing just to say "Yes, I'm here").

ipconfig/ifconfig/ip

The *ipconfig* (Windows), *ifconfig* (macOS and UNIX), and *ip* (Linux) tools give you a lot of information about a computer's IP settings. Executing `ipconfig` alone only gives basic information. Executing `ipconfig /all` gives detailed information (including DNS servers, MAC

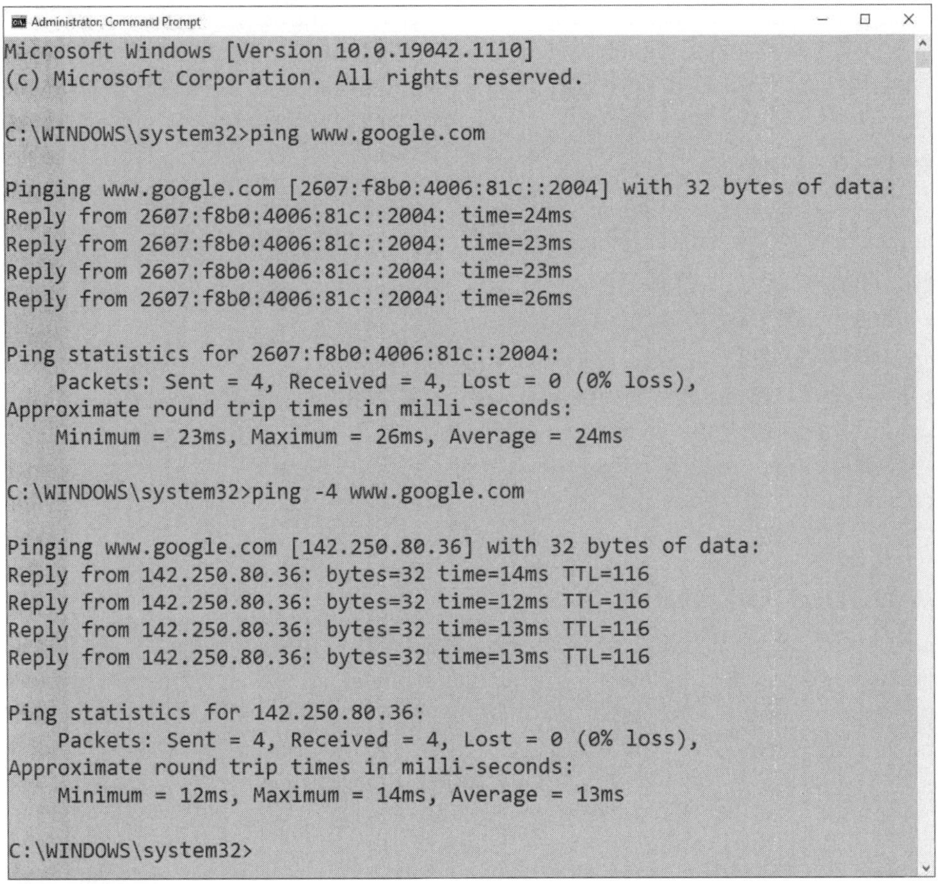
Administrator: Command Prompt
Microsoft Windows [Version 10.0.19042.1110]
(c) Microsoft Corporation. All rights reserved.
C:\WINDOWS\system32>ping www.google.com
Pinging www.google.com [2607:f8b0:4006:81c::2004] with 32 bytes of data:
Reply from 2607:f8b0:4006:81c::2004: time=24ms
Reply from 2607:f8b0:4006:81c::2004: time=23ms
Reply from 2607:f8b0:4006:81c::2004: time=23ms
Reply from 2607:f8b0:4006:81c::2004: time=26ms
Ping statistics for 2607:f8b0:4006:81c::2004:
Packets: Sent = 4, Received = 4, Lost = 0 (0% loss),
Approximate round trip times in milli-seconds:
Minimum = 23ms, Maximum = 26ms, Average = 24ms
C:\WINDOWS\system32>ping -4 www.google.com
Pinging www.google.com [142.250.80.36] with 32 bytes of data:
Reply from 142.250.80.36: bytes=32 time=14ms TTL=116
Reply from 142.250.80.36: bytes=32 time=12ms TTL=116
Reply from 142.250.80.36: bytes=32 time=13ms TTL=116
Reply from 142.250.80.36: bytes=32 time=13ms TTL=116
Ping statistics for 142.250.80.36:
Packets: Sent = 4, Received = 4, Lost = 0 (0% loss),
Approximate round trip times in milli-seconds:
Minimum = 12ms, Maximum = 14ms, Average = 13ms
C:\WINDOWS\system32>

FIGURE 5.3-4 `ping` in action

address, and more). The output can help you troubleshoot, and possibly discover, an incorrect IP address, subnet mask, default gateway IP address, DNS server IP address, and more.

Here's sample `ipconfig` output:

```
Ethernet adapter Main:

   Connection-specific DNS Suffix  . :
    IPv6 Address. . . . . . . . . . . : 2001:470:bf88:1:fc2d:aeb2:99d2:e2b4
    Temporary IPv6 Address. . . . . . : 2001:470:bf88:1:5e4:c1ef:7b30:ddd6
    Link-local IPv6 Address . . . . . : fe80::fc2d:aeb2:99d2:e2b4%8
    IPv4 Address. . . . . . . . . . . : 192.168.4.27
    Subnet Mask . . . . . . . . . . . : 255.255.255.0
    Default Gateway . . . . . . . . . : fe80::223:4ff:fe8c:b720%8
                                        192.168.4.1
```

And here's sample `ifconfig` output:

```
lo0: flags=8049<UP,LOOPBACK,RUNNING,MULTICAST> mtu 16384
        options=3<RXCSUM,TXCSUM>
        inet6 ::1 prefixlen 128
        inet 127.0.0.1 netmask 0xff000000
        inet6 fe80::1%lo0 prefixlen 64 scopeid 0x1
        nd6 options=1<PERFORMNUD>
gif0: flags=8010<POINTOPOINT,MULTICAST> mtu 1280
stf0: flags=0<> mtu 1280
en0: flags=8863<UP,BROADCAST,SMART,RUNNING,SIMPLEX,MULTICAST> mtu 1500
        options=10b<RXCSUM,TXCSUM,VLAN_HWTAGGING,AV>
        ether 3c:07:54:7a:d4:d8
        inet6 fe80::3e07:54ff:fe7a:d4d8%en0 prefixlen 64 scopeid 0x4
        inet 192.168.4.78 netmask 0xffffff00 broadcast 192.168.4.255
        inet6 2601:e::abcd:3e07:54ff:fe7a:d4d8 prefixlen 64 autoconf
        inet6 2601:e::abcd:b84e:9fad:3add:c73b prefixlen 64 autoconf temporary
        nd6 options=1<PERFORMNUD>
        media: autoselect (1000baseT <full-duplex,flow-control>)
        status: active
```

And finally, here's Linux's `ip address` output:

```
1: lo: <LOOPBACK,UP,LOWER_UP> mtu 65536 qdisc noqueue state UNKNOWN group default
    link/loopback 00:00:00:00:00:00 brd 00:00:00:00:00:00
    inet 127.0.0.1/8 scope host lo
       valid_lft forever preferred_lft forever
    inet6 ::1/128 scope host
       valid_lft forever preferred_lft forever
2: eth0: <BROADCAST,MULTICAST,UP,LOWER_UP> mtu 1500 qdisc pfifo_fast state UNKNOWN
group default qlen 1000
    link/ether 00:0c:29:e0:b2:85 brd ff:ff:ff:ff:ff:ff
    inet 192.168.4.19/24 brd 192.168.4.255 scope global eth0
       valid_lft forever preferred_lft forever
    inet6 2601:e:0:abcd:8cfb:6220:ec23:80a/64 scope global temporary dynamic
       valid_lft 86221sec preferred_lft 14221sec
    inet6 2601:e:0:abcd:20c:29ff:fee0:b285/64 scope global dynamic
       valid_lft 86221sec preferred_lft 14221sec
    inet6 fe80::20c:29ff:fee0:b285/64 scope link
       valid_lft forever preferred_lft forever
```

nslookup/dig

nslookup (name server lookup) is a DNS tool, found natively in all operating systems, that allows you to query DNS servers for resource records (discussed in Objective 1.6). *dig* is a more powerful tool, and is also cross-platform, but is not installed by default in Windows OSes. Both tools are great for DNS troubleshooting and educational purposes. dig uses the OS DNS resolver libraries, while nslookup uses its own internal ones.

Figure 5.3-5 shows nslookup returning a list of authoritative DNS servers for the rit.edu and flcc.edu domains.

Figure 5.3-6 shows dig (using DNSSEC) returning information about www.arin.net.

```
Command Prompt - nslookup                                          —    □    ×

Microsoft Windows [Version 10.0.16299.309]
(c) 2017 Microsoft Corporation. All rights reserved.

C:\Users\jswics>nslookup
Default Server:  dns.quad9.net
Address:  9.9.9.9

> set q=ns
> rit.edu.
Server:  dns.quad9.net
Address:  9.9.9.9

Non-authoritative answer:
rit.edu nameserver = accuvax.northwestern.edu
rit.edu nameserver = ns1a.rit.edu
rit.edu nameserver = ns2a.rit.edu
> flcc.edu.
Server:  dns.quad9.net
Address:  9.9.9.9

Non-authoritative answer:
flcc.edu        nameserver = ns.flcc.edu
flcc.edu        nameserver = ns4.flcc.edu
flcc.edu        nameserver = ns7.suny.edu
flcc.edu        nameserver = ns8.suny.edu
flcc.edu        nameserver = ns9.suny.edu
flcc.edu        nameserver = dns3.flcc.edu
>
```

FIGURE 5.3-5 nslookup in action

```
jonathan@kali-weissman:~$ dig +dnssec a www.arin.net.

; <<>> DiG 9.16.3-Debian <<>> +dnssec a www.arin.net.
;; global options: +cmd
;; Got answer:
;; ->>HEADER<<- opcode: QUERY, status: NOERROR, id: 62525
;; flags: qr rd ra ad; QUERY: 1, ANSWER: 2, AUTHORITY: 0, ADDITIONAL: 1

;; OPT PSEUDOSECTION:
; EDNS: version: 0, flags: do; udp: 512
;; QUESTION SECTION:
;www.arin.net.                   IN      A

;; ANSWER SECTION:
www.arin.net.           59      IN      A       199.43.0.47
www.arin.net.           59      IN      RRSIG   A 5 3 60 20200727120008 20
200713110008 44725 arin.net. Clm1VSaFGLghSQ68Wn0+SspqkmkqZLWbtT4NL29/4mys3
C+ZbKgplrn/ stj8MhqCkuxhHPeaGJNmDe02/Xi9EfG5xn3pOGr106EQdr3efLxVzwr4 Ek/tD
Z/24aeK+1Dfsic5bW/yl09NHdv5B2++B4xlPG9SfC2W/FgEXGKF gS4=

;; Query time: 36 msec
;; SERVER: 8.8.8.8#53(8.8.8.8)
;; WHEN: Mon Jul 13 23:21:04 EDT 2020
;; MSG SIZE  rcvd: 225
```

FIGURE 5.3-6 dig in action

traceroute/tracert

The ping tool is a Boolean tool. You either get a response or you don't get a response. The *traceroute/tracert* (tracert on Windows, traceroute on everything else) tool can be even more helpful than the ping tool. If a ping fails, with traceroute/tracert, you'll be able to identify where it failed. The traceroute/tracert tool will produce a list of all routers between you and a destination.

Check out Figure 5.3-7 for a tracert from my home in Rochester, NY to www.google.com.

The first column in the output lists the hop number. The second, third, and fourth columns represent the time in milliseconds it took to hear back from a router at that particular hop. Notice that there are three attempts sent for each hop. The fifth column shows either an IP address or FQDN and IP address (in square brackets) for each hop. A hop is a router/network that your packets pass through. The first hop in the list will always be your default gateway. The last "hop" in the list is the actual destination, so it isn't really a hop, even though the output makes it appear to be one. You can reach any destination machine in the world in usually 15 hops or less.

Windows tracert sends ICMP packets, while UNIX/Linux/Cisco traceroute sends UDP datagrams by default. Sometimes ICMP from a Windows tracert will be filtered, making a non-Windows traceroute more useful. Other times, the port numbers used in traceroute will be filtered, making a Windows tracert more useful.

```
Administrator: Command Prompt                                      —  □  ×
Microsoft Windows [Version 10.0.19042.1110]
(c) Microsoft Corporation. All rights reserved.

C:\WINDOWS\system32>tracert -4 www.google.com

Tracing route to www.google.com [172.217.6.196]
over a maximum of 30 hops:

  1     1 ms     1 ms     1 ms   192.168.0.1
  2     3 ms     5 ms     5 ms   100.65.88.1
  3     4 ms     4 ms     1 ms   172.16.0.3
  4    18 ms     5 ms     5 ms   172.16.0.9
  5    11 ms    15 ms    13 ms   lag-104.ear1.NewYork6.Level3.net [4.30.178.177]
  6     *         *         *    Request timed out.
  7    13 ms    12 ms    14 ms   Google-level3-100G.NewYork6.Level3.net [4.68.75.170]
  8    16 ms    14 ms    16 ms   108.170.225.2
  9    11 ms    13 ms    13 ms   108.170.237.205
 10    12 ms    14 ms    13 ms   lga25s54-in-f4.1e100.net [172.217.6.196]

Trace complete.

C:\WINDOWS\system32>
```

FIGURE 5.3-7   tracert in action

arp

The *arp* tool is used to see a device's ARP cache, which is populated by ARP requests and ARP replies, allowing hosts to find an unknown MAC address for a known IP address, as described in Objective 2.3. As shown in the following Windows output, `arp -a` displays an ARP cache. To delete all entries from the ARP cache, execute `arp -d`.

```
C:\>arp -a

Interface: 10.0.0.61 --- 0x1a
  Internet Address       Physical Address      Type
  10.0.0.1               14-c0-3e-85-54-f2     dynamic
  10.0.0.255             ff-ff-ff-ff-ff-ff     static
  224.0.0.2              01-00-5e-00-00-02     static
  224.0.0.22             01-00-5e-00-00-16     static
  224.0.0.251            01-00-5e-00-00-fb     static
  224.0.0.252            01-00-5e-00-00-fc     static
  239.255.255.250        01-00-5e-7f-ff-fa     static
  255.255.255.255        ff-ff-ff-ff-ff-ff     static
```

netstat

The *netstat* tool enables you to explore the sessions between communicating systems. Check out the netstat output in Figure 5.3-8.

Notice that each connection is represented by a Local Address and Foreign Address. Sockets are endpoints of active communication links between two programs on separate machines, represented by a combination of IP address and port number, as well as the Layer 4 protocol, TCP (Transmission Control Protocol) or UDP (User Datagram Protocol), for both the source and destination. TCP sockets are actual connections between source and destination, whereas UDP sockets are connectionless. The Local Address is on the machine you're using, while the Foreign Address is on the machine you're connected to and communicating with.

 EXAM TIP   Windows still comes with the netstat tool, but with the net-tools package replaced by the iproute2 package in the world of Linux (in fact, net-tools was deprecated in 2011), the ss tool has completely replaced the netstat tool on the Linux side. The ss tool is faster and more powerful than netstat, but is not covered on the CompTIA Network+ exam.

hostname

The *hostname* tool prints out the hostname of the current system. There are other places to check the hostname (especially in the GUI), but being able to check the hostname from the command line comes in handy, especially if you're troubleshooting over SSH. The command is also useful if you have to run a script on many systems that need access to each system's

```
Command Prompt

C:\Users\jswics>netstat -a

Active Connections

  Proto  Local Address          Foreign Address        State
  TCP    0.0.0.0:21             jweissman:0            LISTENING
  TCP    0.0.0.0:135            jweissman:0            LISTENING
  TCP    0.0.0.0:445            jweissman:0            LISTENING
  TCP    0.0.0.0:5357           jweissman:0            LISTENING
  TCP    0.0.0.0:5985           jweissman:0            LISTENING
  TCP    0.0.0.0:47001          jweissman:0            LISTENING
  TCP    0.0.0.0:49664          jweissman:0            LISTENING
  TCP    0.0.0.0:49665          jweissman:0            LISTENING
  TCP    0.0.0.0:49666          jweissman:0            LISTENING
  TCP    0.0.0.0:49667          jweissman:0            LISTENING
  TCP    0.0.0.0:49673          jweissman:0            LISTENING
  TCP    0.0.0.0:49677          jweissman:0            LISTENING
  TCP    10.80.100.3:5040       jweissman:0            LISTENING
  TCP    10.80.100.3:49670      13.89.185.175:https    ESTABLISHED
  TCP    10.80.100.3:49712      13.89.188.5:https      ESTABLISHED
  TCP    10.80.100.3:49718      65.55.44.109:https     TIME_WAIT
  TCP    127.0.0.1:14147        jweissman:0            LISTENING
  TCP    127.0.0.1:49682        jweissman:4243         SYN_SENT
  TCP    127.0.0.1:49693        jweissman:62522        ESTABLISHED
  TCP    127.0.0.1:62522        jweissman:0            LISTENING
  TCP    127.0.0.1:62522        jweissman:49693        ESTABLISHED
  TCP    [::]:21                jweissman:0            LISTENING
  TCP    [::]:135               jweissman:0            LISTENING
  TCP    [::]:445               jweissman:0            LISTENING
  TCP    [::]:5357              jweissman:0            LISTENING
  TCP    [::]:5985              jweissman:0            LISTENING
  TCP    [::]:47001             jweissman:0            LISTENING
  TCP    [::]:49664             jweissman:0            LISTENING
  TCP    [::]:49665             jweissman:0            LISTENING
  TCP    [::]:49666             jweissman:0            LISTENING
  TCP    [::]:49667             jweissman:0            LISTENING
  TCP    [::]:49673             jweissman:0            LISTENING
  TCP    [::]:49677             jweissman:0            LISTENING
  TCP    [::1]:14147            jweissman:0            LISTENING
  UDP    0.0.0.0:500            *:*
  UDP    0.0.0.0:3702           *:*
  UDP    0.0.0.0:3702           *:*
  UDP    0.0.0.0:4500           *:*
  UDP    0.0.0.0:5050           *:*
  UDP    0.0.0.0:5353           *:*
  UDP    0.0.0.0:5355           *:*
  UDP    0.0.0.0:60633          *:*
```

FIGURE 5.3-8   netstat in action

hostname, for example, to gather information about how many systems are configured and save the details in a file named for each host.

Here's sample hostname output from a Windows system:

```
C:\>hostname
jonathan-desktop
```

route

The *route* tool enables you to display and edit the local system's routing table. To show the routing table, execute `route print` or `netstat -r`.

Check out the route output in Figure 5.3-9, showing both the IPv4 and IPv6 Windows routing tables.

FIGURE 5.3-9   route print output

telnet

The *telnet* tool should never be used today under any circumstance, as all communication is transmitted in plaintext. As discussed in Objective 4.3, SSH is the protocol and tool (ssh) that should be used today to remotely connect through a command line interface to another machine, since everything is encrypted to and from the SSH server.

tcpdump

Sometimes a GUI tool like Wireshark won't work because a server has no GUI installed. In situations like this, the *tcpdump* tool is the go-to choice. This great command line tool not only enables you to monitor and filter packets in the terminal, but can also create files you can open in Wireshark for later analysis. Even better, it's installed by default on most UNIX/Linux systems.

nmap

The *nmap* tool, as discussed earlier in this objective, is the de facto standard tool for port scanning.

Basic Network Platform Commands

Basic network platform commands for Cisco routers include show interface, show config, and show route. The first two also apply to Cisco switches. The last two are general references and not the actual commands (to be explained in the sections that follow).

show interface

The *show interface* command can provide important configuration information and statistics. In Objective 3.1, this command was shown in its full version, show interfaces. However, interfaces can be shortened to anything that uniquely identifies that command from other commands in the same mode. In that context in, int, inte, inter, interf, interfa, interfac, interface, and interfaces all are valid and work the same.

show config

There is no *show config* command. The CompTIA Network+ exam objective is using that as a general category. To see the running-config file, stored in dynamic RAM, execute the show running-config command. To see the startup-config file, stored in NVRAM, execute the show startup-config command.

show route

There is no *show route* command. The CompTIA Network+ exam objective is using that as a general category. To see the router's routing table, stored in dynamic RAM, execute the show ip route command.

REVIEW

Objective 5.3: Given a scenario, use the appropriate network software tools and commands

- *Software tools* for troubleshooting include the following: WiFi analyzer, protocol analyzer/packet capture, bandwidth speed tester, port scanner, iPerf, NetFlow analyzers, TFTP server, terminal emulator, and IP scanner.

- A *WiFi analyzer* (CompTIA objectives omit the hyphen in Wi-Fi) is any device that looks for and documents all existing wireless networks in the area.

- A *protocol analyzer/packet capture* program, also known as a packet sniffer, not only intercepts and logs all the 1s and 0s moving in and out of a NIC but also shows its capture in a human-readable format, in addition to binary and hexadecimal.

- A *bandwidth speed tester* enables you to measure the data flow in a network.

- A *port scanner* is a tool that sends packets to a destination machine in order to identify the state of that machine's ports. The process of running such scans is called port scanning. From a cybersecurity perspective, port scanning helps you verify the security of systems under your control. From a cybercrime perspective, it allows attackers to find programs or services with vulnerabilities that can be exploited.

- A tool like *iPerf* (the current version is iPerf3) can actively measure the available and maximum bandwidth on a network.

- *NetFlow analyzers* were covered in Objective 1.3.

- A *Trivial File Transfer Protocol (TFTP) server* uses UDP at Layer 4 and enables you to transfer files from one machine to another.

- A *terminal emulator* program like PuTTY (https://www.putty.org/) allows you to send commands through keystrokes from your machine to a remote router or switch and allows the router or switch to send its output to your monitor.

- An *IP scanner* is a tool that scans a network for IP addresses, MAC addresses, hostname, manufacturer, operating system, ports, and other information.

- Selecting and using the right *command line tool* is a skill that aids greatly in network troubleshooting. These tools include ping, ipconfig/ifconfig/ip, nslookup/dig, traceroute/tracert, arp, netstat, hostname, route, telnet (SSH should be used instead of this CompTIA listed tool), tcpdump, and nmap.

- The *ping* tool is a commonly used test to see if you can communicate with another device.

- The *ipconfig* (Windows), *ifconfig* (macOS and UNIX), and *ip* (Linux) tools give you a lot of information about a computer's IP settings.

- *nslookup* (name server lookup) is a DNS tool, found natively in all operating systems, that allows you to query DNS servers for resource records. *dig* is a more powerful tool, and is also cross-platform, but is not installed by default in Windows OSes.

- The *traceroute/tracert* (tracert on Windows, traceroute on everything else) tool can be even more helpful than the ping tool. If a ping fails, with traceroute/tracert, you'll be able to identify where it failed. The traceroute/tracert tool will produce a list of all routers between you and a destination.
- The *arp* tool is used to see a device's ARP cache, which is populated by ARP requests and ARP replies, allowing hosts to find an unknown MAC address for a known IP address.
- The *netstat* tool enables you to explore the sessions between communicating systems.
- The *hostname* tool prints out the hostname of the current system.
- The *route* tool enables you to display and edit the local system's routing table. To show the routing table, execute `route print` or `netstat -r`.
- The *telnet* tool should never be used today under any circumstance, as all communication is transmitted in plaintext. Use the ssh tool instead.
- Sometimes a GUI tool like Wireshark won't work because a server has no GUI installed. In situations like this, *tcpdump* is the go-to choice. It not only enables you to monitor and filter packets in the terminal, but can also create files you can open in Wireshark for later analysis.
- The *nmap* tool is the de facto standard tool for port scanning.
- The `show interface` command can provide important configuration information and statistics.
- To see the running-config file, stored in dynamic RAM, execute the `show running-config` command. To see the startup-config file, stored in NVRAM, execute the `show startup-config` file.
- To see the router's routing table, stored in dynamic RAM, execute the `show ip route` command.

5.3 QUESTIONS

1. Which of the following is a popular port scanner?

   A. Nmap

   B. Wireshark

   C. ping

   D. traceroute

2. Which tool is used to see bindings of IP addresses to MAC addresses?

   A. arp

   B. netstat

   C. hostname

   D. ipconfig

3. Which of the following tools should never be used today?

   A. telnet

   B. tcpdump

   C. tracert

   D. traceroute

5.3 ANSWERS

1. **A**   Nmap, a port scanner and more, is one of the most often used tools for both pentesters and cybercriminals.

2. **A**   The arp tool shows what your system has learned through ARP requests and replies.

3. **A**   The ssh tool, which uses encryption, replaced the telnet tool, which transmits everything in plaintext, a huge security vulnerability.

Objective 5.4 Given a scenario, troubleshoot common wireless connectivity issues

Wireless is everywhere. It's in our phones and our laptops. It's at home, work, and in schools. Wireless is so transparent and handy we tend to forget that wireless isn't a single technology. There are a number of technologies that collectively make up wireless networking.

Because the networking signal is freed from wires, you'll sometimes hear the term "unbounded media" to describe wireless networking. As such, troubleshooting can be a little more difficult. However, for all their disconnected goodness, wireless networks share more similarities than differences with wired networks. With the exception of the first two OSI layers, wireless networks use the same protocols as wired networks. The components that differ are the type of media—radio waves instead of cables—and the protocols for transmitting and accessing data. Different wireless networking solutions have come and gone in the past, but the wireless networking market these days is dominated by the various IEEE 802.11 wireless standards and Wi-Fi technologies and protocols based on 802.11 standards.

Cross-Reference

Wireless was covered in Objective 2.4. This objective just deals with the troubleshooting of common wireless connectivity issues.

Specifications and Limitations

Wireless technologies, like their wired counterparts, also have *specifications and limitations* in regard to throughput, speed, and distance. However, included in that list for wireless technologies are also received signal strength indication (RSSI) signal strength and effective isotropic radiated power (EIRP)/power settings.

Throughput

In regard to the many speeds listed for 802.11, you need to appreciate that wireless networking has a tremendous amount of overhead and latency. Access points (APs) send out almost continuous streams of packets that do nothing more than advertise their existence or maintain connections. Wireless devices may sometimes stall due to processing or timeouts. The end result is that only a percentage of the total *throughput* is achieved in real data bits getting to the applications that need them.

Speed

802.11n was the first wireless standard with a theoretical *speed* of 100 Mbps. 802.11ac can go up to 1 Gbps, while 802.11ax speeds can approach 10 Gbps!

EXAM TIP   As mentioned in Objective 5.2, speed and throughput are synonyms. CompTIA lists the terms separately here in this objective and in Objective 5.2, though.

Distance

Wireless networking *distance* (range) is hard to define. You'll see most descriptions listed with qualifiers such as "around 150 feet" and "about 300 feet." Wireless distance is greatly affected by environmental factors. Interference from other wireless devices and solid objects affects range.

Received Signal Strength Indication (RSSI) Signal Strength

802.11 is a low-power radio and has a limited range. If the AP doesn't have enough power, you'll have signal attenuation and your device won't be able to access the wireless network. All of the 802.11 standards have distance limitations; exceeding those limitations will reduce performance. Certainly, a quick answer is to move closer to the AP, but there are a number of issues that cause power levels to drop too low to connect beyond the obvious "you're too far away" from the AP.

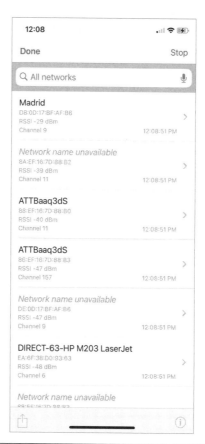

FIGURE 5.4-1 AirPort Utility showing RSSI strengths

Manufacturers use scales called *received signal strength indication (RSSI) signal strength* to show the signal between an AP and a receiver. Every manufacturer uses different RSSI numbers, but they usually show as "how many bars" you have. Running the Wi-Fi Scan feature of the AirPort Utility app in my iPhone, for example, shows my WLAN RSSI as –29 dB, whereas my neighbor's WLAN shows as –40 dB (Figure 5.4-1). (We live close together in my neighborhood.) The closer to 0 dB, the better the signal. The little symbol for Wi-Fi strength shows full strength to my WLAN.

Effective Isotropic Radiated Power (EIRP)/Power Settings

The *effective isotropic radiated power (EIRP)/power settings* refers to the signal strength coming out of an antenna. With a non-directional antenna, the signal in any direction will be the same. Use the EIRP to measure the relative signal strength coming out of a directional antenna, comparing the "strong" end signal with a omnidirectional antenna.

Considerations

Troubleshooting common wireless connectivity issues includes several important *considerations* that are not relevant when troubleshooting cable connectivity issues, such as antennas, channel utilization, AP association time, and the site survey.

Antennas

Important considerations when troubleshooting wireless connectivity issues are the placement, type, and polarization of *antennas*.

Placement

All access points have antennas that radiate the 802.11 signal to the clients, so the optimal location for an AP depends on the area you want to cover and whether you care if the signal bleeds out beyond the borders. You also need to use antennas that provide enough signal and push that signal in the proper direction and alignment.

AP antennas come in many shapes and sizes. In the early days it was common to see APs with two antennas. Some APs have only one antenna and some (802.11n, 802.11ac, and 802.11ax) have more than two. Even an AP that doesn't seem to have antennas is simply hiding them inside the case.

Optimal antenna *placement* varies according to the space to fill and security concerns. You can use the site survey and the same wireless analyzer tools to find dead spots, odd corners, and so on. Use the right kind of antenna on each WAP to fill in the space.

Type

There are three basic types of antennas common in 802.11 networks: omnidirectional, unidirectional, and patch. Each type offers different solutions for coverage of specific wireless network setups. Plus, the signals emanating from the antennas have a feature called polarization that needs to be considered. These antenna types are covered in Objective 2.4. Troubleshooting wireless connectivity issues can be done first by understanding which antenna *type* is being used. For example, an omnidirectional antenna, which radiates signal outward from the access point in all directions, might be used whereas a directional/unidirectional antenna, which focuses a radio wave into a beam of sorts, is called for elsewhere.

Polarization

All radio signals have a property called *polarization*, which describes the orientation of the radio waves. The polarization of a Wi-Fi signal depends on the antenna, though linear polarization (meaning the waves all oscillate in the same direction) is the most common. In addition, these polarized antennas and emitted signals can be oriented in several ways, such as vertically, horizontally, and slanted (like a 45-degree angle).

When you adjust a Wi-Fi antenna or rotate the device it is attached to in physical space, you effectively change the angle (orientation) of its signal. When the receiving antenna aligns with the polarization of the transmitter, this creates the strongest signal. The more out of alignment between receiver and transmitter, the weaker the signal. Misaligned polarization can lower a network's effective range and throughput.

If Ann wants to connect two buildings in her organization via Wi-Fi, with both antennas aligned vertically, the connection will be strong and solid. On the other hand, if she sets one antenna to vertical and the other to horizontal, a 90-degree difference, the signal strength would drop by 18 decibels. Every 3 dB equates to a doubling (or halving) of power, so −18 dB represents a 98.4 percent loss in power.

Channel Utilization

You can use wireless scanning tools to check for wireless *channel utilization*. These are software tools that give you metrics and reports about nearby devices and which one is connected to which AP. These tools enable you to discover overworked APs, saturated areas, and so on, so you can deploy APs to optimize your network.

Wireless networks send out radio signals on the 2.4-, 5.0-, or 6.0-GHz spectrum using one of a number of discrete channels. In early wireless networks, a big part of the setup was to determine the channels used nearby in order to avoid them. In modern wireless networks, we rarely adjust channels manually anymore. Instead we rely on powerful algorithms built into APs to locate the least congested channels automatically. The bigger challenge today is the preexistence of many Wi-Fi networks with lots of clients, creating high device density environments. You need a wireless solution that handles many users running on the few wireless frequencies available.

AP Association Time

Association describes the connection between an AP and a wireless client, a part of the typical 802.11 process. Issues like misconfigurations or authentication servers not being reachable can cause *AP association time* problems, which result in very slow connection times or forced disassociation, meaning a client abruptly loses the Wi-Fi connection.

A few years ago, a popular Wi-Fi manufacturer upgraded AP firmware, which worked great for most users. Some users, however, immediately started complaining that the association process—that previously happened in a couple of seconds—took minutes and often failed altogether. Another firmware upgrade fixed the issue, but didn't quite fix the disgruntled users!

Site Survey

Installing and configuring a Wi-Fi network requires a number of discrete steps. You should start with a *site survey* to determine any obstacles (existing wireless, interference, and so on) you need to overcome and to determine the best location for your access points. You'll need to install one or more access points, and then configure both the access point(s) and wireless clients. Finally, you should put the network to the test, verifying that it works as you intended.

The main components for creating a site survey are a floor plan of the area you wish to provide with wireless and a site survey tool such as NETSCOUT's AirMagnet Survey Pro (Figure 5.4-2). Wireless survey tools help you discover any other wireless networks in the

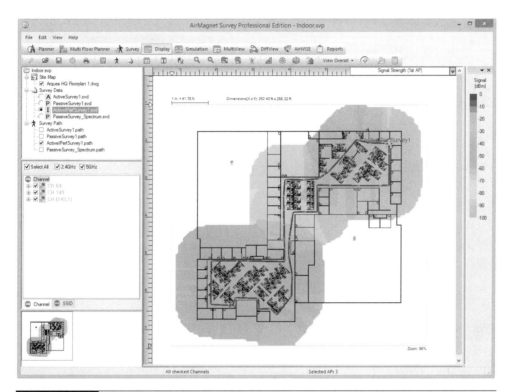

FIGURE 5.4-2 AirMagnet Survey Pro

area and will integrate a drawing of your floor plan with interference sources clearly marked. This enables you to get the right kind of hardware you need and makes it possible to get the proper network coverage.

Discovering any wireless network signals other than your own in your space enables you to set both the SSID and channel to avoid networks that overlap. One part of any good site survey is a wireless analyzer. A wireless analyzer (also known as a Wi-Fi analyzer) is any device that looks for and documents all existing wireless networks in the area. Wireless analyzers are handy tools that are useful for diagnosing wireless network issues and conducting site surveys. You can get dedicated, hand-held wireless analyzer tools or you can run site survey software on a laptop or mobile wireless device. Wireless survey tools like AirMagnet Survey Pro always include an analyzer as well. Figure 5.4-3 shows a screenshot of Acrylic Wi-Fi, a free and popular wireless analyzer.

There are plenty of tools like AirMagnet Survey Pro to support a wireless survey. All good survey utilities share some common ways to report their findings. One of the most powerful reports that they generate is called a heat map. A heat map is nothing more than a graphical representation of the RF sources on your site, using different colors to represent the intensity of the signal. Figure 5.4-4 shows a sample heat map.

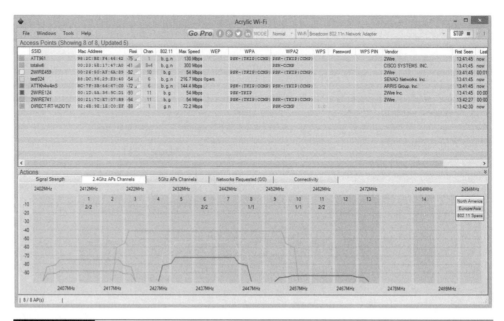

FIGURE 5.4-3 Acrylic Wi-Fi

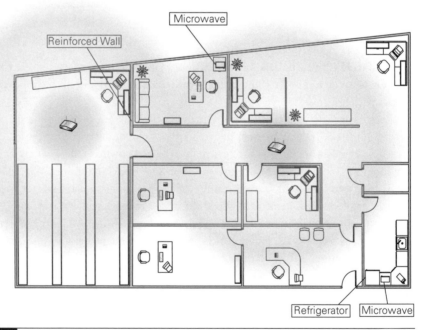

FIGURE 5.4-4 Site survey with heat map

Common Issues

Common issues for wireless connectivity include interference, antenna cable attenuation/ signal loss, RF attenuation/signal loss, wrong SSID, incorrect passphrase, encryption protocol mismatch, insufficient wireless coverage, captive portal issues, and client disassociation issues.

Interference

It might seem like overkill in a small network, but any network beyond a simple one should have a sketched-out site survey with any potential *interference* sources clearly marked. Refrigerators, reinforced walls, metal plumbing, microwave ovens—all of these can create horrible dead spots where your network radio wave can't easily penetrate. With a difficult or high-interference area, you might need to move up to 802.11ac or 802.11ax equipment with three or four antennas just to get the kind of coverage you want. Or you might need to plan a multiple AP network to wipe out the dead zones. A proper site survey gives you the first tool for implementing a network that works.

Channel Overlap

Every Wi-Fi network communicates on a channel, a portion of the available spectrum. For the 2.4-GHz band, the 802.11 standard defines 14 channels of 20 MHz each (that's the channel bandwidth), but different countries limit exactly which channels may be used. In the United States, an AP using the 2.4-GHz band may only use channels 1 through 11, which have *channel overlap*. Therefore, two nearby APs should not use close channels like 6 and 7. Most APs use channels 1, 6, or 11 because they don't overlap. You can fine-tune a network by changing the channels on APs to avoid overlap with other nearby APs. This capability is especially important in environments with many wireless networks sharing the same physical space.

The 5-GHz and 6-GHz bands offer many more channels than the 2.4-GHz band. In general, there are around 40 different channels in the spectrums, and different countries have wildly different rules for which channels may or may not be used. The versions of 802.11 that use the 5- and 6-GHz bands use automatic channel switching, so from a setup standpoint we don't worry about channels when we talk about 5-GHz and 6-GHz 802.11 standards.

Antenna Cable Attenuation/Signal Loss

Antenna cable attenuation/signal loss is caused by inadequate cable connecting an antenna to a WAP. The fix is to simply use a better cable. As a cable run gets longer, the attenuation increases, and the signal becomes weaker.

RF Attenuation/Signal Loss

Glass is notorious for bending radio waves as the waves pass through them. What may look like a straight line between an AP and client suddenly may run into problems if a glass door is placed between them. This phenomenon is called refraction.

Different materials may cause more than one of these effects. A concrete wall may both absorb and reflect radio, whereas a metal framed door with glass inserts may both reflect and refract a radio wave.

Physical obstacles can cause *RF attenuation/signal loss*, as radio waves pass through different mediums. Air and rain can even cause this!

Physical effects prevent clear, strong radio signals from reaching their target devices. These attenuation effects are different in every case and therefore tricky to predict during a site survey, requiring serious troubleshooting after the installation of a wireless network. A solid concrete wall is easy to predict as a problem (and avoid with proper AP placement, for example). A room full of thick-walled, metal-framed room dividers might not be as easy to identify during a survey and won't come to light as a physical problem until the users start complaining about slow connections.

When a tech suspects a physical problem, the first step is to perform another site survey. Find physical barriers that prevent hosts at specific locations that need good access. Often a quick look-around is all that's needed to identify and move a physical barrier or to move or add APs or antennas as needed. Secondly, the tech can install APs with multiple antennas, creating multipath.

Wrong SSID

It's easy to access the *wrong SSID*, so being aware and careful of the SSID you click is important. Some 802.11 devices are notorious for moving their list of discovered SSIDs in such a way that you think you are clicking one SSID when you are actually accidentally clicking the wrong one. The only fix to this is to practice diligence when logging onto a new SSID. For example, who hasn't seen SSIDs such as the infamous "attwifi"? This SSID is AT&T's attempt to use all of its clients as hotspots. Sadly, it's a simple process to create an evil twin SSID (described in Objective 4.2) to mimic the attwifi SSID, and get otherwise unsuspecting people to log into it.

Manually entering an SSID can obviously result in a typo. Luckily, in these cases your typo won't accidentally land you onto another SSID. You'll just get an error.

Incorrect Passphrase

If you've automatically accessed a particular SSID and entered the *incorrect passphrase*, you're not going to connect. Entering the wrong passphrase is the classic no-errors-but-won't-work issue. In older operating systems, you often would only get one chance to enter a key, and if you failed, your only clue was that your client got an APIPA/zeroconf address. More modern operating systems say something clearer, such as a message like "wrong passphrase." Pretty much every wireless NIC is set to DHCP, and if you don't have the right password your client won't get past the AP to talk to anything on the network, including the DHCP server.

Encryption Protocol Mismatch

Entering the wrong encryption type, an *encryption protocol mismatch*, is rare, and only happens when you set up a wireless connection manually.

Insufficient Wireless Coverage

The Received signal strength indication (RSSI) signal strength section, earlier in this objective, discussed the fact that if an access point doesn't have enough power, you'll have signal attenuation and your device won't be able to access the wireless network. That is what CompTIA refers to now with the term *insufficient wireless coverage*.

Captive Portal Issues

Many public facilities, like airports and coffee shops, employ a captive portal to control access to their public Wi-Fi networks. An attempt to connect to the network opens a Web browser that insists you follow the terms of service, acceptable use policy, and more. Captive portals can also be used to control bandwidth. *Captive portal issues* include higher security standards in your Web browser that can block this content, and in essence, your access to the network.

Client Disassociation Issues

Client disassociation issues are similar to deauthentication (they even use the same frame type), as discussion in Objective 4.2. The difference is that deauthentication is a notification, not a request. Deauthentication automatically causes disassociation and can't be refused unless management frame protection is implemented.

When a client is associated to an access point, a disassociation frame can be sent by either side at any time. A client may send a disassociation frame to the access point when it starts roaming. An access point can send a disassociation frame when clients send invalid parameter values.

REVIEW

Objective 5.4: Given a scenario, troubleshoot common wireless connectivity issues

- Wireless technologies, like their wired counterparts, also have *specifications and limitations* in regard to throughput, speed, and distance.
- Only a percentage of the total *throughput* is achieved in real data bits getting to the applications that need them.
- 802.11n was the first wireless standard with a theoretical *speed* of 100 Mbps. 802.11ac can go up to 1 Gbps, while 802.11ax speeds can approach 10 Gbps.
- Wireless *distance* is greatly affected by environmental factors. Interference from other wireless devices and solid objects affects range.
- Manufacturers use scales called *received signal strength indication (RSSI) signal strength* to show the signal between an AP and a receiver.

- The effective isotropic radiated power (EIRP)/power settings is the signal strength coming out of an antenna.

- Troubleshooting common wireless connectivity issues includes several important *considerations* that are not relevant when troubleshooting cable connectivity issues, such as antennas, channel utilization, AP association time, and the site survey. Important considerations when troubleshooting wireless connectivity issues are the placement, type, and polarization of *antennas*.

- The big considerations for *antennas* include placement, type, and polarization.

- Optimal antenna *placement* varies according to the space to fill and security concerns.

- Troubleshooting wireless connectivity issues can be done first by understanding which antenna *type* is being used. For example, an omnidirectional antenna, which radiates signal outward from the access point in all directions might be used where a directional/unidirectional antenna, which focuses a radio wave into a beam of sorts is called for.

- All radio signals have a property called *polarization*, which describes the orientation of the radio waves.

- You can use wireless scanning tools to check for wireless *channel utilization*.

- Issues like misconfigurations or authentication servers not being reachable can cause *AP association time* problems, which result in very slow connection times or forced disassociation, meaning a client abruptly loses the Wi-Fi connection.

- Installing and configuring a Wi-Fi network requires a number of discrete steps. You should start with a *site survey* to determine any obstacles (existing wireless, interference, and so on) you need to overcome and to determine the best location for your access points.

- *Common issues* for wireless connectivity include interference, antenna cable attenuation/ signal loss, RF attenuation/signal loss, wrong SSID, incorrect passphrase, encryption protocol mismatch, insufficient wireless coverage, captive portal issues, and client disassociation issues.

- It might seem like overkill in a small network, but any network beyond a simple one should have a sketched-out site survey with any potential *interference* sources clearly marked.

- In the United States, an AP using the 2.4-GHz band may only use channels 1 through 11, which have *channel overlap*. Therefore, two nearby APs should not use close channels like 6 and 7.

- Antenna cable attenuation/signal loss is caused by inadequate cable connecting an antenna to a WAP. The fix is to simply use a better cable. As a cable run gets longer, the attenuation increases, and the signal becomes weaker.

- Physical obstacles can cause *RF attenuation/signal loss*, as radio waves pass through different mediums. Air and rain can even cause this.
- It's easy to access the *wrong SSID*, so being aware and careful of the SSID you click is important.
- If you've automatically accessed a particular SSID and entered the *incorrect passphrase*, you're not going to connect.
- Entering the wrong encryption type, an *encryption protocol mismatch*, is rare, and only happens when you set up a wireless connection manually.
- If the AP doesn't have enough power, you'll have signal attenuation and your device won't be able to access the wireless network with this *insufficient wireless coverage*.

5.4 QUESTIONS

1. What is RSSI used for?
   - **A.** Measuring throughput
   - **B.** Measuring speed
   - **C.** Measuring distance
   - **D.** Measuring signal strength between an AP and receiver

2. Which of the following is not a consideration for antennas?
   - **A.** Channel overlap
   - **B.** Placement
   - **C.** Type
   - **D.** Polarization

3. Which of the following is the least likely to be the cause of a wireless connectivity issue?
   - **A.** Incorrect passphrase
   - **B.** Insufficient wireless coverage
   - **C.** Encryption protocol mismatch
   - **D.** Captive portal issues

5.4 ANSWERS

1. **D**   Manufacturers use scales called received signal strength indication (RSSI) signal strength to show the signal between an AP and a receiver.

2. **A**   Channel overlap is a configuration issue, not related to antennas themselves.

3. **C**   Entering the wrong encryption type, an encryption protocol mismatch, is rare, and only happens when you set up a wireless connection manually.

Objective 5.5   Given a scenario, troubleshoot general networking issues

Sometimes an issue you're troubleshooting won't fit into the common cable connectivity issues category. It might not even fit into the wireless connectivity issues category. You need to be prepared to troubleshoot general networking issues.

Considerations

Considerations when troubleshooting general network issues include device configuration review, routing tables, interface status, VLAN assignment, and network performance baselines.

Device Configuration Review

Whenever you run into network trouble, it's a good idea to perform a *device configuration review*, as there is a possibility that someone, or maybe even just an update, has changed a device configuration recently. This might've been a documented change, or maybe someone else was trying to troubleshoot a different problem and forgot to revert or document the change. If a user had sufficient permissions on the system, they may have fiddled with settings themselves to try and get things working again. Execute the `show running-config` command mentioned in Objective 5.3 to see.

There's a risk here that someone trying to fix a problem has changed the settings to something that won't work no matter what you do. Especially with user devices, make sure they are configured correctly before you start looking at the network itself.

Routing Tables

If you are troubleshooting a Layer 3 problem, consider the *routing tables* of the various routers, firewalls, and other devices that the packets are moving through. Checking the routing tables directly enables you to see how the packets will be forwarded through the network. This can help point to a direct problem with the entries in the routing tables. For example, a router might not have an entry for a specific destination network. Without a default route, traffic to an unknown destination network will be dropped by the router. Also, you might notice that the packets are taking a path through the network that you didn't know about.

Execute the `show ip route` command mentioned in Objective 5.3 to see.

Interface Status

While it seems simple enough, checking the *interface status* of the systems involved can help resolve many networking issues quickly. So instead of looking first for a more complex cause to your problem, don't forget to consider the interface status of the devices you're troubleshooting. As discussed in Objective 3.1, you want each interface to have an up/up status.

Execute the `show interfaces` command mentioned in Objective 5.3 to see.

VLAN Assignment

Like the other considerations just described, doing a quick review of the *VLAN assignment* is good practice when troubleshooting. You could be dealing with a simple incorrect port assignment, or more complex problems. While this will be most important when troubleshooting Layer 2 issues, VLAN assignment also plays a role is problems further up the OSI stack.

Network Performance Baselines

One of the best things you can do to keep a network in good shape is to invest time now to set up performance monitoring via an NMS (discussed with SNMP in Objective 3.1) or take periodic benchmarks and learn what kind of performance and access patterns are normal when all is well. When vague complaints come in regarding speed or reliability, having access to historical *network performance baselines* can be the difference between knowing where to look and having to let the problem fester until you have enough user reports to connect the dots. The baselines may even help you proactively spot failing or misconfigured devices, catch compromised hosts up to no good, or plan for extra capacity before performance falls off a cliff.

Common Issues

There are *common issues* that every network tech should be aware of when troubleshooting general network issues. Knowing about these common issues allows you to zone in on specific problems early in the troubleshooting process.

Collisions

While *collisions*—multiple devices transmitting on the same wire at the same time—once plagued wired networks, this problem was eliminated when half-duplex technologies were replaced with full-duplex technologies and CSMA/CD went away. However, collisions can still be seen on networks today if a misconfiguration took place.

Continuing the discussion of duplexing issues from Objective 5.2, an incorrect manual configuration could result in a duplex mismatch, where one side of a cable connection is operating at half-duplex with CSMA/CD, detecting collisions, and the other side is operating at full-duplex without CSMA/CD, not even concerned with collisions.

The half-duplex side will incorrectly think collisions are happening, and will stop transmitting, implement the backoff timer and wait, resend the frames, and do that all again many times. Needless to say, this will result in poor performance and latency. Check the speed/duplex settings, as described in Objective 2.3, and find the interfaces that are not set to auto.

Broadcast Storm

A *broadcast storm* is the result of one or more devices sending a nonstop flurry of broadcast frames/packets on a network. The first sign of a broadcast storm is when every computer on the broadcast domain suddenly can't connect to the rest of the network. There are usually no clues other than network applications freezing or presenting "can't connect to..." types of error messages. Every activity light on every node is blinking so wildly that they appear like they're solidly on. Computers on other broadcast domains/networks/subnets/LANs, though, work perfectly well.

The trick is to isolate the problem. You need to break down the network quickly by unplugging devices until you can find the one node causing trouble. Getting a packet analyzer to work can be difficult, but you should at least try. If you can scoop up one packet, you'll know what node is causing the trouble. The second the bad node is disconnected, the network should return to normal. However, if you have a lot of machines to deal with and a bunch of users who can't get on the network yelling at you, you'll need help. Call a supervisor to get support to solve the crisis as quickly as possible.

Duplicate MAC Address

Incorrect configuration of any number of options in devices can stop a device from accessing nearby resources. These problems can be simple to fix, although tracking down the culprit can take time and patience.

A condition where more than one device claims to have the same MAC address is a *duplicate MAC address* problem. It's rare, and can happen when working with virtual machines or as a result of a manufacturing error. Either put the devices (and their NICs with the MAC addresses) on different subnets, configure a new MAC address through software, or swap out NICs to avoid duplication.

Duplicate IP Address

One of the most obvious configuration errors occurs when you're duplicating machines and using static IP addresses. As soon as you configure a *duplicate IP address*, an IP address already assigned to a device on the same network, problems will arise. No two computers can have the same IP address on a broadcast domain. The fix for the problem is to change the IP address on the new machine either to an unused static IP address or to set it to use DHCP.

Multicast Flooding

Related to broadcast storms, though not as destructive, is *multicast flooding*. Multicast is a Layer 3 technology (while each Layer 3 multicast IP address will have a corresponding Layer 2 multicast MAC address). Switches send multicast traffic to all ports in the broadcast domain, unless the multicast is pruned. This becomes a problem if you are using multicast for things like high-bandwidth video. In that case, you can see lots of traffic to every host on the LAN, even if those hosts aren't joined to a particular multicast group (and don't care about the traffic).

To mitigate problems with multicast flooding, you can move all the systems that need to participate in the multicast group to their own VLAN or subnet. This will minimize the flooding to hosts on that broadcast domain. However, this still can saturate any trunk lines that carry that VLAN's traffic.

Another approach to mitigating multicast issues is to enable IGMP snooping on your switches. This will prune multicast traffic and let your switches only forward multicast traffic to ports with hosts that are members of a multicast group. IGMP snooping works by letting the switch "listen" for when the host joins a multicast group, and only then will the switch forward frames from that multicast to that host.

Similarly, an IGMP filter on a router can prevent multicasts from entering a LAN if no devices on that LAN are subscribed to that multicast.

Asymmetrical Routing

Asymmetrical routing, when packets take one path to their destination but the response takes a different path back, isn't necessarily a problem for everyone all the time, but it could still cause network issues. Some networks intentionally use asymmetric routes for performance reasons, but the different routes may confuse security and NAT devices that assume they'll see both halves of a symmetric conversation—or mislead you about the nature of a connectivity problem that is only impacting packets sent in one direction.

Diagnosing a problem asymmetric route often involves using packet captures and traceroute/tracert to determine how the packets are actually flowing through the network. Some advanced networking devices will also detect asymmetric routes automatically and give you a heads-up about potential issues.

Switching Loops

Switching loops (also known as bridging loops) occur when multiple switches are connected together in such a way that causes a circular path to appear. In cases like this, unnecessary duplicate copies of a frame are sent in different directions, taxing bandwidth and device processing. Switching loops are rare because switches use Spanning Tree Protocol (STP), which eliminates loops before they can even form. However, configuration errors can disable parts or all of STP, causing switching loops. The symptoms are identical to a broadcast storm: every computer on the broadcast domain can no longer access the network and link lights are constantly blinking.

The good part about switching loops is that they rarely take place on a well-running network. Someone had to break something, and that means someone, somewhere is messing with the switch configuration. Escalate the problem, and get the team to help you find the person making changes to the switches. Then, reverse the changes.

Routing Loops

Individual routers will happily forward packets down a path that they think is correct, even if that path will actually lead them back around to a router they have already passed through, causing *routing loops*. Once this happens, the packets are doomed to either literally time out, or get dropped after the packet takes as many hops as its TTL value in the IP header allows.

Routing loops are generally a misconfiguration problem between routers, through a manual configuration. As for switching loops, find out who made the incorrect changes and reverse the changes.

Different dynamic routing protocols have different features that attempt to keep these loops from developing in the first place.

Rogue DHCP Server

A *rogue DHCP server* attack was explained in Objective 4.2. As mentioned in Objective 4.3, enabling DHCP snooping is a great way to prevent this attack.

To summarize, a rogue DHCP server is an unauthorized DHCP server that will answer a DHCP Discover with a DHCP Offer containing the normal information given out to the clients in that autonomous system, with one small difference: it lists itself as the default gateway! Now, all remote traffic will be sent directly to the attacker, who can sniff the packets, perform an on-path attack, and perform reconnaissance. This can be mitigated with DHCP Snooping, which drops DHCP Offers coming from an untrusted, since there should be no legitimate DHCP servers connected to that port. Furthermore, the switch port automatically shuts down.

DHCP Scope Exhaustion

DHCP scope exhaustion can be caused by a finite number of available host IP addresses being leased by clients, leaving other potential clients no available IP addresses to lease. For example, on a /24 network, there are 254 usable host addresses, which means if all 254 addresses are currently leased, no other DHCP clients can get an IP address from the DCHP server.

If a DHCP server has a finite number of host addresses to lease to clients, what happens when that number is reached, and a new client sends a DHCP Discover? That client is out of luck. The DHCP server has no more addresses to give out. Normally, the way IP networks are designed and provisioned, this shouldn't be an issue. However, this can result from new network uses or changes in implementations. If a company sets up an imaging bench and runs through 50–100 devices a day, using a 7-day lease, the company could exhaust its address pool. Issues could also arise when a large number of visitors enter and exit a company in a short amount of time.

DHCP scope exhaustion can also be the result of an attack by an attacker who sends an overwhelming number of DHCP Discovers with random spoofed MAC addresses. The DORA process will complete for all of those spoofed MAC addresses, and the DHCP server will be fresh out of IP addresses to lease to legitimate clients. That's a form of a denial of service (DoS) attack known as a DHCP starvation attack, because there are no more IP addresses for clients to "eat."

Cross-Reference

Objectives 1.6 and 4.3 have additional DORA coverage.

Tools like Gobbler, Yersinia, and Metasploit automate DHCP starvation attacks. Besides a DoS attack, a DHCP starvation attack can be used in tandem with a rogue DHCP server. Deplete the corporate DHCP server's IP address pool, and clients will have no choice but to accept the rogue DHCP server's parameters. To mitigate this attack, when a tool like Gobbler, which uses different source MAC addresses for each DHCP Discover, is used, configure port security (discussed in Objective 4.3 as a mitigation technique for a CAM overflow attack).

However, if the DHCP starvation attack uses the same MAC address in the Ethernet frame, and simply changes the MAC address in the DHCP payload, port security won't help, because as far as the switch goes, it's one source MAC address sending traffic into the port. In this case, mitigate the attack with DHCP snooping (discussed in Objective 4.3 as a mitigation technique for a rogue DHCP server attack), which will be configured to verify that the source MAC address in the frame matches the MAC address in the DHCP payload.

IP Setting Issues

Various *IP setting issues*, like an incorrect gateway, incorrect subnet mask, incorrect IP address, and incorrect DNS, can be common issues you'll be troubleshooting.

Incorrect Gateway

If the default gateway address for a client (configured statically or dynamically) is incorrect, an *incorrect gateway* issue, the client won't be able to send traffic off of its subnet.

Incorrect Subnet Mask

An *incorrect subnet mask* will stop even local traffic from the client, since it will incorrectly deduce that destinations on the same subnet are on different subnets. Furthermore, remote traffic won't be able to be sent either, since the client won't be able to reach its default gateway, which now won't be on the same subnet (per the incorrect mask) as the client.

Incorrect IP Address

An *incorrect IP address* that's not in the valid range of host addresses for the subnet will cause all communication to fail, as once again the host will not be able to reach any local device, including its default gateway.

Incorrect DNS

A client with *incorrect DNS* server IP addresses won't be able to resolve FQDNs into their corresponding IP addresses, and thus will not be able to access devices by name. This may be more subtle, such as only internal DNS names failing, if the address is a valid DNS server, just not the right one.

 **EXAM TIP** Being able to ping by IP address but not by name is indicative of a DNS issue.

Missing Route

A router misconfiguration can lead to a *missing route* that makes some destination networks unreachable for certain networks.

Low Optical Link Budget

Installing and troubleshooting fiber adds a few wrinkles that we don't have to worry about with copper cable. One of those wrinkles is the optical link budget, which is the difference between the maximum power a transceiver can transmit and the minimum power it needs to receive a signal. This budget, basically, is how much the signal can attenuate before you run into trouble. A *low optical link budget* indicates that too much power has been lost.

Attenuation is affected by factors such as the number and type of connectors, cable length and quality, and how many times it is spliced or patched. Assuming your network was properly designed and installed, you should not run into link budget issues. Otherwise, these issues might accumulate until eventually the light is too dim for the receiver on the other end to cleanly detect the signal, at which point it may start having frame errors or completely lose connectivity.

If you suspect a problem, a good place to start is with the diagnostics built into more advanced switches. These diagnostics will tell you about the module's minimum, maximum, and current transmit/receive power. If you have a network monitoring system set up, it should trigger an alarm if any of these thresholds are exceeded. Here is the diagnostics output from my Juniper switch:

```
Virtual chassis port: vcp-255/2/3
    Laser bias current                        :  6.204 mA
    Laser output power                        :  0.3300 mW / -4.81 dBm
    Module temperature                        :  30 degrees C / 86 degrees F
    Module voltage                            :  3.3460 V
    Receiver signal average optical power     :  0.3190 mW / -4.96 dBm
    . . .
    Laser output power high alarm threshold   :  1.9950 mW / 3.00 dBm
    Laser output power low alarm threshold    :  0.1170 mW / -9.32 dBm
    Laser output power high warning threshold :  1.5840 mW / 2.00 dBm
    Laser output power low warning threshold  :  0.1860 mW / -7.30 dBm
    Laser rx power high alarm threshold       :  1.9953 mW / 3.00 dBm
    Laser rx power low alarm threshold        :  0.0490 mW / -13.10 dBm
    Laser rx power high warning threshold     :  1.5849 mW / 2.00 dBm
    Laser rx power low warning threshold      :  0.0776 mW / -11.10 dBm
```

Beyond what is built into the switch, you'll want to turn to dedicated hardware diagnostic devices such as optical power meters and fiber inspectors. These tools can be used by technicians to help hunt down the source of any attenuation issues in the fiber run.

Certificate Issues

TLS certificates have expiration dates and companies need to maintain them properly. If you get complaints from clients that the company Web site is giving their browsers untrusted TLS certificate errors, chances are that the certificate has expired. The fix for these *certificate issues* is pretty simple—update the certificate. Keep in mind, though, that depending on security settings, this fix can prevent communications or authentication if the certificates are used for VPNs or other authentication systems.

Hardware Failure

A *hardware failure* can certainly make a network device unreachable. Fall back on your Comp-TIA A+ training for troubleshooting. Check the link lights on the NIC. Try another NIC if the machine seems functional in every other aspect.

Pay attention to link lights when you have a hardware failure. The network connection light-emitting diode (LED) status indicators—link lights—can quickly point to a connectivity issue. Try known-good cables/NICs if you run into this issue.

Host-Based/Network-Based Firewall Settings

Incorrect *host-based/network-based firewall settings* could produce false positives, where legitimate traffic is filtered, and false negatives, where malicious traffic is let through. After configuring a host-based on network-based firewall, run some tests to ensure the configuration is as it's supposed to be in terms of permitting and denying.

Blocked Services, Ports, or Addresses

A firewall or ACL might be incorrectly configured, which can lead to *blocked services, ports, or addresses* that shouldn't be blocked.

Incorrect VLAN

Configuring a port to be a member of an *incorrect VLAN* can cause the device plugged into that port to lose some or all network access.

DNS Issues

If you can ping a file server by IP address but not by name, this points to *DNS issues*. Similarly, if a computer fails in discovering neighboring devices/nodes, like connecting to a networked printer, DNS misconfiguration could be the culprit.

NTP Issues

Most devices these days rely on the NIST time servers on the Internet to regulate time. When machines that are isolated from the Internet, and thus removed from a time server and the ubiquitous Network Time Protocol (NTP), go out of sync, *NTP issues* can stop services from working properly.

BYOD Challenges

BYOD was covered in Objective 3.2, and has benefits and challenges. The benefits are fairly obvious. The organization saves money because employees pay for their own devices.

Employees get the devices they prefer, which can increase employee happiness and productivity. The flip side of this, *BYOD challenges*, revolves around security, end-user support, and privacy. If a user's mobile device gets lost or stolen, that puts at risk both company information and private information. Does the support staff know how to provide help with *x* or *y* device? What if it's a later model than they've worked with in the past? What do they do then? Finally, what about monitoring software installed on the mobile device? Does it stay active during employee non-work time? How do you make that call? What about users who unwittingly bring in devices that are already compromised, putting the security of other devices—not to mention the organization's data—at risk?

Licensed Feature Issues

Once you move beyond SOHO gear, many of the features on network devices require specific licenses. This is important to keep in mind when you are purchasing new equipment or want to start using additional features your exiting gear supports. There is no technical fix for *licensed feature issues*. You just need to make sure you have bought, or have an active subscription for, the correct license to enable the features you need and have registered those licenses on the devices.

Network Performance Issues

Connectivity problems are bad for user productivity, but most of them have a clear resolution. Once someone tracks down the problem and implements a solution, we can close the ticket and move on. In contrast, *network performance issues* can be harder than connectivity problems to diagnose. A performance problem could just as easily be caused by a pipe that's just too small, a router that's running too hot, new sources of interference, ailing network devices, too many coworkers watching Netflix or Twitch while they work, poor QoS policies, backups running during your daytime peak instead of at night, an office that's simply outgrowing its infrastructure, or a compromised host exfiltrating petabytes of your organization's most precious data.

Network performance baselines are great to have for many kinds of troubleshooting—but they're really great when it comes to spotting performance issues before people are cranky enough to start complaining. In all of these cases, monitoring is your friend. Monitor everything you can!

Monitor your devices and network, obviously—but don't be shy about throwing in anything you have instruments and storage space to track. Things like temperature, humidity, the weather, indoor and outdoor air quality, the quality of electricity from your power company, the number of active Wi-Fi clients, the amount of ambient noise, and the number of active DHCP leases. Once you have all this data feeding into your network security monitor (NSM), make sure to set up thresholds so that you are notified when critical systems are running outside of their optimal performance range.

You won't need most of this data most of the time. But it's the kind of thing that can help you work your way back from complaints on Monday afternoons about Wi-Fi in the break room to the WAP on the ceiling going on the fritz when your water delivery service props the door open for 10 minutes on a muggy, sweltering Friday afternoon.

REVIEW

Objective 5.5: Given a scenario, troubleshoot general networking issues

- *Considerations* when troubleshooting general network issues include device configuration review, routing tables, interface status, VLAN assignment, and network performance baselines.
- Whenever you run into network trouble, it's a good idea to perform a *device configuration review*, as there is a possibility that someone (or maybe even just an update) has changed a device configuration recently.
- If you are troubleshooting a Layer 3 problem, consider are the *routing tables* of the various routers, firewalls, and other devices that the packets are moving through.
- Checking the *interface status* of the systems involved can help resolve many networking issues quickly.
- Doing a quick review of the *VLAN assignment* is good practice when troubleshooting. You could be dealing with a simple incorrect port assignment, or more complex problems. While this will be most important when troubleshooting Layer 2 issues, VLAN assignment also plays a role is problems further up the OSI stack.
- When vague complaints come in regarding speed or reliability, having access to historical *network performance baselines* can be the difference between knowing where to look and having to let the problem fester until you have enough user reports to connect the dots.
- There are *common issues* that every network tech should be aware of when troubleshooting general network issues.
- While *collisions*—multiple devices transmitting on the same wire at the same time—once plagued wired networks, this problem was eliminated when half-duplex technologies were replaced with full-duplex technologies and CSMA/CD went away. However, collisions can still be seen on networks today if a misconfiguration took place.
- A *broadcast storm* is the result of one or more devices sending a nonstop flurry of broadcast frames/packets on a network.
- A condition where more than one device claims to have the same MAC address is a *duplicate MAC address* problem.
- As soon as you configure a *duplicate IP address*, an IP address already assigned to a device on the same network, problems will arise.

- Related to broadcast storms, though not as destructive, is *multicast flooding*. Switches send multicast traffic to all ports in the broadcast domain, unless the multicast is pruned. This becomes a problem if you are using multicast for things like high-bandwidth video. In that case, you can see lots of traffic to every host on the LAN, even if those hosts aren't joined to a particular multicast group (and don't care about the traffic).

- *Asymmetrical routing* is when packets take one path to their destination but the response takes a different path back. This isn't necessarily a problem for everyone all the time, but it could still cause network issues.

- *Switching loops* (also known as bridging loops) occur when multiple switches are connected together in such a way that causes a circular path to appear. In cases like this, unnecessary duplicate copies of a frame are sent in different directions, taxing bandwidth and device processing.

- Individual routers will happily forward packets down a path that they think is correct, even if that path will actually lead them back around to a router they have already passed through, causing *routing loops*.

- A *rogue DHCP server* attack can be prevented by enabling DHCP snooping.

- *DHCP scope exhaustion* can be caused by a finite number of available host IP addresses being leased by clients, leaving other potential clients no available IP addresses to lease. For example, on a /24 network, there are 254 usable host addresses, which means if all 254 addresses are currently leased, no other DHCP clients can get an IP address from the DCHP server. DHCP scope exhaustion can also be the result of an attack.

- Various *IP setting issues*, like an incorrect gateway, incorrect subnet mask, incorrect IP address, and incorrect DNS, can be common issues you'll be troubleshooting.

- If the default gateway address for a client (configured statically or dynamically) is incorrect, an *incorrect gateway* issue, the client won't be able to send traffic off of its subnet.

- An *incorrect subnet mask* will stop even local traffic from the client, since it will incorrectly deduce that destinations on the same subnet are on different subnets.

- An *incorrect IP address* that's not in the valid range of host addresses for the subnet will cause all communication to fail, as once again the host will not be able to reach any local device, including its default gateway.

- A client with *incorrect DNS* server IP addresses won't be able to resolve FQDNs into their corresponding IP addresses, and thus will not be able to access devices by name.

- A misconfiguration can lead to a *missing route* that makes some destination networks unreachable for certain networks.

- A *low optical link budget* indicates that too much power has been lost.

- The fix for *certificate issues* is pretty simple—update the certificate.

- A *hardware failure* can certainly make a network device unreachable. Check the link lights on the NIC. Try another NIC if the machine seems functional in every other aspect.

- Incorrect *host-based/network-based firewall settings* could produce false positives, where legitimate traffic is filtered, and false negatives, where malicious traffic is let through.

- A firewall or ACL might be incorrectly configured, which can lead to *blocked services, ports, or addresses* that shouldn't be blocked.

- Configuring a port to be a member of an *incorrect VLAN* can cause the device plugged into that port to lose some or all network access.

- If you can ping a file server by IP address but not by name, this points to *DNS issues*.

- When machines that are isolated from the Internet—and thus removed from a time server and the ubiquitous Network Time Protocol—go out of sync, *NTP issues* can stop services from working properly.

- *BYOD challenges* revolve around security, end-user support, and privacy.

- There is no technical fix for *licensed feature issues*—you just need to make sure you have bought (or have an active subscription for) the correct license to enable the features you need and have registered those licenses on the devices.

- *Network performance issues* can be harder than connectivity problems to diagnose.

5.5 QUESTIONS

1. Which of the following represents the simplest item to check when troubleshooting general networking issues?
    A. Device configuration review
    B. Routing tables
    C. Interface status
    D. VLAN assignment

2. Which of the following is eliminated with STP?
    A. Routing loops
    B. Switching loops
    C. Duplicate MAC address
    D. Duplicate IP address

3. Which of the following likely is the issue if you can ping by IP address and not by name?
    A. NTP issue
    B. Duplicate IP address
    C. Incorrect gateway
    D. DNS issue

5.5 ANSWERS

1. **C** Checking the interface status is the simplest item listed. Eliminating simple and easy issues first is a good troubleshooting strategy.

2. **B** Spanning Tree Protocol (STP) eliminates switching loops.

3. **D** If you can ping a file server by IP address but not by name, this points to a DNS issue.

About the Online Content

This book comes complete with the following online content:

- TotalTester Online customizable practice exam software with more than 100 practice exam questions
- More than 20 sample simulations from Total Seminars' TotalSims
- More than an hour of video training episodes from Mike Meyers' CompTIA Network+ Certification series
- Links to a collection of Mike's favorite tools and utilities for network troubleshooting

System Requirements

The current and previous major versions of the following desktop Web browsers are recommended and supported: Chrome, Edge, Firefox, and Safari. These browsers update frequently and sometimes an update may cause compatibility issues with the TotalTester Online software or other content hosted on the Training Hub. If you run into a problem using one of these browsers, please try using a different Web browser until the problem is resolved.

Your Total Seminars Training Hub Account

To get access to the online content, you will need to create an account on the Total Seminars Training Hub. Registration is free and you will be able to track all your online content using your account. You may also opt in if you wish to receive marketing information from McGraw Hill or Total Seminars, but this is not required for you to gain access to the online content.

Privacy Notice

McGraw Hill values your privacy. Please be sure to read the Privacy Notice available during registration to see how the information you have provided will be used. You may view our Corporate Customer Privacy Policy by visiting the McGraw Hill Privacy Center. Visit the **mheducation.com** site and click **Privacy** at the bottom of the page.

Single User License Terms and Conditions

Online access to the digital content included with this book is governed by the McGraw Hill License Agreement outlined next. By using this digital content you agree to the terms of that license.

Access   To register and activate your Total Seminars Training Hub account, simply follow these easy steps.

1. Go to this URL: **hub.totalsem.com/mheclaim**.

2. To register and create a new Training Hub account, enter your email address, name, and password on the **Register** tab. No further information (such as credit card number) is required to create an account.

   If you already have a Total Seminars Training Hub account, enter your e-mail address and password on the **Log in** tab.

3. Enter your Product Key: **2b59-6f57-0s46**

4. Click to accept the user license terms.

5. For new users, click the **Register and Claim** button to create your account. For existing users, click the **Log in and Claim** button.

   You will be taken to the Training Hub and will have access to the content for this book.

Duration of License   Access to your online content through the Total Seminars Training Hub will expire one year from the date the publisher declares the book out of print.

Your purchase of this McGraw Hill product, including its access code, through a retail store is subject to the refund policy of that store.

The Content is a copyrighted work of McGraw Hill and McGraw Hill reserves all rights in and to the Content. The Work is © 2022 by McGraw Hill.

Restrictions on Transfer   The user is receiving only a limited right to use the Content for user's own internal and personal use, dependent on purchase and continued ownership of this book. The user may not reproduce, forward, modify, create derivative works based upon, transmit, distribute, disseminate, sell, publish, or sublicense the Content or in any way commingle the Content with other third-party content, without McGraw Hill's consent.

Limited Warranty   The McGraw Hill Content is provided on an "as is" basis. Neither McGraw Hill nor its licensors make any guarantees or warranties of any kind, either express or implied, including, but not limited to, implied warranties of merchantability or fitness for a particular purpose or use as to any McGraw Hill Content or the information therein or any warranties as to the accuracy, completeness, correctness, or results to be obtained from, accessing or using the McGraw Hill Content, or any material referenced in such content or any information entered into licensee's product by users or other persons and/or any material available on or that can be accessed through the licensee's product (including via any hyperlink or otherwise) or as to non-infringement of third-party rights. Any warranties of any kind, whether express or implied, are disclaimed. Any material or data obtained through use of the McGraw Hill Content is at your own discretion and risk and user understands that it will be solely responsible for any resulting damage to its computer system or loss of data.

Neither McGraw Hill nor its licensors shall be liable to any subscriber or to any user or anyone else for any inaccuracy, delay, interruption in service, error or omission, regardless of cause, or for any damage resulting therefrom.

In no event will McGraw Hill or its licensors be liable for any indirect, special or consequential damages, including but not limited to, lost time, lost money, lost profits or good will, whether in contract, tort, strict liability, or otherwise, and whether or not such damages are foreseen or unforeseen with respect to any use of the McGraw Hill Content.

TotalTester Online

TotalTester Online provides you with a simulation of the CompTIA Network+ exam. Exams can be taken in Practice Mode or Exam Mode. Practice Mode provides an assistance window with hints, references to the book, explanations of the correct and incorrect answers, and the option to check your answers as you take the test. Exam Mode provides a simulation of the actual exam. The number of questions, the types of questions, and the time allowed are intended to be an accurate representation of the exam environment. The option to customize your quiz allows you to create custom exams from selected domains or chapters, and you can further customize the number of questions and time allowed.

To take a test, follow the instructions provided in the previous section to register and activate your Total Seminars Training Hub account. When you register you will be taken to the Total Seminars Training Hub. From the Training Hub Home page, select your certification from the Study drop-down menu at the top of the page to drill down to the TotalTester for your book. You can also scroll to it from the list of Your Topics on the Home page, and then click on the TotalTester link to launch the TotalTester. Once you've launched your TotalTester, you can select the option to customize your quiz and begin testing yourself in Practice Mode or Exam Mode. All exams provide an overall grade and a grade broken down by domain.

Pre-Assessment Test

In addition to the sample exam questions, the TotalTester also includes a CompTIA Network+ pre-assessment test to help you assess your understanding of the topics before reading the book. To launch the pre-assessment test, click **Network+ Pre-Assessment**. The Network+ pre-assessment test has 50 questions and runs in Exam mode. When you complete the test, you can review the questions with answers and detailed explanations by clicking **See Detailed Results**.

Other Book Resources

The following sections detail the other resources available with your book. You can access these items by selecting your certification from the Study drop-down menu at the top of the page and then expanding your book's options and selecting the Book Resources link. If you are on the TotalTester tab, click on the Book Resources tab. The menu on the right side of the screen outlines all of the available resources.

TotalSims for Network+

Click the TotalSims tab to see what is available for free. There are over 20 free simulations available for reviewing topics referenced in the book, with an option to purchase access to the full TotalSims for Network+ (N10-008) with more than 120 simulations.

Mike's Video Training

More than an hour of training videos, starring Mike Meyers, are available for free. Click the TotalVideos tab to see what is available for free. Along with access to the free videos, you'll find an option to purchase Mike's complete video training series.

Mike's Cool Tools

Mike loves freeware/open source networking tools! To access the utilities recommended click the Resources tab, and then select **Mike's Cool Tools**.

Technical Support

For questions regarding the TotalTester or operation of the Training Hub, visit **www.totalsem .com** or e-mail **support@totalsem.com**.

For questions regarding book content, visit **www.mheducation.com/customerservice**.

Index

2.4 GHz band, 179–180
3G technology, 188
4G technology, 188
5.0 GHz band, 179–180
5G technology, 188
10BASE-LR standard, 51–52
10BASE-SR standard, 51–52
10BASE-T standard, 47–48
10GBASE-T standard, 50
40GBASE-T standard, 50
66 blocks, 46
100BASE-FX standard, 50–51
100BASE-SX standard, 51
100BASE-T standard, 48–49
110 blocks, 46
802.11 standards, 175
    802.1Q, 161–162
    802.1X authentication, 246–247
    802.11a, 175–176
    802.11ac, 178
    802.11ax, 178–179
    802.11b, 176
    802.11g, 176–177
    802.11n, 177–178
1000BASE-LX standard, 51
1000BASE-SX standard, 51
1000BASE-T standard, 49–50

A

A and AAAA (Address) DNS records, 103–104
A flag (Address Autoconfiguration flag) in
    router advertisement, 79
acceptable use policies (AUPs), 209
access control
    acceptable use policies, 209
    hardware, 304–306
access control lists (ACLs), 284
access control vestibules, 306
access/edge layer in datacenters, 110

access points (APs)
    association time, 364
    description, 133
    ransomware, 259–260
    rogue, 259
ACK flag in TCP, 11, 92
ACLs (access control lists), 284
Acrylic Wi-Fi tool, 365–366
actions in troubleshooting, 319–320
active-active clusters, 228
active-passive clusters, 228
ad-hoc (independent basic service set)
    nodes, 182
Address (A and AAAA) DNS records,
    103–104
Address Autoconfiguration flag (A flag)
    in router advertisement, 79
Address Resolution Protocol (ARP)
    dynamic inspection, 280
    overview, 170–173
    spoofing, 256–257
addresses
    blocked, 379
    IP. See IP addresses
    MAC. See media access control (MAC)
        addresses
administrative distance, 156–157
ADSL (asymmetric DSL), 31
Advanced Encryption Standard (AES), 185–186
Advanced Research Projects Agency Network
    (ARPANET), 82
adware, 268–269
AES (Advanced Encryption Standard), 185–186
aggregation, port, 162
aggregation layer in datacenters, 110–111, 113
agreements
    MOUs, 219
    NDAs, 218
    SLAs, 218–219

AH (Authentication Header), 94
Aircrack-ng tool, 249
AirMagnet Survey Pro tool, 365
alerts, interface, 199–200
ALGs (application layer gateways), 139
American Registry for Internet Numbers
    (ARIN), 73
AND operations, 170–172
angled physical contact (APC) connectors, 43
anomaly-based IDSs, 141
antennas
    cable attenuation, 367
    placement, 286–287, 363
    polarization, 363–364
    types, 183–184, 363
anycast addresses, 66
APC (angled physical contact) connectors, 43
APIPA (Automatic Private IP Addressing),
    59–60
application layer gateways (ALGs), 139
Application layer in OSI model, 8
application plane in SDN, 113
APs. *See* access points (APs)
areas in OSPF, 154
ARIN (American Registry for Internet
    Numbers), 73
ARP (Address Resolution Protocol)
    dynamic inspection, 280
    overview, 170–173
    spoofing, 256–257
arp tool, 354
ARPANET (Advanced Research Projects
    Agency Network), 82
assessment reports, 217
asset disposal, 307–308
asset tags, 303
asymmetric DSL (ADSL), 31
asymmetrical routing, 375
attacks
    human and environmental, 269–274
    questions, 276
    review, 274–276
    technology-based. *See* technology-
      based attacks
attenuation in cable, 328
audit log reviews, 197

audit reports, 217
AUPs (acceptable use policies), 209
authentication
    802.1X, 246–247
    deauthentication, 264–266
    EAP, 245–246
    Kerberos, 244–245
    LDAP, 244
    local, 245
    multifactor, 242
    overview, 242
    RADIUS, 243
    remote access, 300
    SSO, 243–244
    TACACS+, 243
Authentication Header (AH), 94
authoritative name servers, 102–103
authorization for remote access, 300
auto-medium-dependent interface crossover
    (MDI-X), 166
Automatic Private IP Addressing (APIPA),
    59–60
automation in infrastructure as code, 124
availability, 192
    baselines, 201
    environmental factors and sensors,
      200–201
    high. *See* high availability (HA)
    interface errors and alerts, 199–200
    interface statistics and status, 198–199
    NetFlow data, 202
    network device logs, 196–198
    performance metrics and sensors,
      192–194
    questions, 204–205
    review, 203–204
    SNMP, 194–196
    uptime and downtime, 202–203

B

backbones in datacenters, 111, 114
backdoors, 268
backups
    configuration, 283
    datacenters, 116
    network devices, 230

badge readers, 304–305
bandwidth
    managing, 157–158
    OSPF, 154
    performance metrics, 193
    speed testers, 346–347
baseband networks, 37
baselines
    configuration documentation, 217–218
    creating, 201
basic service set identifiers (BSSIDs), 182
basic service sets (BSSs), 182
bastion hosts, 240
best practices for hardening techniques, 277–285
BGP (Border Gateway Protocol), 155–157
bidirectional wavelength division multiplexing, 53
biometrics, 305–306
BIX (Building Industry Cross-connect) blocks, 46
blocks in SANs, 116
Bluetooth for WPANs, 22–23
Border Gateway Protocol (BGP), 155–157
botnets, 255
Bottom of Label Stack in MPLS headers, 23
bottom-to-top OSI troubleshooting model, 315–316
branch offices for datacenters, 115
bridge protocol data units (BPDUs), 168–169
bridges, 133
bridging loops, 375
bring your own device (BYOD) policies, 210, 379–380
broadband networks, 37
broadcast messages, 62–63
broadcast storms, 374
brute-force password attacks, 262–263
BSSIDs (basic service set identifiers), 182
BSSs (basic service sets), 182
Building Industry Cross-connect (BIX) blocks, 46
bus topology, 16
business continuity plans, 207
business risk assessments, 249–250

BYOD (bring your own device) policies, 210, 379–380
byte counts in interfaces, 199

C

C&C (command and control), 255
cabinets, locking, 306
cable companies for Internet connections, 32–33
cable connectivity issues
    application, 324–327
    attenuation, 328
    common, 327–330
    considerations, 323–324
    decibel loss, 329–330
    duplexing, 331
    interference, 328–329
    optical, 331–332
    questions, 343
    review, 340–343
    specifications and limitations, 321–323
    status indicators, 330–331
    tools, 332–340
cable crimpers, 332
cable modems, 32–33, 135–136
cable strippers, 339
cable testers, 336–337
cable types and connectors, 35
    connectors, 42–44
    copper, 35–40
    Ethernet standards, 47–53
    fiber, 40–42
    managing, 44–46
    questions, 54
    review, 53–54
caching, DNS, 103
CAM (content addressable memory) tables. *See* media access control (MAC) address tables
cameras, 143, 303
campus area networks (CANs), 23
canonical name (CNAME) resource records, 104
captive portals
    issues, 369
    purpose, 289

carrier-sense multiple access with collision avoidance (CSMA/CA), 6
carrier-sense multiple access with collision detection (CSMA/CD), 6, 169–170
categories of copper cabling, 36–37
CDMA (code-division multiple access), 187
cellular technologies, 186–188
central processing unit (CPU) performance metrics, 192–193
certificate issues, 378–379
change determination, 313
change management, 206
channels
    bonding, 181
    description, 180–181
    overlap, 367
    utilization, 364
chassis performance metrics and sensors, 192–193
CIA (confidentiality, integrity, and availability) triad, 234–235
classes of IP addresses, 73–74
Classless Inter-Domain Routing (CIDR), 75–76
classless subnets, 74–75
client issues in wireless
    disassociation, 369
    isolation, 288
client-server networks, 21
client-to-site VPNs, 296–297
clientless VPNs, 296
clients in NTS, 107–108
cloud, 119
    backup sites, 228
    connectivity options, 124–125
    deployment models, 120–121
    elasticity, 126
    multitenancy, 125
    questions, 127–128
    review, 127
    scalability, 125–126
    security, 126
    service models, 121–124

clusters for redundancy, 223–224, 228
CNAME (canonical name) resource records, 104
coarse wavelength division multiplexing (CWDM), 53
coaxial cabling, 37–39
code-division multiple access (CDMA), 187
cold aisles, 213
cold sites, 227
collisions
    CSMA/CD, 169–170
    Layer 2 switches, 131
    troubleshooting, 373
colocation for datacenters, 115
Combs, Gerald, 346
command and control (C&C), 255
command line tools
    arp, 354
    hostname, 354–355
    ipconfig, 349–351
    netstat, 354–355
    nslookup and dig, 351–352
    ping, 349
    questions, 358–359
    review, 358–359
    route, 356
    tcpdump, 357
    telnet, 357
    traceroute and tracert, 353
common agreements
    MOUs, 219
    NDAs, 218
    SLAs, 218–219
common documentation
    audit and assessment reports, 217
    baseline configurations, 217–218
    physical network diagrams, 211–215
    site survey reports, 216
    wiring diagrams, 215–216
Common Vulnerabilities and Exposures (CVE) database, 236–237
commonly used ports, 86–89
community cloud deployment, 121
complexity for passwords, 282

concentrators, VPN, 141

confidentiality, integrity, and availability (CIA) triad, 234–235

configuration

    backups, 230, 283

    ports, 161–163

    reviews, 372

    wipe, 307–308

connection-oriented protocols, 94

connectionless protocols, 94

connectivity

    cable. *See* cable connectivity issues

    cloud options, 124–125

    wireless. *See* wireless connectivity

connectors and connections

    cable types, 42–44

    SANs, 117–118

consent to monitoring in acceptable use policies, 209

console cable, 325

content addressable memory (CAM) tables. *See* media access control (MAC) address tables

control layer in SDN, 112–113

control plane policing, 280

copper cabling, 35

    10BASE-T, 47–48

    10GBASE-T, 50

    40GBASE-T, 50

    100BASE-T, 48–49

    1000BASE-T, 49–50

    categories, 36–37

    coaxial/RG-6, 37–39

    termination standards, 39–40

    twinaxial cable, 39

    twisted pair, 35–36

core layer in datacenters, 111

costs in OSPF, 154

coverage issues in wireless connectivity, 369

CPU (central processing unit) performance metrics, 192–193

CRCs (cyclic redundancy checks)

    errors, 200

    interfaces, 199

    OSI model, 6

crimpers, cable, 332

crossover cable, 325–327

crosstalk, 328–329

CSMA/CA (carrier-sense multiple access with collision avoidance), 6

CSMA/CD (carrier-sense multiple access with collision detection), 6, 169–170

cutters, 338

CVE (Common Vulnerabilities and Exposures) database, 236–237

CWDM (coarse wavelength division multiplexing), 53

cyclic redundancy checks (CRCs)

    errors, 200

    interfaces, 199

    OSI model, 6

cycling device logs, 196

D

DaaS (Desktop as a Service), 123–124

DAC (direct attached cable), 39

DARPA (Defense Advanced Research Projects Agency), 82

data encapsulation and decapsulation in OSI model, 8–11

Data Link layer in OSI model, 4–6

data loss prevention (DLP), 211

Data Offset field in TCP headers, 90–91

data virtual local area networks, 160–161

datacenters

    layout, 212–214

    location, 115

    questions, 119

    review, 118

    SANs, 116–118

    SDN, 111–113

    spine and leaf, 113–114

    three-tiered, 109–111

    traffic flows, 114–115

    UPSs, 225

dB (decibel) loss, 329–330

DCI (Deep Content Inspection), 139

deauthentication, 264–266

decapsulation in OSI model, 8–11

deception software, 241

decibel (dB) loss, 329–330
Deep Content Inspection (DCI), 139
Deep Packet Inspection (DPI), 139
default gateways for IP addresses, 67
default passwords, 281–282
default routes, 156
default VLANs, 282
Defense Advanced Research Projects Agency (DARPA), 82
defense in depth, 239–241
demarcation points, 25
demilitarized zones (DMZs), 239–240
denial-of-service (DoS) and distributed denial-of-service (DDoS) attacks, 254–255
dense wavelength division multiplexing (DWDM), 53
deployment models for cloud, 120–121
Desktop as a Service (DaaS), 123–124
destination LAN IPs in routing, 150–152
detection methods in physical security, 302–303
devices, networking, 130
    access points, 133
    ALGs, 139
    backups and restores, 230
    bridges, 133
    cable modems, 135–136
    cameras, 143
    configuration reviews, 372
    doorbells, 145
    DSL modems, 136
    firewalls, 137–138
    hubs, 132–133
    HVAC sensors, 144
    industrial control systems, 145–147
    IoT, 144
    IPS/IDS, 139–141
    Layer 2 switches, 130–131
    Layer 3 capable switches, 132
    load balancers, 134
    media converters, 136–137
    network logs, 196–198
    networked, 142–145
    performance metrics and sensors, 192–193
    physical access control, 143
    printers, 142
    proxy servers, 135
    questions, 148–149
    refrigerators, 144
    repeaters, 136
    review, 147–148
    routers, 132
    speakers, 145
    thermostats, 145
    UTM appliances, 139
    voice gateways, 136
    VoIP phones, 142
    VPN headends, 141
    WLCs, 133–134
DHCP. *See* Dynamic Host Configuration Protocol (DHCP)
dictionary password attacks, 261–262
Diffie-Hellman key exchange (DHKE), 298–299
dig tool, 351–352
digital subscriber line (DSL), 31–32
dipole antennas, 183–184
direct attached cable (DAC), 39
directional antennas, 184
disabling unneeded devices and services, 281
disaster recovery plans, 207
Discover, Offer, Request, and Ack (DORA) steps in DHCP, 96–97
disposal of asset, 307–308
distance considerations
    cable connectivity, 323
    wireless connectivity, 361
distance vector routing protocols, 155–156
distribution layer in datacenters, 110–111
diverse paths for routers, 228
divide and conquer troubleshooting approach, 315–316
DKIM (DomainKeys Identified Mail), 106
DLP (data loss prevention), 211
DMARC (Domain-based Message Authentication, Reporting and Conformance), 106
DMZs (demilitarized zones), 239–240
DNS. *See* Domain Name System (DNS)

documentation
    common. *See* common documentation
    in troubleshooting, 319–320
Domain-based Message Authentication,
    Reporting and Conformance (DMARC), 106
Domain Name System (DNS)
    global hierarchy, 100–103
    incorrect, 377
    internal vs. external, 107
    issues, 379
    overview, 99
    poisoning, 257
    ports, 87
    record types, 103–106
    recursive lookup, 103
    reverse and forward lookup, 106–107
    TTL, 103
    zone transfers, 99–100
DomainKeys Identified Mail (DKIM), 106
doorbells, smart, 145
DORA (Discover, Offer, Request, and Ack)
    steps in DHCP, 96–97
DoS (denial-of-service) and distributed
    denial-of-service (DDoS) attacks, 254–255
downtime, 202–203
DPI (Deep Packet Inspection), 139
DSL (digital subscriber line), 31–32
DSL modems, 136
dual stack in IPv6, 76
duplex
    cable connectivity issues, 331
    interfaces, 198–199
    ports, 162
duplicate IP addresses, 374
duplicate MAC addresses, 374
duplicating problems for problem
    identification, 314
DWDM (dense wavelength division
    multiplexing), 53
dynamic ARP inspection., 280
dynamic assignment in DHCP, 97
Dynamic Host Configuration Protocol
    (DHCP)
    dynamic assignment, 97
    exclusion ranges, 97
    IPv4, 59–60
    leases, 96–97
    ports, 87
    reservations, 97–98
    rogue, 258–259, 376
    scope, 96
    scope exhaustion, 376–377
    snooping, 282
    static assignment, 97
    subnets, 98–99
dynamic ports, 85
dynamic routing, 152–156

E

EAP (Extensible Authentication Protocol),
    245–246
EAP-TLS, 246
east-west traffic in datacenters, 115
echo requests in ICMP, 92–93
ECPM (Equal-Cost Multipath), 114
effective isotropic radiated power (EIRP), 362
EGP (Exterior Gateway Protocol), 157
EIA (Electronic Industries Alliance) standards,
    39–40
EIGRP (Enhanced Interior Gateway Routing
    Protocol), 155–156
EIRP (effective isotropic radiated power), 362
elasticity in cloud, 126
electrical loads, sensors for, 200–201
electromagnetic interference (EMI)
    100BASE-FX, 50
    coaxial cable, 38
    description, 328
    fiber cable, 40
    twisted pair cable, 323
Electronic Industries Alliance (EIA) standards,
    39–40
employee training, 304
Encapsulating Security Payload (ESP), 94
encapsulation
    errors, 200
    OSI model, 8–11
encryption
    protocol mismatches, 368
    wireless standards, 184–186

enhanced form-factor pluggable (SFP+) transceivers, 43
Enhanced Interior Gateway Routing Protocol (EIGRP), 155–156
enhanced quad small form-factor pluggable (QSFP+) transceivers, 44
environmental factors and sensors, 200–201
Equal-Cost Multipath (ECPM), 114
equipment requirements in SLAs, 218
error display for interfaces, 199–200
ESP (Encapsulating Security Payload), 94
ESSs (extended service sets), 182
ESX hypervisors, 27–28
Ethernet standards
    cables and connectors, 47–53
    headers, 8, 10
Ethernet switching features, 160
    ARP, 170–173
    CSMA/CD, 169–170
    data virtual local area networks, 160–161
    jumbo frames, 165
    MAC address tables, 166–167
    NDP, 173
    PoE, 167
    port configurations, 161–163
    port mirroring, 163
    port security, 164–165
    questions, 174–175
    review, 174
    STP, 168–169
    Voice VLANs, 161
EUI-64 (Extended Unique Identifier), 60–62
evil twin attacks, 259
exclusion ranges in DHCP, 97
experimental bits in MPLS headers, 23
explicit deny statements, 285
exploits, 237–238
extended service sets (ESSs), 182
Extended Unique Identifier (EUI-64), 60–62
Extensible Authentication Protocol (EAP), 245–246
Exterior Gateway Protocol (EGP), 157
exterior routing protocols, 157
external DNS, 107
external threats, 235–236

F
F connectors, 38–39, 43
facilities and infrastructure support, 224
    fire suppression, 227
    generators, 226
    HVAC, 226–227
    PDUs, 226
    UPSs, 225
factory resets, 307–308
far-end crosstalk (FEXT), 328–329
Fast Ethernet, 48
FAST (Flexible Authentication via Secure Tunneling), 246
FC (Fibre Channel), 117
FCoE (Fibre Channel over Ethernet), 117
federated authentication, 243–244
FEXT (far-end crosstalk), 328–329
FHRP (first hop redundancy protocol), 80, 228–229
fiber cabling, 331–332
    10BASE-LR, 51–52
    10BASE-SR, 51–52
    100BASE-FX, 50–51
    100BASE-SX, 51
    1000BASE-LX, 51
    1000BASE-SX, 51
    distribution panels, 46
    multimode, 41–42
    overview, 40–41
    single-mode, 41
    WDM, 53
fiber light meters, 339
Fibre Channel (FC), 117
Fibre Channel over Ethernet (FCoE), 117
Figueroa, Edgar, 179
File Transfer Protocol (FTP) ports, 85–86
filters
    firewall, 137–138
    MAC addresses, 286
FIN flag in TCP, 12
findings in troubleshooting, 319–320
fire suppression systems, 227
firewalls, 137–138
    Layer 7, 139
    redundancy, 224

rules, 285

    settings, 379

firmware management, 282–284

first hop redundancy protocol (FHRP), 80, 228–229

flags

    fragmentation, 13

    router advertisement, 79

    TCP, 11–12, 90–92

Flexible Authentication via Secure Tunneling (FAST), 246

flooding

    multicast, 374–375

    sensors, 200–201

floor plans, 212

flow control in ports, 163

forward lookup in DNS, 106–107

forward proxy servers, 135

Fox and Hound tone generators, 333–334

FQDNs (fully qualified domain names), 100

fragmentation

    Layer 3, 7

    MTUs, 13–14

frames

    giant and runt, 200

    jumbo, 165

    OSI model, 5–6

frequencies, wireless, 179–180

FTP (File Transfer Protocol) ports, 85–86

full tunnel VPN connections, 296–297

fully qualified domain names (FQDNs), 100

fusion splicers, 337

G

Gateway Load Balancing Protocol (GLBP), 80

gateways

    default, 67

    incorrect, 377

    routing, 150–151

    voice, 136

gathering information for problem identification, 313

general data protection regulation (GDPR), 217

generators, 226

Generic Routing Encapsulation (GRE) protocol, 94

geofencing, 288–289

giant frames, 200

Gigabit Ethernet standard, 49–50

GLBP (Gateway Load Balancing Protocol), 80

global hierarchy in DNS, 100–103

Global System for Mobile Communications (GSM), 187

global unicast addresses (GUAs), 62, 66

GRE (Generic Routing Encapsulation) protocol, 94

GSM (Global System for Mobile Communications), 187

GUAs (global unicast addresses), 62, 66

guest network isolation, 288

H

HA. *See* high availability (HA)

hard drives in datacenters, 116

hardening and security policies

    acceptable use, 209

    BYOD, 210

    data loss prevention, 211

    onboarding and offboarding, 210–211

    overview, 208–209

    passwords, 209

    remote access, 210

    security, 211

hardening techniques, 277

    access control lists, 284

    best practices, 277–285

    control plane policing, 280

    default passwords, 281–282

    default VLANs, 282

    DHCP snooping, 282

    dynamic ARP inspection., 280

    explicit deny statements, 285

    firewall rules, 285

    implicit deny statements, 285

    IoT access considerations, 289–292

    password complexity, 282

    patch and firmware management, 282–284

    port security, 278–279

hardening techniques *(cont.)*
    private VLANs, 280–281
    questions, 294
    RA Guard, 277–278
    review, 292–294
    role-based access, 285
    secure SNMP, 277
    unneeded devices and services, 281
    wireless, 285–289
hardware
    access control, 304–306
    failures, 379
    redundancy, 223–224
hardware-based firewalls, 138
hashes in dictionary password attacks, 261–262
headends, VPN, 141
headers
    MPLS, 23–24
    OSI model, 8–11
    TCP, 90–92
    UDP, 92
Health Insurance Portability and
    Accountability Act (HIPAA), 217
heat maps, 365–366
heating, ventilation, and air conditioning
    (HVAC)
        purpose, 226–227
        sensors, 144
Hello packets in OSPF, 154
hexadecimal letters in IPv6, 77
HIDSs (host-based IDSs), 141
high availability (HA)
    facilities and infrastructure support,
        224–227
    load balancing, 222
    multipathing, 222–223
    network device backups, 230
    NIC teaming, 223
    overview, 222
    questions, 232
    redundancy, 223–224, 227–230
    review, 231–232
High-Speed Packet Access (HSPA+), 188
HIPAA (Health Insurance Portability and
    Accountability Act), 217
honeypots, 241

host-based firewalls
    description, 138
    settings, 379
host-based IDSs (HIDSs), 141
host calculations in subnetting, 69–70
hostname tool, 354–355
hot aisles, 213
hot sites, 227
Hot Standby Router Protocol (HSRP), 80
HSPA+ (High-Speed Packet Access), 188
HTTP (Hypertext Transfer Protocol)
    ports, 87
HTTPS (Hypertext Transfer Protocol Secure)
    ports, 88
hub-and-spoke topology, 19
hubs, 132–133
human and environmental attacks
    phishing, 271–273
    piggybacking, 274
    shoulder surfing, 274
    social engineering, 269–271
    tailgating, 273–274
humidity sensors, 200–201
HVAC (heating, ventilation, and air
    conditioning)
        purpose, 226–227
        sensors, 144
hybrid cloud deployment, 120–121
hybrid routing protocols, 155–156
hybrid topology, 17–19
Hydra tool, 261
Hypertext Transfer Protocol (HTTP) ports, 87
Hypertext Transfer Protocol Secure (HTTPS)
    ports, 88
hypervisors in virtual networks, 27–28

I

IaaS (infrastructure as a Service), 122–123
IaC (infrastructure as code), 124
IANA (Internet Assigned Numbers
    Authority), 73
ICA (Independent Computing Architecture), 297
ICANN (Internet Corporation for Assigned
    Names and Numbers), 73
ICMP (Internet Control Message Protocol),
    92–93

ICSs (industrial control systems), 145–147
identifying problems, 312–314
IDF (intermediate distribution frame)
    documentation, 212–214
IDS (intrusion detection system) devices,
    139–141
IETF (Internet Engineering Task Force), 94
ifconfig tool, 349–351
IGMP (Internet Group Management
    Protocol), 63
IGRP (Interior Gateway Routing Protocol), 155
illegal use in acceptable use policies, 209
IMAP (Internet Message Access Protocol)
    ports, 87
IMAP over SSL ports, 88
implicit deny statements, 285
IMT-2000 (International Mobile
    Telecommunications-2000) standard, 188
in-band remote access management, 300
incident response plans, 206–207
independent basic service set (ad-hoc)
    nodes, 182
Independent Computing Architecture
    (ICA), 297
industrial control systems (ICSs), 145–147
infrared (IR) in WPANs, 22–23
infrastructure as a Service (IaaS), 122–123
infrastructure as code (IaC), 124
infrastructure layer in SDN, 112–113
infrastructure-level changes, 206
insufficient wireless coverage, 369
interface identifiers (interface IDs), 61
interfaces
    errors and alerts, 199–200
    routing, 151–152
    statistics, 198–199
    status, 198–199, 372
interference
    100BASE-FX, 50
    cable connectivity, 328–329
    coaxial cable, 38
    description, 328
    fiber cable, 40
    twisted pair cable, 323
    wireless, 367

Interior Gateway Routing Protocol
    (IGRP), 155
interior routing protocols, 157
intermediate distribution frame (IDF)
    documentation, 212–214
internal DNS, 107
internal threats, 235
International Mobile
    Telecommunications-2000 (IMT-2000)
    standard, 188
Internet Assigned Numbers Authority
    (IANA), 73
Internet Control Message Protocol (ICMP),
    92–93
Internet Corporation for Assigned Names and
    Numbers (ICANN), 73
Internet Engineering Task Force (IETF), 94
Internet Group Management Protocol
    (IGMP), 63
Internet Message Access Protocol (IMAP)
    ports, 87
Internet of Things (IoT)
    access considerations, 289–292
    description, 144
Internet Protocol (IP) headers, 8, 10
Internet Protocol Security (IPsec), 94
Internet service providers (ISPs), 228
Internet Small Computer Systems Interface
    (iSCSI), 117–118
intrusion detection system (IDS) devices,
    139–141
intrusion prevention system (IPS) devices,
    139–141
IoT (Internet of Things)
    access considerations, 289–292
    description, 144
IP addresses
    anycast, 66
    APIPA, 59–60
    broadcasts, 62–63
    default gateways, 67
    DHCP, 96–99
    duplicate, 374
    EUI-64, 60–62
    firewalls, 137

IP addresses *(cont.)*
    IPv4 vs. IPv6, 59–67
    IPv6, 76–79
    loopback, 66–67
    multicasts, 63–65
    NAT, 56–57
    PAT, 57–59
    public vs. private, 55–59
    questions, 81
    review, 81
    RFC 1918, 55–56
    router advertisement, 78–79
    routing. *See* routing
    scanners, 349
    settings, 377
    spoofing, 263–264
    subinterfaces, 80
    subnetting, 67–76
    unicast, 65–66
    virtual IP, 79–80
IP helpers in DHCP, 98
IP (Internet Protocol) headers, 8, 10
IP packets in OSI model, 7
IP protocol types
    AH/ESP, 94
    connectionless vs. connection-oriented, 94
    GRE, 94
    ICMP, 92–93
    IPsec, 94
    TCP and UDP, 89–92
ip tool, 349–351
ip routing tool, 132
ipconfig tool, 349–351
ipconfig /all command, 4–5
iPerf tool, 348
IPS (intrusion prevention system) devices, 139–141
IPsec (Internet Protocol Security), 94
IR (infrared) in WPANs, 22–23
iSCSI (Internet Small Computer Systems Interface), 117–118
ISO/IEC 27001 standard, 217
ISO/IEC 27002 standard, 217
ISPs (Internet service providers), 228
iterative lookups in DNS, 103

J
jitter, 194
jumbo frames, 165

K
Kerberos authentication, 244–245
Krone LSA-PLUS connectors, 46

L
labels in MPLS headers, 23
LACP (Link Aggregation Control Protocol), 162
LANs. *See* local area networks (LANs)
latency performance metrics, 193
Layer 1 OSI model, 3
Layer 2 OSI model, 4–6
Layer 2 OSI model switches, 130–131
Layer 3 OSI model, 7
Layer 3 OSI model switches, 132
Layer 4 OSI model, 7
Layer 5 OSI model, 7
Layer 6 OSI model, 8
Layer 7 OSI model, 8
Layer 7 OSI model firewalls, 139
LCs (local connectors), 42
LDAP (Lightweight Directory Access Protocol)
    description, 244
    ports, 88
LDAPS (Lightweight Directory Access Protocol over SSL)
    description, 244
    ports, 88
LEAP (Lightweight EAP), 246
leased lines, 33
leases in DHCP, 96–97
least privilege principle, 238
LED (light-emitting diode) status indicators for cable connectivity, 330–331
legacy systems, 208, 283
length of passwords, 282
lessons learned in troubleshooting, 319–320
levels in device logs, 197–198
licensed feature issues, 380
light-emitting diode (LED) status indicators for cable connectivity, 330–331
light meters, 339

Lightweight Access Point Protocol (LWAPP), 134
Lightweight Directory Access Protocol (LDAP)
    description, 244
    ports, 88
Lightweight Directory Access Protocol over
  SSL (LDAPS)
    description, 244
    ports, 88
Lightweight EAP (LEAP), 246
limitations
    cable connectivity, 321–323
    wireless connectivity, 361
Link Aggregation Control Protocol (LACP), 162
link budgets, optical, 378
link-local IP addresses, 59–60
link-local unicast addresses, 66
link state, 198
link state advertisement (LSA) packets, 154
link state routing protocols, 155–156
LLC (Logical Link Control) layer in OSI
  model, 6
load balancers, 134, 222
local area networks (LANs)
    data virtual, 160–161
    description, 22
    virtual. *See* virtual local area networks
      (VLANs)
    wireless controllers, 133–134
local authentication, 245
local connectors (LCs), 42
location of datacenters, 115
lockers, smart, 307
locks, 306
logic bombs, 267
Logical Link Control (LLC) layer in OSI
  model, 6
logical network diagrams, 215
logs for network devices, 196–198
Long Term Evolution (LTE) technology,
  187–188
lookups in DNS, 103, 106–107
loop networking issues, 375–376
loopback adapters, 334–335
loopback addresses, 66–67
LSA (link state advertisement) packets, 154

LTE (Long Term Evolution) technology,
  187–188
LWAPP (Lightweight Access Point Protocol), 134

M

M flag (Managed Address Configuration flag)
  in router advertisements, 79
MAC addresses. *See* media access control
  (MAC) addresses
MAC (media access control) address tables
    Layer 2 switches, 130
    overview, 278–279
    port security, 164–165
MAC (Medium/Media Access Control) layer in
  OSI model, 6
macro viruses, 267
mail exchange (MX) resource records, 104–105
main distribution frame (MDF)
  documentation, 212–214
malware
    adware, 268–269
    logic bombs, 267
    overview, 266
    RAT, 268
    rootkits, 268
    spyware, 269
    Trojan horses, 267–268
    viruses and worms, 266–267
man-in-the-middle attacks, 255
Managed Address Configuration flag (M flag)
  in router advertisements, 79
management information bases (MIBs) in
  SNMP, 194
management plane in SDN, 113
MANs (metropolitan area networks), 22
mantraps, 306
mass storage devices in datacenters, 116
Matherly, John, 291
MAUs (multistation access units), 17–19
maximum transmission units (MTUs), 13–14
MD5 (Message Digest version 5), 246
MDF (main distribution frame)
  documentation, 212–214
mean time between failure (MTBF), 229
mean time to repair (MTTR), 229

Mechanical Transfer Registered Jack (MT-RJ) connectors, 42
media access control (MAC) address tables
    Layer 2 switches, 130
    overview, 278–279
    port security, 164–165
media access control (MAC) addresses
    ARP spoofing, 256–257
    DHCP, 99
    duplicate, 374
    EUI-64, 61
    filtering, 286
    Layer 2 switches, 130–131
    OSI model, 4–5
    overview, 166–167
    port security, 278–279
    ports, 163–164
    spoofing, 263
media converters, 43, 136–137
Medium/Media Access Control (MAC) layer in OSI model, 6
Medusa tool, 261
memoranda of understanding (MOU), 219
memory performance metrics, 193
Merdinger, Shawn, 291
mesh topology, 19–21
Message Digest version 5 (MD5), 246
Metasploit tool, 249
metro-optical links, 33–34
metropolitan area networks (MANs), 22
MFA (multifactor authentication), 242
mGRE (multipoint generic routing encapsulation) protocol, 24
MIBs (management information bases) in SNMP, 194
MIMO (Multiple Input, Multiple Output), 188–189
mirroring ports, 163
missing routes, 378
mixed mode in 802.11g, 176
MLD (Multicast Listener Discovery), 63
MMF (multimode fiber), 41–42
modems
    cable, 32–33, 135–136
    DSL, 136

modes in fiber cabling, 41–42
motion detection, 303
MOU (memoranda of understanding), 219
MPLS (Multiprotocol Label Switching), 23–24
MT-RJ (Mechanical Transfer Registered Jack) connectors, 42
MTBF (mean time between failure), 229
MTTR (mean time to repair), 229
MTUs (maximum transmission units), 13–14
Multi-user MIMO (MU-MIMO), 188–189
multicast flooding, 374–375
Multicast Listener Discovery (MLD), 63
multicast messages, 63–65
multifactor authentication (MFA), 242
multilayer switches, 132
multimeters, 336
multimode fiber (MMF), 41–42
multipathing, 222–223
multiple approaches in troubleshooting, 315
Multiple Input, Multiple Output (MIMO), 188–189
multiple Internet service providers, 228
multiple problems in problem identification, 314
multipoint generic routing encapsulation (mGRE) protocol, 24
Multiprotocol Label Switching (MPLS), 23–24
multistation access units (MAUs), 17–19
multitenancy in cloud, 125
MX (mail exchange) resource records, 104–105
MySQL ports, 89

N

NAC (network access control), 241
name server (NS) resource records, 106
NAT (network address translation), 56–57
native mode in 802.11g, 176
Ncrack tool, 261
NDAs (non-disclosure agreements), 218
NDP (Neighbor Discovery Protocol), 64, 173
near-end crosstalk (NEXT), 328
Neighbor Discovery Protocol (NDP), 64, 173
NetFlow data, 202
netstat tool, 354–355
network access control (NAC), 241

network address translation (NAT), 56–57
network-based firewall settings, 379
network-based IDSs (NIDSs), 141
network device logs, 196–198
network function virtualization (NFV), 30
network interface cards (NICs)
    OSI model, 4–5
    teaming, 223
    vNICs, 28–29
Network layer in OSI model, 7
network performance metrics and sensors,
   193–194
network segmentation enforcement, 239
network services
    DHCP, 96–99
    DNS, 99–107
    NTS, 107–108
    questions, 108–109
    review, 108
Network Time Protocol (NTP)
    description, 107–108
    issues, 379
    ports, 87
networking issues
    asymmetrical routing, 375
    broadcast storms, 374
    certificates, 378–379
    collisions, 373
    DHCP scope exhaustion, 376–377
    duplicate IP addresses, 374
    duplicate MAC addresses, 374
    hardware, 379
    IP settings, 377
    link budgets, 378
    loops, 375–376
    missing routes, 378
    multicast flooding, 374–375
    overview, 372–373
    performance, 380–381
    questions, 383–384
    review, 381–383
    rogue DHCP servers, 376
next-generation firewalls (NGFWs), 139
NEXT (near-end crosstalk), 328
NFV (network function virtualization), 30

NGFWs (next-generation firewalls), 139
NICs (network interface cards)
    OSI model, 4–5
    teaming, 223
    vNICs, 28–29
NIDSs (network-based IDSs), 141
Nmap scanner, 347–348
non-disclosure agreements (NDAs), 218
north-south traffic in datacenters, 114
NS (name server) resource records, 106
nslookup tool, 351–352
NTP (Network Time Protocol)
    description, 107–108
    issues, 379
    ports, 87

O
O flag (Other Configuration Flag) in router
   advertisement, 79
object identifiers (OIDs) in SNMP, 194
obvious issues in troubleshooting, 315
offboarding policies, 210–211
OIDs (object identifiers) in SNMP, 194
omni antennas, 183–184
on-path attacks, 255
on-premises datacenters, 115
onboarding policies, 210–211
open cable connections, 330
Open Shortest Path First (OSPF) protocol,
   154–155
Open Systems Interconnection (OSI) model
    data encapsulation and decapsulation,
      8–11
    headers, 8–11
    Layer 1, 3
    Layer 2, 4–6
    Layer 3, 7
    Layer 4, 7
    Layer 5, 7
    Layer 6, 8
    Layer 7, 8
    overview, 2–3
    questions, 15
    review, 14
    TCP flags, 11–12

Opportunistic Wireless Encryption (OWE), 265
optical cables. *See* fiber cabling
optical link budget, 378
optical time-domain reflectometers (OTDRs),
    335–336
optimal media in datacenters, 116
orchestration in infrastructure as code, 124
organizational documents and policies, 205
    common agreements, 218–219
    common documentation, 211–218
    hardening and security policies,
        208–211
    plans and procedures, 205–208
    questions, 221
    review, 219–221
OSI model. *See* Open Systems Interconnection
    (OSI) model
OSPF (Open Shortest Path First) protocol,
    154–155
OTDRs (optical time-domain reflectometers),
    335–336
Other Configuration Flag (O flag) in router
    advertisement, 79
out-of-band remote access management, 300
outcomes in troubleshooting, 319–320
OWE (Opportunistic Wireless Encryption), 265
ownership in acceptable use policies, 209

P
PaaS (platform as a service), 123
packet capture programs, 344–346
packet injector tools, 265
packets in IP addresses, 92
PANs (personal area networks), 22–23
passwords
    attacks, 260–263
    complexity, 282
    default, 281–282
    local authentication, 245
    policies, 209
    wireless, 368
PAT (port address translation), 57–59
patch management, 282–284
patch panels, 44–45

payloads in headers, 8
Payment Card Industry Data Security Standard
    (PCI DSS), 217
PDUs (power distribution units), 226
PEAP (Protected EAP), 245–246
peer-to-peer networks, 21
penetration testing, 249
Per-VLAN Spanning Tree+ (PVST+), 169
performance issues and metrics
    baselines, 201
    devices, 192–193
    networking, 193–194, 380–381
personal area networks (PANs), 22–23
phishing attacks, 271–273
physical access control devices, 143
Physical layer in OSI model, 3
physical network diagrams
    description, 211
    floor plans, 212
    IDF/MDF, 212–214
    logical network diagrams, 215
    rack diagrams, 214–215
physical security
    asset disposal, 307–308
    detection methods, 302–303
    prevention methods, 303–307
    questions, 309
    review, 308–309
piggybacking, 274
ping command, 92, 349–350
pinouts, cable, 330
plans and procedures, 205
    business continuity, 207
    change management, 206
    disaster recovery, 207
    incident response, 206–207
    standard operating procedures, 208
    system life cycle, 208
plans of action in troubleshooting, 317–318
platform as a service (PaaS), 123
platform commands, 357
plenum cable, 324
PoE (Power over Ethernet), 167, 327
point-to-multipoint bridges, 133
point-to-point bridges, 133

pointer (PTR) resource records, 105
poisoning
        ARP, 256
        DNS, 257
polarization in antennas, 363–364
policies
        hardening and security. *See* hardening
            techniques
        organizational. *See* organizational
            documents and policies
POP3 (Post Office Protocol v3)
        POP3 over SSL, 88
        ports, 87
port address translation (PAT), 57–59
port scanners, 347–348
ports
        aggregation, 161–162
        blocked, 379
        cable connectivity, 330
        commonly used, 86–89
        configurations, 161–163
        mirroring, 163
        overview, 82–84
        questions, 95
        review, 94–95
        security, 164–165, 278–279
        states, 85–86
        types, 84–85
Post Office Protocol v3 (POP3)
        POP3 over SSL, 88
        ports, 87
posture assessment, 249
power distribution units (PDUs), 226
power levels in wireless security, 287
Power over Ethernet (PoE), 167, 327
power settings, wireless, 362
Presentation layer in OSI model, 8
preshared keys (PSKs)
        EAP, 245
        encryption, 288
prevention methods
        physical security, 303–307
        in troubleshooting, 318–319
printers, 142
privacy in acceptable use policies, 209

private cloud deployment, 120
private-direct connection to cloud providers, 125
private IP addresses, 55–59
private VLANs, 280–281
probable causes in troubleshooting, 315–316
problem identification in troubleshooting,
        312–314
process assessments, 250
protect mode in ports, 165, 279
Protected EAP (PEAP), 245–246
protocol analyzers, 344–346
protocol packets in interfaces, 199
protocols
        dynamic routing, 152–156
        IP types, 89–94
        overview, 82–84
        questions, 95
        review, 94–95
provider links
        cable companies, 32–33
        DSL, 31–32
        leased lines, 33
        metro-optical, 33–34
        overview, 30
        satellite, 30–31
proximity readers, 304–305
proxy servers, 135
PSH flag in TCP, 12
PSKs (preshared keys)
        EAP, 245
        encryption, 288
PTR (pointer) resource records, 105
public cloud deployment, 120
public IP addresses, 55–59
punchdown blocks, 46
punchdown tools, 332–333
PVST+ (Per-VLAN Spanning Tree+), 169

Q

quad small form-factor pluggable (QSFP)
        transceivers, 44
quadruple-amplitude modulated (QAM), 178
quality of service (QoS) policies, 158
questioning users in problem identification, 313

R

RA (Router Advertisement) Guard, 277–278
racks
 diagrams, 214–215
 locking, 306
radio-frequency identification (RFID) cards, 304
radio grade 6 (RG-6 cabling), 37–39
RADIUS (Remote Authentication Dial-In User Service), 243
range, wireless, 179–180
ransomware, 259–260
RAs (router advertisements), 78–79
RATs (remote administration tools), 268
RDC (Remote Desktop Connection), 297–298
RDP (Remote Desktop Protocol), 89
Real-Time Streaming Protocol (RTSP), 90
receive traffic information for interfaces, 199
received signal strength indication (RSSI), 287, 361–362
record types in DNS, 103–106
recovery point objective (RPO), 229–230
recovery time objective (RTO), 229
recursive DNS lookups, 103
redundancy for high availability, 223–224, 227–230
refrigerators, 144
Registered Jack (RJ) connectors, 42
registered ports, 84
regulatory impacts for wireless channels, 181
relay agents in DHCP, 98
remote access
 authentication and authorization, 300
 client-to-site VPNs, 296–297
 in-band vs. out-of-band management, 300
 overview, 295
 policies, 210
 questions, 301–302
 Remote Desktop Connection, 297–298
 Remote Desktop Gateway, 298
 review, 301
 site-to-site VPNs, 296
 SSH, 298–299
 virtual desktop, 299–300
 VNC, 299

remote administration tools (RATs), 268
Remote Authentication Dial-In User Service (RADIUS), 243
Remote Desktop Connection (RDC), 297–298
Remote Desktop Gateway, 298
Remote Desktop Protocol (RDP), 89
remote terminal units (RTUs) in SCADA, 147
repeaters, 136
reports
 audit and assessment, 217
 site surveys, 216
reservations in DHCP, 97–98
Reserved field in TCP headers, 90
restores for network devices, 230
restrict mode for ports, 165, 279
reverse DNS lookup, 106–107
reverse proxy servers, 135
RF attenuation in wireless, 367–368
RFC 1918, 55–56
RG-6 cabling (radio grade 6), 37–39
ring topology, 16–17
Rios, Billy, 291
RIP (Routing Internet Protocol), 152–154
riser-rated cable, 324
risk management, 247–250
RJ (Registered Jack) connectors, 42
 RJ11, 43
 RJ45, 43, 48
roaming in wireless, 183
rogue access points, 259
rogue DHCP, 258–259, 376
role-based access, 238, 285
rollover cable, 325
root DNS servers, 101–102
rootkits, 268
route tool, 356
Router Advertisement (RA) Guard, 277–278
router advertisements (RAs), 78–79
routers
 description, 132
 diverse paths, 228
 redundancy, 224

routing
administrative distance, 156–157
asymmetrical, 375
default routes, 156
dynamic, 152–156
missing routes, 378
overview, 149–152
questions, 159–160
review, 158–159
static, 156
Routing Internet Protocol (RIP), 152–154
routing loops, 375–376
routing tables, troubleshooting, 372
RPO (recovery point objective), 229–230
RSSI (received signal strength indication), 287, 361–362
RST flag in TCP, 12
RTO (recovery time objective), 229
RTSP (Real-Time Streaming Protocol), 90
RTUs (remote terminal units) in SCADA, 147
rules for firewall, 285
runt frames, 200

S
SaaS (software as a service), 121–122
SAE (Simultaneous Authentication of Equals) protocol, 265
sanitizing devices, 308
SANs (storage area networks), 23, 116–118
satellite links, 30–31
SATs (source address tables), 130, 164, 166
SC (subscriber connector) types, 42
SCADA (Supervisory Control and Data Acquisition), 145–147
scalability in cloud, 125–126
scanners
IP, 349
port, 347–348
scareware, 272
scope in DHCP
description, 96
exhaustion, 376–377

screened subnets, 239–240
SDN (software-defined networking)
control layer, 112–113
overview, 111
spine and leaf architecture, 114
SDSL (symmetric DSL), 31
SDWANs (software-defined wide area networks), 24
Secure File Transfer Protocol (SFTP), 86
Secure Shell (SSH)
overview, 298–299
ports, 85–86
secure SNMP, 277
Secure Sockets Layer (SSL) ports, 88
security
authentication methods, 242–247
CIA triad, 234
cloud, 126
defense in depth, 239–241
exploits, 237–238
hardening. *See* hardening and security policies
least privilege principle, 238
overview, 234
physical. *See* physical security
ports, 164–165
questions, 253–254
review, 251–253
risk management, 247–250
role-based access, 238
SIEM, 250–251
threats, 235–236
vulnerabilities, 236–237
wireless. *See* wireless security
zero trust, 238–239
security information and event management (SIEM), 250–251
segmentation enforcement, 239
send traffic information for interfaces, 199
Sender Policy Framework (SPF), 105
sensors
environmental, 200–201
HVAC, 144
performance, 192–194

separation of duties, 240–241
Sequence Number field in TCP headers, 91
Server Message Block (SMB) ports, 88
service-level agreements (SLAs),
   218–219
service models in cloud, 121–124
service-related entry points, 24–26
service set identifiers (SSIDs)
   evil twin attacks, 259
   overview, 181–182
   wireless connectivity, 368
service (SRV) resource records, 106
services
   blocked, 379
   SLAs, 218
   unneeded, 281
Session Initiation Protocol (SIP) ports, 89
Session layer in OSI model, 7
severity levels in device logs, 197–198
SFP (small form-factor pluggable)
   transceivers, 43
SFTP (Secure File Transfer Protocol), 86
shielded cable, 323
shielded twisted pair (STP) cable, 323
Shodan search system, 289–291
shorted cable connections, 330
shorthand notation for IPv6, 77–78
shoulder surfing, 274
show config command, 357
show interface command, 357
show interfaces IOS command, 198
shutdown mode in port security, 279
SIEM (security information and event
   management), 250–251
signal loss in wireless, 367–368
signature-based IDSs, 141
Simple Mail Transfer Protocol (SMTP)
   ports, 86
Simple Network Management Protocol (SNMP)
   overview, 194–196
   ports, 88
   secure, 277
Simultaneous Authentication of Equals (SAE)
   protocol, 265
single-mode fiber (SMF), 41
single sign-on (SSO), 243–244

SIP (Session Initiation Protocol) ports, 89
site surveys
   reports, 216
   steps, 364–366
site-to-site VPNs, 296
SLAAC (stateless address autoconfiguration),
   61, 78–79
SLAs (service-level agreements), 218–219
small form-factor pluggable (SFP)
   transceivers, 43
smart devices, 145
smart lockers, 307
smartjacks, 26
SMB (Server Message Block) ports, 88
SMF (single-mode fiber), 41
smishing attacks, 271
SMTP (Simple Mail Transfer Protocol)
   ports, 86
snips, 338
SNMP (Simple Network Management
   Protocol)
   overview, 194–196
   ports, 88
   secure, 277
snooping, DHCP, 282
SOA (start of authority) resource records, 105
social engineering attacks, 269–271
software as a service (SaaS), 121–122
software-based firewalls, 138
software-defined networking (SDN)
   control layer, 112–113
   overview, 111
   spine and leaf architecture, 114
software-defined wide area networks
   (SDWANs), 24
software tools, 344
   bandwidth speed testers, 346–347
   IP scanners, 349
   port scanners, 347–348
   protocol analyzers, 344–346
   questions, 359–360
   review, 358–359
   terminal emulators, 349
   Trivial File Transfer Protocol servers,
     348–349
   WiFi analyzers, 344

solutions in troubleshooting, 318
source address tables (SATs), 130, 164, 166
Spanning Tree Protocol (STP)
    overview, 168–169
    switching loops, 375
speakers, smart, 145
spear phishing, 272
specifications
    cable connectivity, 321–323
    wireless connectivity, 361
spectrum analyzers, 337–338
speed
    bandwidth testers, 346–347
    cable connectivity, 322
    interfaces, 198–199
    ports, 163
    wireless connectivity, 361
SPF (Sender Policy Framework), 105
spine and leaf architecture in datacenters,
    113–114
split tunnel VPN connections, 296–297
spoofing
    ARP, 256–257
    IP, 263–264
    MAC, 263
spyware, 269
SQL (Structured Query Language) Server
    ports, 88
    RPO and RTO, 230
SQLnet ports, 88
SRV (service) resource records, 106
SSH (Secure Shell)
    overview, 298–299
    ports, 85–86
SSIDs (service set identifiers)
    evil twin attacks, 259
    overview, 181–182
    wireless connectivity, 368
SSL (Secure Sockets Layer) ports, 88
SSO (single sign-on), 243–244
ST (straight tip) connectors, 42
standard operating procedures, 208
star topology, 19–20
start of authority (SOA) resource records, 105
state data backups, 230

stateful packet filtering, 138
stateless address autoconfiguration (SLAAC),
    61, 78–79
stateless packet filtering, 138
states of ports, 85–86
static assignment in DHCP, 97
static routing, 156
statistics for interfaces, 198–199
status indicators for cable connectivity,
    330–331
status of interfaces, 198–199, 372
storage area networks (SANs), 23, 116–118
STP (shielded twisted pair) cable, 323
STP (Spanning Tree Protocol)
    overview, 168–169
    switching loops, 375
straight tip (ST) connectors, 42
strata in NTS, 107–108
strategic-level changes, 206
Structured Query Language (SQL) Server
    ports, 88
    RPO and RTO, 230
subinterfaces for IP addresses, 80
subnets and subnet masks
    calculating, 71–72
    classful, 73–74
    classless, 74–75
    DHCP, 98–99
    host calculations, 69–70
    incorrect, 377
    making, 70–71
    overview, 67–69
    routing, 150–151
subscriber connector (SC) types, 42
Supervisory Control and Data Acquisition
    (SCADA), 145–147
switches
    Layer 2, 130–131
    Layer 3 capable, 132
    redundancy, 224
    vSwitches, 29
switching, Ethernet. See Ethernet switching
    features
switching loops, 375
switchports, unneeded, 281

symmetric DSL (SDSL), 31
symptom identification, 313
SYN (Synchronize) flag in TCP, 11, 91
syslog log reviews, 197
Syslog ports, 88
system life cycle, 208

T

TACACS+ (Terminal Access Controller Access Control System Plus), 243
tagging
    asserts, 303
    port, 161–162
tailgating, 273–274
tamper detection, 303
tape backups for datacenters, 116
taps, cable, 337
TCP (Transmission Control Protocol)
    flags, 11–12
    headers, 8–10
    overview, 89–92
TCP/IP (Transmission Control Protocol/ Internet Protocol), 82
tcpdump tool, 357
TDMA (time-division multiple access), 187
technical support in SLAs, 218
technology-based attacks
    ARP spoofing, 256–257
    deauthentication, 264–266
    DNS poisoning, 257
    DoS/DDoS, 254–255
    evil twin, 259
    IP spoofing, 263–264
    MAC spoofing, 263
    malware, 266–269
    on-path, 255
    password, 260–263
    rogue access points, 259
    rogue DHCP, 258–259
    VLAN hopping, 257–258
Telecommunications Industry Association (TIA) copper cabling standards, 39–40
telnet tool
    plaintext communication, 357
    ports, 86

temperature sensors, 192, 200–201
Temporal Key Integrity Protocol (TKIP), 185
Tentler, Dan, 290–291
Terminal Access Controller Access Control System Plus (TACACS+), 243
termination standards for copper cabling, 39–40
testing
    penetration, 249
    troubleshooting theories, 316–318
text (TXT) resource records, 105–106
TFTP (Trivial File Transfer Protocol)
    ports, 87
    servers, 348–349
theories in troubleshooting
    establishing, 315–316
    testing, 316–318
thermostats, smart, 145
threats
    assessment, 248
    security, 235–236
three-tiered datacenters, 109–111
three-way handshakes in TCP, 11–12, 90–92
throughput
    cable connectivity, 321–322
    testers, 346–347
    wireless connectivity, 361
TIA (Telecommunications Industry Association) copper cabling standards, 39–40
time-division multiple access (TDMA), 187
Time to Live (TTL) field
    DNS, 103
    MPLS headers, 23
    routing protocols, 157
TKIP (Temporal Key Integrity Protocol), 185
TLDs (top-level domains), 100–102
TLS (Transport Layer Security) in EAP, 246
tone generators, 332–334
top-level domains (TLDs), 100–102
top-of-rack switching in datacenters, 114
top-to-bottom OSI troubleshooting model, 315–316
topologies and network types
    bus, 16
    CANs, 23
    client-server, 21

hub-and-spoke, 19–20
hybrid, 17–19
LANs, 22
MANs, 22
mesh, 19–21
mGRE, 24
MPLS, 23–24
overview, 15–16
PANs, 22–23
peer-to-peer, 21
provider links, 30–34
questions, 34–35
review, 34
ring, 16–17
SANs, 23
SDWANs, 24
service-related entry points, 24–26
star, 19–20
virtual network concepts, 26–30
WANs, 22
WLANs, 22
traceroute tool, 353
tracert tool, 92, 353
traffic flows in datacenters, 114–115
traffic log reviews, 197
traffic shaping, 158
training, employee, 304
transceivers
    cable connectivity, 331
    description, 43
transfers in DNS, 99–100
Transmission Control Protocol (TCP)
    flags, 11–12
    headers, 8–10
    overview, 89–92
Transmission Control Protocol/ Internet
    Protocol (TCP/IP), 82
transmit and receive (TX/RX) reversed
    issues, 331
Transport layer in OSI model, 7
Transport Layer Security (TLS) in EAP, 246
traps in SNMP, 194–196
Trivial File Transfer Protocol (TFTP)
    ports, 87
    servers, 348–349

Trojan horses, 267–268
troubleshooting cable connectivity. *See* cable
    connectivity issues
troubleshooting methodology
    documentation, 319–320
    overview, 312
    probable causes, 315–316
    problem identification, 312–314
    questions, 320–321
    review, 320
    theory testing, 316–318
    verifying functionality, 318–319
TTL (Time to Live) field
    DNS, 103
    MPLS headers, 23
    routing protocols, 157
Tunneled TLS (TTLS), 246
tunneling in IPv6, 76
twinaxial cable, 39
twisted pair copper cabling, 35–36
TX/RX (transmit and receive) reversed
    issues, 331
TXT (text) resource records, 105–106
Type 1 hypervisors, 27–28
Type 2 hypervisors, 27–28
types, antenna, 363–364

U
UC (unified communication), 142
UDP (User Datagram Protocol)
    DHCP forwarding, 98
    headers, 8–10
    overview, 89–92
ultra-physical contact (UPC) connectors, 43
unicast addresses, 65–66
unified communication (UC), 142
unified threat management (UTM)
    appliances, 139
uninterruptible power supplies (UPSs), 225
unique local addresses, 66
unneeded devices and services, 281
unshielded twisted pair (UTP) cable, 35–36,
    323–324
up/down state, 198
UPC (ultra-physical contact) connectors, 43

UPSs (uninterruptible power supplies), 225
uptime, 202–203
URG flag in TCP, 12
User Datagram Protocol (UDP)
    DHCP forwarding, 98
    headers, 8–10
    overview, 89–92
UTM (unified threat management)
  appliances, 139
UTP (unshielded twisted pair) cable, 35–36,
  323–324

V

variable-length subnet masks (VLSMs),
  75–76, 153
vendor assessments, 250
verifying functionality in troubleshooting,
  318–319
virtual desktop, 299–300
virtual IP (VIP), 79–80
virtual local area networks (VLANs)
    assignment review, 372
    data, 160–161
    default, 282
    hopping, 257–258
    incorrect, 379
    private, 280–281
Virtual Network Computing (VNC), 299
Virtual Network Interface Cards (vNICs),
  28–29
virtual networks
    hypervisors, 27–28
    NFV, 30
    overview, 26
    vNICs, 28–29
    vSwitches, 29
virtual private networks (VPNs)
    client-to-site, 296–297
    cloud, 124–125
    headends, 141
    site-to-site, 296
Virtual Router Redundancy Protocol (VRRP),
  80, 228–229
viruses, 266–267
vishing attacks, 271

VLANs. *See* virtual local area networks (VLANs)
VLSMs (variable-length subnet masks),
  75–76, 153
VNC (Virtual Network Computing), 299
vNICs (Virtual Network Interface Cards),
  28–29
voice gateways, 136
Voice over Internet Protocol (VoIP) phones, 142
Voice VLANs, 161
VPNs. *See* virtual private networks (VPNs)
VRRP (Virtual Router Redundancy Protocol),
  80, 228–229
vSphere Client, 28
vSwitches, 29
vulnerabilities, 236
    assessment, 248
    CVE, 236
    zero-day, 236–237

W

WANs (wide area networks), 22
WAPs. *See* wireless access points (WAPs)
warm sites, 227
wavelength division multiplexing (WDM), 53
well-known ports, 84
whaling attacks, 272
Wi-Fi 4 standard, 177–178
Wi-Fi 5 standard, 178
Wi-Fi 6 standard, 178
Wi-Fi Protected Access 2 (WPA2), 185–186
wide area networks (WANs), 22
WiFi analyzers, 344
WiFi Protected Access (WPA), 185
wipe configuration, 307–308
wire maps, 336
wireless access points (WAPs)
    association time, 364
    description, 133
    ransomware, 259–260
    rogue, 259
wireless analyzers, 365–366
wireless connectivity
    common issues, 367–369
    considerations, 363–366
    deauthentication attacks, 264–266

overview, 360
questions, 371
review, 369–371
RSSI, 361–362
specifications and limitations, 361
wireless LAN controllers (WLCs), 133–134
wireless local area networks (WLANs), 22
wireless mesh networks, 21
wireless security
    antenna placement, 286–287
    captive portals, 289
    client isolation, 288
    geofencing, 288–289
    guest network isolation, 288
    MAC filtering, 286
    overview, 285–286
    power levels, 287
    pre-shared keys, 288
wireless standards and technologies
    802.11, 175–179
    antenna types, 183–184
    cellular, 186–188
    channel bonding, 181

    channels, 180–181
    encryption, 184–186
    frequencies and range, 179–180
    MIMO and MU-MIMO, 188–189
    questions, 189–190
    review, 189
    SSIDs, 181–183
Wireshark tool, 346
wiring diagrams, 215–216
wiring rooms, 213
WLANs (wireless local area networks), 22
WLCs (wireless LAN controllers), 133–134
worms, 266–267
WPA (WiFi Protected Access), 185
WPA/WPA2-Enterprise, 186
WPA2 (Wi-Fi Protected Access 2), 185–186
WPA2 Personal, 185

Z

zero-configuration networking (zeroconf), 60
zero-day vulnerabilities, 236–237
zero trust concept, 238–239
zone transfers in DNS, 99–100